FAMILY DEVELOPMENT
IN THREE GENERATIONS

A Longitudinal Study of Changing Family Patterns of Planning and Achievement

REUBEN HILL

With Chapters in Collaboration with

NELSON FOOTE

JOAN ALDOUS

ROBERT CARLSON

ROBERT MACDONALD

SCHENKMAN PUBLISHING CO., INC.
CAMBRIDGE, MASS., U.S.A.
AND LONDON, ENGLAND

Library of Congress Catalog Card #78-127047
Copyright © 1970
SCHENKMAN PUBLISHING COMPANY, INC.
Cambridge, Massachusetts 02138
PRINTED IN THE UNITED STATES OF AMERICA

Preface

THIS IS A RESEARCH REPORT of changes in family patterns of planning and achievement over three generations. Because of the high interest in three generation families the study has been identified almost from the first day as "The Three Generation Family Study." For many the subject matter has been less salient than the three generation research design. Everyone has ideas about generational differences! Drop in on any multi-generational gathering and you will hear about how much better or worse life was for families in grandfather's day than today. Everyone has ideas about how faithfully families transmit the cultural heritage from generation to generation. It is asserted by economists that both poverty and success run in families. Occupational specialists have speculated about how much the success of the new generation is due to help in getting started by the older generation, "It isn't what you know, but who you know that counts in getting ahead." Among sociologists a debate has been continuous for a number of years about the issue of how much mutual aid persists among the generations of the same family line and whether the modern industrial society isn't better served by a more autonomous nuclear family. Public welfare policy confronts the issue of filial obligations for the support of the elderly before public assistance can be given. Fiscal policy with respect to tax deductions for dependents enters into the formula of how much support must be given to one's married children or one's aged parents before a tax deduction may be taken.

Even our cooperating families were motivated to submit to five interviews over a year's period because this was a three generation family study and they felt it was high time someone did a book about them. They felt, moreover, that this would be one book they could read and understand because it would deal with how the generations cope with their day-to-day problems.

The proposal to study three generations of the same family line initially was more a design for collecting depth data over time and to hold constant the variability of family culture than a source of theoretical problems to be explored and tested. It was only after the research problem had been formulated, its research design completed, the interview guides developed, the first waves of interviews completed and preliminary results tabulated that the research team began to see the theoretical possibilities of the three generation idea. The plans for the fourth interview were consequently reformulated to include data about intergenerational transactions and the degree of interdependency for mutual aid. Doctoral dissertations were organized from these data focussing on two of the most pressing theoretical issues; conditions associated with intergenerational helping patterns and the antecedents and consequences of continuity from generation to generation. With these dissertations under way the study finally could justify its three generation moniker.

The more perduring theme of this study has been the issue of family consumership, the phenomenon of the efficient utilization of resources in getting ahead as a family which it was assumed would yield more if it were studied intergenerationally. The reader may wish a quick review of how these research ideas about consumership evolved, leaving to the first chapter the details of the strategies undertaken to render them researchable.

The initial interest in looking into family consumership, the phenomenon of families managing their resources effectively to achieve their collective goals, emerged from discussions between Nelson Foote, sociologist in the Research Division of Marketing Services of General Electric Company, and Reuben Hill, family sociologist and Director of the Family Study Center of the University of Minnesota. Foote saw possibilities in applying longitudinal research methods to the study of family earning, saving and buying to ascertain the timing and sequences of financial planning and action. Hill was challenged by the prospects of testing propositions he had developed in his Puerto Rican research on the family as a decision-making unit in fertility planning and control in the new context of family consumption and was particularly interested in Foote's concepts of long-term family career planning. The early discussions covered many areas of economic activity: residence location, redecorating-remodeling, durable goods and automobile purchases, retirement and protection insurances, savings and investments and educational planning:

1. Do families follow similar patterns in the acquisition of durable goods and automobiles as in acquiring children, negotiating residential moves or making changes in the family's financial portfolio?
2. What are the predominant styles of problem-solving behavior for the generations?
3. Do these styles run in families?

4. How planful are families in the major areas of decision making?
5. What are the outcomes of different types of planning and non-planning?
6. Who are the most successful planners?

These research ideas were eventually formalized as research objectives for discussion with a research sponsor. They were not yet clearly researchable ideas but, as stated, they could be appraised for their possible contributions to knowledge and for their researchability. We reproduce this statement of research objectives below:

Changing Patterns of Family Policy Formation
A Project Proposal for a Longitudinal and Intergenerational
Study of Long-Term Financial Planning and Consumption

A. Specific Aims
  1. To describe broadly the processes of family planning and decision making with respect to long-term goals from data collected from three generations of the same line.
  2. To discover about what types of issues and problems families are most likely to be planful, what they leave to chance, and what they tend to handle impulsively.
  3. To describe from retrospective data patterns of family income, family expenditures and family acquisitions over their entire life cycle for the grandparents, over the phases through the middle years for the parents, and for the beginning phase of getting established for the young married children.
  4. To describe major sources of influences in setting of long-term goals and in the choice of action plans: immediate family, kinsmen, neighbors, age peers, mass media, professionals.
  5. To describe the process of structuring the future through family policy formation.
     (a) Do couples begin with rudimentary career images for their future family which guide their subsequent planning?
     (b) Does a consistent set of family policies with respect to housing, education, health and acquisition of durable goods develop only after considerable trial and error experience?
     (c) How are past experiences evaluated and crystallized into policies?

(d) Do policies have significant influence in arriving at long-term purchase commitments compared with the appeals of the mass media advertising or the momentary climate of opinion about shortages, inflation and so on?

' 6. To discover the range of planfulness and the length of horizon spans for key issues at different stages of family development.

7. To test hypotheses from previous studies about the family correlates of planfulness, length of planning spans, use of credit, and success in carrying through purchase plans.

B. Types of Data to be Collected and Analyzed

1. Whereas most data on consumer behavior are cross-sectional in character, it is proposed that basic data for this study be sequential in character.

2. The main subject matter will be "longitudinal" patterns of earning, saving, spending, buying and financial planning generally; the main objective will be to ascertain the correlations and causal connections among these sequences, to emphasize the dimension of time and timing in the understanding of household decision making.

3. In analysis of the data, methods of discerning analysis will be used for change data. Patterns of family spending and consumption change over time, partly because family members grow older and partly because historical circumstances shift. We hope to find, using these methods, recognizable continuity and development in these changes, which may be generalized in terms of family style types made up of long-term objectives, policies or commitments. If such generalized patterns can be discerned, they will help both to account for and to predict a wide range of concrete buying decisions.

With this initial crystallization of the research ideas we wished to pursue, the task of rendering these ideas researchable was undertaken. Consultants from marketing and from academic economics, sociology and statistics were involved in the formulation of a researchable problem and in developing an efficient, economical and appropriate sampling and research design. An accounting of that process is undertaken in the first chapter.

The project was funded by the Marketing Research Division of the General Electric Company for whom three reports for internal consumption have been produced jointly by Nelson N. Foote and Lee Wiggins of General Electric Company and Reuben Hill and Robert Carlson of the Minnesota Family Study Center. In addition to these internal reports three doctoral dissertations by R. H. Rodgers,[1] Joan Aldous,[2] and Robert Macdonald[3] and one masters thesis by Arlene Davis Goodman[4] have been completed as well as several professional articles.[5] These advance publications have relieved somewhat the pressure to finish this final and more complete report.

The volume begins with an introduction of three chapters exposing the reader to the research problem and the vicissitudes of organizing and executing the research, and second to the cooperating families to acquaint him at the outset with the three generations of families that make up the cast of actors in this drama. The third chapter looks more closely at the interdependence of these generational groups as hypothesized "modified extended family networks."

With introductions out of the way the book continues in six chapters to describe the planning careers of each generation from the

[1] Roy H. Rodgers, "Improvements in the Construction and Analysis of Family Life Cycle Categories," Ph.D. Dissertation, University of Minnesota, 1962, published by Western Michigan University Press, Kalamazoo, Michigan, 1962.

[2] Joan Aldous, "Family Continuity Patterns Over Three Generations: Content, Degree of Transmission and Consequences" unpublished Ph.D. Dissertation, University of Minnesota, 1963.

[3] Robert Macdonald, "Intergenerational Family Helping Patterns." Unpublished doctoral dissertation, University of Minnesota, 1964.

[4] Arlene Davis Goodman, "Marital Adjustment in a Three Generational Sample," unpublished masters thesis, University of Minnesota, 1968.

[5] Hill, Reuben, "Patterns of Decision-Making and the Accumulation of Family Assets," in Nelson N. Foote, ed., *Household Decision Making*, Vol. IV of the Consumer Behavior Series, (New York: New York University Press, 1961); "Judgment and Consumership in the Management of Family Resources," *Sociology and Social Research*, Vol. 47, No. 4, July 1963, pp. 446-460; "Methodological Problems with the Developmental Approach to Family Study," *Family Process*, Vol. 3, No. 1 (1964), pp. 5-22; "The American Family of the Future," *Journal of Marriage and the Family*, Vol. 26, No. 1 (February, 1964) pp. 20-28; "Decision Making and the Family Life Cycle," in Ethel Shanas and Gordon Streib, eds., *The Family and Social Structure: Generational Relations*, (Englewood Cliffs, N.J.: Prentice Hall, 1965, pp. 113-139; "The Three Generation Technique for Studying Social Change" in Reuben Hill and Rene Konig, eds., *Families in East and West: Socialization Processes and Kinship Ties* (Paris: Mouton and Company, 1970).

Joan Aldous, "The Consequences of Intergenerational Continuity," *Journal of Marriage and the Family*, XXVII, (Nov. 1965) pp. 462-68; "Intergenerational Visiting Patterns: Variation in Boundary Maintenance as an Explanation," *Family Process*, Vol. 6, No. 2, 1967, pp. 235-251.

Joan Aldous and Reuben Hill, "Social Cohesion, Lineage Type, and Intergenerational Transmission," *Social Forces*, Vol. 43, 4 (May 1965) pp. 471-482.

R. H. Rodgers, "Some Factors Associated with Homogeneous Role Patterns in Family Life Cycle Careers," *Pacific Sociological Review* (1964) 7, pp. 38-48.

beginning of marriage to the day of the first study interview, as well as a detailed examination of family achievements occurring during the twelve months study period. Covered in five chapters are family composition changes, occupational career patterns, housing careers, financial career planning, and the acquisition of a durable goods inventory. The sixth chapter assesses the extent to which achievements in one career area stimulate or depress achievements in other areas and also examines the consistency with which the same families tend to lead, to be on schedule or to lag in the several areas of achievement. There appears to be more of a tendency for all three generations of the same family line to be leaders of their respective generations than there is for them to be laggers.

The next major section of the book seeks explanations for success or failure in family consumership in four chapters in which the several phases of the consumption process are assessed: (1) identification of unmet needs, (measured by volume of plans expressed), (2) choosing a course of action or process of decision, (measured by a rationality of decision-making score), (3) action-taking (measured by volume of actions and proportion of preplanned actions), (4) evaluation of adequacy of actions taken (measured by degree of satisfaction with outcome). This section looks first at the relative explanatory power of the several antecedents grouped as incentives and contraints, indices of development, indices of social competence, value orientations, restrictiveness of family organization and marital climate. The correlates of family consumership vary by generation but are less variable for successful than for unsuccessful family lines. In successive chapters the linkages between planning career achievements over the life span and family consumership during the twelve months of the study are explicated for each of the three generations.

In the final part the implications of this study for family development and intergenerational theory are spelled out along with types of programmatic applications which might be undertaken. Programs of family service are suggested which would treat the kinship structure more as the client family's first line of defense than as a threat to its autonomy, as well as programs of training in family life education to raise the level of consumership among newly married couples.

To list all of the people to whom acknowledgements of help received on this project would be endless. Foremost among those to whom the project is indebted is Dr. Nelson N. Foote, Community Consultant, General Electric Company, who has served virtually as co-director of the study from its inception, acting as liaison and monitor and final editor of all internal reports for the funding agency. Dr. Foote gave selflessly of his counsel at every stage in the research process including significant help in the preparation of this final report. Chief among those who served as architects of the study are Howard Stanton of the University of Puerto Rico with whom I worked in an unpublished three generation study of social and cultural change in Puerto Rico which inspired our adoption of its intergenerational design, and several consultants, Lee Wiggins of General Electric, Orville Brim Jr. of the Russell Sage Foundation, Scott Maynes and Roy Francis of the University of Minnesota, and James Morgan of the University of Michigan. R. H. Rodgers and Robert E. Carlson served as field and data processing supervisors with Rodgers responsible for interviewer training and quality control and Carlson for coding, tabulation and analysis. Joanne Hirt Lecander served as office manager and accountant. Ten interviewers underwent rigorous training and participated in the first waves. The four intrepid interviewers who persisted for the entire twelve months of data collection included Mildred O. Roe, Martha B. Kidd, Marion F. Greer, and Jeannette G. Anderson. Research assistants during the analysis phase have included Myrna Eickhoff, Arlene Davis Goodman, and William Silverman. Mary Ann Ellingson has supervised the processing of the manuscript for publication. No more dedicated research team has ever been assembled.

Perhaps our greatest debt is to those three hundred and twelve generationally linked families who opened their homes for more than twelve hours of intensive interviews extended over several months of panel interviewing. They have generously shared with us their trials and achievements, their frustrated and fulfilled plans as well as their satisfactions and disappointments with the consumption process. The data which they have freely and anonymously given constitute the precious lore about family careers across the generations from which this story has been written.

REUBEN HILL

Contents

Charts

Tables

INTRODUCTION

CHAPTER I

Family Development and Consumership

ISSUES OF THEORY AND RESEARCH DESIGN

JUST AS THE ARENA of the family has attracted a number of academic disciplines, notably anthropology, economics, psychology and sociology, so has the phenomenon of consumer behavior. In a money economy, consumer behavior consists heavily of choices in the use of time and money. Economists have been interested not only in aggregate expenditure patterns of categories of consumers at any one time, but also in changes over time. Psychologists have until recently shown less interest in expenditures, as such, than in the motivational factors which account for specific commodity choices. Sociologists have been more far ranging, looking at the consumption function macroscopically, as a basic family function which has become more important today in integrating family activities than economic production in most of the countries of the world. Sociologists have also used family expenditures and time allocation patterns as the basis for inferring the value orientations of social classes. Rural sociologists and home economists have drawn policy inferences from these patterns by comparing levels and standards of living among significant sectors of the society.

More recently the work of sociologists, psychologists and economists have converged on the issues of consumer decision making, planning, and the fulfillment of plans. The multiplicity of factors involved in these issues is well stated in the diagram formulated by

James Morgan in his review of research on consumer behavior, see Chart 1.01, A Diagram of Factors Affecting A Consumer's Choice.[1]

Morgan, it will be noted, identifies consumer choice as an individual's choice, thus opening the way for large contributions from personality variables of basic motives, needs, goals and perceptions on the one hand and decision-making abilities of information seeking and problem solving on the other. The situational variables of income, educational level and occupational class used most frequently by economists are treated conceptually in Morgan's chart as incentives or constraints.

Morgan's review transcends the parochialisms of the disciplines whose work on consumer behavior is covered, to note both convergences and divergences in interests and concepts used. Since his dependent variables is individual consumer behavior, he makes reference only in passing to the possibility of research on primary groups like the family as planning, decision-making and spending units, suggesting that the decisions of the family group might be more stable and easier to predict than if one looked only at individuals.[2] This is not a bad springboard from which to launch our discussion of a family level study of consumership, the effectiveness with which families manage their resources to achieve family goals. The balance of this chapter is devoted to a discussion of the strategies for rendering such a research idea theoretically interesting and methodologically researchable.

Strategies Employed

To bring the research idea into sharper focus, making it simultaneously more theoretically relevant and more manageable we need to consider a number of alternative strategies: (1) the range of conceptual approaches which can be brought to bear upon the problem of family consumership, (2) the building of a theoretical model based upon the approach chosen which identifies the crucial analytic categories and their relationships to the dependent variable chosen for study, and (3) the developing of a research design, including the methods of sampling, data collection and analysis needed to test the propositions of the theoretical model.

---

[1] James Morgan, "A Review of Recent Research on Consumer Behavior," in Lincoln Clark, editor, *Consumer Behavior: Research on Consumer Reactions* (New York: Harper & Brothers, 1958), p. 100.

[2] *Ibid.,* p. 104.

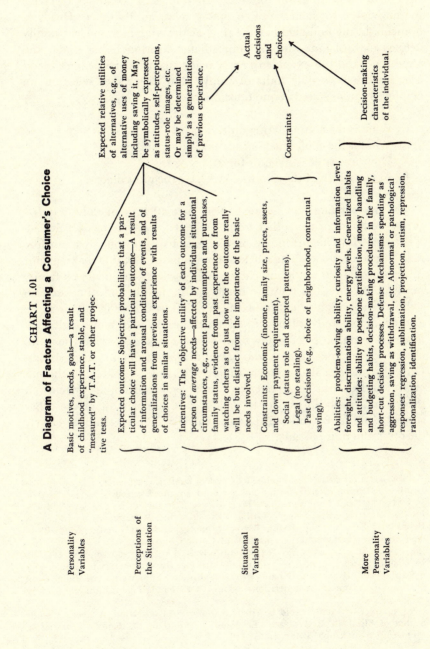

CHART 1.01
A Diagram of Factors Affecting a Consumer's Choice

Personality Variables

Basic motives, needs, goals—a result of childhood experience, stable, and "measured" by T.A.T. or other projective tests.

Perceptions of the Situation

Expected outcome: Subjective probabilities that a particular choice will have a particular outcome—A result of information and arousal conditions, of events, and of generalizations from previous experience with results of choices in similar situations.

Incentives: The "objective utility" of each outcome for a person of average needs—affected by individual situational circumstances, e.g., recent past consumption and purchases, family status, evidence from past experience or from watching others as to just how nice the outcome really will be but distinct from the importance of the basic needs involved.

Situational Variables

Constraints: Economic (income, family size, prices, assets, and down payment requirement).
Social (status role and accepted patterns).
Legal (no stealing).
Past decisions (e.g., choice of neighborhood, contractual saving).

More Personality Variables

Abilities: problem-solving ability, curiosity and information level, foresight, discrimination ability, energy levels. Generalized habits and attitudes: ability to postpone gratification, money handling and budgeting habits, decision-making procedures in the family, short-cut decision processes. Defense Mechanisms: spending as aggression, saving as withdrawal, etc. Abnormal or pathological responses: regression, sublimation, projection, autism, repression, rationalization, identification.

Expected relative utilities of alternatives, e.g., of alternative uses of money including saving it. May be symbolically expressed as attitudes, self-perceptions, status-role images, etc. Or may be determined simply as a generalization of previous experience.

Constraints

Decision-making characteristics of the individual.

Actual decisions and choices

A first issue in the formulation of a research problem is the question of the optimum unit of study. In studies of consumer behavior the individual consumer is often the behaving unit studied. Heads of households, the household at the time of the study, the nuclear family defined as husband, wife and immediate offspring living under the same roof, and the extended family made up of all immediate blood kin, are other possible units of study.[3] The criteria of selection we employed can be stated as questions:

1. What is the accumulating unit?
2. What is the choice-making and decision-making unit?
3. How accessible is the unit for study?
4. About which of these units do we have the most theory?

The nuclear family, it seemed to us, met all four of these requirements better than any other units suggested. Let us consider its advantages: (1) The inventory of acquisitions over time is a nuclear family inventory. (2) The nuclear family is the decision-making unit in asset accumulation. Many choices and decisions are made by family heads, to be sure, but they are made *for* the family and often involve some participation from children.[4] (3) The nuclear family is more accessible for study than the extended family and more easily definable for purposes of study than is the household, which may include roomers and servants who have little part in family acquisitions. Only the individual consumer is more accessible. (4) Finally, the nuclear family serves as a referent in several conceptual systems of theory and has been subject to greater study than most of the other suggested units. By these criteria the nuclear family would be clearly the optimum unit of study.

---

[3] Another alternative, the modified extended family, a confederation of nuclear families in helping exchanges had not yet been advanced seriously as researchable. Its advantages and limitations have been discussed by Litwak in a series of papers. For the most recent see Eugene Litwak, "Extended Kin Relations in an Industrial Democratic Society," and Irving Rosow, "Inter-generational Relationships: Problems and Proposals," in Ethel Shanas and Gordon F. Streib, *Social Structure and the Family* (Englewood Ciffs, N.J.: Prentice-Hall, 1965) pp. 290-326, and 341-378. In chapter 3 we explore the extent to which our three generation sample confirms the viability and functionality of this family form, but we do not think it can be seriously advanced as a decision-making or accumulating unit in our society, see pp. 59-80.

[4] A number of studies could be cited to support this assertion. A relevant study is that of Elizabeth H. Wolgast, "Economic Decisions in the Family," *Journal of Marketing*, 23, (October 1958) pp. 151-158.

Alternative Conceptual Frameworks

Having selected the nuclear family as the unit for study, a number of alternative conceptual frameworks for viewing the family needed to be considered. Sociology, cultural anthropology, psychology and consumption economics have developed approaches which differ almost as much as the proverbial three blind men's perceptions of the elephant. Eight relatively differentiated conceptual frameworks had been identified from analysis of several hundred pieces of research on marriage and the family, primarily in the United States, using as criteria for classification the definitions of the family implied, the key concepts and their interrelationships and the peculiar foci employed.[5] Generalizations arising from these different approaches cannot always be added to each other to form cumulative theories, and students who learn the concepts and techniques of only one approach are handicapped in making sense out of marriage and family writings.

Table 1.01 provides a list of the competing frameworks for family study with the disciplines which originated and elaborated them and the names of men whose research best exemplify them. Of these eight conceptual approaches, the institutional-historical is eliminated as a possibility for this research problem because of its macroscopic scope and institutional focus. The situational approach suffers from too great specificity. The learning theory approach is unable to handle the plurality of actors involved in family acquisitions and focuses too narrowly on the personality development of children. The household economics approach is also ineligible because of its focus on the household as a firm in its close alliance with farm management type concepts and its lack of concepts in family organization. The household economics framework is essentially a balance sheet approach balancing the resources of time, money and energy with expenditure outputs. It is probably inappropriate, therefore, for a study of decision making and choice making. It is essentially a normative and non-operational model seeking to prescribe rules which, if followed, would enable consumers to maximize their satisfactions.

The three approaches which survived our scrutiny all dealt with the nuclear family as the focus of interest and brought to the research rich concepts and theories that would be useful to consider:

---

[5] For more detailed discussion of five of these frameworks, see Reuben Hill and Donald A. Hansen, "The Identification of Conceptual Frameworks Utilized in Family Study," *Marriage and Family Living*, Vol. XXII, No. 4 (November 1960), pp. 299-311.

the structure-function, the symbolic-interactionist and the family development approaches.

The structure-function approach, which views the family as a social system, has its roots in anthropology and sociology and is rapidly winning adherents among family researchers everywhere in the world. Elaborated in the United States in more recent years by Harvard and Columbia sociologists, notably Talcott Parsons, Kingsley Davis, Robert Merton, George Homans and Marion Levy, it has been applied to the family profitably at several levels from broad macroanalysis to intensive microanalysis: in the interplay between changes in the family and society in changing China,[6] in the strains induced between the occupational structure's demands of the family farm on the farm family,[7] in the analysis of power allocation among families of four differently oriented cultural groups,[8] and in the analysis of relative stress of economic deprivation and political terrorism among families of political refugees.[9] This conceptual framework has the advantage of providing descriptive categories within a scope wide enough to encompass the interplay between the family system and larger systems like the community and the society; the interplay between the family and collateral systems like the school, the occupational world and the marketplace; and the transactions between the family and the smaller subgroups of the husband-wife dyad, the sibling cliques and the individual personality systems of family members.

The symbolic-interactionist approach, first developed in sociology and social psychology, has been more frequently employed and has a larger history of use in American family sociology than the structure function framework. The approach was a direct outgrowth of the work of George Herbert Mead and the University of Chicago group of symbolic interactionists, of which Ernest W. Burgess was a prominent member. It was Burgess who first suggested the feasibility of viewing the family as an interacting entity in 1928, and subsequent applications have gradually refined the interactional conceptual framework for microanalytic studies of the family. It assumes the

---

[6] Marion Levy, *The Family Revolution in Modern China* (Cambridge: Harvard University Press, 1949).

[7] Eleanor Godfrey, *A Construction of Family Typologies and Their Initial Verification* (Cambridge: Radcliffe College, 1951).

[8] Fred L. Strodtbeck, "Husband-Wife Interaction Over Revealed Differences," *American Sociological Review* (August 1951), pp. 468-473.

[9] Kent Geiger, "Deprivation and Solidarity in the Soviet Urban Family," *American Sociological Review,* Vol. 20 (January 1955), pp. 57-68.

TABLE 1.01

Approaches to the Study of the Family Competing for Adherents in America*

Conceptual Framework	Originating in Disciplines of:	Exemplified in Researches by:
The institutional-historical approach	Sociology and Historical Sociology	C. C. Zimmerman and associates, and John Sirjamaki
The structure-function approach	Sociology and Social Anthropology	K. Davis, K. Geiger, W. J. Goode, M. Levy, C. McGuire, G. Murdock, T. Parsons, F. Strodtbeck, L. Simmons, L. Warner and others
The symbolic interactionist approach	Sociology and Social Psychology	R. C. Angell, E. W. Burgess, R. Cavan, L. S. Cottrell, T. D. Eliot, N. Foote, R. Hill, M. Komarovsky, E. Koos, E. T. Kreuger, H. Mowrer, S. Stryker, W. Waller, and Paul Wallin
The situational-psychological habitat approach	Developed independently by Sociology and Psychology	W. I. Thomas, L. J. Carr, J. H. S. Bossard and associates, R. Blood, and R. G. Barker and H. F. Wright
The learning theory approach	Psychology	R. Sears and John Whiting; and Robert Dalton
The psychoanalytic approach	Psychology	Limited research on families as such, see writings of Flügel, Ackerman, English, Murray, Winch and others
The household economics approach	Consumption Economics and Home Economics	H. Kyrk, J. Morgan, L. Gordon, P. Nickell, Margaret Reid and Alice Thorpe
The family development or family life cycle approach	Interdisciplinary, borrowing from Rural Sociology, Child Psychology, Human Development, and Sociology	Limited research completed as yet, approximations seen in work of Harold Feldman, Wells Goodrich, P. Glick, R. Hill, J. Lansing, E. LeMasters, J. Morgan, R. Rapoport, R. Rodgers, M. Sussman, L. Stott and writings of R. Cavan and E. Duvall.

* Developed by Reuben Hill and associates for the Inventory of Marriage and Family Research from careful analysis of the definitions of the family implied, the key concepts used and the peculiar foci employed in more than two hundred pieces of research on marriage and the family during the last twenty years. This listing of approaches to the study of the family obviously does not do justice to the various approaches to consumer behavior except as caught by the household economics approach. Excluded are, for example, the distinctive Gestalt psychological framework of Katona and associates, and the Lewinian approach of Bilkey. Detailed discussion of five of these frameworks, their properties and limitations may be found in Reuben Hill and Donald A. Hansen, *op. cit.*, pp. 229-301. The article contains an annotated bibliography of works illustrating the products of the several frameworks.

family to be a relatively closed system of interaction. It is thus narrower in scope than the structure-function approach which, as Homans in *The Human Group* has indicated, has both an internal system for regulating relations within the family and an external system
for dealing with the transactions between the family and non-family
agencies and events. The scope of the interactional approach corresponds roughly to the internal system of the structure-function
schema. As a consequence it has stimulated hundreds of inner-oriented
studies of marriage and the family but has not spawned many
family-in-the-community studies. Three orders of concepts are illustrative: (a) status and inter-status relations, which become the
bases for authority patterns and initiative taking; (b) role, role conceptions, role expectations and role differentiation; and (c) processes
of communication, conflict, compromise and consensus, of problem
solving, decision making and action taking.

The family development approach, youngest and least seasoned of
the frameworks, is not really in competition with the other seven
since it was created to remedy the deficits of the other approaches
and where possible to incorporate their strengths into one unified
scheme. From rural sociologists it borrowed the concept of stages of
the family life cycle. From child psychology and human development have come the concepts of developmental needs and tasks. From
the sociologists engaged in work on the sociology of the professions
has been borrowed the concept of career and the view of the family
as a convergence of intercontingent careers of husband and wife, later
of children. From the structure-function and interactional schools
have been borrowed the concepts of age and sex roles, plurality
patterns and the many concepts associated with the family as a system of interacting actors. The resulting frame of reference furnishes
an opportunity for the accretion of generalizations about the internal
development of families from their formation in the engagement and
wedding to their dissolution in divorce or death. An integration of
the scattered writings on family development has been recently completed by Hill and Rodgers.[10] This approach to family study implies
use of the longitudinal method of research, which because of its expense and slow yield has seen limited use in family research to date.

In quick summary, three approaches are both appropriate and suggestive of concepts and ideas for our research problem. The symbolic

[10] Reuben Hill and Roy H. Rodgers, "The Developmental Approach" in Harold T.
Christensen, ed., *Handbook of Marriage and the Family* (Chicago: Rand McNally,
1964) pp. 171-211.

interaction approach is rich in concepts related to decision making and goal setting, and offers help especially in relating internal family organization to success in making family acquisitions. The structure-function approach offers, in addition, leads about the transactional behavior of the nuclear family unit with outside agencies like the school, the church and the marketplace. Transactional concepts will be important in the exchanges between the nuclear family and kinship extensions in studying intergenerational transfers, gift giving and receiving, styles of conspicuous consumption and living up to or down to the Joneses. As an approach, family development has the advantage of incorporating most of the relevant concepts about the family from both the interactional and structure-function frameworks including the all important concepts dealing with family transactions while adding the dimension of family growth over time, coping as it does with the orderly and predictable changes which occur over the family's life cycle. Of the eight approaches we have considered, family development offers the most for this research.

Family development views the nuclear family as a small group system, intricately organized internally into paired positions of husband-father, wife-mother, son-brother and daughter-sister. Norms prescribing the appropriate role behavior for each of these positions specify how reciprocal relations are to be maintained as well as how role behavior may change with changing ages of the occupants of these positions. This intimate small group has a predictable natural history designated by stages beginning with the simple husband-wife pair, and becoming more and more complex with each additional position that is activated, then becoming less complex as members are launched into jobs and marriage and the group contracts in size to the husband-wife pair once again. As the age composition of the family changes, so do the expectations for the occupants of the positions in the family change, and so does the quality of interaction between family members.

Coping with the demands of the community and of family members, families may develop policies which not only help in making choices in the present but give direction and structure to the future. As the family develops in stature and competence from wedding day on, it builds a history of problem solutions, a pattern of decision making and a set of rudimentary family policies by which actions can be judged. These policies, moreover, include the family's time schedule for reaching important goals and objectives, owning a home, closing the family, launching children into jobs and marriage, and retirement. These are the contents of the family culture which, if we knew them, would make family behavior more predictable.

Scope and Focus of the Research Problem

With the choice of the nuclear family as the unit of study and the family development approach as the conceptual framework within which to work, the focus and scope of the research problem could be more readily delineated. We shall be studying quite directly family exchange behavior, both acquisitive and transmissive. The behaving units will be nuclear families with variable histories and at differing stages of their careers. The extent and quality of acquisitions and other actions will be expected to vary greatly by stage of the family cycle, and at any given stage should be highly related to the effectiveness with which the family has managed its many resources to date (which we have chosen to call "consumership").

Using the lenses provided by family development concepts, variables are suggested which may be expected to account for the success or failure of families in managing and getting ahead. Beginning with the assumption that the family is a purposive system and that its members are goal oriented, we hypothesize that motivations for planfulness, accompanied by knowledge and skill in manipulating the means of planning, combined with good group organization for action, should include the essentials for effective long-range planning effectiveness.

Motivationally, families will vary in their valuing of planfulness as a mode of living. Most families will fall in between the extremes of Benjamin Franklin-type prudence and the fatalistic acceptance of one's lot in life characteristic of depressed families. Furthermore, families will vary in the degree to which they value services, travel and education more than durable goods such as houses, cars and appliances. Additionally, we expect families to vary greatly in their orientation to time, some looking to the past, many to the present and some to the future for the good life. It will be interesting to correlate these orientations toward time with planning effectiveness.

Knowledge about the methods of problem solving, of rational decision making, may be expected to be unequally distributed among families. The skills of management may be transmitted, as are other aspects of the culture, from the parental families. The research should explore the possibility that knowledge about the procedures of problem solving runs in families like speech forms and table manners. Intergenerational comparisons will be extremely useful here.

There are close parallels between the problem of accounting for fertility planning effectiveness and effectiveness in long-range planning in the present projected study. Families in Puerto Rico that were not only highly motivated, but also possessed a knowledge of the means of fertility control and were internally well organized to act upon this knowledge were also more likely than others to be regular and effective users of birth control methods.[11]

To be efficient and effective in stewarding one's resources, a family must be a well-organized team, and the relationships between spouses should be especially adequate. How effective, for example, is the family as a group in perceiving, discussing and arriving at consensus about what to do in vital areas of family planning? Families may be expected to vary in their power structure, in the openness of the channels of communication within the family, in the adequacy of communication between members and in the accuracy of perception of the wishes and desires of other members. These are illustrative of the action potentials which are brought to bear when the family is viewed as an organization for meeting problems and taking action.

Finally, the family development approach suggests the great gain to be obtained from a historical-longitudinal view of family success and failure in coping with crucial problems. Just as marital success can best be predicted by the pair's success in engagement achievement, and parole behavior best previewed by the prisoner's criminal career, so also can a family's effectiveness in long-range planning be anticipated best by an analysis of its past successes in management. Such successes can be represented by the family's residential history, its income and wealth curves and the occupational and education careers of the breadwinners.

The outlines of a theoretical schema of analytic categories which will be useful in explaining family effectiveness in long-range planning have begun to shape up from our discussion of the contributions of family development thinking to the problem at hand. The advantages of the framework will be even clearer as we complete the theoretical schema (Chart 1.02) and indicate the methods suggested by the framework for rendering it researchable. The schema is termed an "accounting model" because it is an open ended attempt to specify the many types of explanatory variables which "account" for variance in the dependent variable. It is multi-variate and uni-directional.

[11] Reuben Hill, J. Mayone Stycos and Kurt W. Back, *The Family and Population Control* (Chapel Hill: University of North Carolina Press, 1959).

An Accounting Model of Analytic Categories

In the schema of analytic categories we have prepared (Chart 1.02), the demographic background variables used by the economist to account for variance in most of his dependent variables are placed on the extreme left of the schema and the dependent variable which we wish to explain, namely, effectiveness of planning, is on the extreme right. Intervening between these two major blocks of variables are categories of explanatory variables which become increasingly specific and dimensionally similar to the dependent variables as we move from left to right.

The block of dependent variables, Block G in our accounting model, is evaluative of the consumption process which we have conceptualized in phases as follows: Needs → Articulated Plans → Decision-Making → Action → Satisfaction with Action Taken. Evaluation of the phases of the consumption process is shown in this block of variables as a series of measures constituting a profile of *family consumership:* a measure of risk taking (volume of plans and actions), a measure of the rationality of choice making and decision-making, a measure of planfulness (degree of preplanning of actions taken and fulfillment of plans articulated) and a measure of the satisfaction with actions taken. The complexities of operationalizing the dependent variables will be detailed further in Part Two of the monograph.

As we look at the categories of explanatory variables on the left of the dependent variable, Block G, we identify Block E, Marital Climate (family action potentials) and Block F, Cumulative Career Patterns, conceptual categories which should have high predictive value. Block E reflects the adequacy of internal organization for action in problem solving, including measures of husband-wife communication, marital agreement and marital integration. Block F involves career profiles cumulating the family's history in choice making with respect to such crucial issues as where to live, what jobs to keep or leave and how large a durable goods inventory to acquire. The resulting profiles should predict planning effectiveness with more accuracy than measures of family attributes alone could ever do.

Block C, Developmental and Intergenerational Properties, groups together first several variables which reflect the family's developmental history—years married, stage of life cycle and age of spouses at marriage. Also included in Block C are designations of intergenerational properties including generation, lineage type, intergenerational helping patterns and degree of intergenerational continuity.

CHART 1.02

Schema of Analytic Categories Specifying Interrelations Anticipated in Family Consumership Study (an accounting model)

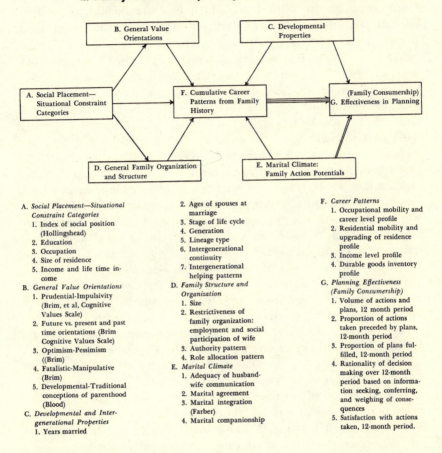

A. *Social Placement—Situational Constraint Categories*
1. Index of social position (Hollingshead)
2. Education
3. Occupation
4. Size of residence
5. Income and life time income

B. *General Value Orientations*
1. Prudential-Impulsivity (Brim, et al, Cognitive Values Scale)
2. Future vs. present and past time orientations (Brim Cognitive Values Scale)
3. Optimism-Pessimism ((Brim)
4. Fatalistic-Manipulative (Brim)
5. Developmental-Traditional conceptions of parenthood (Blood)

C. *Developmental and Intergenerational Properties*
1. Years married

2. Ages of spouses at marriage
3. Stage of life cycle
4. Generation
5. Lineage type
6. Intergenerational continuity
7. Intergenerational helping patterns

D. *Family Structure and Organization*
1. Size
2. Restrictiveness of family organization: employment and social participation of wife
3. Authority pattern
4. Role allocation pattern

E. *Marital Climate*
1. Adequacy of husband-wife communication
2. Marital agreement
3. Marital integration (Farber)
4. Marital companionship

F. *Career Patterns*
1. Occupational mobility and career level profile
2. Residential mobility and upgrading of residence profile
3. Income level profile
4. Durable goods inventory profile

G. *Planning Effectiveness (Family Consumership)*
1. Volume of actions and plans, 12 month period
2. Proportion of actions taken preceded by plans, 12-month period
3. Proportion of plans fulfilled, 12-month period
4. Rationality of decision making over 12-month period based on information seeking, conferring, and weighing of consequences
5. Satisfaction with actions taken, 12-month period.

The intergenerational variables are new in family research and their impact will be watched closely.

Block D, Family Structure and Organization, is a more general and theoretical category of variables than Block E and would have greater theoretical usefulness than some of the more specifically relevant variables in Block E if our research shows it predicts planning effectiveness. How do families with restrictive type organization, cloistering the wife at home, highly centralized in power structure and possessing a rigidly segregated sex division of labor, compare with families with open permissive organization in which the wife works gainfully and is active in community affairs, characterized by equalitarian distribution of power and high sharing of duties and responsibilities within the family? In Puerto Rico restrictiveness of family organization, indicated by high husband dominance, restrictions on the wife working and participating socially, was found negatively related to success in fertility planning.[12]

Block A, Social Placement-Situational Constraints Category, has been widely used to explain economic behavior of families but has meager relevance to any body of middle-range theory. These demographic background variables reflect the vagaries of life conditions and the environmental limitations under which families operate. They become meaningful theoretically in our model when they are translated into the values which families of similar situational circumstances share, shown in the schema as Block B, General Value Orientations. People reared in the open country share a set of values that will be somewhat more traditional, fatalistic and magical than will people reared in a metropolitan environment. It isn't the country air but the country associations which differentiate rural from urban residents. Likewise, education and occupation are social placement variables which, when used to classify families, segregate those who are restrictive and severe in their disciplinary practices and conceptions of parenthood from those who are permissive and developmental. By combining education, occupation and area of city lived in, an Index of Social Position can be computed which segregates families into social classes sharing a common subculture.[13] Our schema will permit the testing of the relationships between Block A and Block B variables to ascertain whether or not the predictive value of the former lies largely in the value orientations of families rather than in the happenstance of their social placement in the community.

The schema in Chart 1.02 allows for historical and cross-sectional analysis, since the conceptual categories provide both time depth variables and contemporary attribute type variables. It is possible to undertake both discerning analysis through progressive cross-classification of variables and factor analysis. The model, finally, permits the testing of our basic formula: that high motivation (appropriate value orientations and goals), acquaintance with and cumulative experience in manipulating the means and adequate organiza-

---

[12] Hill, Stycos and Back, *op. cit.,* pp. 203-214.
[13] See the work of August B. Hollingshead and Frederick C. Redlich, *Social Class and Mental Illness* (New York: John Wiley and Sons, 1958), pp. 387-397.

tion to take action are necessary for optimum effectiveness in long-range planning.

A Research Design

A number of strategies are open to us as we attempt to render the accounting model outlined in Chart 1.02 manageable within the limitations of our time and money budget. The choice of a population of families to be studied, the sampling design employed, the methods of data collection and data analysis are among the means we employ to keep the problem within the bounds required.

Let us again phrase the research problem. We have, basically, a problem in explanation leading to prediction rather than solely description. *We wish to account for the success or failure of families in structuring and controlling the future.* The main subject matter will be longitudinal patterns of earning, saving, buying and financial planning; the basic data are sequential rather than cross-sectional in character. The dimension of time and timing are crucial in the understanding of family planning; postponement of expenditures is as important to predict as purchases. Our research design will need to make possible long-run observations of families through history taking, and shorter run observations forward in time through waves of interviews with a panel of families.

Who Have Been Studied?

Within the limitations of our budget, a number of possibilities for research populations occurred to us: (1) a cross-sectional sample of families at all stages of family development broadly representative of Minnesota, (2) a sample of metropolitan Twin Cities families encompassing two or more generations but unrelated, (3) an intergenerational sample of intact three-generation families representative of Minneapolis-St. Paul.

Although we recognized the possibilities of the bias of greater residential stability in the third alternative, we also saw that the advantages it offered for our family development framework were substantial. The population of families could be regionally homogenous, largely urban and intergenerationally linked, thus holding constant the variables of region, urbanity and variations in private family culture. Moreover, it would offer depth historically and permit the type of intergenerational comparison which no study yet had undertaken.

We were fortunate in being able, through the generous cooperation of the research department of the Minneapolis *Star and Tribune,* to tap a series of area probability samples of families in the Twin Cities in surveys undertaken during the period of our tooling up in which respondents were asked about their membership in three-generation families. Roughly four per cent of 3,000 opinion poll respondents reported such three-generation linkages with their kin resident within 50 miles' radius of the Twin Cities. This has made possible identifying 360 nuclear families linked by threes, 120 grandparent families, 120 parent families and 120 young married children families.

Through this device of three-generation families, it was believed that the excessive cost and awkwardness of a truly longitudinal study, which would try to follow families for an entire generation, could be avoided without sacrificing more than a few of the benefits of a longitudinal study.[14] It will be seen that all stages of the family cycle will be represented in the grandparent families, most of the stages of the cycle in the parent generation and the first stage of family development in the young marrieds. Looked at cross-sectionally the variance in the stages of the life cycle will be held constant, but using retrospective histories, the depth of life cycle analysis is possible for two of the three generations.

By means of intergenerational data collection, whatever continuity in family culture is transmitted can be compared and held constant in intergenerational analyses. Such data also permit us to take into account changes due to historical circumstances such as wars, depressions and periods of inflation. Patterns of family spending and consumption change over time, partly because family members grow older and partly because historical circumstances shift. From intergenerational data drawn from the same family lines it was hoped we could identify the continuity and growth changes which could be generalized as part of life cycle development and those which were adventitious or due to historical circumstances.

The sample because of its special character differs in certain

[14] Other trials and tribulations of longitudinal studies which we have avoided through the three-generation device can be noted from the recent evaluation of the longitudinal method in child development and physical growth research, see Dankward Kodlin and Donovan J. Tompson, *An Appraisal of the Longitudinal Approach to Studies of Growth and Development* (Lafayette, Indiana: Society for Research in Child Development, 1958). The author has described elsewhere the relative advantages and disadvantages of five methodological short cuts that have been devised to circumvent costs and travail of longitudinal research with families, see his "Methodological Issues in Family Development Research," *Family Process* (1964), 3, pp. 186-206.

major respects from the population living in the Minneapolis-St. Paul Standard Metropolitan Statistical Area (Table 1.02). Yet when plotted by location the families are ecologically dispersed in all of the major neighborhoods. Drawing a sample by generational cohorts created some distortion in the age composition which in turn affects the occupational and educational composition of the sample. For example, the inclusion of the grandparent generation skews the sample to the older ages with a consequent lower average income and educational attainment than is found in the SMSA population. The presence of three generations of the same family living in the area means that the respondents have also been less mobile geographically. There is also an overrepresentation of persons claiming affiliation with the Roman Catholic faith. Though differing from the general population, the sample is representative of the universe of intergenerationally linked families living within the same metropolitan area.

How Have Families Been Studied?

A number of strategies were open to us in the choice of methods of data collection. Interviews, tests, questionnaires, diaries, records and projectives had all been suggested. Choice of informant was an issue, whether to use husband or wife or both in joint interviews. Panel interviews, poll type interviews or depth interviews constituted still another dimension to consider.

We decided that our chief reliance in technique would be on standard semi-structured interviewing procedures. Respondents would be interviewed in their own homes, where interviewers could obtain the data necessary for interviewer ratings from direct observations at the same time that they conducted formal interviews. A system of sequential interviews combining the advantages of the panel and the longitudinal method seemed indicated in which families would be interviewed in four waves, once every three months, covering a twelve-month period. One purpose of repeated interviewing for the period of a year is to encompass a complete annual cycle, thus accounting for seasonal variations in routine.[15] The repeated inter-

---

[15] Unfortunately the full advantage of seasonal variations was not achieved because the interviewing was spread out over the entire wave and the last families interviewed in Wave I were already in a season different from the first families interviewed. A much larger interviewing staff would be necessary to correct for this elongation of the interviewing period. Ideally enough interviewers should be utilized to conduct all interviews for each wave within the first week, thus assuring uniformity of season, of historical events, and other environmental features which might affect consumership.

TABLE 1.02

**A Comparison of the Composition of the Three-Generation Sample
and of the Population of the Standard Metropolitan Statistical Area
for Minneapolis-St. Paul, 1959**[a]

| | Three Generation Sample | | Standard Metropolitan Statistical Area |
	f	*%*	*%*
Age of Male			
Under 20	3	1.1	40.7[b]
21–30	71	26.9	12.6
31–40	16	6.1	13.6
41–50	37	14.0	11.5
51–60	42	15.9	9.2
61–70	19	7.2	7.2
71–80	55	20.8	3.9
80 and over	21	8.0	1.1
Occupation of Male			
Professional, Technical	16	10.1	14.6[c]
Mgrs., Officials and Prop.	34	21.5	12.6
Clerical and Kindred	9	5.7	10.0
Sales	12	7.6	9.4
Craftsmen, Foremen	35	22.2	21.3
Operatives and Service except Household Workers	38	24.1	24.7
Farmers	10	6.3	1.1
Laborers	4	2.5	6.2
Residential Mobility			
Same House as in 1955	139	63.8	48.0[d]
Different House, Same County	62	28.4	30.8
Different House and County, Same State	14	6.4	10.8
Different House, County, and State	3	1.4	8.1
Residence in 1955 not Reported	—	—	1.5
Education (25 years and older)			
No school	15	3.3	.7[e]
1–6	78	17.2	5.9
7–8	121	26.7	23.8
9–11	65	14.3	17.0
12	119	26.2	30.0
13 or over	56	12.3	22.6
Income			
Under 2000	22	10.2	5.6[f]
2000–3999	41	19.1	10.4
4000–5999	71	33.0	22.3
6000–7999	43	20.0	26.0
8000–9999	13	6.1	16.0
10,000 and over	25	11.6	19.8

| *Religious Affiliation* | Sample St. Paul | | Population St. Paul[g] | Sample Minneapolis | | Population Minneapolis[g] |
	f	*%*	*%*	*f*	*%*	*%*
Roman Catholic	64	61.5	45.0	51	40.1	33.3
Protestant	40	38.5	50.0	71	55.9	66.6

viewing also enables us to conform to the principles of a longitudinal study for the year of data gathering supplemented for the past with retrospective history taking. We have had to rely for the past on respondents' memories and powers of verbalization, as assisted and checked by the testimony of the prior and succeeding generations.

Interview content for successive waves of interviews is designated in Chart 1.03. which outlines the content of each wave of interviewing. The chart indicates that content divides into a part that is repeated at each wave and a part that is different; the former deals primarily with recent and immediately prospective purchase plans, or other changes in status, and their fulfillment or modification, while the latter deals with the intergenerational history of the family and its long-range financial goals and commitments. At each interview, data about family attributes (termed cross-sectional explanatory variables in the chart) were elicited by pencil-paper tests or questionnaires.

During each wave after the initial wave, one-third of the families were seen in a joint interview with both husband and wife present, during which they discussed their family goals and policies and crucial issues of authority, decision making, division of labor as well as those items such as the financial aspects on which the husband is likely to be the more expert informant. From the joint interview the interviewer observed husband-wife interaction directly on a number of issues devised by Nelson Foote, requiring reconciliation of differences to give him the basis for rating the adequacy of communication between husband and wife, the degree of consensus they demonstrated, who took the initiative and the location of power in decision making in the family.

[a] The N's on the various comparisons differ with the proportion of individuals in the sample falling into the particular categories.

[b] U.S. Bureau of the Census, U.S. Census of Population: 1960, General Population Characteristics, Minnesota, Final Report PC (1)-25B (Washington, D.C.: U.S. Government Printing Office, 1961), p. 54, Table 20.

[c] U.S. Bureau of the Census, U.S. Census of Population: 1960, General Social and Economic Characteristics, Minnesota, Final Report PC (1)-25c (Washington, D.C.: U.S. Government Printing Office, 1961), p. 237, Table 74.

[d] Ibid., Table 72, p. 227.

[e] Census, General Social and Economic Characteristics, op. cit., p. 232, Table 73.

[f] Ibid., p. 247, Table 76.

[g] Minneapolis and St. Paul Council of Churches. The St. Paul Catholic Chancery gives different percentages for Catholics, as follows: St. Paul, 41%; Minneapolis, 26%.

CHART 1.03

Content of Interviews and Tests for Four Waves Family Consumership Study

Type of Variables Treated	Wave 1	Wave 2	Wave 3	Wave 4
Cross-Sectional Explanatory Variables a. Self-reporting b. Observer rating based on joint interview	a. (1) Role allocation (2) Power structure	a. (1) Brim Cognitive Values Test (2) Conceptions of Parenthood Test b. 1/3 of sample, joint interviews (1 Foote test of: Authority pattern Demonstration of affection Communication pattern (2) Family goals and achievements	a. (1) Communication (2) Social participation (3) Farber marital integration test b. 1/3 of sample, joint interviews (1 Foote test of Authority pattern Affectional pattern Communication pattern (2) Family goals and achievements	a. (1) Intergenerational Visiting and Interaction Patterns b. 1/3 of sample, joint interviews (1) Foote test of Authority pattern Affectional pattern Communication pattern (2) Family goals and achievements
Historical Environmental Variables	1. Residential status and history 2. Family composition status 3. Occupational and educational status 4. Financial status	1. Checking changes and reasons for changes 2. Family composition history and changes in 3. Changes in occupational status 4. Changes in financial status	1. Changes in residential status 2. Checking family composition history and changes 3. Employment history and changes in 4. Changes in financial status	1. Changes in residential status 2. Changes in family composition 3. Checking job changes 4. Financial history and changes in
Longitudinal Dependent Variables	1. Inventory of current durable possessions 2. 1/2 of history of inventory acquisitions 3. Expections of purchases next 3 mos.	1. Changes in inventory since Wave 1 (outcome) (a) Confrontation of discrepancies (b) What happened? 2. Completion of history of inventory acquisition 3. Expectations of purchases 4. Interviewer check on decision-making pattern followed 5. Interviewer check on satisfaction with outcome of actions taken	1. Changes in past 3–4 mos. (a) Confrontation of discrepancies (b) What happened? 2. Expected changes 3. Interviewer check on decision-making pattern followed 4. Interviewer check on satisfaction with outcome	1. Changes in past 3–4 mos. (a) Confrontation of discrepancies (b) What happened? (c) Impact of interview on plans 2. Interviewer's check on decision-making pattern followed 3. Satisfaction test on actions over period 4. Summary of all help exchanges among generations and with other kin, with peers, specialists and agencies for entire study year.

With the exception of this joint interview, the wife has been the spokesman for the family. Previous studies have verified the high reliability of the wife as informant for the family. Elizabeth Wolgast found the wife equally well informed and more accurate in predicting the fulfillment of purchase plans than the husband.[16] From the standpoint of expediency, the wife would be by far the most accessible family informant for repeated interviews.

Beginning with the first interview, history taking for one of the crucial status variables was undertaken, starting with residential status and history in the first meeting and ending with financial history in the fourth wave. Expected changes in each of the four statuses were noted to be checked in subsequent waves. Thus in four waves life cycle sequences for each family on residential mobility, family composition, occupational careers and financial growth were elicited.

The data on acquisition of durable goods were gathered longitudinally by interview exclusively, obtaining in the first wave the inventory of durable possessions and making a beginning on the history of each possession. The inventory was a selected sample of the durable items listed by the *Life* study and included items from the categories of labor-savers, comforts, time-fillers and status items. Additionally at each wave, expectations of purchases during the next three months were elicited and the extent of commitment to the expenditure probed. On the second and subsequent waves, changes in the inventory were noted and discrepancies between expectations and outcomes discussed. A process account of the reasons for postponement, the change in importance now ascribed to the expected but postponed purchase, and the interplay of members about the purchase or failure to buy were obtained. This has been done over the year's period for each of the six areas of discussion: acquisition of durables and automobiles, redecorating or remodeling, changes of residence, of job, and changes in the family's financial portfolio.

This concentration on *what happens in between waves* is what distinguishes the longitudinal panel study of decision-making from most panel studies which merely verify changes in opinion on issues at different points in time or collect evidence of fulfillment or non-fulfillment of purchase plans at specified points in time. The advantage of taking soundings at different points of time is lost unless linkages of a process nature are made *in between* to account for change or non-change.

At the end of each confrontation interview in which discrepancies between plans and fulfillment were discussed, the interviewer has ob-

[16] Wolgast, *op. cit.*

tained information on the decision-making effectiveness of the family for the period covered. This evaluation has taken into account the adequacy of information on which decisions were based, the degree of consultation inside and outside the family, and the extent to which long-range and short-range outcomes were used in arriving at decisions.

Problems of attrition were expected to be great for this study, since every family we lost for whatever reason represented a total loss of twelve interviews. We felt keenly the importance of minimizing panel attrition. A number of steps were taken in that direction. Our initial contact with the families was a letter from the Director of the Minnesota Family Study Center of the University of Minnesota telling them of the purpose of the study and its importance. Much was made of the fact that this was a pioneering study of three-generations of the same family lines, that such families were hard to find and that they, the selected families, were rare and important people. Interviewers found the doors open when they arrived and were able to move ahead quickly to obtain commitments to participate through the high interest of these families in intergenerational comparisons.

Interviewers themselves were carefully selected and trained. They were exposed to much more difficult stress situations than they were likely to encounter in field situations. Taped interviews with tricky responses were used to develop skill in clarification probes and accuracy in recording. An important part of the interviewer training has been the involvement and commitment of the interviewers to the research idea, which has been made possible by their participation in the final stages of constructing and pretesting the original interview schedules. Interviewers were expected to develop high rapport with their families, since they were to remain with the same families for twelve months, barring unforeseen contingencies. A supervisor operated as troubleshooter when emergencies arose, to follow up on reluctant families. Attrition has been held to a minimum (see Chart 1.04), ending the interviewing with 312 surviving families of 336 located in the first interview, a much lower figure than that reported by Ferber's pioneering study.[17]

Our attrition from the first, most difficult, contact amounted to thirty-nine families because we dropped all three generations if one could not be located or induced to cooperate (7 refusals in the first wave resulted therefore in losing 21 families). After the first wave

[17] Robert Ferber, *Factors Influencing Durable Goods Purchases* (Urbana: Bureau of Economic and Business Research, 1955), pp. 10-12.

was completed, we held on to all generations which continued to co-operate even if one member of the trio dropped out. The major attrition after the first wave was due to dishonest reporting by one interviewer, resulting in the loss to the study of twenty families and more than twenty interviews. This was discovered by random call-backs between waves. In the 939 interviews with wives and the 300 additional joint interviews with both spouses obtained after Wave I, only seven refusals were encountered. This is a refusal rate of less than one per cent and a remarkable tribute to the effectiveness of the interviewer training program and the high caliber performance by most of the interviewers. In effect, the study suffered attrition from refusals to cooperate only at the beginning and held the families remarkably well once the initial interview was completed.

An equally serious problem with our type of research design is the possible *training* effect of being interviewed on the planning effectiveness of families over the twelve months covered by the longitudinal interviews. This problem of conditioning panel families has not been given the attention it deserves, but a beginning has been made. Sandage found no marked evidence of bias developing in panel members either in beliefs or information about cooperatives and chain stores as a consequence of prolonged membership of up to seven years in a consumer panel of farm families, when compared with newly added panel members.[18] Ferber, however, found his more frequently interviewed panel members purchased more and were more accurate as a consequence of being studied. He has no measures to indicate that they also became more planful or that they became more effective in fulfilling their purchase plans.[19] We were able to make the same tests of reflexivity that Ferber did, but have gone further. As part of the fourth interview, we asked the respondent if any discussions in the family in between waves made mention of the interview or the interviewer and what difference, if any, this made in the plans arrived at. The evidence at hand suggests there is no improvement in planfulness over the time period studied and little impact of the interview on discussion about future plans.

Problems of operationalizing conceptual variables are great for certain parts of the theoretic model depicted in Chart 1.02. Many of the self-reported items among the cross-sectional variables in the top row of Chart 1.03 have been collected by tests and scales already used

---

[18] C. H. Sandage, "Do Research Panels Wear Out," *Journal of Marketing*, (April 1956), pp. 399-401.

[19] Ferber, *op. cit.*, p. 11.

CHART 1.04

**Flow Chart Showing Sources and Amounts of Attrition
From Original Intergenerationally Linked Sample
and
Reserve Sample Replacements Made Before Completing First Interviews**

	Located and Successfully Interviewed Wave I	Successfully Interviewed Wave II	Successfully Interviewed Waves III-IV	
360 Families Expected in Original Sample 375	 336	 315	 312	107 child generation families
I. Replacements from Reserve Sample 15 —				105 parent gen. families
II. Sources of Attrition				100 grandparent generation families
1. Migration of one or more generation from area, thus disqualifying all three generations	12	1. Refused to cooperate beyond Wave I 4	1. Refused to cooperate beyond Wave II 3	
2. One generation or more refused to be interviewed or weren't home after repeated calls	21	2. Dishonestly reported as interviewed, but no interviews beyond Wave I 17		
3. Grandparents too senile to be interviewed, disqualifying all generations	3			
4. Dishonestly reported by interviewer as interviewed but checkbacks proved otherwise	3			

in other studies, and employing them has served to further standard-
ize their use. A test by Orville Brim and colleagues, the Cognitive
Values test, was particularly appropriate for our study.[20] We have also
utilized previously developed tests for power structure, role allocation, conceptions of parenthood, social participation, communication, marital integration and marital consensus.

How Have The Data Been Analyzed?

Because the project's unique research design called for such a far-
ranging variety of methods, employing the method of the cross-
sectional survey, longitudinal sequential interviewing, as well as simultaneous history taking with three generations, the possiblities of
data analysis have been enormous.

There are rich materials for sheer description of the processes of
family planning and decision-marking comparing three generations
of the same family line. Descriptive analysis has clarified the types of
issues and problems families have been most planful about, what
they have left to chance and what they have tended to handle impulsively.

At the more analytic level, the schema depicted in Chart 1.02 provides a model for zero order cross-classification of variables to explain consumership. It also provides a model for factor analysis
by blocks of variables, and for multiple and partial correlation analysis of the variance in the dependent variables explained by all
blocks and by each block of explanatory variables.

Summary

This initial chapter has constituted an account of the choices made
and actions taken as the research problem evolved from an initial
interest in the range of patterns by which families structure the
future (and the possibility of utilizing the methods of longitudinal
research in studying this) to the completion of a research design
ready for application in the field. The strategies employed have included:

1. Choice of the nuclear family as the unit of study rather than the
    individual or the household since it is the unit of decision

---

[20] The properties of the Cognitive Values test (labelled Test of Epistemological and
Instrumental Beliefs by the authors) can be examined in Orville Brim, Jr., et. al.,
Personality and Decision Processes (Stanford: Stanford University Press, 1962)
pp. 71-74, pp. 309-311. See also Appendix B for a list of the specific items used in this
study, pp. 414-417.

making in asset accumulation, is easily accessible for study, and is a referent of several conceptual systems of theory.

2. Choice of the family development framework from eight alternative approaches, since it views the family as an interacting and transacting small group system and is able to cope with episodes of interaction of decision-making length as well as larger units of time such as stages of development over the family's life span.

3. Development of an accounting model of analytic categories which specifies the chief dependent variable of family consumership and the major explanatory variables and their interrelationships.

4. The formulation of a sampling design which would maximize the possibilities of data collection longitudinally and intergenerationally, producing an intergenerational sample of 312 intact families linked through three generations, and living accessibly within 50 miles of Minneapolis-St. Paul.

5. The decision to obtain longitudinal data by combining *history taking* in several areas of decision from the beginning of the marriage with *panel interviewing* forward in time over a year's period in four waves of interviews.

6. The diversification of methods of data collection to cope with the diverse problems of data accessibility:
   (a) Four semi-structured interviews with wives
   (b) One joint interview with both spouses
   (c) Pencil-paper tests filled out by both spouses
   (d) Direct observation of stress situations involving observation guides and ratings by interviewers.

7. The choice of a wide range of methods of data coding, analysis and summarization.

The choice of the longitudinal dimension of family consumption has not been undertaken lightly. It has been consciously and reluctantly neglected by previous investigators because of the high cost entailed, yet all authorities agree on the desirability of such studies. By joining the theoretical interests of family sociology in the intriguing regularities of family development and the methodological interest in intergenerational comparisons, we have provided a device for obtaining the benefits of longitudinal study without having to follow the same lineal families for twenty or more years. By comparing generations of the same lineal families over their histories from marriage to the present and by observing their consumption behavior forward in time over a year's period, an effective compromise of the longitudinal and the panel studies has been achieved. If in analysis these data do join meaningfully, the path will have been broken for future longitudinal studies more within the limits of existing resources. Many existing cross-sectional data will become more meaningful, and some of the errors from generalizing longitudinal conclusions from cross-sectional data may be detected and corrected.

CHAPTER II

The Families Studied:

THREE GENERATIONS OF THE SAME FAMILY LINES

BEFORE CONSIDERING THE ISSUE of the timing of plans and actions, which constitutes the basic substance of the planning careers of families, we want in two chapters to describe our cast of actors in this drama. The more than three hundred families who joined us as collaborators in this study were convinced by our letter of invitation that it was indeed time some attention be given to three-generation families. They took us on faith and opened their homes to our questions. Since our cooperating families were promised anonymity in joining the study, we shall identify them not as individual families but as generational groups, giving the study thereby the three-generation stamp of which they approved so highly.

The grandparent generation is concentrated in the ages sixty and over, with about two-thirds in the 71-80 years bracket. These couples have been married on the average fifty years or more. The parent generation is more varied with respect to age, ranging from forty-one to seventy, but is concentrated in the ages 46-55 (with wives about five years younger than their husbands). Over two-thirds of this generation have been married long enough to celebrate their silver (25th) wedding anniversary. The married child generation is not young by teen-age marriage standards, with 85 percent of husbands and 82 percent of wives in the 21-30 age bracket. They have been married on the average of five and a half years.

The grandparent generation entered marriage just before World War I and was at the end of the child-rearing period before the great depression set in. The parent generation married in the midst of the depression and was well along in the child-rearing phase when

World War II started. The married child generation was born in the aftermath of the depression and has been reared under conditions of war stress and warborn prosperity. Marriage for this third generation began under conditions of relative affluence in the period immediately following the Korean War.

To what extent historical circumstances have affected these three generations will be difficult to disentangle from other influences which come with maturation and aging. The comparisons of the three generations which we will undertake in this chapter, however, should be read with the above historical contexts in mind.

Ecological setting. The environmental setting in which the study takes place is metropolitan Minneapolis-St. Paul and hinterland extending outward along a radius of roughly eighty miles. The three hundred families are widely distributed within this area, with many more grandparent generation units at the rural periphery and somewhat more married child generation units in the suburbs. Fifteen percent of the grandparents live outside a fifty-mile radius of the city compared with just 3 percent of their married grandchildren units.

The ecology of metropolitan Minneapolis-St. Paul is greatly affected by the meandering waterways of the Minnesota and the Mississippi rivers and by the more than thirty lakes within its borders. These waterways and lakes are linked together by parks and playgrounds which give a distinct cast to the zoning of residential, business and industrial areas. Residential zones border the waterways and the lakes and extend out into the suburbs. Deteriorated areas border the industrial, railroad and central business sections of the two cities, and dwelling units there today are of uniformly poor quality.

From an analysis of the location of families by socio-economic status of census tracts, it is apparent that the parent and child generation units predominate in the upper economic areas. The grandparent generation units are both most numerous in the middle and the lowest group and would appear to be most deprived in their living setting. The overpowering impression, however, is one of great dispersion of families of every generation in all sectors of the metropolitan area.

When the generations expressed their preferences of areas to live in, the married child generation clearly prefers the suburbs (33 percent) or the "city further out" (24 percent); the parent generation divides quite equally between suburbs, country, small town and city outskirts; the grandparent generation provides a substantial vote for the country (27 percent), with small minorities voting for other sectors.

When the interviewers made their first visits they rated the neighborhoods in which families lived on several dimensions of desirability:

1. Upkeep of streets, sidewalks, trees
2. Size of lots, spaciousness, upkeep of yards, lawns
3. Freedom from industrial and business encroachments
4. Friendliness and neighborliness
5. Overall desirability.

The generations differ in the ratings of neighborhoods lived in very much as their distribution by socio-economic status of census tract would indicate. Two-thirds of the grandparent generation are living in the two lowest categories of neighborhoods, C and D areas, with only 3 percent living in A grade neighborhoods. Parent generation units are better located, with 10 percent in A grade areas and only 58 percent in C-D grade neighborhoods. The married children units are in between, with more living in D grade areas than the older generations but more also located in B grade neighborhoods. In time it can be anticipated that the married child generation will surpass the other two generations in the quality of their living spaces.

A test of the extent to which neighborhood grades run in families is provided in Table 2.01.

TABLE 2.01

Shifts in Neighborhood Grade by Generation

	Percentage of Families in Better Neighborhoods %	Percentage of Families in Poorer Neighborhoods %	Percentage Remaining the Same %	Total %
From Grandparent to Parent Generation	38.0	23.9	38.0	100
From Grandparent to Married Grandchild Generation	36.6	29.0	34.4	100
From Parent to Married Child Generation	21.0	31.6	47.4	100
Number of Families	89	79	112	

Examination of this table suggests that there is a significant tendency for neighborhood grades to be the same from generation to generation; that is, married child, parent and grandparent units will be living in similar type neighborhoods. The correspondence is greatest between parents and married children where 47.4% were similarly graded. There is slightly more similarity between grandparent and parent (38%) than between grandparent and their married grandchildren (34.4%).

The dissimilarity between generations is due to the improvement in neighborhoods from grandparent to parent and from grandparent to grandchild. Parents, however, are living in significantly better neighborhoods than their children. One might speculate that this relationship may change in time because of the upward movement of the married child generation.

Residential mobility. The movement of families from one neighborhood to another is not possible to trace directly with the data we have. We know that twenty-seven married child units moved in the six months preceding the first interview, and another thirteen at that time were poised to move again. This is over six times the mobility of the grandparents and five times the movement of parents over the same period. During the year of the study, 72% of the child generation made plans to move and 35% actually did move. This was roughly four times the mobility of the more settled parents and grandparents. The pressure to move, for the married child generation, is primarily to meet space deficiencies with the addition of children and, incidentally, to do this by shifting from rental to home ownership.

The movement of families has been increasingly from rural to urban places by generation. About half the grandparents were reared in rural areas, about a third of the parent generation and less than one-tenth of the married child generation. But fewer than a fourth of the grandparents have spent 50 percent or more of their years in rural areas, and only five percent of the parent generation units have been so long in rural areas. Ninety-one percent of the married child generation has never spent any time in rural areas. The movement is clearly from rural to urban, even for the grandparents, and the other two generations are almost entirely urban in their orientation.

The mobility of the youngest generation has been largely intra-city mobility, averaging three-fourths of a move per year of marriage, with forty-seven couples moving one or more times per year of marriage. This is four times the mobility of the parent generation and outdistances the grandparents even more.

This picture of the three generations is one of increasing movement in space, of residential upgrading and of improving the adequacy of the neighborhoods in which families live. The grandparent generation is most rural in background, most deprived in adequacy of neighborhood, and most residentially stable. The parent generation is almost entirely urban in background and residence, best located by socioeconomic area, and next most stable residentially. The married child units are entirely urban and residentially highly mobile.

Situational Incentives and Constraints

Families are small group associations for which high expectations are held in our society. They are supposed to be the means for their members getting ahead in the world, yet they must also meet the everyday emotional needs of members and maintain a reputation of integrity and self-dependence economically. Since children are no longer potential assets who can be expected early to earn their keep, but liabilities for most of their days with mouths to feed, bodies to clothe and minds to educate, the number of children a family has becomes a significant situational incentive and/or constraint to family action. The three generations differ in their valuing of family size and the numbers they have contracted for.

Number of children. All three generations identify the four-child family most frequently as the preferred size. The grandparent generation valued more children on the average than the two younger generations, with the parent generation being least child oriented. With respect to sex distribution, the predominant answer is "no preference" or "equal numbers of boys and girls." Girl children are more frequently preferred by the married child generation than the two older generations. Spacing of children was not too well understood by the grandparents, and many parents were vague about this issue. In contrast, the married child generation shows marked preference for intervals of one or two years between marriage and first child and two- and three-year intervals between subsequent children.

In family size expressed as number of children ever born, the grandparent generation averaged 5.2 children, with over a fourth bearing eight or more children. This is higher than their preferred family size of four children. The parent generation restricted family size to 3.5 children, with over half of the families found in the two- and three-child categories. The married child generation is just beginning its childbearing cycle but already averages 2.4 children per family with twenty years of childbearing still ahead. As will be shown in more detail later, this generation leads the parent generation in the first five years of marriage in number of children born and if it continues at this rate may be expected to surpass its antecedents in size before closing the family.

Present household size. At this point in time the grandparent generation has contracted sharply in size to 2.73 persons; virtually all children have been launched. The parent generation units also are in the last stages of the life cycle, one-third of their children married and out of the home, averaging 3.71 persons in the household. In contrast, the married child generation is still expanding in size and averages 4.14 persons, each with everchanging needs. Only one-tenth have no children yet, two-thirds have pre-school age children and one-fifth have children of school age under twelve.

Stage of family development. To give numerical expression to the stages in which the units of the three generations find themselves, Table 2.02 has been prepared:

TABLE 2.02

Distribution of Families by Stage of Family Development and by Generation

	Grandparent %	Parent %	Married Child %
Childless, marriage to birth of first child	—	—	8.7
Expanding, birth of first child to birth of last child	—	—	89.7
Stable, birth of last child to launching of any child	—	1.0	—
Contracting, first launched to last launched	11	70.3	—
Aging companions, no children in home	81	24.8	—
Divorced or one partner deceased	8	1.0	1.9
	100	100	100
Number of families	100	105	107

From Table 2.02 it is clear that the pressure of population on space and other family resources will be heaviest in the married child generation. These families can be expected to be more dissatisfied with their residential arrangements, income and jobs than the other two generations, which are contracting in size and in responsibilities.

Educational status and aspirations for children. The avenue of upward mobility, of increased productivity and of increased competence to deal with the exigencies of living appears to be education. On no single index do the generations differ more sharply. See Table 2.03.

TABLE 2.03

**Percentage Distribution of Years of Education
of Husband and Wife by Generation**

	Grand-parent		Parent		Married Child		Total	
	H	W	H	W	H	W	H	W
7 years of school or less	56	49	16	6			23	17
8	28	33	31	26	6	1	21	19
9–11	7	10	21	25	20	24	16	20
12	4	5	23	35	44	55	24	32
13–15	5	3	8	8	15	16	9	9
16–17+			2	1	15	6	6	2
Total	100	100	100	100	100	100	100	100

Standard education for the grandfathers was eight years or less (84 percent). In the parent generation 47 percent of husbands reached this level and 23 percent graduated from high school. For the youngest generation only 6 percent stopped with 8 years of schooling, 44 percent graduated from high school and 30 percent have had some college training. This is a remarkable shift in three generations of the same family line.

The same story appears to hold for wives, with 82 percent of grandmothers, 32 percent of the parent generation and only 1 percent of the child generation stopping with eight grades. A slightly lower proportion of wives received higher education than husbands in the youngest generation, whereas the pattern among parents and grandparents was just the opposite.

The aspirations for one's children have also increased tremendously by generation. We asked each couple to think back to when they were first married and had first decided on the amount of education they wanted for their children. This was a difficult task for the older couples, of course, and the answers are undoubtedly biased by the actual achievements of their children, but we provide their answers as an indication of change in educational aspirations. Grandparents reported they were satisfied to have their children finish high school, and 20 percent saw elementary school as sufficient. Aspirations for sons were slightly higher than for daughters. (Actually their daughters exceeded their sons in the years of schooling completed. See Table 2.03). Half the parent generation units reported that at marriage they wanted their daughters to finish high school and half set college graduation as aspirations for their sons. The generation of young marrieds is quite uniform in setting college graduation as the norm for its children; two-thirds of sons and one-half of daughters are so destined.

A backward glance at Table 2.03 suggests that if we take the parent generation as representative of the children of the grandparent generation, the former exceeded the latter's aspirations for them. The daughters of the middle generation also exceeded their parents' aspirations, but the sons did not, since two-thirds of the parents had set college graduation as the norm for them to attain.

A more precise expression of movement in education from generation to generation is provided in Table 2.04, which shows the degree of advancement or retardation of the most educated adult child over or under that of his father.

TABLE 2.04

Degree of Advancement or Retardation of Most Educated Adult Child Finished with School Over or Under That of Father

		Grandparent %	*Parent* %
	—5 or less	63	28
Father	—4	11	32
Less	—3	4	4
Education	—2	9	9
	—1	3	7
Same Education	0	4	11
Father	+1	1	5
More	+2	2	2
Education	+3	1	—
	+4	1	1
	+5 or more	—	1
	Total	100	100

It is quite clear that the upgrading in education is greatest between the grandparent generation and the parent generation. Almost two-thirds of the best educated sons exceed their fathers by five or more years of school, and only 5 percent had less education. In the next generation the movement is also in the direction of greater education, but the gap is not so large for so many sons. One-third have had four years more, but 23 percent have had roughly the same education, plus or minus one year.

When the education of husbands is compared from generation to generation of the same family line to discover the extent to which amount of education runs in families, Table 2.05 is produced.

TABLE 2.05

**Shifts in Educational Status Categories
by Generation from Education of Husband**

	Percentage of Families Improved Education	Percentage of Families Retarded Education	Percentage Remaining the Same	Total
	%	%	%	%
From Grandparent to Parent Generation	27.8	7.2	64.9	100
From Grandparent to Grandchild Generation	72.2	1.0	26.8	100
From Parent to Child Generation	61.9	1.0	37.1	100
Number of families	157	9	125	291

In this table, similarity of educational level is not nearly as marked from generation to generation as neighborhood grade was in Table 2.01. Indeed, only in the link from grandparent to parent generation do the similars exceed the dissimilars; for example, 64.9 percent are of the same educational level in both the grandparent and parent generation. Twenty-seven have less and 7 grandfathers more education than the men in the parent generation. The other comparisons suggest that upgrading is the norm, with 61.9 percent of married children better educated and only 1 percent poorer educated than parents. The balance of 37.1 percent is of the same educational level. From grandparent to grandchild the movement is even more marked, with 72.2 percent of children better educated and only 26.8 percent of the same educational level. This is indeed a remarkable record of upgrading of the educational level of the population and will be referred to in subsequent analyses of consumership behavior by generation and by educational level.

Occupational status and aspirations. Changes in occupational location have also been characteristic of the generations we are studying. A comparison of the three generations, taking the job last held for the grandparent generation, is given in Table 2.06.

TABLE 2.06

**Percent Distribution of Families by Occupation
of Husband and by Generation**

	Grandparent Percent	Parent Percent	Married Child Percent
Professional	0.0	2.0	3.0
Semi-professional and managerial	7.0	12.0	23.0
Clerical, skilled trades and retail business	14.0	31.0	12.0
Farmers	24.0	10.0	4.0
Semi-skilled, minor clerical	21.0	28.0	34.0
Slightly skilled	18.0	12.0	17.0
Day laborers	7.0	1.0	2.0
Other	9.0	4.0	7.0
Total	100.0	100.0	100.0
N	97	97	97

A shift in composition is evident from the blue collar and farming sections of the work force to the white collar and semi-professional type occupations. This is generally in line with husbands' aspirations for themselves—since the married child generation aspires to the professional (10 percent), managerial (9 percent) and clerical (22 percent) occupations, with twice as many pointing to these upper level white collar jobs as the parent generation and three times as many as the grandparents. Interestingly enough, the largest proportion of each generation prefer the type of work in which they are presently engaged (37 percent of grandparents, 45 percent of parents and 42 percent of married children).

Wives too are in the labor force, with the highest proportion currently employed in the parent generation (47 percent employed). If employed, wives of the married child generation are found more frequently than other wives in higher class employment, as full-time professional or clerical workers.

In justifying the wife working, the generations emphasized different points. The youngest generation was alone in asserting maternal employment fitted well with raising a family (9 percent). Thirty-four percent of both the middle and younger generation said the major justification was that the "wife enjoys or has a talent for her work." The middle generation was also more likely to stress the financial return, "pays bills." Very few wives of the oldest generation were employed, but the stress here, too, was the monetary one.

Examination of the changes in occupational composition from generation to generation suggests more movement upward and less similarity in type of occupations as we move from oldest to youngest generation; Table 2.07 has been prepared to summarize these shifts.

TABLE 2.07

Shifts in Occupational Status Categories by Generation from Occupation of Husband

	Percentage of Families Upward Mobile %	Percentage of Families Downward Mobile %	Percentage Remaining the Same %	Total %
From Grandparent to Parent Generation	57.9	23.2	18.9	100
From Grandparent to Grandchild Generation	48.5	24.7	26.8	100
From Parent to Child Generation	31.3	46.9	21.9	100

Obviously the married child generation may yet surpass the parent generation in job level, since it is at the beginning of its career and brings a superior education to bear. There is no evidence here to support a theory of class rigidity, since movement is more characteristic than conformity from generation to generation. The overwhelming impression is one of great change upward from the grandparent to the parent generation, similar but not such marked upward change from grandparent to grandchild (just beginning a career) and change in both directions from parent generation to child generation, with more beginning their cycle behind their parents than ahead. This may account for the tendency of many parents to equalize this situation by gifts and loans to the married children at the beginning of their careers.

Income adequacy. There are marked differences in income by generation. Grandparents range from $1000 to $6000, with one-half under $2000. Parents are best off with incomes ranging from $1000 to

$20,000, one-half under $6500. Married children range from $2000 to $12,000, with one-half under $5500. The need for income, of course, is greatest for the married children units in the expanding stage of family development.

TABLE 2.08

Shifts in Income Categories by Generation from Classification of Total Family Income in 1958

	Percentage of Families w/higher Incomes	Percentage of Families w/lower Incomes	Percentage Remaining The Same	Total
	%	%	%	%
From Grandparent to Parent Generation	88.7	2.1	9.3	100
From Grandparent to Grandchild Generation	81.4	6.2	12.4	100
From Parent to Child Generation	20.6	44.3	35.1	100

Does high or low income run in families? Analysis of income categories of the generation representatives of the same family line is made in Table 2.08. We see that income levels are not the same but tend to be higher for parents and married children than for grandparents. In view of the pattern of upgrading in the first two generations, it can be expected that the married child generation will ultimately change the picture of their inferior income and level with respect to their parents as they age and mature economically.

One expression of income adequacy is the subjective definition of the income as adequate for necessities only or for luxuries too. Families were asked to express their feelings about the family's income in these terms. Table 2.09 tabulates the responses of the three generations in percentage form and suggests that the grandparents generation feels the financial squeeze more than the other two generations. Half of them are barely meeting the necessities, but 15 percent are on easy street.[1] Three-fourths of the married child group checked

---

[1] The responses of the grandparent generation are quite comparable to the perception of adequacy of income in a Grand Rapids, Michigan, survey of people 60 and above who reported as follows:
    15% couldn't make ends meet

TABLE 2.09

Percent Distribution of Responses on Adequacy
of Family Income by Generation

	Grandparents Percent	Parents Percent	Married Children Percent
1. Do without many needed things	28.0	4.7	1.2
2. Have the things we need, but none of the extras	23.5	5.9	4.8
3. Have the things we need and a few of the extras	30.5	61.0	76.0
4. Have things we need and any extras we want	3.5	14.2	16.8
5. Have the things we need and any extras we want, and still have money left over to save or invest	14.5	14.2	1.2
Total	100.0	100.0	100.0
Number of families	85	85	83

the expression, "We have the things we need and a few of the extras." Only one couple in this generation, however, feels really "flush." It will be interesting to see how this compares with their buying and planning behavior. The parent generation is not only factually better off, they feel more comfortable, distributing their answers toward the luxuries end of the scale.

Ethnic and religious background. Some of the handicaps in education, occupational level and income for the grandparent generation stem from the rural and immigrant backgrounds of that generation. Eighty percent of the grandparent generation were immigrants or first generation compared with 48 percent of the parent generation and 15 percent of the married child generation. The ethnic background is predominantly North European (75 percent), one-fourth of which is Scandinavian.

Religious affiliation is quite similar for husband and wife by gen-

---

66% just enough to get along on
15% had more than was needed.
See Richard Williams, "Changing Status, Roles and Relationships," in Clark Tibbitts, *Handbook of Social Gerontology* (Chicago: University of Chicago Press, 1961), pp. 283-284.

erations as shown in Table 2.10. This is one heritage which appears to be transmitted without marked change from generation to generation, see Table 2.11.

There is no support for the often advanced assertion that families change their religious affiliations toward the churches of higher social standing as they advance economically. The predominant pattern among these families is to stay put, especially among wives of the married child generation (80% remaining stable). Movement is toward the numerically dominant but socio-economically heterogeneous Catholic and Lutheran groups over the other Protestant and Jewish denominations.

TABLE 2.10

Religious Affiliation of Husband and Wife by Generation

	Grandparent		Parent		Married Child	
	Husband %	Wife %	Husband %	Wife %	Husband %	Wife %
Religious Group						
Roman Catholic	39.1	38.5	44.0	44.1	44.1	46.8
Lutheran	22.7	24.8	25.7	26.1	26.1	29.7
Other Protestant	29.1	33.9	24.8	27.0	25.2	20.7
Jewish	1.8	.9	.9	.9	.9	.9
Other	1.8	.9	.9	.9	1.8	1.8
Total	100	100	100	100	100	100
N	110	109	109	111	111	111

We have learned a good bit about the three generations of families participating in this study from the device of locating them in the social structure of the metropolitan community in which they are living. We have looked at their distribution by neighborhoods and socio-economic areas, by educational and occupational status, by family composition and income and, finally, by ethnic and religious background. On many of these locational factors the grandparent generation has been disadvantaged compared with the two younger generations, and the youngest generation has appeared to experience the greatest deprivations arising from the discrepancy between aspirations and achievements. To fill out the picture we will turn to additional data in Chapter 3 about the easing of these deprivations by mutual aid among the generations.

TABLE 2.11

Changes in Religious Affiliation by Generation for Husband and for Wife

							Shift to Other Protestant, Jewish or				
	Remaining the Same		Shift to Catholic		Shift to Lutheran		to Non-Affiliation			Total	
	Husb.	Wives	Husb.	Wives	Husb.	Wives	Husb.	Wives	Husb.		Wives
	%	%	%	%	%	%	%	%	N	%	N %
From Grandparent to Parent Generation	70.1	69.1	13.4	12.4	8.2	10.3	8.2	8.2	107	100	107 100
From Grandparent to Grandchild Generation	55.7	63.9	16.5	15.5	16.5	14.4	11.3	6.2	107	100	107 100
From Parent to Child Generation	68.0	79.4	10.3	7.2	12.4	8.2	9.3	5.2	107	100	107 100

Value Orientations

With this backdrop of information about the social structural and economic constraints within which the generations have been functioning we now turn to the ideologies and beliefs of the three generations for further understanding of their behavior. These have been obtained by opinionnaires filled out at the time of the interviews and are based on the Cognitive Value Scales developed by Orville Brim and his associates at the Russell Sage Foundation.[2] In this discussion we have selected scores on fatalism, impulsivity, pessimism and time orientation for comparing the respondents of the three generations; we also have included a Conception of Parenthood Scale developed by Robert Blood from Duvall's developmental typology to show generational similarities and differences over parent-child issues.

Table 2.12 provides a profile of the median scores and the range in

[2] The scales ingeniously draw from proverbial-type statements about life in each of the dimensions tapped. They are introduced by the statement, "These are proverbs and statements about life. You will find you agree with some and disagree with others." See Orville Brim, *et. al., Personality and Decision Processes* (Stanford: Stanford University Press, 1962), pp. 309-312.

scores for three generations on the several scales used.[3] One is impressed in scanning this table not so much with the differences among the generations, although these shall be noted, but by the similarities. There appears to be high transmission of value orientations from generation to generation.

TABLE 2.12

Value Orientations Profile of Three Generations

Scale	Grandparents Median	Range	Parents Median	Range	Married Children Median	Range
Fatalism-Manipulative	54.4	49-64	52.6	43-58	52.3	40-58
Prudential-Impulsivity	45.1	37-52	45.4	37-55	46.0	37-55
Optimism-Pessimism	18.0	15-21	18.4	16-21	18.0	14.19
Future vs. Present Time Orientation	12.5	9-14	12.9	10-16	13.4	8-18
Developmental-Traditional Conception of Parenthood	6.7	4-8	8.4	6-12	9.3	5-13

Fatalism-Manipulative Attitudes. All three generations are more inclined toward fatalism than "man can manipulate his own future" type proverbs. There are fifteen statements on this dimension which have been scored: strongly-agree-with fatalism-type proverbs and strongly-disagree-with manipulative-type statements would add up to a possible score of 75 (each strongly-agree-with or strongly-disagree-with is worth five points). The median scores of 52.3 to 54.4 are expressive of at least moderate agreement with the fatalist position, grandparents being somewhat more fatalistic than parents or married children. This attitude is even clearer in examining the ranges of the three generations. The types of proverbs with which respondents were agreeing follow:

1. Man's existence is completely under the control of destiny.
2. There is a divinity that shapes our ends, rough-hew them as we will.
3. Nothing comes to pass but what fate wills.
4. Whatever may happen to thee, it was prepared for thee from all eternity.

Prudential-Impulsivity. All generations lean more toward prudential-type statements than those glorifying spontaneity and impulsivity. Statements expressing both sides of this continuum follow:

[3]For range in scores in Table 2.12 we have listed the extreme scores achieved by seven or more families.

1. For every action there's a limited number of outcomes; it's smart to consider them all beforehand.
2. Nothing is less in our power than the heart, and far from commanding it, we are wiser to obey it.
3. Happiness comes from impulse rather than reason.
4. In deciding whether or not to do something, it's wise to make as long a list as you can of all the outcomes.

Optimism-Pessimism. There are fewer statements on which to score the two dimensions of optimism and time orientation so that the highest score possible would be 25 instead of 75. All three generations lean toward optimism rather than pessimism. Statements which reflect these views are as follows:

1. The highest wisdom is continual cheerfulness.
2. To fear the worst is to go through life with an unnecessary burden.
3. It is worth a thousand dollars a year to have the habit of looking on the bright side of things.

Future vs. Present Time Orientation. From the median scores and ranges it appears that the three generations are right in the middle of the future-present orientation, neither predominantly future nor present oriented. The married child generation has a longer range but a higher median score on the question suggesting, as would be expected, higher future orientation. The grandparents are less so, leaning toward present and past orientations. Statements with which they agreed and disagreed follow:

1. Happiness comes from living day to day.
2. Our grand business is not to see what lies dimly at a distance, but to do what clearly lies at hand.
3. The pleasures of one today are worth those of two tomorrows.
4. To live each day as if it were the last would soon lead one to disaster.

Developmental-Traditional Conceptions of Parenthood. In this test developed by Robert O. Blood[4] from Duvall's typologies of parenthood and childhood ideologies, the respondent may make a score of 15 by agreeing with all of the developmental statements from a list of 30 items evenly divided between developmental and traditional statements. There are ten characteristics which describe the ideal father, ten for the ideal mother, and ten for the ideal child. The developmental statements emphasize the importance of growth and de-

---

[4] For a copy of the scale, see Appendix B, pp. 417-418 and Robert O. Blood, Jr., *Teachers Manual* (Glencoe: Free Press, 1956) pp. 46-47.

velopment of the child's personality, the wife's rights to growth as a person, and the father's gains from working with them. The traditional statements emphasize the conception of the child as obedient, respectful of adults, honest, polite, respectful of property, dependable— a "little adult"; the conception of the mother is that of a good housekeeper, cleanliness oriented and focused on habit training; the father is conceived as a breadwinner, disciplinarian, rule enforcer and source of gifts, whose job is "to bring home the bacon" and keep things peaceful.

TABLE 2.13

Shifts in Beliefs About Childhood and Parenthood by Generation

	Percentage Shifts Toward More Developmental Beliefs %	Percentage Shifts Toward More Traditional Beliefs %	Percentage Remaining the Same %	Total %
From Grandparent to Parent Generation	63.9	18.6	17.5	100
From Grandparent to Grandchild Generation	67.0	16.5	16.5	100
From Parent to Child Generation	38.1	24.7	37.1	100

The grandparents are clearly most traditional of the three generations, averaging less than half developmental responses and having a range pretty well limited to the lower half of the scale. The parent generation is more developmental, with several parents falling in the clearly developmental side of the scale. The married child generation has the longest range and the highest average score, suggesting that it is most developmental of all. Of all the ideologies tapped in this list, there is more evidence of social change affecting the generations in the beliefs about childhood and parenthood than in the other areas we have touched.

Further analysis of the shift in beliefs about childhood and parenthood is possible by examination of Table 2.13. Here we show that the shift to developmentalism is greatest from grandparents to parents, and persists to the third generation. Only in the last generation do we have continuity in beliefs to any extent, and this is a continuity of developmental views about childhood and parenthood. This pattern of greater differences between the two older generations is in line with the educational and occupational differences we have observed earlier in this chapter.

In quick summary we might characterize the grandparent generation as predominantly fatalistic, prudential, optimistic, present or past oriented and traditional in parental ideologies. The parent generation is predominantly fatalistic, prudential, optimistic, present oriented and shows mixed developmental-traditional in parental ideologies. The child generation is least fatalistic of the three, prudential, moderately optimistic, most future oriented and the most developmental in parental ideologies.

Marital and Family Organization by Generation

How do the generations compare in the ways their families are organized maritally? Are the relationships between the spouses open and communicative, companionable and affectionate? How adequate is the division of roles and tasks in getting the family's work done? What is the system of decision making employed? Answers to these questions may tell us how flexible and responsive the family will be in meeting the exigencies of living. Has there been movement toward greater companionship and effectiveness, more democratic relationships and higher communication in the younger as against the older generations?

Marital Authority Patterns. We obtained two appraisals of the locus of power in decision making. In one we asked the spouses to indicate who usually makes the final decision with respect to six problems: what house or apartment to take, how much life insurance and what type, whether the wife shall work gainfully, whether the husband changes his job or not, whether or not a doctor is called when a family member is ill, and where to spend vacations. The responses were scored in such a way that husband-centeredness, wife-centeredness and equalitarian patterns were identified in decision making. Interviewers were also asked to record who did most of the talking, who exercised most influence, and who seemed to have the last word in a series of problems posed to the families in a joint interview. These interviewer-observed patterns provide a second set of data on which to classify the same families by husband-centeredness, wife-centeredness and equalitarian patterns. The results are shown in Table 2.14.

There is a clear trend to equalitarian patterns by generation in the self-reported authority patterns. This may reflect partly the changing

TABLE 2.14

**Percentage Distribution of Families by Generation
on Authority Patterns in Husband-Wife Relations**

	Self-Reported			Observer Reported		
	Grand-parent	Parent	Married Child	Grand-parent	Parent	Married Child
Husband-Centered	22	12	15	34	24	41
Equalitarian	69	82	80	28	47	42
Wife-Centered	9	6	5	38	29	18
Total	100	100	100	100	100	100
No. of Families	94	100	107	74	90	96

beliefs about how decisions ought to be made. The interviewer's reports show greater proportions of husband-centeredness in the married child generation and much greater wife-centeredness in all generations than is reported by the families themselves. The observer reports shows wife-centeredness in decision making decreasing by generation and some tendency toward husband-centeredness and equalitarian patterns to increase.

Role Allocation Patterns. Traditionally there has been a clear-cut division of tasks and responsibilities by gender within the family. The husband was the breadwinner, worked in the yard, did the repair jobs around the house, and the wife was housekeeper, cook and nurse. With many wives now gainfully employed, husbands have been involved in crossing the sex line to undertake housekeeping tasks formerly done only by women, creating a fluidity of role allocation and considerably more sharing of tasks together. Table 2.15 provides two expressions of this phenomenon by generation, role specialization and role conventionality. Spouses were asked who it is who usually does the following jobs:

1. Who gets the husband's breakfast?
2. Who washes the supper dishes?
3. Who straightens up the living room when company comes?
4. Who mows the lawns?
5. Who shovels snow from the sidewalks?
6. Who keeps track of money and bills?

From the answers to these questions it has been possible to classify families on the consistency with which husbands and wives always do the same jobs, *role specialization,* and the extent to which the sexes are rigidly tied to doing only the appropriate jobs for their specific gender, *role conventionality*.

TABLE 2.15

**Percentage Distribution of Families by Generation
on Role Specialization and Role Conventionality**

Role Specialization	Grandparent Percent	Parent Percent	Married Child Percent
High specialization, husband or wife always do certain household tasks	78	65	57
Medium specialization, spouses usually but not always do the same specified tasks	14	29	37
Low specialization, great shifting about, in who does tasks	8	6	6
Total	100	100	100
Number of families	99	100	107
Role Conventionality			
Both conventional in doing sex-typed tasks, and combination where wife conventional, husband crossing line	42	21	17
Husband conventional and wife crossing line, and combinations where both cross line	33	62	70
Combinations of conventionality, line crossing and systematic role reversals	26	17	13
Total	100	100	100
Number of Families	98	100	107

Examination of Table 2.15 reveals that all generations follow a pattern of medium to high role specialization, with the specialization higher for the grandparent generation than the younger generations. The married child generation is most flexible in this respect. Role conventionality is less universally practiced, with much crossing of the sex lines and even reversals of traditional roles. Curiously, the grandparent generation is both most conventional in role allocation and also has the highest proportion of combinations in which role reversals occur—brought about possibly by periods in which one spouse or the other is sick and can't perform his usual roles. With both spouses retired, there is also more time and opportunity to try out opposite gender roles. The youngest generation is least conventional in role allocation and highest in wife crossing the line to do men's tasks or both crossing the line on occasion. This may be related to the situational problems facing this generation, with heavy demands on two parents for child care services, housekeeping services worked out with split second timing and full-time employment of husband.

Material Consensus and Role Integration. From Farber[5] we have borrowed measures of consensus on the ranking of family values (Marital Consensus) and of role tension and integration involving identifying desirable and undesirable role attributes in the spouse (Role Integration). In Table 2.16 the median scores for these two measures are shown in a profile of marital organization. Consensus on family values improves by generation, but role integration deteriorates by generation. The grandparent generation does not appear to share the same values to the same extent as the other generations, but they see one another in a more kindly light as this is reflected in low role tension.

Marital communication scores are especially low in the grandparent generation—perhaps they do not have the same need to communicate on issues after many years of meeting common problems. The best communicators are the young married children, according to the interviewers, who rate them as highest both on marital communication and companionship. In the self-reported scales on communication and agreement the older generations are higher in agreement and lower in communication.

TABLE 2.16

Profile of the Generations on Marital Consensus, Role Integration, Communication and Agreement

	Grandparent Median Score	Parent Median Score	Married Child Median Score
Marital Consensus (Agreement on Family Values)	0.25	0.28	0.44
Role Integration (Absence of Undesirable Role Attributes)	33.0	24.0	18.5
Marital Communication	4.6	15.4	16.3
Marital Agreement	36.5	27.9	25.0
Marital Companionship and Communication (Observer Reported)	7.20	7.86	8.10

[5] Bernard Farber, "An Index of Material Integration," *Sociometry* (1957, 20), pp. 117-134. See also Appendix B for copies of scale used p. 410.

Marital Conflict and Resolving of Conflict. In the observations made by the interviewers in the joint interview in which differences between the spouses were generated by posing difficult questions which they were expected to answer as a pair, the interviewers found a greater readiness to enter into conflict among the youngest generation. The parent generation couples were very loath to enter into conflict over differences and in the expression of hostility toward one another, but were also lower on expressed consensus on the issues raised. The pattern of the youngest generation was frequently one of identifying differences, engaging in conflict and then locating a basis for agreement, with one party undertaking to smooth over the differences and seeking to save face. Among the generations the husband was more likely to play the peacemaker in the young married child generation, with the wife acting as the "idea person" who identifies the differences between them. Altogether the interviewers found the sessions with the youngest generation the most colorful and interesting. They were both most likely to produce conflict and gestures of hostility, but also most likely to conclude with consensus and gestures of affection.

Achievements of Families in Housing, Inventory Accumulation, and Financial Security

In looking back over their careers, the generations took quite different perspectives. The two older generations, of course, were at the end of their achievement spurts and had leveled off. The youngest generation was just well started. They were, therefore, asked different questions: To the grandparents and parents the question was put as follows: "Looking back over your marriage, how close would you say you've come to realizing your desires for your family?" To the children generation the question was, "In your marriage so far, where would you say you are in your 'timetable' for achieving your desires for the family?"

More grandparents found it impossible to answer the question (23 percent of grandparents, 14 percent of parents, 12 percent of married children). About 20 percent of responding grandparents felt they had achieved "about half and half," 72 percent had achieved all and 6 percent felt they had overachieved. Parents' goals were higher originally, and 31 percent felt they had achieved "about half and half," 63 percent had achieved all and 6 percent agreed they had overachieved. The children responded well to the notion of a timetable or schedule of achievement:

53 percent felt they were about on schedule

34 percent felt they were ahead of schedule

11 percent felt they were behind schedule

2 percent felt they probably would never get there.

In closing this chapter let us turn to the tangible accomplishments in the economic areas of housing, accumulation of a durable goods inventory and financial holdings to assess the relative position of these three sets of families in July 1958 as the study was launched.

Housing Adequacy. The three generations differ sharply in the types and adequacy of their present housing. Remembering that present residential status reflects the accumulation of benefits as well as handicaps since marriage, as well as the amount of discretionary income that can presently be devoted to housing, the findings are interesting to examine.

Using type of dwelling as a rough index of adequacy, all three generations are predominantly housed in single unfurnished units, but the parent generation leads with 88 percent so located (grandparent 75 percent, children 59 percent). The grandparents lead in unfurnished duplexes with 13 percent, and children in multi-unit unfurnished quarters with 16 percent (grandparents 7 percent, parents 4 percent). This links with number of rooms occupied, tenure and housing adequacy. Grandparents average fewer rooms than parents (M = 4.9), but their needs for space are lower. Parents average most rooms (M = 5.6) and lead in home ownership of quarters (93 percent). Children are least adequately housed given needs for space (M = 4.6 rooms) and are more frequently located in rented quarters than the other generations (45 percent compared with grandparents 22 percent and parents 7 percent).

Using rental value of quarters as an index of housing adequacy, the grandparent generation occupies quarters of lowest rental value (M = $48); indeed, 45 percent live in quarters valued at less than $50 a month (parents 15 percent, children 12 percent). It must be remembered that grandparents are more likely to be at the rural periphery of the cities geographically and to live in less adequate neighborhoods. The parent generation leads in rental value, with 37 percent living in homes exceeding $125 a month compared with grandparents of only 14 percent and married children of 29 percent.

The most sensitive index of housing adequacy compiled by the present study takes into account bedrooms per person resident, bathrooms per persons beyond preschool age, presence or absence of dining room, and telephone facility. When the three generations are compared on this index they are amazingly similar in the median scores and differ primarily in the range achieved:

		Housing Adequacy Index	
	Median Score	Mean Score	Range
Grandparent generation	25.23	24.72	12-31
Parent generation	25.20	24.98	14-34
Married grandchildren	25.30	25.32	16-31

The impression of inadequacy of housing for the grandparents is caught from the representatives in the lower sections of the range, but using the median as an average these extremes don't affect the average. Using the mean, a somewhat different picture of housing adequacy emerges in which each succeeding generation appears more adequately housed than its predecessor.

Acquisition of Durable Goods Inventory. It has been said that nothing's emptier than an unfurnished house! Couples begin accumulating items required for housekeeping well before marriage, and they are listed high in the gifts obtained at wedding receptions. Some families point to their inventory of durable goods as others do to their automobile or house as symbols of "having arrived." We see durable goods as serving symbolic status functions, as providing short cuts to recreation and ways of saving time, as well as sheer comfort. As such they appear to families as indices of accomplishment of family objectives.

We have drawn our list of durable goods from a much larger listing in the nationwide LIFE *Study of Consumer Expenditures* (1957). Several dimensions of goods were sampled in arriving at the final listing: small and large ticket items; necessities and luxuries; items of high, medium and low saturation; items that bring comfort, prestige, save time and fill time (recreation). Among comforts we included air conditioners, electric blankets, several types of floor coverings and several types of sofas. Among time savers we included several types of stoves, refrigerators and freezers, sewing machines, washing machines and dryers, vacuum cleaners, dishwashers, garbage disposals, electric fry pans and coffeemakers. Among recreational time fillers we included several types of radios, television sets, record players and high fidelity equipment and musical instruments.

Table 2.17 presents a list of 24 items ranked by saturation of item for the sample as a whole. The parent generation leads the three in the proportion of the total possible items present in the family inventory with the average parent generation family having 36.7 percent of the 24 items compared with the average married child generation family with 33.3 percent and the grandparent group with 29.9 percent. This ranking of acquisitions by generation parallels closely earlier rankings of present income, occupational level and rental value of dwelling lived in.

TABLE 2.17

**Percentage of Families Possessing Durable Goods Items
Listed by Generation (1958)**

		Grand-parent	Parent	Married Child	Total	
Rank	Item	%	%	%	%	N
1	Refrigerator	98	100	98	99	287
2	Sofa	90	98	97	95	276
3	Television	87	99	93	93	270
4	Radio	92	93	96	93	272
5	Washing machine	85	96	91	90	263
6	Vacuum cleaner	79	95	75	83	242
7	Sewing machine	82	91	64	79	230
8	Range, other (gas)	76	78	74	76	222
9	Dining room table	76	84	56	72	209
10	Floor cover—carpeting	64	76	70	70	204
11	Electric coffee maker	39	60	69	56	163
12	Electric fry pan	21	47	45	38	110
13	Floor covering, other	40	27	39	35	103
14	Food freezer	22	42	28	31	89
15	Musical instruments	23	39	27	30	86
16	Range, electric	25	26	27	26	75
17	Record player	7	37	28	24	70
18	Dryer, gas	4	20	28	17	50
19	Dryer, electric	6	12	20	13	37
20	Electric blanket	11	16	7	12	34
21	Hi-fi equipment	3	12	14	10	29
22	Garbage disposal	3	11	5	7	19
23	Air conditioner	3	10	1	5	14
24	Dishwasher	1	4	5	3	10
	% of Total by Generation	29.9	36.7	33.3		

The parent generation exceeds each of the other two generations in the proportion possessing luxury items in which saturation is low: air conditioners, garbage disposals, food freezers, electric blankets and record players as well as a few luxuries which have high saturation such as vacuum cleaners, sewing machines, floor carpeting and dining room tables. Children lead the three generations on coffeemakers, clothes dryers, radios and hi-fi equipment which, with one exception, were recent entries into the market. Grandparents lag behind in the proportion owning any of the items in the inventory except the cheaper type of floor covering, linoleum or throw rugs.

The remarkable finding in this table is not that parents lead the three generations on so many counts, but that the married child generation units after only five and one-half years of marriage have acquired so much of their total inventory. As we shall see later, they began the first year of marriage with very nearly as large a collection of durable goods items as their parents and grandparents acquired in the first two decades of marriage. It is little wonder that 82 percent of them feel they are either ahead or about on schedule in the meeting of their objectives.

Financial Security. The simplest of indicators are used in assessing the financial security of the three generations: number and composition of financial holdings in the form of insurances, savings and investments and retirement provisions. Dollar amounts are not shown, but the range of protective devices utilized and the utilization of institutionalized financial mechanisms for reducing the risks held by the future, have been emphasized.

On sheer number of financial policies and investment accounts, the parent generation leads the three groups substantially with 9 items and 40 percent of families have eight or more in their financial portfolio. The married child generation follows with 7.00 and is bi-modally distributed with 38 percent at the upper end of eight or more and 36 percent with only five or six such policies or plans. The grandparent generation lives in another world entirely with only 4.45 items of protection and investment and is concentrated in the four or fewer grouping.

Scanned for type of item: 77 percent of the grandparent generation have no investments set aside for retirement either through insurances, property, business interests or other investments compared with 37 percent of the parent generation and 47 percent of the married child generation. Sixty-two percent of grandparents are covered by Social Security, which is virtually their sole source of retirement income.

Life insurance combined with retirement benefits are found in 49 percent of the parent generation and in 35 percent of the married child generation. The grandparent generation is badly provided, with 55 percent with life insurance only and 34 percent without even life insurance.

In liquid assets Table 2.18 provides a picture which compares the three generations in striking fashion. A third of the grandparent generation have no liquid assets, and another third have only savings. A small minority of the grandparents, about one-fifth have savings, government bonds and some investments in stocks or corporate bonds. Children maintain the most liquid of assets, savings accounts

TABLE 2.18

Percentage Distribution of Types of Liquid Assets by Generation

	Grand-parent Percent	Parent Percent	Married Child Percent	Total Percent
None	32	18	22	24
Savings account	37	36	42	38
Stocks or corporate bonds	2	4	1	2
Government bonds	4	4	4	4
Savings account and stocks or corporate bonds	5	9	8	7
Savings account and government bonds	17	24	17	19
Government bonds and stocks or corporate bonds	0	1	0	
Government bonds and stocks or corporate bonds and savings	3	5	6	5
Total	100	100	100	100
Number of Families	100	104	106	310

(42 per cent) with roughly a fifth having both government bonds and savings. It is the parent generation again which is possessed with enough disposable income to be able to invest it in broad categories including stocks, corporate bonds, government bonds as well as savings. Fewer of the parents are without any liquid assets. This distribution of assets confirms nicely the subjective picture families gave of the felt margin earlier in the chapter: grandparents having only enough for the necessities and no luxuries, married children enough for the necessities and occasional extras and the parent generation with enough for necessities and luxuries too, and "still have enough left over to save or invest."

This concludes our overview of the generational differences in achievement in housing, inventory accumulation and financial holdings. Superficial though it has been, the same picture comes through: the grandparent generation is disadvantaged in housing adequacy, in durable goods accumulation and in utilization of the insurances and protection mechanisms to minimize the risks of the future. All this has been foretold by the previous description of occupational history, income and educational level and current dependency observed in the help given and received record of this generation. The parent generation shows up as advantaged on all counts, with more of a demonstrated margin in some areas of activity than others, yet the accomplishments of the married child generation in its short span of

marriage are so great that it is safe to predict the parent generation will be surpassed in a very few years in the adequacy of housing,
in the size of the durable goods inventory and in the magnitude of
investments and protections acquired.

Incentives to Action and Outlook

What has this panoramic view of three generations of families living in the Twin Cities of Minneapolis-St. Paul in the late 1950's told
us about the incentives they have for planning and acting to change
their lot?

Sheer pressure of population on size of quarters and size of pay-
check should make the married child generation the most mobile
occupationally, the most needful consumer group and the most pressured to bring about change, since family size is largest, quarters are
small and rented and liquid assets are marginal. Moreover, aspirations for children's education and for added children are highest for
this generation. There is, however, no evidence of panic in this group,
since they estimate they are either on schedule or slightly ahead of
schedule and as we shall see in the next chapter, they are more nearly
in reciprocity in help given and received within the intergenerational
network.

In comparison, the two older generations appear lower in motivation. They find themselves at the point in their own cycle of development when they are disengaging from commitments rather
than striving to get ahead. This is true despite the critical disadvantages recorded in the grandparent generation on almost every index of well-being utilized in the chapter.

Given this greater incentive to act, to plan and to strive in the
married child generation, how do they compare in outlook? How do
they compare in their attitudes toward taking action on one's lot, in
their attitudes about living for the future, in their attitudes on prudentiality and planfulness? In this respect the married child family
units are slightly more oriented to manipulate their world, to act
prudentially and plan for the future. The less powerfully motivated
grandparent generation is more traditional, fatalistic and past oriented.
The parent generation occupies the middle ground in this respect.

Given the favorable motivation and the presence of values which
support planful action in the married child generation, what have we
learned about the types of family structure and marital relationships
in this young generation compared with the other two generations
of families? We know the married child units are better educated and

are more flexibly organized as decision-making units. The spouses are more flexible in the allocation of tasks and duties, are more companionable and more communicable. They are, however, more prone to conflict, mutual criticism (role tension) and expression of hostility than the older generations. Nevertheless, they have higher marital consensus (agreement on family values) and appear to be better equipped to meet new and unusual problems because of their sense of common direction (shared goals), their superior ability to communicate and their greater adaptability.

The attempts to trace the carryover of family patterns from one generation to another shows that some patterns are transmitted faithfully but many are not. Religious affiliations tend to be transmitted, as are neighborhood location and value orientations toward fatalism and prudentiality, but educational level, occupational and income category and conceptions about parenthood and childhood have been transformed by the generational process. The patterns of authority in the family, the division of labor between spouses and the ways of resolving conflict are also patterns which appear to be in flux. This story of change and continuity over three generations provides some evidence of generational continuity, but more evidence of upgrading, innovating and creating of new patterns. It is expected from the initial profiles built of the three generations in this chapter that the young married child generation will be especially well prepared to cope with the exigencies of family living during the year they are to be studied. This we shall examine in greater detail in subsequent chapters.

CHAPTER III

Interdependence Among The Generations[1]

IN THIS SECTION we carry the description of the families studied one step farther than was feasible in the previous chapter. From a comparison of the properties and achievements of each of the three generation groups we move to an examination of their transactions with each other and the extent of interdependence which binds them together. Will this examination reveal that our sample of lineages of three nuclear families linked intergenerationally are more insulated each from the other than they·are confederated interdependencies? Are the boundaries which separate the families of each generation maintained in a policy of separateness or are they frequently crossed through intergenerational visiting, participation in celebrations and common social activity and the exchanging of money, goods and services? In an examination of the social network of families in each generation it should be possible to establish how important kinsmen of the other generations are, compared with one's siblings and friends, as well as private, public and commercial agencies, in the solutions of critical family problems.

Boundary Maintenance vs. Boundary Crossing

It has been firmly established by dozens of studies in Europe and the United States that urbanization has not destroyed the kinship ties which link the generations insofar as this is indicated by amount of contact and the exchange of goods and services between parents

[1] We are deeply indebted to Robert Macdonald for many of the tables, analyses, and interpretations of the data presented in this chapter. As indicated in the preface Macdonald's doctoral thesis was built from data collected in the fourth wave of interviews of this research for which he served as field supervisor. See Robert Macdonald, "Intergenerational Family Helping Patterns," Unpublished Ph.D. dissertation, University of Minnesota, 1964.

and their married offspring.[2] The present study, however, is the only one to date to collect data about these inter-family transactions in three-generation depth with respondents from each generation reporting on their own behavior and demarcating their own networks of transaction. In most two generation studies, interviews are with representatives of only one generation who are asked to report for both generations. This study is in a position to verify whether the network of nuclear families to which Litwak has given the term "modified extended family" is more than two generations in depth and whether or not families of other vertical kin (uncles and aunts) are reckoned in the network of the younger generations along with the families of horizontal kin (brothers and sisters and cousins). Discussions of the scope of the modified extended family to date have been largely theoretical speculating about the functionality of different family types and their relative adaptability to industrial living.[3] In this chapter it should be possible to make some empirical contributions about the scope, as well as the mode of functioning of the modified extended family network.

Extent of Inter-kin Contact. Two types of data are available to assess the stance of the three generations with respect to kinship interaction: Ideological beliefs about how much contact there should be and behavioral counts of inter-kin contacts during the year of the study. From an opinionaire administered to the respondents in the final interview normative views were elicited about the issue of the desirability of greater separateness or connectedness among the generations which yielded the following results:

Opinion		Percent Endorsement by Generations		
		Grandparent %	Parent %	Children %
A young couple and their parents-in-law should go their separate ways and see each other only occasionally	Agree	60	42	36
	Disagree	29	46	42
	Undecided	11	12	22
Children who move up in the world tend to neglect their parents	Agree	22	20	9
	Disagree	64	69	74
	Undecided	14	11	17
A young man has a real responsibility for keeping in touch with parents-in-law	Agree	65	65	74
	Disagree	13	21	14
	Undecided	22	14	12

The response to the first of these statements suggests greater ideological support for boundary establishment and maintenance by the oldest than by the youngest generation. This is accompanied by a consensus among all three generations that there is no neglecting of parents by the upwardly mobile and that young couples should take the initiative to maintain parental contacts. These endorsements don't provide much normative support for trends toward greater insulation of nuclear families. Indeed, the youngest generation is the most negative to the idea of each generation going its separate way. If there is any trend by generation it is away from separateness toward maintaining intergenerational transactions.

The behavioral information on the extent of kinship interaction was obtained by asking respondents for the frequency of contact with the other two generations (both maternal and paternal lines) and the siblings on both sides of the family. Contacts could be a visit, telephone call, or letter (although they were mostly visits and phone calls). Respondents indicated if the contacts were daily, weekly, monthly, quarterly or yearly.

We found, in fact, a high degree of contact with kin for this sample of families. The average family contacted a kinsman at least weekly with the married child and parent generation having higher contact scores with kinsmen than the grandparent generation.

Focussing on intergenerational visits only, a table prepared for an earlier publication by my colleague Joan Aldous,[4] depicts the range and distribution of visiting by gender (see Table 3.01). The most frequent visiting is between adjacent generations, first between the married child and parent generations, and second between the parent and grandparent generations. Seventy percent of the married children saw their parents weekly or oftener. However, the amount of visiting between the youngest and oldest generations is also substantial with roughly a third visiting weekly. The visiting network

[2] This literature has been codified by Marvin Sussman and Lee Burchinal in two position papers, "Kin Family Network: Unheralded Structure in Current Conceptualizations of Family Functioning," *Marriage and Family Living* XXIV, 2 (Aug., 1962), pp. 231-240 and "Parental Aid to Married Children: Implication for Family Functioning," *Marriage and Family Living*, XXIV, No. 4 (Nov., 1962), pp. 320-332.

[3] Eugene Litwak, "Extended Kin Relations in an Industrial Democratic Society" and commentary by Irving Rosow, "Intergenerational Relationships: Problems and Proposals" in E. Shanas and G. F. Streib, eds., *Social Structure and the Family: Generational Relations*, (Prentice-Hall, 1965), pp. 290-323, 341-378.

[4] Joan Aldous, "Integenerational Visiting Patterns: Variation in Boundary Maintenance as an Explanation," *Family Process*, Vol. 6, No. 2 (Sept., 1967) pp. 235-251.

TABLE 3.01

Intergenerational Visiting According to Gender*

	Parent-Grandparents		Child-Parents		Child-Grandparents	
	Male	Female	Male	Female	Male	Female
	%	%	%	%	%	%
Daily	6	15	32	21	6	6
Weekly	30	39	42	48	26	35
Monthly	52	39	23	25	16	15
Quarter-yearly	9	6	—	6	36	33
Yearly	3	—	3	—	16	10
N. cases	33	46	31	48	31	48

* The percentage totals do not always add to 100 because of rounding.

appears from these data to be three rather than only two generations in depth.

It is the parent generation, however, which serves as the lineage bridge across the three generations. With its nuclear family boundaries contingent to those of the other two generations the parent generation is most often involved in intergenerational contacts. To function in three generation depth the modified extended family network would seem to require an active "kinkeeping" middle generation.

Examining Table 3.01 for differences by gender, it is clear that daughters are more likely to be the kinkeepers than sons since there is more frequent visiting between daughters and their parents and grandparents than between sons and their progenitors.

The amount of intergenerational visiting in this sample has been shown by Joan Aldous,[5] to be related to social class with working class men engaging in more intergenerational interaction than white collar men. In the youngest generation both upward mobility and downward mobility were found by Dr. Aldous to attenuate kinship contacts. The upward mobile members of the parent generation, in contrast, were more likely than others to be in frequent contact with their parents.

Still another correlate of intergenerational visiting is the phenomenon of a shared tradition of common religious affiliation, common educational achievements, and common marital structures within the same family line, which we have termed intergenerational continuity (r = + 0.15 between family continuity and visiting between

[5] Ibid, p. 240.

children and parents, but no relation was found between family continuity and visiting between grandchildren and grandparents).[6]

Beyond the frequency count of visits and telephone calls as an indicator of inter-kin contact we also have data showing the extent to which the generations share social activities together, such as birthdays and other anniversaries, holidays, vacation trips, sports, picnics, religious observances and club activities. Responses were summarized to include the categories of immediate family, married children, parent, grandparent, horizontal kin, and friends. Respondents were asked for each activity not only with whom they participated but whether they "always" participated or "almost always" or only "sometimes" participated. A typical or modal case shows the family sharing special events such as Thanksgiving, Christmas, Mother's or Father's Days, birthdays and so on, always with the immediate family, almost always with the other two generations on at least one major special event per year. Recreation is shared always with the immediate family, almost always with the other two generations. Religion is shared always with the immediate family, almost always or sometimes with the other two generations, and at least sometimes with one's peers.

From these findings of extensive intergenerational visiting three generations in depth, and high participation in common social activities, we must conclude that the vast majority of the families in this three generation sample are caught up in an extended network of kin which resembles more closely the modified extended family than the type of discrete boundary maintaining insulated nuclear families which Parsons has alleged would best fit our urban industrial society.[7]

Interdependence for Mutual Aid

The most extensive data which we have in this study about intergenerational transactions are drawn from questions regarding help given or received involving exchanges of money, goods, services or

[6] It may be that the married grandchildren are bound to their grandparents by ties of kinship rather than economic or sociability bonds. If so, factors such as the family life cycle stage of the youngest generation, as well as the health and the number of other kinsmen and friends the older generation can call upon will have more to do with the grandchildren-grandparent visiting patterns than a common heritage. See Joan Aldous, "The Consequences of Intergenerational Continuity," *Journal of Marriage and the Family*, Vol. XXVII, No. 4, November, 1965, pp. 462-468.

[7] Talcott Parsons and Robert F. Bales, *Family, Socialization and Interaction Process*, (New York: Free Press of Glencoe, 1955), pp. 3-19.

knowledge. The occasion on which the help was given plus the conditions (that is, loan, exchange, or gift) and the circumstances (whether a specific crisis situation) surrounding the help were noted. In addition respondents were asked a specific question about where they turned in time of trouble. "For the family and personal problems you met or solved during the past year or are presently working on, to whom did you go for advice or counseling?"

TABLE 3.02

Help Source Sought or Source Family Would Seek Regarding Family or Personal Problems

Generation	Dr.	Law.	Sch. Nurse	Soc. Wkr.	Relig. Ldr.	Family Member	None of These	No Problem
Grandparent Per Cent (of 85)	8.2	4.7		1.2	20.0	48.2	17.6	55.3
Parents Per Cent (of 85)	10.6	5.9		2.4	25.9	34.1	21.2	64.7
Children Per Cent (of 85)	4.7	2.4	1.2	4.7	16.5	48.2	22.4	55.3
Per Cent (255)	7.8	4.3	0.4	2.7	20.8	43.5	20.4	58.4

N = 85 Sets or 255 Families

The responses to this question (Table 3.02) enable us to see to what extent respondents tended to turn outside the family networks for counsel. Note that in all generations more than half stated they had no family or personal problems requiring counsel during the year. The parent generation was apparently freest of such problems.

For those acknowledging problems, "members of the family" are most frequently turned to for counsel of all the several possible advisors listed. [Grandparents, 48.2%; parents 34.1%; children 48.2%) followed at some distance by religious leaders (21%) and none of these (20%)]. All other types of counselors received meager patronage from this sample of ordinary families.

If we can accept these answers as valid, there is no serious competitor for kinsmen as advisors for the majority of these families.

In support of the validity of this finding is the count made of help received from "non-kin only" over the 12 months of the study which shows even lower utilization of help from non-kin than is shown in Table 3.02 (grandparents 12%; parents, 14%; and married children, 20%).

Extent of Mutual Aid. To document the full extent of intergenera-- tional transactions we turn to the accounting requested of each generation of the help given and received during the year from all sources including immediate and extended kin, peers, church, social agencies, private specialists, and commercial sources in the problem areas of illness, child care, household management, emotional gratification, and economic assistance. The three generations reported an involvement in a vast nexus of transfers of one sort or another during the year, over five thousand, of which 3,781 were quite clearly help exchanges. Table 3.03 has been prepared to demonstrate the social networks within which help is exchanged. First of all, we note that help exchanges within the vertical kin (giving and receiving help, other generations) exceeds all other categories in the social networks for each of the generations. This is especially true for the grandparents for whom 65 per cent of the instances of help received was familial [from their children (the parent generation) or their grandchildren] compared with 53 per cent for the parent generations and 44 per cent for the married grandchildren. The married child generation operates in a wider flung network of exchanges with a less concentrated pattern, especially of giving within the vertical kin line (only 28%), and gives proportionately more than the other generations to horizontal and vertical kin once removed (siblings, cousins, aunts, uncles, nieces, and nephews), 25% compared to 14% for the parent generation and only 9% for the grandparents. To all other sources (religious organizations, health and welfare agencies, and other specialists), the grandparents give proportionately the most (29%) followed by the other two generations at 25% each. Age mates are least likely to be recipients of help from the parent and child generation, whereas for the aged generation the horizontal and vertical kin once removed are least seen as targets for help.

In general we note that help instances given exceed those received for all generations and for virtually all categories of the social network. The level of giving is highest for the parent generation and lowest for the grandparents. The child generation leads in volume of receiving as might be expected, given its heavy needs.

The data arrayed in Table 3.03 has provided us with a picture of the scope of the modified extended family network when charted by

TABLE 3.03

Comparison of Help Instances Given to Help Instances Received by Generation and by Various Sources Over a Year's Period*

generation	source or recipient	per cent of help instances:		total instances of help
		given	received	
	Total	100	100	
	Other generations	47	65	521
Grandparent	Peers	15	16	148
	Horizontal and vertical kin once removed	9	8	80
	All other agencies	29	10	206
	N = 574	381	955	
	Total	100	100	
	Other generations	44	53	637
Parent	Peers	17	21	246
	Horizontal and vertical kin once removed	14	20	212
	All other agencies	25	6	252
	N = 890	457	1347	
	Total	100	100	
	Other generations	28	44	516
Married children	Peers	22	20	316
	Horizontal and vertical kin once removed	25	27	380
	All other agencies	25	9	267
	N = 844	635	1479	
	Total instances of help	2308	1473	3781

* Per cents may not total 100 due to rounding

giving and receiving of help transactions. The scope is clearly three generations in depth both in giving and receiving help, and for roughly one fifth of the instances of help extended outward to siblings, cousins, aunts, uncles or nieces and nephews. Together these kin exchanges account for 70% of the total of 3,781 instances of help experienced by this sample of families over a year's period. This is hardly support for the assertion that urban families are living in vulnerable isolation shorn of kinship supports. For none of the three generations does this assertion hold. In mutual aid as well as in visiting patterns and sharing in common activities the three generations are linked together in a symbiotic network of multiple services and transfers.

TABLE 3.04

**Comparison of Help Received and Help Given
by Generation for Chief Problem Areas***

	economic		emotional gratifi-cation		household manage-ment		child care		illness	
	gave per cent	re-ceived per cent	gave per cent	re-ceived per cent	gave per cent	re-ceived per cent	gave per cent	re-ceived per cent	gave per cent	re-ceived per cent
Total	100	100	100	100	100	100	100	100	100	100
Grandparents	26	34	23	42	21	52	16	0	32	61
Parents	41	17	47	37	47	23	50	23	21	21
Married children	34	49	31	21	33	25	34	78	47	18

Type of crisis is the overall heading over the type-of-crisis columns.

* Per cents may not total 100 due to rounding.

In Table 3.04 we can examine much more intensively the 1,674 exchanges which occurred exclusively among the three generations by type of help provided and received. The parent generation, within this narrower network, is again the most active in giving help and the married child generation the most frequent recipient of help. The grandparent generation both gave and received least of the three generations in help items of all kinds. Grandparents are not, however, on the periphery of these changes since they were involved in 521 instances of help given or received over the year's period. The parent generation appears again, as in visiting patterns earlier, as the lineage bridge, the sociometric star of the interchanges, giving more to the married children and to the grandparents than either gives to the other. The parent generation also receives in exchange more from the grandparents and from the married children than either receives in their interchanges.[8]

Examining the exchanges in Table 3.04 by area of need highlights

[8] The two generation studies to which we have referred earlier showed mutual aid exchanges running primarily from parents to married children which is consonant with our findings, see Marvin Sussman, "Intergenerational Family Relationships and Social Role Changes in Middle Age," *Journal of Gerontology,* XV (1960) pp. 71-75. The advantage of our three generation design is that we are able to identify the middle generation as the patron of the other two generations and the lineage bridge between them.

the functions which the modified extended family network fulfills for its constituent nuclear families about which there has been much speculative debate. By area of need grandparents required heavy help with the problems of illness (61%), household management (52%) and emotional gratification (42%) for which it would have been difficult to secure aid from non-kin sources. These are precisely the areas in which the married child generation responded by giving heavily. The married child generation in turn required help especially in the problem areas of child care (78%) and of economic assistance (49%) in which the parent generation gave heavily. The ingenuity of the modified extended family linking three generations into one network is that there is defense in depth through the middle generation to help the very vulnerable married child generation get started (only 21% of this generation required no help of a crisis nature during the year) while helping the grandparent generation at its level of need. We might term the several crises listed in Table 3.04 as problems requiring modified extended family functioning which the constituent nuclear families had been unable to solve by themselves.

To highlight this idea of the kin network functioning to pool resources of the constituent generations let us examine the findings in Table 3.04 which compare percentages receiving and giving help in five categories by generation. The parent generation quite clearly gives more help than it receives in all five areas of exchange. The grandparents, in sharp contrast, receive substantially more help than they give in all areas except child care where they have, obviously, no need of help. The married child generation gives more than it receives in three areas—emotional gratification, household management, and illness. This generation, on the other hand, receives more than it gives in the economic-assistance and child-care areas. We get from this table a most interesting picture of changes in symbiosis over the generations. In the beginning of the life span the married child generation is apparently quite willing to receive various kinds of help and perceives itself more or less in equilibrium in its giving and receiving. It appears to benefit more from exchanges that are reciprocal than does the grandparent generation. The grandparents perceive themselves as both meager givers and high receivers, almost in a dependency status, whereas the parent generation, in contrast, is high in giving and modest in receiving, a patron-type status. Only the married child generation appears high both in giving and receiving, a status of high reciprocity and interdependence within its social network.

Associated with these statuses of dependent, patron, and reciprocator are the classifications chosen by the generations themselves when
specifying the conditions governing the transfers of help. We found
that the grandparents tend to classify themselves as "givers" rather
than "exchangers" or "loaners" in terms of giving to others. Similarly
the grandparents tend to classify help received by them as gifts more
often than expected, in comparison to the other two generations
rather than classifying these as "exchanges" or "loans." The parents
see themselves as "givers" in help given to others, but more often
than expected the parents see themselves as receiving transfers of an
"exchange" nature. The married child generation primarily classifies their help items, both given and received, as "exchanges" and
"loans" more often than expected in comparison to the other two
generations.

Preferred Sources for Help. Are there differences among the generations as to preferred sources of help under circumstances of
crisis? We found grandparents tended to turn first to their children
(the parent generation), second to their peers, third to health and
welfare agencies, fourth to private specialists and fifth to their married grandchildren. The parent generation in contrast looked to the
kinship and friendship network almost exlusively: first to their parents, second to their married children, third to their peers, fourth
to private specialists and fifth to siblings. The child generation
brought the private specialist in earlier than the other generations,
second only to parents, and turned third to peers, fourth to siblings,
and fifth to grandparents. All three generations place the friendship
network in third rank among sources to which to turn in crisis
while differing sharply on the use of other non-kin sources.

The kinship and friendship networks provide the major nexus of
help exchanges in this sample. There is alleged frequent giving to
health and welfare agencies (financial, goods, and services) but
scanty acknowledgment of help received from these sources. Only 13
per cent of the three generation sample of families (18 grandparent
couples, 8 parent couples and seven couples of married children)
reported receiving help from health and welfare agencies. This is additional evidence that the majority of the families in the sample are
linked together as modified extended families rather than being
boundary maintaining nuclear in form.

Some Typical Family Reactions to Help Exchanges. In closing
this discussion of the extent of mutual aid among the three generations we are listing some of the typical family reactions to the help
exchanges. Interviewers were often impressed by the good feeling and

extent of expressed interdependence of these families. This is not to say, of course, that there were no situations in which animosity amongst families was present nor that there were no situations in which help given was unwillingly received or not welcomed. Many help items seem to have been given despite the recipient's protests. Many items were given to meet stressor situations with the recipient feeling that the help item was unnecessary, unwanted, or inadequate.

One of the women in the grandparent generation whose family was extremely active in helping other kin, and particularly involved in mutual help with the children generation and neighbors, had this to say:

"The children see to it I don't get anything too old fashioned and no dull colors. Why I ain't even got a black dress! Sometime I'm going to sneak away and get me a nice black dress."

Regarding knowledge help she might seek for family or personal problems, she commented:

"I think any mother would go to her family before she'd go to strangers. She could talk it over in the family. They sure wouldn't give me any wrong advice because my in-laws are so good to me."

Somewhat different is a parent generation family in which the wife commented that she got most help from a social worker who visited periodically. In this family, the parents have experienced serious marital difficulties which presumably have culminated in several overt fights during the past few years. The wife talked of knowledge help she got

". . . from a woman from the court who comes here about once a week. She wants to know how we are getting along. She's mostly interested in the kids. I ask her lots of questions."

The children generation in the same family grouping talked of loaning money frequently to the parents

". . . when things get real rough over there . . . once we paid an electric bill or their electricity would have been shut off."

The children generation in this family also commented about giving frequent marital advice, but neither this nor the financial help was even mentioned by the parent generation respondents.

In another family grouping, the grandparent generation appeared to be somewhat aloof, and perhaps bitter towards the other two generations, commented that they did not believe in lending money to relatives because they had worked hard for their money and besides it was not good in their opinion for young people to have everything handed to them. This attitude seemed to prevail regarding help given to them, apropos of which they commented:

"When my wife couldn't walk, the children came up and sat with her and helped me with the work." The grandmother added: "We really didn't need them. I just wanted to be left alone. My husband was perfectly able to take care of me."

That not all help is given without reservations is illustrated by the remarks of one of the parent generation mothers who commented:

"We're always loaning money or advancing it to people who work for us. We don't have a credit union like some firms. We know all the people who work for us and what their troubles are. My husband is more generous than I am. He's taken in by any hardluck story. Some months it sums into the hundreds. We don't always get it back either."

When asked regarding services help given, this mother commented that everyone seemed to call on her asking her to help on some drive or other to which she usually responded by sending a check instead. When asked as to whether she did any babysitting or helped her daughters by giving any services, she commented: "Certainly not! They have their own maids or housekeepers and they can afford other help if they need it. My babysitting days are over!" And finally regarding knowledge help given, the respondent commented:

"It seems to me that I spend half my life advising people. We employ mostly women. And let's face it, some of them aren't as smart as they could be. Sometimes it's unmarried girls who are pregnant. Sometimes it's husbands who drink or run around. I give them the best advice I can but usually they go ahead and do what they want to anyway."

Regarding her daughters, the respondent said that if they had any real problems, they would not discuss them with their parents.

One of the children generation families commented that, except for special occasions, ". . . . we don't accept or expect gifts from our relatives. There's always too many strings attached." In this family grouping, the parent generation said they gave $500 to the children in this family, which, it should be noted, was not acknowledged by them.

One family, which in many respects is more typical of the majority of the sample, presents a picture in marked contrast to the vignettes above.

The grandparents in this linkage received four phone calls during the course of the interview. Two were from the daughters, one was from the granddaughter-in-law and one was from the husband's sister-in-law. Although this family was existing on a marginal income, they insisted the interviewer have coffee and a light lunch with them, commenting that the electric meter man always has coffee and toast each month when he comes to read the meter. The grandmother, a kindly matriarch, described her attitude this way:

"We try to show a kind face or to be a hero to our relations, so we pinch ourselves black till it hurts. We enjoy more seeing the children pleased and proud than having enough to eat ourselves." The grandfather commented: "We try to make everyone think we're rich and don't need nothing."

In regard to services help during the past year, this family received help from the children generation and the parent generation specifically with respect to remodeling and redecorating the house, with occasional household management help and with frequent transportation provided by kin. They apologized picturesquely regarding their inability to return services to the other generations saying: "I tell you gentleman, last year we were both under the air (sick) so couldn't give it for others (services help)." In regard to the fairly frequent discussion of knowledge sharing or advice giving given amongst the three generations in this family grouping, the grandparents emphasized that they never ask their children what they do, they never pry and do not believe in ".... poking into their business." When asked, and when they are sure their kin want advice, they do give it. They are particularly close with one of their two sons and the granddaughter-in-law. The husband commented he could discuss any problems with his son. "Go to my son it's safe like a hundred locks, go to the daughters, they all tell each other."

Frequency of Intergenerational Contacts and Extent of Help Exchanged

We have found substantial intergenerational contacts through visiting and telephone calls and through participation together in anniversaries, special holidays, and social activities. To what extent is such interaction between the generations associated with the phenomenon of help exchanges under critical circumstances?

In testing the degree of association between kin contact and stressor help patterns, the concept of "reciprocal help transaction" will be employed to classify the different help patterns. A reciprocal help transaction is one in which an instance of help is given to a recipient who in turn gives one or more instances of help to the initiator of the exchange. The categories of reciprocal transactions form a series from full reciprocity to non-participation: (1) Gave help, received help; (2) Gave help, received none; (3) Gave none, received some; (4) Gave none; received none.

Two measures of kinship contact are used: A kinship activity score based on the number of activities shared with kinsmen, and an intensity of kinship interaction score based on the frequency of visits and telephone calls.

Kinship Activity and Reciprocal Exchanges. Table 3.05 cross classifies the kin activity scores with the types of reciprocal transaction patterns for all three generations. It will be noted that reciprocity

TABLE 3.05

Stressor Help Patterns Between Kin by Kin Activities Scores

Kin Activity Score (Three Generations)	Number of Families in Each Stressor Help Pattern Category				
	Gave Some Rec'd. Some	Gave Some Rec'd. None	Gave None Rec'd. Some	Gave None Rec'd. None	Total
	%	%	%	%	%
Kin Activity Score Above Median (15 or more)	45	58	36	35	46.8
Kin Activity Score Below Median (0 to 14)	55	42	64	65	53.2
Total	100	100	100	100	100
N	85	83	47	40	255

Chi square = 8.509
p < .05 > .02

behavior (gave and received some help) is a pattern of high incidence (33.3% of families are so categorized compared with lower frequencies in the non-reciprocating and non-participant categories).

The positive relationship between high kin activity and high reciprocity of help exchanges which might have been expected doesn't appear. A subtler relationship characterizes these two processes. Families of high kin activity scores are more frequently initiators only (i.e. gave some, received none) whereas families of low kin activities scores are more frequently "non-reciprocating receivers" or "neither givers nor receivers." Within the grandparent generation this pattern is especially marked with two thirds of the non-reciprocated initiators having high kinship activity scores compared with forty per cent of the "reciprocators" and twenty eight per cent of the non-reciprocating receivers.

If the kinship activity scores of all families in Table 3.05 receiving no help from kin in crisis situations are compared with those who acknowledged receiving such help, Table 3.06 is produced. In this table high activity scores are disproportionately found among "self reliant" families who received no help from kin in crisis situations

TABLE 3.06

Number of Families in All Three Generations Receiving Stressor Help from Any Source by Kin Activities Scores

Kin Activity Score (Three Generations)		"Self-Reliant" No Stressor Help Rec'd	Stressor Help Rec'd from Kin and/or Others	Total
		%	%	%
Kin Activity Score Above Median (15 or more)		58	40	46
Kin Activity Score Below Median (0 to 14)		42	60	54
	Total	100	100	100
	N	84	171	255

Chi square $= 7.47$
$p < .01 > .001$

whereas low activity scores are found among recipients of such help. Does dependency perhaps beget avoidance?

Intensity of kinship interaction and reciprocal exchanges. The kin interaction score differs from the kinship activity score since it is derived from the frequency of visits and other contacts between a family and their immediate kin. The median score for the sample is 6.4 which represents roughly weekly contacts between a family and its immediate kin. In Table 3.07 a cross-classification of kinship contact scores and types of reciprocity patterns provides relationships very similar to those of Table 3.05 which linked kin activity scores with help exchanges. Although not statistically significant, high kin-

TABLE 3.07

Stressor Help Patterns Between Kin by Kin Contact Scores

Number of Families in Each Stressor
Help Pattern Category

Kin Contact Score	Gave Some Rec'd. Some %	Gave Some Rec'd. None %	Gave None Rec'd. Some %	Gave None Rec'd. None %	Total %
Kin Contact Score Above Median (6.5 or more)	50	58	47	35	49.8
Kin Contact Score Below Median (6.4 or less)	50	42	53	65	50.2
Total	100	100	100	100	100
N	85	83	47	40	255

Chi square = 5.834
p < .20 > .10

ship interaction is found most frequently among non-reciprocated initiators and low contact scores are found among non-reciprocating receivers and among those who neither gave nor received help.

When, however, grandparents are studied separately, a positive and statistically significant relationship emerges between reciprocity of giving and receiving and intensity of kinship interaction; see Table 3.08. Sixty per cent of the full fledged reciprocators were high in kinship interaction compared with 28% of the "gave none, received some" and 17% of the "gave none—received none" families. The latter are good examples of Parsons' independent nuclear families since they both have low kinship contact and have also participtated in no help exchanges whatsoever.

It remains to examine how the kin contact score differentiates between families giving help to "kin only," to "mixed kin and peers," to "peers only" and to "neither kin nor peers." Table 3.09 combines the findings for all three generations to demonstrate a positive and statistically significant relationship between kin contact score and preference in giving to the kinship over the friendship network. Fifty six per cent of "kin only" givers have high kin contact scores compared with 27% of "peers only" givers.

TABLE 3.08

Stressor Help Patterns Between Grandparent Generation and All Other Kin by Kin Contact Scores

*Number of Grandparent Families
in Each Stressor Help
Pattern Category*

Kin Contact Score (Grandparents Only)	Gave Some Rec'd. Some	Gave Some Rec'd. None	Gave None Rec'd. Some	Gave None Rec'd. None	Total
	%	%	%	%	%
Kin Contact Score Above Median (6.5 or more)	59	47	28	17	36.5
Kin Contact Score Below Median (6.4 or less)	41	53	72	83	63.5
Total	100	100	100	100	100
N	22	15	25	23	85

Chi square = 9.93
p < .02 > .01

Thus in a number of analyses there does appear to be a positive relation between *giving help to kin and the intensity of their kinship contacts. Receiving help,* in contrast, is more frequently negatively related to both kinship activity and kinship contact scores as is nonparticipation in either giving or receiving help.

In general, this suggests that those families who share activities frequently are more likely to be independent of one another in regard to help in crises than are those families who share activities infrequently. Indeed, those families who were highest on kin activities tended to be initiators of helping activities which were not reciprocated.

Full reciprocity in help exchanges appears randomly distributed with respect to kinship interaction except within the grandparent generation where it is associated significantly with high kinship contacts scores. In short, there appears to be support for the generalization that dependency does beget avoidance and that high kinship contact is compatible only for those self-reliant families who turn elsewhere in preference to kin in time of trouble.

Several writers have suggested that helping behavior is governed

TABLE 3.09

Number of Families Giving Stressor Help to Kin and Peers by Kin Contact Scores for the Three Generations Combined

Number of Families Giving To

Kin Contact Score	Kin Only*	Mixed Kin & Peers	Peers Only	Neither: No Stressor Help Given**	Total
	%	%	%	%	%
Kin Contact Score Above Median (6.5 or more)	55	53	28	50	49.4
Kin Contact Score Below Median (6.4 or less)	45	47	72	50	50.6
Total	100	100	100	100	100
N	81	87	39	48	255

Chi square $= 8.723$
$p < .05 > .02$

* "Kin" includes other generations, plus vertical and horizontal kin.
** Excludes help to Religious Institutions, Health and Welfare Agencies and Other Specialists.

by a general norm of reciprocity.[9] The present study provides evidence that this norm is operative in family exchanges but suggests also that other norms appear as alternatives to govern helping transactions between families in a kinship network. In analysis of our several tables and case history material it would appear that each generation has developed some consensus about help exchange patterns which enables members of the cohort to maintain some measure of meaningful continuity with the other two generations. The inference to be drawn is that the nuclear family, when involved with kinsmen in reciprocal exchanges, becomes an even stronger unit in facing crisis situations. Simultaneously, the family is weaker and more unstable on crisis occasions if the help flows predominantly one way. It may be that three prevalent norms run throughout the life cycle. These are the norms of reciprocity, filial responsibility, and "noblesse

[9] Alvin Gouldner, "The Norm of Reciprocity," *American Sociological Review*, Vol. 25, No. 2, (April, 1960), pp. 161-178 and George Homans, "Social Behavior as Exchange," *American Journal of Sociology*, Vol. 64, No. 6 (May, 1958), pp. 597-606.

oblige." To be more explicit, it may be that help given or received is governed first by the norm of reciprocity which places constraints and obligations on both the giver and the receiver, and second by the norm of responsiblity of children for their parents (in this case the norm is seen reflected primarily in transfers from parent to grandparent). Thirdly, the helping behavior observed may stem from the desire and sense of obligation of the more advantaged family to aid those perceived to be in less fortunate circumstances. It would seem timely that future research into family helping patterns should examine more closely than has been done to date what combination of norms are associated with the giving and taking of help within the kinship network.

Summary and Conclusions

There has been much discovery in this disquisition dealing with the ties that bind the three generations in the study. Abundant evidence has been arrayed in support of the existence of modified extended family networks seen in the interdependence of the three generations and against the thesis of high incidence of independent boundary maintaining nuclear families in this urban sample.

The intergenerationally linked sample design has permitted the collection of data about inter family transactions in three generation depth for the first time in the history of family research with respondents from each generation reporting on their own behavior and demarcating their own networks of transaction. This study has consequently been able to establish for the first time empirically that the scope of the much debated "modified extended family" is actively three generations in depth both in high frequency of shared kinship activities, in almost weekly interkin visiting, and in a vast nexus of help exchanges of mutual aid.

In mode of functioning the study has demonstrated that the modified extended family network relies on the middle or parent generation to serve as the lineage bridge across the generations. With its nuclear family boundaries contingent to those of the other two generations the parent generation is most often involved both in intergenerational contacts and in help exchanges. We are prepared to hypothesize from these findings that the modified extended family would seem to require an active "kinkeeping" middle generation in order to function in three generation depth.

Who needs such an extended family network? Apparently all

three generations do for they turn predominantly first to immediate kin when trouble strikes. Kinship exchanges accounted for 70% of the total of 3,781 instances of help in the year's period. The married child generation with its pressures of children on resources was most needful and received most help. Whereas the relatively affluent parent generation was least in need of help and received least. Moreover, less than a fifth utilized "non-kin only" for help during the year of the study.

It is in the analysis of the 1,700 help exchanges during the year which were exclusively undertaken among the three generations that the functional and symbiotic character of the modified extended family network is best highlighted because these exchanges also specify the area of need in which help was given and received. By area of need grandparents required disproportionate help with problems of illness, household management, and emotional gratification which are difficult to obtain from non kin. These are precisely the areas in which the married child generation gave more than would have been expected. The married child generation, in turn, required help especially with problems of child care and economic assistance to which the parent generation gave disproportionately. Thus each generation turns to the network for help in solving problems it can't solve for itself. By linking three generations into one functioning network, the modified extended family, through its middle generation, is able to help the very vulnerable married child generation get started while also meeting the grandparent generation at its level of need.

The balance between giving and helping, however, is so asymetrical within the intergenerational network that some strains are introduced. Parents who give to both younger and older generations more than they receive from either are in a *patron*-like status, while grandparents who give much less than they receive find themselves in a *dependent* status. Only the married children appear high in both giving and receiving. They also benefit more from exchanges that are reciprocal than do the grandparents and therefore perceive themselves in the very healthy status of *reciprocators*.

In a further analysis of the phenomenon of giving and receiving help the nature of the strains introduced by non-recipocity were most apparent with respect to receiving without giving. This was associated with low shared activities and infrequent visiting with kin —as if dependency begets avoidance. Non-reciprocated giving in contrast tended to be positively associated with high kinship interactions whereas full reciprocity of giving and receiving was randomly associated with such cultivation of kinship contacts.

These findings lead us to conclude that although intergenerational transactions do appear to be governed in part by the norm of *reciprocity* that two other norms are even more apparent, namely the norms of *filial obligation* and of *noblesse oblige*. These latter norms appear to be sufficient to motivate an optimum level of kin keeping activities designed to maintain viable modified extended family networks.

PART ONE

PLANNING CAREERS

An Overview of the Timing of Actions

IN THIS DESCRIPTION of the planning careers of representatives of three generations we are looking for the order in which events have occurred from early marriage onward, seeking to discover the patterns of timing employed. Families form in marriage, have babies, rear and launch them in a rhythm of growth and contraction that has been called, "The Family Life Cycle." How do the imperious demands of numbers of children at different stages of development affect the decisions of family heads in making residential moves, purchasing a home, acquiring durable goods including cars, or undertaking investments and savings? In what sequence do these several decisions occur? Does the addition of the first child precipitate a change in residence which, if to an unfurnished dwelling, requires adding durable goods, in turn affecting the financial portfolio? Are occupational changes linked with income and residence changes? Do all three generations show the same patterns of sequential change? Do their careers follow the same curves of rapid accumulation in the early years, leveling off in the middle years and dropping off in the later years? (The child generation can't be observed in these later stages, of course, since its most seasoned couples are just finishing their first ten years of marriage.)

To make a beginning at answering these several questions, the histories of each generation of families have been plotted on each of the areas of economic activity in which we are interested. After they have been examined separately, they will be interrelated to discover to what extent activity in one area is contingent upon activity in a second area at a given point in time. We will also check to see to what extent families which, over the marriage, consistently lead their generation in one activity also lead in the other activities being studied.

Finally, we are also interested in knowing how well a family's career in the various activities before the study began previews its planning and actions during the year of study. This we shall examine separately for each area of economic activity. Does lagging one's generation over most of one's career make for greater or lesser effectiveness in planning over the twelve months covered by our interviews?

The sequence of our interests in this discussion of careers links in tandem the three-part focus of the great French sociographer, Frederic LePlay, "Family, Work, and Place," since we will look at family composition changes, occupational career, and residence histories. These three aspects of family development are closely interlinked but are also more frequently precipitators of economic activities than consequences. Family additions, job changes (including wife working), and residential changes tend to precede as incentives or constraints rather than follow the other areas of economic activity of our study, namely, financial portfolio changes and durable goods acquisitions. These latter are more clearly contingency variables, dependent upon preceding incentives or constraining actions. Perhaps this justifies in part the order in which we shall examine the areas of economic decision: family composition changes, occupational changes, residential changes, financial portfolio changes, and acquisitions of durable goods.

CHAPTER IV

Changes in Family Composition and Occupational Career Patterns

CONCERN OVER THE CONTROL of family size has been so great in recent years that the term "family planning" has almost been preempted to mean fertility control. The present research makes no exhaustive analysis of family size planning, but we do attempt to interrelate changes in family size with actions in other areas of family living. In this chapter we will begin with a description of changes in family composition over the life span, noting similarities and differences among the three generations studied, and after an examination of activity during the year of the study will assess the comparable changes in the occupational career patterns by generation.

Changes in Family Composition Over The Life Span

Chart 4.01 has been prepared to demonstrate the similarities and differences between the generations in the timing of family composition changes from age at marriage to launching of last child.

The generations began marriage at radically different points in historical time. The average grandfather married in 1907 at age 25.3 years, somewhat younger than the U.S. 1890 family head (26.1 years). The next generation married in 1931 with the husband 25 years of age, somewhat older than the U.S. 1940 family head of 24.3 years. The married child generation husband married in 1953 at age 22.4 years, just a bit younger than the U.S. figure for 1950 of 22.8. The age at marriage is, therefore, lower for husbands in each succeeding generation, despite the fact that years of schooling have increased sharply over the same period of time. For each succeeding generation the husband enters marriage with less time in the labor force in

CHART 4.01

Profile of the Timing of Family Composition Changes by Generation

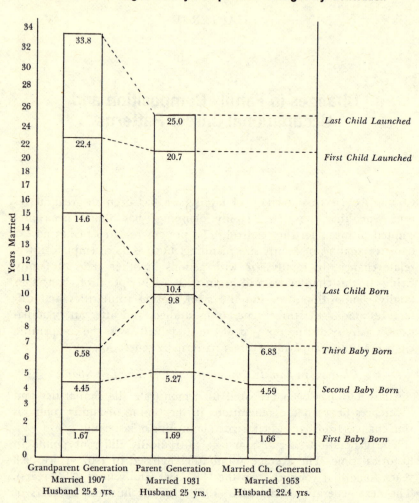

| | Grandparent Generation
Married 1907
Husband 25.3 yrs. | Parent Generation
Married 1931
Husband 25 yrs. | Married Ch. Generation
Married 1953
Husband 22.4 yrs. |

which to have accumulated the wherewithal to marry and support a family.

Although beginning marriage in different historic epochs, and with differing education and skills, the three generations spent very nearly the same time span childless, the median interval between marriage and birth of first child being 1.67, 1.69, and 1.66 years respectively as we move from grandparents to married grandchildren.

It looks as if all three generations married with hopes for children early in the marriage. Differences of some magnitude, however, appear in the spacing of subsequent births. The grandparent generation had its second child 4.45 years and the third child 6.58 years after marriage whereas the depression-oriented parent generation waited until 5.27 years for the second and 9.8 years for the third. The married child generation shows more optimism, with its second child coming after 4.59 years and its third just 6.83 years after marriage.

The grandparent generation closed its family at 5.2 children, with over a fourth bearing eight or more children. The last child was born after 14.6 years of marriage, which stretches childbearing over almost a decade and a half. The parent generation closed its family at 3.5 children, with over half of its numbers closing in the two and three child categories. The last child was born after 10.4 years of marriage, shortening the childbearing span by more than four years over the preceding generation. The married child generation still has over twenty years of possible childbearing ahead but has already produced more than two-thirds the numbers of the parent generation, averaging 2.4 children at the beginning of the study. This generation will doubtless exceed the parent generation in numbers, eventually, but may not extend its childbearing over as long a period as the previous generations.

Timing of launching children into jobs and/or marriage may also be noted on our marriage chronograph. The launching of the first child (defined as leaving the home to live independently of the family of orientation) by the grandparent generation occurs at 22.4 years compared with 20.7 for the parent generation. This is the point at which the family begins contracting in size, a process which will continue until the last child is launched. For the grandparent generation this occurs after 33.8 years of marriage, stretching leave-taking over more than a decade. For those families in the parent generation now in the post-parental stage, by contrast, the launching period has extended over a period of only five years, the last child being launched 25 years after marriage.

Summarizing our preceding discussion of the timing of family composition changes based upon Chart 4.01, we may note that the grandparent generation entered marriage at a later age, began childbearing with about the same time interval after marriage as the other generations, bore children at closer intervals, but extended childbearing over a longer period of time, producing more children in total. The child generation resembles the grandparents more closely than it does the parent generation in numbers and spacing of children in the early years of marriage, but is probably more likely to have been voluntary in its child planning than the grandparent generation. The grandparent generation launched its first child into marriage later and extended the launching period over a longer time span than the parent generation. This adds up to a longer period of childbearing, of child rearing, and of leave taking for the grandparent generation.

A second chart (Chart 4.02) confirms, independently, many of the generalizations we have made in the foregoing discussion. It shows the grandparent generation leading the other generations in the size of its household over most of the life span. Beginning together, the two younger generations diverge after the third year of marriage, with the child generation bearing more children thereafter into the second half of the first decade. Following into the later years of marriage, household size turns downward in the 16-20 years period and drops precipitously for both older generations beyond the fourth decade. The parent generation stops in that decade with slightly more than one dependent still unlaunched.

If the economy were geared to need rather than purchasing power, these two charts would suggest that the married child generation is in a rising crescendo of consumption with more than a decade to go. The pressing demands of the other two generations are subsiding and consolidating, thus decreasing the range and intensity of consumption. Deviations from this hypothesized pattern will be detailed later in the analysis of planning and consumption during the year of study.

Stages of Family Development. Still another way of illuminating the changes in family composition over the life span is to look at the stages of family development in a process known as family life cycle analysis. Roy H. Rodgers has subjected our data to special analyses that identify the typical duration of each successive stage of family development for the sample as a whole and for each generation separately.[1] Utilizing the family development conceptual framework, Rodgers saw the family as a set of role complexes changing with the addition and the withdrawl of positions in the system. A simple way of breaking up the life span would follow from changing size alone: Stage I, Childless Couple; Stage II, Expanding Family; Stage III, Stable Family; Stage IV, Contracting Family; Stage V, Childless

---

[1] *Improvements in the Construction and Analysis of Family Life Cycle Categories,* (Kalamazoo, Michigan: Western Michigan University, 1962.)

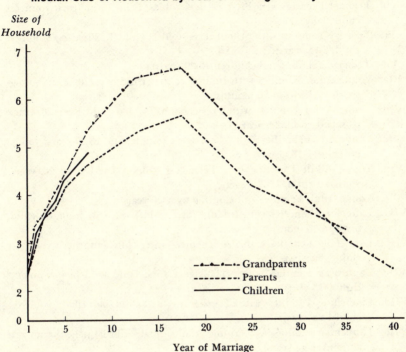

CHART 4.02

Median Size of Household by Year of Marriage and by Generation

Aging Couple. Rodgers, however, noted the changes in role expectations for parents and children which occurred with the changing ages of the oldest and youngest child by dividing up the age roles into those for infants, for pre-school children, school age children, teenagers, and young adults. He obtained from this sytem several stages of family development as follows:

   I. Beginning Families (defined as childless couples)

  II. Families with Infants (all children less than 36 months old)

IIIa. Preschool Families with Infants (oldest child, 3-6 years; youngest child, birth to 36 months)

IIIb. Preschool Families (all children 3-6 years)

IVa. School-age Families with Infants (oldest child, 6-13 years; youngest child, birth to 36 months)

IVb. School-age Families with Pre-Schoolers (oldest child, 6-13 years; youngest child, 3-6 years)

IVc. School-age Families (all children 6-13 years)

Va. Teenage Families with Infants (oldest child 13-20 years; youngest child, birth to 36 months)
Vb. Teenage Families with Pre-Schoolers (oldest child 13-20 years; youngest child, 3-6 years)
Vc. Teenage Families with School-agers (oldest child 13-20 years; youngest child, 6-13 years)
Vd. Teenage Families (all children 13-20 years)
VIa. Young Adult Families with Infants (oldest child over 20 years; youngest child, birth to 36 months)
VIb. Young Adult Families with Pre-Schoolers (oldest child over 20 years; youngest child, 3-6 years)
VIc. Young Adult Families with School-agers (oldest child 13-20 years; youngest child, 6-13 years)
VId. Young Adult Families with Teenagers (oldest child over 20 years; youngest child, 13-20 years)
VIe. Young Adult Families (all children over 20 years)
VIIa. Launching Families with Infants (first child launched; youngest child, birth to 36 months)
VIIb. Launching Families with Pre-Schoolers (first child launched; youngest child 3-6 years)
VIIc. Launching Families with School-agers (first child launched; youngest child 6-13 years)
VIId. Launching Families with Teenagers (first child launched; youngest child 13-20 years)
VIIe. Launching Families with Young Adults (first child launched; youngest child over 20 years)
VIII. Middle Years (all children launched through to retirement of breadwinner)
IX. Aging Couple (retirement to death of one spouse)
X. Widowhood (death of first spouse to death of survivor)

Table 4.01 presents data for the sample as a whole about the percentage of families falling into each of the above stages by duration of marriage. By using the category in which 50% or more of the cases occur, or by using as many categories as necessary to reach the 50% level, we can describe a "typical family life cycle" for the sample as a whole. These median values are indicated in the table by printing the percentage value in italics.

Most families had their first child by the end of the second year of marriage. They remained in the Families with Infants category through the fourth year of marriage, roughly three years of caring for infants, all of whom are below three years of age. In the fifth year of marriage, two categories are typical, II and IIIa, while years 6 and 7 found most families shifting into category IIIa, Preschool

TABLE 4.01

Percentage Distribution of Family Life Cycle Categories by Year of Marriage, Total Sample

Family Life Cycle Category	Year of Marriage

Family Life Cycle Category	1	2	3	4	5	6	7	8	9	10	11	12	13	14	15	16	17	18	19	20	21-25	26-30	31-35	36-40	41-45	46-50	51-60
I	88	33	15	06	04	03	02	01	—	—	—	—	—	—	—	—	—	—	—	—	—	—	—	—	—	—	—
II	12	67	85	83	31	13	05	03	02	01	01	—	—	—	—	—	—	—	—	—	—	—	—	—	—	—	—
IIIa	—	—	—	10	47	59	54	23	10	06	03	01	01	—	—	—	—	—	—	—	—	—	—	—	—	—	—
IIIb	—	—	—	02	18	22	20	09	04	02	02	02	—	—	—	—	—	—	—	—	—	—	—	—	—	—	—
IVa	—	—	—	—	01	02	14	39	49	50	51	48	38	14	07	01	01	—	—	01	—	—	—	—	—	—	—
IVb	—	—	—	—	—	01	03	18	23	28	21	24	22	09	03	02	01	01	01	—	—	—	—	—	—	—	—
IVc	—	—	—	—	—	01	01	07	11	13	24	25	25	12	05	08	02	02	01	—	—	—	—	—	—	—	—
Va	—	—	—	—	—	—	—	—	—	—	—	—	05	26	27	30	26	28	23	16	02	—	—	—	—	—	—
Vb	—	—	—	—	—	—	—	—	—	—	—	—	—	18	21	20	21	10	09	12	02	—	—	—	—	—	—
Vc	—	—	—	—	—	—	—	—	—	—	—	—	—	18	33	34	33	34	27	18	02	04	—	—	—	—	—
Vd	—	—	—	—	—	—	—	—	—	—	—	—	—	04	05	08	15	18	20	16	03	—	—	—	—	—	—
VIa	—	—	—	—	—	—	—	—	—	—	—	—	—	—	—	—	—	—	—	01	03	01	—	—	—	—	—
VIb	—	—	—	—	—	—	—	—	—	—	—	—	—	—	—	—	—	—	—	01	03	01	—	—	—	—	—
VIc	—	—	—	—	—	—	—	—	—	—	—	—	—	—	—	—	—	—	—	—	04	—	—	—	—	—	—
VId	—	—	—	—	—	—	—	—	—	—	—	—	—	—	—	—	—	—	—	01	08	04	02	—	—	—	—
VIe	—	—	—	—	—	—	—	—	—	—	—	—	—	—	—	—	—	—	—	—	01	15	23	03	—	—	—
VIIa	—	—	—	—	—	—	—	—	—	—	—	—	—	—	—	—	—	—	—	05	14	28	28	23	—	—	—
VIIb	—	—	—	—	—	—	—	—	—	—	—	—	—	—	—	—	—	—	—	07	09	26	11	06	—	—	—
VIIc	—	—	—	—	—	—	—	—	—	—	—	—	—	—	—	—	—	—	—	14	19	09	30	53	05	—	—
VIId	—	—	—	—	—	—	—	—	—	—	—	—	—	—	—	—	—	—	—	09	23	14	06	14	07	—	—
VIIe	—	—	—	—	—	—	—	—	—	—	—	—	—	—	—	—	—	—	—	—	03	01	—	—	—	03	—
VIII	—	—	—	—	—	—	—	—	—	—	—	—	—	—	—	—	—	—	—	01	04	—	—	—	55	48	24
IX	—	—	—	—	—	—	—	—	—	—	—	—	—	—	—	—	—	—	—	—	—	—	—	—	33	49	76
Total*	100	100	100	100	100	100	100	100	100	100	100	100	100	100	100	100	100	100	100	100	100	100	100	100	100	100	100
N =	289	283	272	262	249	232	220	210	207	197	193	188	185	183	183	183	182	182	182	181	176	135	109	92	85	45	33

* Percents may not total 100 due to rounding

Families with Infants. In the eighth year the category IVa, School-age Families with Infants appears typical, with years nine and ten having high percentages in both categories IVa and IVb. Note that the most typical categories continue to be those carrying subscript *a* designating "Infants present" into the 14th year of marriage. This should tell us something of the needs of families in the first decade of marriage, since they tend to remain dominated by the needs of infants.

In the 14th year of marriage there is a shift to category V, Families with Teenagers, with over 60 percent of the cases falling in that stage, but with 40 percent of the families still having infants present in the family. The 15th through the 19th years of marriage continue to show subtypes of category V as typical, with category Vc, Teenage Families with Schoolagers, being most representative, but Va continuing to show for about 25 percent of the cases. In the 20th year, although many families are rearing teenagers (Vb, Vc, and Vd), a shift occurs to young adulthood and launching (VI and VII) with a large spread in the distribution of families by categories. This wide scatter of cases continues well beyond the 30th year of marriage, but with increasing movement toward the launching category. VIIc and VIId categories predominate from the 21st through the 25th years. Although launching combined with rearing schoolagers (VIIc) and teenagers (VIId) continues to predominate, 14 percent of the families have reached the postparental stage (VIII), with all children launched, by the 26-30 years of marriage period. By the years 36-40, 53 percent of the cases appear to have completed the launching process.

For 10 years, from the 36th to the 45th year, category VIII predominates but with a substantial number of cases of retired husbands appearing (category IX). The majority enter that final stage of Retired Childless Couples in the 47th year and thereafter.

These data demonstrate how heterogeneous the families appear by duration of marriage. No simple classification can do justice to the variety of situations making up the careers of families over time. Rodgers has shown in Table 3.01 that the complications are most varied in the middle of the cycle and less involved at both extremes. At the beginning of the family's life span, virtually all couples are childless or pregnant, homogeneously facing the same issues and expectations. The number and the spacing of children, however, is sufficiently variable that by the 14th year of marriage, the cohort of married couples which started out together find themselves already widely dispersed with respect to family responsibilities. In that year, for example, 35 percent are School Age Families, 14 percent with infants, 9 percent with Preschool Children, and 12 percent with School Age Children only. The balance of 65 percent are variably engaged in rearing Teenagers; 26 percent with Infants as well as one or more Teenagers; 18 percent with Preschool children and one or more Teenagers; 19 percent with School Age children and one or more Teenagers; and 4 percent with Teenagers only. The heterogeneity of the cohort of families which started out together becomes even greater in the third decade of marriage. By the 21st year of marriage, families are strung out along the stages of development like cross country runners carrying variable handicap loads into a total of *thirteen different categories.*

Still another way of highlighting the variation which exists in the family life categories is to note the perseveration of categories in Table 3.01 by noting when a category first appears and when it disappears along the marriage time span. Beginning with Category I, it can be seen that, while it is the typical category for only the first year of marriage, childless couples continue to appear through the 8th year of marriage. Category II is typical for four years, but occurs from the first to the 11th year. Category III occurs for the period from the 4th through the 13th year, although it is typical only for the 5th through the 8th years. In at least one of its three variations, Category IV appears from the 5th year to the 20th year, but is most frequent only from the 8th to the 13th year. In like manner, Category V spans the years from 12 to 27, though the majority of cases fall in the years from 14 to twenty-one. Category VII stretches from the 16th through the 50th years. In terms of span of years represented, however, Category VIII is clearly the most lengthy. The first case of the Post-Parental Middle Years appears at the 20th year of marriage and the last year of marriage in which a case occurs is the sixty-second. As might be expected, the retirement stage is also quite long in terms of the period in which cases appear. The first case appears in the 24th year of marriage and the last case is in the 63rd year of marriage. A check of the cases of retirement appearing before the 30th year of marriage (3 in number) reveals that two of the cases involve disability and that one of the cases involves a situation in which the couple married somewhat later in life.

It is probably obvious that the heterogeneity of composition of the marriage cohort over its life cycle is a function of the numbers of children and their spacing. If all families limited themselves to one child and that child appeared within the first two years of marriage, there would be a smooth progression of the entire group within the uncomplicated categories (I, II, IIIb, VIc, Vd, VIe, VIIe, VIII, IX).

But families are quite variable in the number and spacing of children, and our sample is no exception (see our earlier discussion at the beginning of this chapter). Rodgers has documented the decisive contribution made by number and spacing of children to the heterogeneity of the family life cycle categories by comparing separately the variability of these categories for differently sized families, and for differently spaced birth orders.[2]

Three of Rodgers' findings about the families in our sample warrant reproduction here. Table 4.02 summarizes the data for the two generations on which we have complete family life cycle data; the married child generation is only beginning its cycle. Rodgers found no clear relationship between birth order and spacing; that is, no apparent evidence that lower order births occur closer together than higher order births. There is more variability in the spacing of the grandparent generation families than in the parent generation, which tends to be somewhat more systematically spaced. Last born children were not, as has been supposed, spaced a greater distance from their predecessors than other children were. In both generations the last born child is born closer in time to his predecessor than was true of earlier births. There is support from these data for the frequent allegation that the last born child is unplanned.

Age at Marriage and Family Size. From other analyses carried out on our data by Rodgers, we find suggestions that age at marriage may affect the planning careers of families. Age at marriage of wife is particularly related to number of children produced in both the grandparent and the parent generation. The impact of age at marriage of husband is negligible in contrast, suggesting that family size is less a function of the husband's economic productivity (which is positively related to age at marriage) than of his wife's longer exposure to the possibilities of conceiving and to her educational achievements (which are related to her age at marriage). Early marrying wives average 7.3 children, median marrying averaged 5.5 children and late marrying wives 4.7 children in the grandparent generation. The differences are not so extreme for the parent generation: early marrying wives, 4.2 children; median marrying wives, 3.8 children; and late marrying wives, 3.5 children.

The timing of marriage may also be expressed by the historical period in which marriage falls. Certain outstanding historical events have occurred during the life time of the families studied, most out-

[2] Rodgers, *Op. cit.,* pp. 122-153.

TABLE 4.02

Child Spacing by Ordinal Position and Generation

Ordinal Position	>1	1	2	3	4	5	6	7	8	9	9+	Total
					Years Spacing							
					Grandparents							
1	14	45	18	4	3	1	1	—	—	—	—	86
2	1	22	34	12	7	2	1	1	1	1	2	84
3	2	12	27	18	8	3	—	2	—	1	—	73
4	1	7	29	9	5	3	1	3	—	1	2	61
5	2	8	21	3	5	2	4	1	1	—	2	49
6	—	3	19	3	5	—	1	2	3	—	1	37
7	1	2	13	4	3	4	2	1	—	—	—	30
8	2	3	14	6	—	1	—	—	—	—	—	26
9	—	2	9	2	2	—	—	—	1	—	—	16
10	1	2	4	3	1	1	—	—	—	—	1	13
11	—	3	1	4	1	—	1	—	—	—	—	10
12	—	3	1	—	1	—	—	—	—	—	—	5
13	—	2	—	—	—	—	—	—	—	—	—	2
14	—	2	—	—	—	—	—	—	—	—	—	2
15	—	—	2	—	—	—	—	—	—	—	—	2
16	—	—	—	1	—	—	—	—	—	—	—	1
Total	24	116	192	69	41	17	11	10	6	3	8	497
					Parents							
1	9	52	23	7	2	1	1	—	1	—	—	96
2	1	11	26	20	11	8	7	3	1	1	—	89
3	1	10	12	9	8	6	5	3	3	—	9	66
4	—	11	13	8	1	2	4	1	—	—	—	40
5	1	10	4	4	1	2	1	2	—	—	1	26
6	—	2	7	3	1	—	1	2	—	—	1	17
7	—	1	5	1	—	—	1	1	—	—	1	10
8	—	2	2	—	1	—	—	—	—	—	—	5
9	—	2	1	1	—	—	—	—	—	—	—	4
10	—	1	—	—	—	1	—	—	—	—	—	2
11	—	1	—	—	—	—	—	—	—	—	—	1
12	—	1	—	—	—	—	—	—	—	—	—	1
Total	12	104	93	53	25	20	20	12	5	1	12	357

standing being World Wars I and II and the economic depression of the 1930's. In examining the date of marriage, it was found that all of the grandparent generation families were married prior to 1916 and all but eight were married between 1900 and 1910; hence, no good comparisons could be drawn on a pre and post World War I division. The parent generation, on the other hand, was much more heterogeneous with regard to their marriage dates, and an analysis based on time of marriage appeared worthwhile. Forty-five couples were married between 1921 and 1930, and 50 couples were married between 1931 and 1940. This provided two historically distinct groups: one post World War I and predepression, contrasted with one group married during the depression and prior to World War II. The mean number of children born to the predepression families was 4.1, compared to 3.1 for the depression families. Moreover, the analysis of the family life cycle categories in which these two contrasting groups of families fell over their life span showed the predepression group to be much more heterogeneous, spreading out over the various categories by duration of marriage in much more elongated fashion. Chi-square analysis applied to these data demonstrated that the two groups were sufficiently different in their performance to constitute samples of different universes ($P = 0.001$).

Activity During the Year of Study

The changes in family composition during the twelve months of the study were relatively modest except in the married child generation, which added thirty-one children. This generation, it may be remembered, is still in the childbearing stage of its life span. It is of interest that couples anticipated more children than actually arrived, even when the time span for their arrival was corrected for the dates in which the interviews occurred. Forty-eight couples anticipated children arriving during the months covered by the study. Of these couples, twenty-nine fulfilled their plans and nineteen were unsuccessful. One couple had a baby which they didn't report in advance to interviewers. Analysis of the interviews suggests there was some inhibition in reporting the expected addition before the other children.

The married child generation also added relatives to the home, but in much less planned fashion. Only three plans were made for additions of relatives. One of these didn't materialize, but five relatives were absorbed without advance planning.

A similar story is true for the parent generation, in which seven plans for addition of relatives were made, four of which materialized. However, eleven unplanned accessions to the household occurred during the year, seven of whom were adult children who had been inadequately launched.

The grandparent generation, in contrast, was virtually undisturbed by accessions to the household with only two additions, both unplanned, occurring during the year of study.

This picture of changes in family composition is one of contrast but, except for the married child generation, one of relative stability. The absorption of relatives is primarily of adult children rather than aging parents or grandparents or affinal kindred.

Occupational Career Patterns

In an earlier chapter the occupational composition of the three generations was presented (Table 2.06). The grandparent generation ended its career predominantly in the blue collar occupations of the slightly skilled, day laborers, and farmers. The parent generation, with greater education and larger urban residence, had moved predominantly out of farming, unskilled, and slightly skilled work into the semi-skilled and skilled, the clerical and retail trades, and had representation in the managerial occupations. The married child generation just beginning its career was already more highly represented in the semi-professional and managerial but was also heavily engaged in the semi-skilled trades.

In this analysis we look at the changes which have occurred since marriage for each generation, the amount of occupational mobility, the participation of the wife in gainful employment, and the shifts in occupation composition of the generations over their cohort histories.

Occupational Mobility. How much job changing occurs over a family's life span? Chart 4.03 shows the median number of jobs held since marriage by the husband for each year of marriage by generation. The amount of mobility appears to increase from generation to generation. We must remember that the breadwinner in the grandparent generation started marriage at age 25.3, after having been out of school several years. We can suppose he was more stable occupationally at marriage than his descendants; we know he was more likely to be in farming and less likely to have other job opportunities freely available to him. Chart 4.03 confirms this supposition, showing the median breadwinner still in his first job after marriage until the second half of the first decade. Almost 50 percent of the married child generation, in sharp contrast, enters the second job the second year of marriage, and 40 percent are in the fourth or higher jobs by the end of the first decade. The grandparent took a lifetime to make this many job changes. Indeed, the median breadwinner in the grandparent generation finished his occupational career after having held no more than four positions.

Job mobility for all three generations appears associated with periods of known prosperity. The parent generation's job changing increases during the second and third decade of their marriage, which

CHART 4.03

**Median Number of Jobs Held by Husband Since Marriage
by Year of Marriage and by Generation**

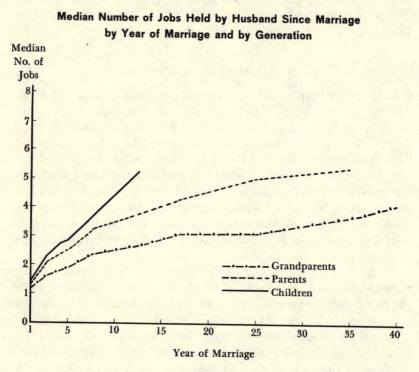

Year of Marriage

was in the war and postwar prosperity period. The only evidence of mobility for the grandparents is in the last twenty prosperous years. The married child generation's entire career, of course, has come during this period, and the impact on its job mobility has been very dramatic.

Chart 4.04 depicts the participation of wives in the labor force for each generation since the beginning of marriage. Women in the grandparent generation, it would appear, had few opportunities for employment outside of home-based industries. They were busily engaged as wives and mothers for a longer period of time in child-bearing and child rearing, as our Chart 4.01 demonstrated earlier in this chapter. It is not until the postparental period that as many as 20 percent of the mothers of this generation entered the labor force. In interesting contrast, 20 percent of the parent generation wives were in the labor force at marriage, about half dropping

CHART 4.04

History of Gainful Employment of Wife by Generation

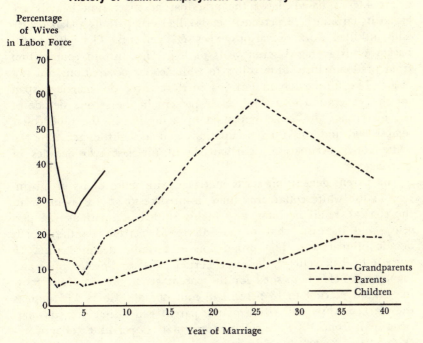

out for the childbearing period but returning in the second half of the first decade. Thereafter they were heavily engaged in gainful employment, reaching a peak of 49 percent employed in the third decade of marriage (their postparental period), dropping thereafter to about 30 percent. This is a radical change in the division of the breadwinning function from the grandparent to the parent generation. The pattern continues in even more exaggerated form in the married child generation, which dramatically begins marriage with over 60 percent of wives working. The decline in numbers during the childbearing period never hits very low and turns up again after only four years of marriage to almost 40 percent employed in the second half of the first decade of marriage. It was undoubtedly the possibility of the wife working which permitted the third generation to marry earlier, with a minimum of time to accumulate the necessities for setting up housekeeping.

An equally striking shift in occupation structure is caught in

Chart 4.05, which depicts the changing composition of each generational cohort over the marriage life span. The basic table on which Chart 4.05 is based shows the grandparent generation heavily engaged in farming (28 percent), semi-skilled occupations (33 percent), and unskilled work of various types (17 percent). The educational backgrounds averaged seven years or less. The shift in composition from predominantly blue collar to white collar occupations did not occur. The proportion in farming increases over the marriage span for this generation to as high as 35 percent in the second decade of the marriage. This is accompanied by a decline in the blue collar semi-skilled and unskilled occupations and a slight increase in the white collar occupations, particularly in the last two decades of marriage.

The parent generation starts marriage with more of its breadwinners in the white collar area than its predecessor, twice as many in the clerical, retail business, and highly skilled occupations (24 percent), and increases that proportion to 34 percent by the fourth decade of marriage. The proportion in farming declined from 15 percent to 9 percent in the same period. The semi-professional and managerial fields flourished for the parent generation fourfold, moving from 4 percent to 16 percent in four decades. Chart 4.05 depicts the marked white collarizing of the parent generation over its marriage span from .42 white collar representatives per blue collar worker to 1.04, a remarkable shift in occupational careers in one lifetime.

The married child generation begins marriage with the best educational background but with the least prior job experience, since the husbands married earliest of the three generations and have been out of school for the shortest period of time. This shows up in Chart 4.05 in their disadvantaged position at marriage in the proportion in the less skilled occupations compared with their parents when they set up housekeeping. Examination of the basic table on which Chart 4.05 is based tells us, however, that this disadvantaged picture is not due to high proportions in farming (only 5 percent) nor in day laborer work (1 percent), but in the numbers who started marriage in the semi-skilled (47 percent) and slightly skilled jobs (23 percent). Over the first ten years the picture changed rapidly, with the married child group moving into the semi-professional and managerial (from 12 percent to 26 percent in five years), into the clerical and retail business fields (from 8 percent to 15 percent in ten years), and out of the semi-skilled and unskilled work (from 70 percent down to 44 percent in ten years). This shift shows up in Chart 4.05 as an acceleration in white collarizing of the generation com-

CHART 4.05

Ratio of White Collar to Blue Collar Occupations by Year of Marriage and by Generation

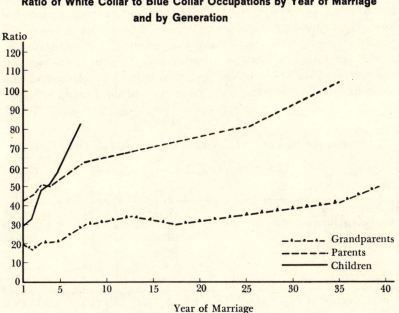

Year of Marriage

pared with the two preceding generations. Accompanied by necessary job mobility and the continued high gainful employment of wife (already documented), we would expect greater movement in other aspects of family living and greater propensity to acquire home, car, durable goods, and financial protections than in the earlier generations. We will also, of course, expect higher occupational movement by this generation during the study year. We turn now to this analysis.

146981

Job Changes Over the Year's Observations

Changes in work by families over a year's period are relatively infrequent. We have, to the best of our ability, noted every change in breadwinning activity of either spouse: entering the labor force, retiring from the labor force, or changing jobs.

Volume of job changes by generation. As expected, the child generation is much the most active of the three generations, see Table 4.03. Almost 60 percent of all job changes during the year were undertaken by this generation. By type of job change the child generation leads in husband changing jobs (75.6 percent) and in the wife entering (53.8 percent) and leaving (62.5 percent) the labor force. In only one category of job change, husband retiring from labor force, does another generation contribute more. This is where the grandparent generation is heaviest (50 percent of all changes). The parent generation is heaviest in wife changing jobs (54.5 percent) and intermediate between the highly volatile child generation and the static grandparent group on all other types of job changes.

TABLE 4.03

Number and Type of Job Changes by Generation over Study Year

Type of Job Change	Grandparent		Parent		Child		Total	
	f	%	f	%	f	%	f	%
Husband changed jobs	2	4.4	9	20.0	34	75.6	45	100.0
Wife changed jobs	0	0.0	6	54.5	5	45.5	11	100.0
Husband started work	1	14.4	3	42.8	3	42.8	7	100.0
Wife started work	2	15.3	4	30.8	7	53.8	13	99.9
Husband retired	6	50.0	2	16.7	4	33.3	12	100.0
Wife retired	1	12.5	2	25.0	5	62.5	8	100.0
Total Changes	14	14.3	26	26.5	58	59.2	98	100.0

In an examination of the husbands' job changes it is noteworthy that the husbands in the semi-skilled and minor clerical strata contribute disproportionately to job mobility, accounting for 55 percent of all husband changes in the child generation and 50 percent of the parent generation changes, although this category only characterized about one-third of the two generations at the start of the study (see Table 2.06). No other job category is so volatile, suggesting possibly lower job satisfaction in this category of work.

In this study we have not only recorded the changes in each of several areas of economic activity in the family but have also made inquiries of each family in advance to discover plans for change. In each of the first three interviews of the panel, respondents were asked whether or not the family was seriously considering making a job change, doing any remodeling or redecorating, or taking action in any of the other areas we are studying. If the answer was affirmative, the respondent was then asked if he had a definite time in mind for the contemplated action. The responses were then coded into the following categories:

Within 3 months

4-6 months
7-9 months
10-12 months
More than 12 months
No definite time

In what follows we shall refer to responses in the category "within 3 months" as "immediate plans." Responses in the categories from "4-6 months" through "more than 12 months" we shall refer to as "longer plans" as contrasted with the category "no definite time," which will be called "indefinite plans."

Types of plans and extent of plan fulfillment. Planning in advance for a job change is apparently difficult to do. In every generation more families made job changes than made plans for them in advance:

	Made Plans	Made Job Changes	Ratio of Plans/Changes
Grandparent generation	6	10	.60
Parent generation	6	26	.23
Child generation	30	55	.54

The volume of planning doesn't correlate with the amount of job mobility by generation. The parent generation enunciates one plan for every four changes, whereas the other generations anticipate job changes more readily. Nevertheless, the amount of planning in this area of family life looks modest indeed. An examination of the types of plans made by generation and their success in fulfilling those plans may throw some light on this issue.

The types of plans made in the occupational area are disproportionately (60 percent) of the indefinite variety, without a specified time for their enactment. However, for those seventeen plans that were indefinite, many more, 76 percent, are immediate, short-run plans of the "three month or less" horizon than longer run plans. Thus we see planning to be both more indefinite than definite, and, if definite, to be short run in type.

Table 4.04 has been prepared to assess the relative success of these types of plans in foretelling job changes during the study year. In over-all performance the grandparent generation foretells 60 percent of its job changes compared to only 43 percent of the child generation. The definite type plan predicts better than the indefinite, and the immediate type definite plan does best of all.

TABLE 4.04

Plan Fulfillment Ratios for Types of Plans
for Occupational Changes by Generation

Ratio	Grandparent Generation	Parent Generation	Child Generation	All Three Generations
Immediate Plans Fulfilled Immediate Plans	1.00	0.67	0.45	0.53
Longer Plans Fulfilled Longer Plans	0.00	0.00	0.40	0.29
Definite Plans Fulfilled Definite Plans	0.50	0.50	0.44	0.46
Indefinite Plans Fulfilled Indefinite Plans	0.67	0.40	0.42	0.50
Total Plans Fulfilled Total Plans	0.60	0.56	0.43	0.48

The differential performance of the three generations in plan fulfillment is due to the type of plans they have made and to their differential volume of activity. The child generation undertakes heavy job changes, 77 percent without previous planning, plans actively but indefinitely with low fulfillment (only 43 percent). The parent generation is not as active in job changes but most of them are unplanned (79 percent), makes very few plans with a higher proportion fulfilled (56 percent). The grandparent generation is low in job changes, two-thirds are unplanned, makes few plans but has a high rate of fulfillment (60 percent).

CHAPTER V

Planning Residential Location and Home Improvements

WHY FAMILIES MOVE is an intriguing title of a research monograph by Peter Rossi which addresses itself to many of the issues of this chapter.[1] Rossi asserts that residential mobility is the mechanism whereby family needs and housing are brought into adjustment with each other. The high level of mobility in America appears to be a function of the inflexibility of the housing stock, which forces families to change their residence when their needs shift. We will be interested in documenting this thesis for each of our three generations from analyses of their residential histories. If the thesis is sound, mobility should be greater during the stages of additions of children to the household and presumably greater before home ownership is achieved than later.

Because of the peculiar requirements of a sample of linked generations, we must anticipate that residential mobility will be limited pretty largely to intrametropolitan moves; otherwise all three generations would not have been present at the time of our interview. This requirement sets limits on the generalizations we might make to a larger universe in comparing mobility by generation. We ask the reader to take this into account in any inferences that are made about residential mobility.

We begin with an analysis of changes in residential arrangements over the life span covering rates of change, ordinal moves, and sequences of room acquisitions and facilities, rent to own, and furnished to unfurnished by years married. With this picture of the families' residential careers, we turn to changes in location and home improve-

---

[1] Peter H. Rossi, *Why Families Move* (Chicago: Free Press, 1955).

ments during the year of study, with some attention to the extent of planfulness shown in undertaking these changes.

Generational Changes in Residential Arrangements

In Rossi's study mentioned earlier, data were obtained from a sample of Philadelphia families on the number of moves of residence they made during the first ten years of marriage. He found substantially lower mobility among the families founded before 1910 than those formed later. Seventy-one percent of the families formed before 1910 (roughly comparable to our grandparent generation families) made no more than two moves during the first decade, whereas only 40 percent of families founded 1930-40 (comparable to our parent generation) made so few moves.[2] Our data for the three generation sample do not confirm such a trend toward increasing mobility by generation except for the first two years of marriage. For example, in the first year of marriage 12% of the grandparent generation, 21% of the parent generation, and 24% of the married child generation moved at least once. In the second year the mobility increases sharply for all generations, but converges, with 42% of the grandparent generation, 48% of the parent generation and 50% of the married child generation moving. Thereafter the mobility patterns appear quite similar.

In Chart 5.01 we have reduced residential mobility to a percentage moving per year over the life span. Families in all three generations followed a similar pattern of mobility for most of the first decade of the marriage (with exceptions noted above). Most couples stayed put in the first year of marriage, but nearly half moved one or more times in the second year, quite possibly precipitated by the arrival of the first child midway in the second year (see Chart 4.01). Thereafter, the number of moves per year diminishes steadily to as low as 4 percent a year in the later years of the grandparent generation.

There is ever so slight evidence of greater mobility in the child generation during the first five years of marriage, but a more defensible conclusion would be that all three generations are following the same pattern of shifting locations until their needs for space and facilities are brought into some equilibrium with the size of household.

It is interesting to compare the residential mobility histories for these three generations (Chart 5.01) with a cross-sectional analysis of

---

[2] See Figure 15 in Nelson Foote, *et al, Housing Choices and Constraints* (New York: McGraw Hill, 1960) p. 161. This figure is reproduced from an unpublished draft by Rossi not included in his published version of *Why Families Move, op. cit.*

CHART 5.01

**Residential Mobility (% moving per year)
by Year of Marriage and Generation**

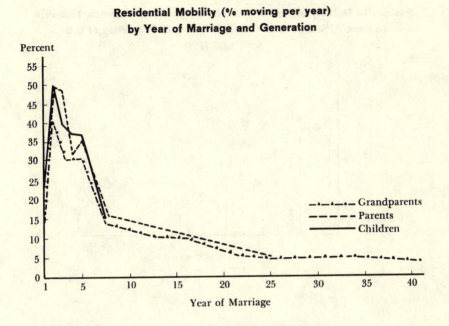

residential mobility of the U.S. population by age of household head, see Chart 5.02. Assuming an age at marriage of 20-24, the first column corresponds roughly to the first four years of marriage in Chart 5.01. At each age level the cross-sectional sample shows higher mobility than the comparable age period for any one of the three generational cohorts. This may be due to the intrinsic differences between cross-sectional and longitudinal parameters or to the fact that a three-generation linked sample is more residentially stable than the population as a whole.

Any theory linking changing family size with residential change would have to take into account the fact that families increase in size over a much longer period than the phenomenon of residential location changes. Compare Chart 4.01 with Chart 5.01. A more detailed analysis to be discussed later will show residential moves associated with shift from the stage of childlessness to parenthood but will suggest subsequent orders of children are less important.

A second expression of residential mobility is found in the ordinal number of dwellings lived in by duration of marriage, which cumulates the effects of prior moves over the life span. Chart 5.03

CHART 5.02

**Residential Mobility by Age of Household Head, United States, 1958-1959
(Source: U.S. Bureau of Census, Mobility of Population of U.S.,
April 1958-1959)**

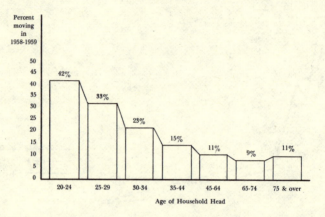

CHART 5.03

Median Number of Dwellings Lived in by Year of Marriage and by Generation

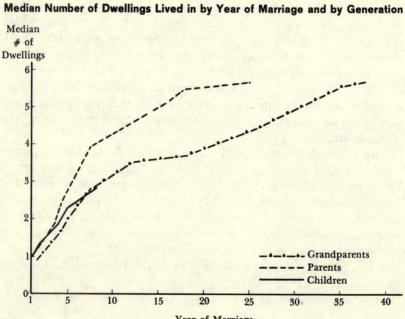

depicts this phenomenon, showing the parent generation to be much the most mobile cumulatively by year of marriage. The child generation actually lags the parent generation in the number of dwellings occupied in the first decade, probably for reasons quite different from those of the grandparent generation, as we shall see shortly. The grandparent generation makes changes in ordinal dwelling more rapidly in the later than in the middle years of marriage, suggesting more constraints operating upon them in their middle years than was true of the parent generation.

How does occupational mobility compare with residential mobility over the life span? A comparison of Chart 4.03 and Chart 5.03 suggests that residence changes occur more rapidly in all generations, especially in the grandparent generation, than do job changes. A more definitive test of the phenomenon of concurrent job and residence changes by year of marriage will be taken up in a later chapter.

Sequences in residential perquisites. In what order have the three generations changed their housing perquisites? How have space and facilities for living changed over the life span by generational cohort? The differences between Charts 5.04 and 5.05 offer dramatic evidence

CHART 5.04

Median Number of Rooms in Dwelling by Year of Marriage and by Generation

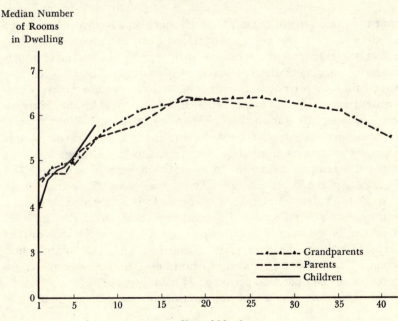

CHART 5.05

Adequacy of Housing by Year of Marriage and by Generation

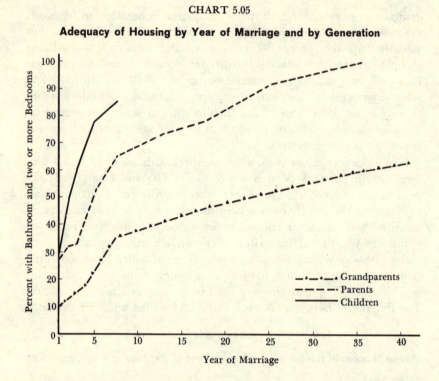

Year of Marriage

that the three generations differ much more year by year of marriage in the quality than in the quantity of space employed. Chart 5.04 shows the grandparent generation with ever so slightly more rooms than the other generations at each stage of marriage. Chart 5.05 demonstrates that the percent with bathrooms and two or more bedrooms increases from generation to generation and rises sharply for the child generation, especially during the first decade of marriage. What appears to be an acceleration phenomenon is present in the rapid rise for this youngest generation from about 28 percent to 85 percent with bathroom and multiple bedrooms in the first ten years of marriage. The increase for the other two generations was from 27 percent to 64 percent for parents and from 10 percent to only 35 percent for the grandparent generation for the same period. Much of the improvement in bedroom and bathroom space in the older generations occurred only in the later years of marriage after the children had departed and may be acquisitions postponed until the financial recovery of the post parental period made them possible.

An interesting picture of the housing career of our families is caught by tracing the modal category of housing for each generation by year of marriage using the dimensions of presence or absence of bathroom, number of bedrooms, and residential tenure. Typically, the grandparent generation remained renters with no bathroom and one or more bedrooms for the first *four* years of marriage. In the fifth year they shifted to home ownership (51 per cent), but still were typically bathroomless and limited to one bedroom into the third decade, when the majority pick up a bathroom and two or more bedrooms—too late, however, for their children to take advantage of these amenities.

Chart 5.06 permits us to see the change in residential tenure of the three generations, showing the parent generation lagging the other two in acquiring a home. Typically, the parent generation rented a place with bath and one bedroom for the first *four* years and in the fifth year another bedroom was added, but it was not until the second

CHART 5.06

Residential Tenure by Year of Marriage and by Generation

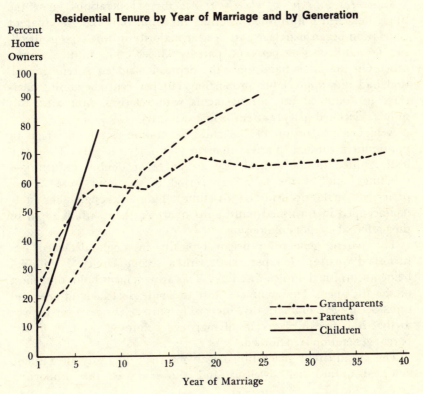

Percent Home Owners

Year of Marriage

decade that the majority of the parent generation became home owners. The homes acquired were equipped with bathroom and two or more bedrooms. Year for year, however, they lagged the child generation in acquiring a bathroom and in the number of bedrooms. The parent generation was behind both the grandparents and the child generation in achieving home ownership. This is the generation which married in the depression, of course, and its effects now show up in postponements of adequate housing just as we perceived them earlier in postponed childbearing (see Chart 4.01).

Typically, the child generation begins marriage in rented quarters with bathroom and one bedroom, shifting to two bedrooms and bathroom the *third* year, two years ahead of the parents. The majority become home owners in the *fifth* year with no loss in bathrooms or bedrooms, more than *five* years ahead of their parents. These acquisitions are the more remarkable because the child generation is younger at marriage, has had less work experience, and year for year has had more children to support than its predecessors.

Sequences in type of dwelling. All three generations favor the single detached unfurnished dwelling unit, but only the grandparent generation began marriage with a near majority in this type of dwelling (grandparents 49 per cent, parents 33 per cent, children 14 per cent). On the other hand, only the depression-ridden parent generation had any appreciable proportion (10 per cent) beginning marriage in "doubled up" arrangements with relatives. Moreover, this number declined sharply after the first two years.

A higher proportion of the child generation began marriage in multi-unit furnished quarters than in any other category. They typically shifted in the second year to single or double unfurnished dwellings, and by the 6-10 year period 86 per cent were in the preferred single unfurnished dwelling. Thus, although they start handicapped in furnished multi-units quarters, their shift is rapid to the preferred category of housing.

The parent generation began typically in single detached unfurnished quarters (33 per cent) with a second choice of families being unfurnished duplex dwellings. This arrangement holds over most of the life span. The complete shift to single detached unfurnished units occurs less dramatically, increasing only a few per cent a year, so that it is the third decade of marriage before 80 per cent of the parent generation is so housed.

The grandparent generation began marriage typically in a single detached unfurnished dwelling and also increased the proportion slowly in this type of dwelling, a minority of about 20 per cent continuing in duplex unfurnished units for several years.

When we add what we have learned from earlier analyses to this profile, we conclude that the grandparent generation obtained unfurnished space equal to the other generations and moved to home ownership early, but that on all counts of quality of facilities and amenities, the child generation leads all three generations in the first decade of marriage despite its youth at marriage and more modest work experience.

One way to express the qualitative dimension of the housing spaces utilized by the generations is caught in the rental value of their dwellings over time (see Chart 5.07). We have corrected for the changing purchasing power of the dollar by recalculating all rental value estimates in 1957-59 dollars.

CHART 5.07

Monthly Rental Value of Dwelling by Year of Marriage and by Generation*

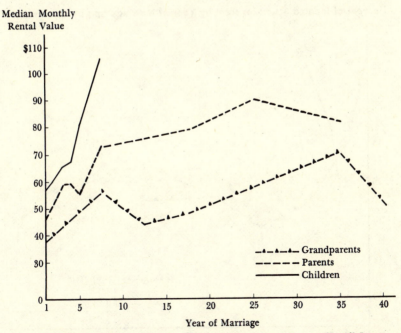

* Constant Dollar—1957-1959. Consumer Price Index, Minneapolis, All Items, 1957-59 = 100.

In Chart 5.07 it can be seen that all three generations increase the rental value of their living quarters over the marriage, even after correcting for the changing value of the dollar represented by different time spans for each generation. The three generations began marriage at about the same level of expenditures for housing spending within twenty dollars of each other, but the upgrading of their dwellings proceeded at quite different rates of speed. By the eighth year of marriage the child generation had jumped from $57 to $105 a month, whereas the parent generation had increased from $44 to $73 a month and the grandparent generation had moved from $38 to $57 a month. The child generation is upgrading its quarters much more rapidly than the other two generations.

The difference in generations is large enough in residential upgrading to ask how they have differed in the proportion of monthly income devoted to housing over the life span. Chart 5.08 has been

CHART 5.08

Percent of Income Spent for Rent by Year of Marriage and by Generation

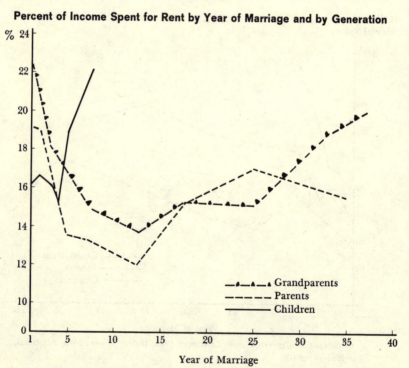

Year of Marriage

constructed for this purpose. It tells us that the two older generations began high in their ratios of rental value to income (at 19-22% of income) and have put progressively smaller proportions of income into housing over the first fifteen years of marriage (dropping to 12-14% at the lowest point) after which they increase the housing component steadily into the last years of marriage. In contrast the married child generation began low at 16% of income spent for housing and upgraded to 19% in five years and on to 22% in the 6-10 year period. The career pattern is diametrically opposed to that followed for the two older generations, thus explaining the differences observed in Chart 5.07 among the generations. The married child generation not only spends more on housing in its accelerated upgrading but is spending more relative to its income than the other generations did.

Thus the generational similarities noted in space obtained in sheer numbers of rooms in Chart 5.04 may now be seen as masking the great differences in quality of housing differences acquired in the early years of marriage by the generational cohorts (see Charts 5.05, 5.06, 5.07, and 5.08).

Congruity of housing goals and achievements. Residential careers may be summarized by relating the housing goals families may have to their present accommodations. In an interview with both husband and wife present, the question was asked: "Do you (or did you, if respondent was older) have a clear picture of a 'dream house' which you have felt it was reasonable to expect you might live in someday? Tell me about it." Many couples found the question difficult to answer, but comparable data were obtained from about two-thirds of the couples. Those not answering may possibly be less rather than more adequately housed than the average. Probes were designed to catch the type of dwelling (apartment, duplex, single family dwelling), number of bedrooms, bathrooms, dining room, family room, and other spaces, including total number of rooms. We have also recorded the present accommodations of each family as a measure of the correspondence between aspirations and achievements to date.

Table 5.01 places these two sets of data in juxtaposition to provide us with the percent of each generation which appears underhoused or overhoused, and what proportion have been able to bring their housing accommodations in line with their "dream house" goals. Most families in all generations preferred a single detached dwelling, but some few did not. The number and types of rooms were quite variable —the dining room was one type of room not checked frequently by the younger respondents. In Table 5.01 it is clear that the child genera-

TABLE 5.01

Percent Underhoused, Congruent, and Overhoused in Comparing Housing Goals with Housing Achievements by Generation

	Goals and Present Housing											
	Underhoused			Congruent Accommodations			Overhoused			Totals		
Housing Goals	Grand-parents	Parents	Child-ren	Grand-parents	Parents	Child-ren	Grand-parents	Parents	Child-ren	Grand-parents	Parents	Child-ren
	%	%	%	%	%	%	%	%	%	%	%	%
Desired type of dwelling unit—most want a single detached dwelling	16	17	34	84	80	66	0	2	0	100	100	100
Desired no. of total rooms	52	42	93	27	38	5	20	20	2	100	100	100
Desired no. of bedrooms	20	14	75	57	58	20	24	28	5	100	100	100
Desired no. of bathrooms	11	21	49	70	60	49	18	19	2	100	100	100
Dining room, if desired	15	17	37	72	57	45	13	26	18	100	100	100

tion, a quarter-way in its residential career and with higher aspirations than the other two generations, sees itself as critically underhoused on total number of rooms, desired number of bedrooms, and even desired number of bathrooms. Size of family is pressing hard on available space for this generation.

Grandparents express higher aspirations than they have achieved, primarily in total number of rooms, but lead the three generations on most other measurements of congruency between goals and achievements. Parents appear almost not at all in the underhoused bracket, and a substantial proportion are in the happy situation of having present accommodations congruent with "dream house" aspirations. Indeed, this generation has more families with more facilities than they dreamed of having. Twenty percent or more have more total rooms, more bedrooms, more bathrooms, and more dining facilities than were to have been in their "dream house." In this sense they lead the parade in being "overhoused".

Much of this difference in generations may be due to the stage of family development in which their families are concentrated—the married children still bearing and rearing children, the parent generation launching children into jobs and marriage, and the grandparent generation in companionate retirement. Yet, if this were the major explanation, the grandparent generation rather than the parent generation should have been the most overhoused. A second intervening variable is the level of housing aspirations of the three generations, which is highest for the child generation, second for the parent generation, and lowest for the grandparents. With achievements in housing adequacy higher than the grandparents and very nearly as high as the parents (see Chart 5.05), the higher level of the child generation's aspirations accounts for its much greater sense of deprivation compared to its predecessors.

Residential Changes over the Year's Observations

Activity in changing residential location and making home improvements are found in all three generations during the year of observation. Indeed, the amount of activity in reducing the frustrations from inadequate housing is second only to durable goods acquisitions among the areas of economic activity studied. For the grandparents and parents it is the chief area of activity in which change occurred. Let us look at the alternatives families face in dealing with their housing deficiencies. A family can meet its housing frustrations in various ways: it can redecorate, it can remodel (if the dwelling is theirs), and/or it can move to other more suitable quarters, or it can plan to follow one of these routes without actually carrying through the plan. We have families who chose each of these paths during the year of the study.

Let us restate the relative position of the three generations with respect to housing at the beginning of the study year. The child generation was much the most restless and dissatisfied with its housing. Twenty-four percent had moved during the six months preceding the study compared with 4 percent of the parent generation and even fewer of the grandparents. They moved to deal with space deficiencies, to meet changing needs of children, and to become home owners. Analysis of the consequences of their moves suggests they were upwardly mobile shifts rather than downward or horizontal changes.

That mobility is continuous for at least the child generation is evident from the number of plans to move as the study began. Despite 24 percent mobility in the past six months, 25 percent of the child generation were poised to move within the next few months (grandparents 9 percent, parents 9 percent). The great push to move is to achieve home ownership (one-third of all plans) and to find more suitable and spacious quarters for children. The child generation is much more definite about its plans to move (75 per cent definite) compared with the older generations (grandparent 50 percent, parent 55 percent). We can, therefore, anticipate greater activity during the year from this generation; there is much reshuffling ahead for them before they will be settling down permanently.

In the six months preceding the study, remodeling and redecorating taken together was much more frequent than changing location of residence for all generations. Fifty per cent of the child generation, 46 percent of the parents, and 24 percent of the grandparents renovated their quarters during the six months preceding the study, and many of these had still further plans afoot. The amount of continual upgrading of living quarters was substantial, especially for the younger generations. Moving, to be sure, does not preclude renovation; indeed it may precipitate a whole series of consumption actions which we will want to analyze in some depth later in this report.

The sheer quantity of plans expressed and actions taken during the year appears in Table 5.02 below. All three generations expressed more intentions to move and more plans to renovate than did so. As predicted by their history and their actions in the previous six months, the child generation was the most mobile, 71 percent planning and 35 percent actually moving during the year. One-fourth of the older generation families enunciated plans, showing dissatisfaction with present quarters, but less than 10 percent actually changed residences.

TABLE 5.02

Number of Residential Location and Redecorating-Remodeling Plans and Changes over Year of Study by Generation

Generation	Residential Location Plans		Ratio of Plans/Residence Changes	Remodeling- Redecorating Plans		Ratio of Plans/Actions
	Plans	Actions	Changes	Plans	Actions	Plans/Actions
Grandparent Generation	22	9	2.44	78	54	1.44
Per Family (N = 100)	.22	.09		.78	.54	
Parent Generation	26	10	2.60	163	93	1.75
Per Family (N = 105)	.25	.10		1.55	.89	
Child Generation	77	37	2.08	196	110	1.78
Per Family (N = 107)	.72	.35		1.83	1.03	
Total	125	56	2.23	437	257	1.70

Many more families in the older generations undertook renovations of their quarters than moved; indeed, this may be their way of solving the housing problem. Over half of the grandparents and almost 90 percent of the parents did some renovating during the year. The child generation was also active in home improvements, proof that both residential mobility and home renovations were undertaken by some families.

Looking at the ratios of plans expressed to actions taken, it appears clear that more families make plans than really carry them out in residential changes and home improvements, whereas in job changes (see Table 4.04) the opposite situation held. Renovations are carried through into action, moreover, more frequently than changes in house location. The child generation appears to have plans and actions in closer congruity than the older generations in this respect. To be certain of this point we should examine the types of plans enunciated and their rates of fulfillment by generation.

Types of plans and extent of plan fulfillment. In Table 5.03 we see that plans to change residential location were more frequently in-definite, without a definite time horizon, than renovation plans. Moreover, a higher proportion of renovation plans were of the immediate type with fulfillment expected within three months. This is true for all three generations. By generation, the child generation is most frequently definite in residence change plans and leads in longer plans for both renovation and residence moves. Knowing as we do that the fulfillment of definite plans is greater than indefinite types of plans, we can expect the child generation to perform better in this area of decisions than the older generations.

Examination of the planning completion ratios in Table 5.03 shows that the child generation does fulfill a higher percentage of its residential location plans (38 percent) but that its record for re-modeling-redecorating is surpassed by the grandparent generation (41 percent vs. 30 percent). Perhaps the most remarkable thing about the planning completion section of Table 5.03 is the very high ful-

TABLE 5.03

**Types of Plans Made for Changed Residential Location
and Home Improvements and Rate of Fulfillment by Generation**

| | Residential Changes | | | Remodeling-Redecorating | | |
| | Grand-parents | Parents | Children | Grand-parents | Parents | Children |
Type of Plans	% Ratio	% Ratio	% Ratio	% Ratio	% Ratio	% Ratio
Immediate Plans	32	15	27	42	34	31
Longer Plans	14	27	31	24	34	37
Indefinite Plans	55	58	42	33	31	32
All Plans	100	100	100	100	100	100
Planning Completion Ratios						
Immediate Plans Fulfilled Immediate Plans	.71	1.00	.81	.67	.50	.54
Longer Plans Fulfilled Longer Plans	.33	.14	.22	.16	.20	.22
Indefinite Plans Fulfilled Indefinite Plans	.25	.00	.22	.27	.22	.16
Total Plans Fulfilled Total Plans	.41	.19	.38	.41	.31	.30

fillment of immediate type plans for residential change for all generations (71-100 percent) and the very low fulfillment of indefinite type plans with no specified time horizon (0-25 percent fulfillment). This is the clearest case to be made in this study for the value of setting a definite deadline for undertaking action in foretelling that an action will indeed take place.

What we don't know as yet about the planfulness of our families in residence changes and renovations is the number of unplanned actions which occurred during the year. In Table 5.02 it was apparent that more plans were made than actions taken in this area, and in Table 5.03 it is even clearer that only a small minority of indefinite type and longer but definite type plans were fulfilled. How did the number of actions preceded by no plans compare with planned actions by generation? Table 5.04 provides this information in ratio form along with other comparisons of interest to us.

First of all, the relative amount of action taken without prior planning is almost 50 percent of all residential activity. This varies by generation, with the parent generation heaviest in impulsive residence changes (50 percent) compared with 22 percent for the child generation and none for the grandparents. *The grandparents planned all of the residence moves made, and two-thirds were definite planned actions.* The allegedly volatile child generation planned for 78 percent of its moves, and 62 percent of these were definite type plans. In comparison with renovation activity, preplanned actions were heavier in residence changes (with the exception of the parent generation).

From the data in Table 5.03 and Table 5.04 we get some idea of the modest amount of planfulness in the general area of residence changes. Many more plans are made than are carried through, 32

TABLE 5.04

**Ratios of Types of Actions to Types of Plans
for Residential Location and Home Improvements by Generation**

Ratios	Residential Changes			Remodeling-Redecorating		
	Grandparents	Parents	Children	Grandparents	Parents	Children
Unplanned Actions All Actions	.00	.50	.22	.41	.46	.46
Planned Actions Unplanned Actions	.00	1.00	3.63	1.45	1.16	1.16
Definite Planned Actions All Actions	.67	.50	.62	.46	.45	.45
Indefinite Planned Actions All Actions	.33	.00	.16	.13	.09	.09

percent fulfilled in residence moves and 34 percent in renovation. Then when the actions that occur are taken as a base we find 77 percent of residence moves preplanned and 55 percent of renovations pre-planned. There are fewer unplanned actions than there are non-fulfilled plans, but together they make a substantial set of discrepancies to be accounted for if our theory required one hundred percent correspondence between plans and actions.

Linkage of residence change and renovation of quarters (redecora-ing-remodeling). We have asked ourselves earlier how change of residence and renovation of quarters are related. Does a family move instead of renovating, renovate instead of moving, or renovate after moving? Does action in one area precipitate action in the other area or suppress it? We can make a partial test of this by noting whether a residential change and a redecorating action occur in the same time period (roughly four months) or are both absent in the same time period. Reciprocally, we can ascertain whether residence moves occur more frequently in time periods when no renovation occurs. Finally, if actions occur we can test whether they have been preceded by plans or are unplanned, which may tell us which are more likely to be planned, the co-actions or the substitutive actions.

Table 5.05 depicts the linkages between residence change and re-decoration and between residence change and remodeling within the same time intervals. There is no support for the thesis that residence change precipitates renovation in the same quarterly interval. On the contrary, the majority of changes in residential arrangements appear to be substitutive, if redecoration then no residence move, if remodeling then no residence move, and if a residence move then no redecorating or remodeling. This is true for all three generations over the waves in which records were made of residential changes. Table 5.05 indicates that redecoration rather than remodeling instead of a residence move is more likely to occur and that residence moves instead of redecorating or remodeling is the least likely substitutive action of the three. Only the child generation undertook any number of simultaneous renovating and residence moves together, and this generation also was more likely than the other generations to move rather than to redecorate or remodel.

Having established that renovating is substitutive rather than linked to residence mobility, it will be of interest to discover how planful the phenomenon of substitution is. Which is most planned, the simultaneous residence move and renovation, the residence move as substitute for renovation, or the renovation action as substitute for moving? Table 5.06 indicates the percentage planned is highest in the residence moves as substitutes for renovations, is next highest for reno-vation substitutions, and is lowest for the linked actions. This increases

TABLE 5.05

Extent of Linkage or Substitution Between Renovation of Quarters (Redecorating or Remodeling) and Change of Residence During Year of Study

	Residence Move and Redecoration Together		Residence Move But No Redecoration		No Residence Move But Redecoration		Total		Residence Move and Remodeling Together		Residence Move But No Remodeling		No Residence Move But Remodeling		Total	
	f	%	f	%	f	%	f	%	f	%	f	%	f	%	f	%
Grandparent Generation	1	2.2	8	17.4	37	80.4	46	100	1	4.5	8	36.5	13	59.0	22	100
Parent Generation	1	1.8	8	14.0	48	84.2	57	100	1	2.0	8	16.5	40	81.5	49	100
Child Generation	8	7.8	30	29.5	64	62.7	102	100	1	1.4	37	50.6	35	48.0	73	100

the confidence we may feel for the discovery that substitution rather than linkage is the predominant pattern, since the substitutions are so frequently planned rather than unplanned actions.

TABLE 5.06

Percentage of All Substitutions Planned Compared with Percentage of Linkages Planned Between Residence Moves and Renovation (Remodeling-Redecorating) of Quarters

Generation	Residence Move and Remodeling-Redecorating Together % Planned	Residence Move But No Renovating Action % Planned	No Residence Move But A Renovating Action % Planned
Grandparents	*	100.0	60.0
Parents	*	62.5	56.0
Children	44.5	71.5	59.5

* Too few cases

CHAPTER VI

Financial Planning

WE HAVE DISCOVERED in the course of several studies that respondents tend to be more sensitive about revealing their income and the disposition made of it than they are to talk about their sexual experiences. Indeed, it has been suggested that American men are more ego-involved in the amount of income they earn and the assets they have accumulated than they are in their more intimate family relations. If this be true, this study of the changing financial career patterns should be psychologically as well as sociologically provocative.

In this chapter we will consider in sequence the income fluctuations, the changing financial holdings, and the pattern of income management for each generational cohort since marriage. We will also examine the changes made in the financial portfolio of the families during the year of observation by generation. Our objective will be to discover how the generations compare in the volume of plans made in this area of decision, the volume of changes made which are and are not preceded by plans, and the types of plans which have the highest rate of fulfillment during the year of study.

Financial Career Patterns

The fluctuations in family income over the life span have usually been described as a modified parabola, starting low in the early years of marriage and increasing by increments to a plateau during the stage of child rearing and child launching and then dropping precipitously with retirement and layoffs in the later years.[1] Such an impression

[1] When children were sources of income as farm hands or factory workers, the couple with a large family reached its peak income during the late years of child rearing before the children married and left the home. With child labor laws and

is supported by a cross-sectional analysis of incomes reported for the U.S. in the Surveys of Consumer Finance shown below as Table 6.01. Even when broken down by education of head there appears to be a parabolic rise, leveling off, and then dropping of income as one moves from young heads to oldest heads. Would the same phenomenon appear if the income histories of the oldest groups had been shown from early marriage to the present time? Income histories are the type of data we shall be examining in this chapter (see Chart 6.01).[2]

TABLE 6.01

Wage-Salary Income by Amount of Education and Age Heads of Spending Units*

Amount of Education of Head

Age	1-8 Yrs.	9-11 Yrs.	High School Graduate	13-15 Yrs.	16+ Yrs., Col. Grad.
18-24	$1460	$1560	$2800	$2300	$5045
25-34	3220	4245	4500	5025	6245
35-44	3540	4315	4685	6185	8345
45-54	3725	3885	4990	6185	8345
55-64	2900	3660	4185	4190	6480

* Source: 1957, 1957 Surveys of Cons. Fin.; Study 687, Nov. 9, 1960,
University of Michigan.

Examination of Chart 6.01 suggests that the parabola is characteristic only of the grandparent generation. This generation increases its income over the first ten years of marriage and then virtually levels off until the 35th year of marriage when it shows a sharp reduction, at what appears to be the retirement period (40 years and over). We shall show later that this parabolic shape doesn't hold for the generation when it is divided up into a younger married and an older married cohort.

All three generations increase their incomes rapidly in the first five years of marriage, but the parent generation persists in its upgrad-

---

the lengthy period of education for children intervening to prohibit children from working gainfully while holding them in school through high school, this family income pattern is no longer characteristic of any sector of the population.

[2] In order to compare each of the three generations with comparable dollar values over their life spans the income figures have been calculated in 1957-59 dollars. The Minneapolis Commodity Price Index was used for most conversions. For the first ten years of the grandparent generation's marriage the U.S. Commodity Price Index was used because the Minneapolis Index did not extend back that far in time.

ing longest and appears to have maintained an income level (in constant dollars) almost 50% higher than the grandparent generation over its life span. The married child generation starts its marriage highest of the three generations but advances more slowly over the first ten years of marriage than the parent generation while remaining substantially higher than the grandparent generation in its earliest years.

In Chart 6.02 we have plotted the median incomes[3] of four cohorts of families, two for the grandparent and two for the parent generation, by the device of dividing them into those married more than the median years and those married less than the median years for their generation. A number of observations may be made:

1. The parabolic pattern of income increasing, stabilizing and declining which we noted in the grandparent generation in Chart 6.01 shows up as

CHART 6.01

Median Income by Year of Marriage and by Generation*

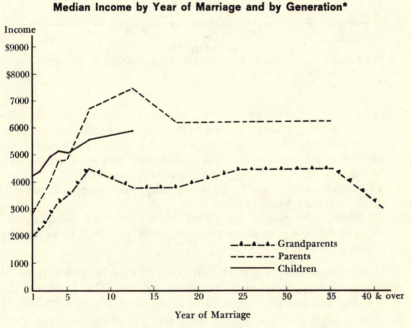

Year of Marriage

* Constant Dollar—1957-59. Consumer Price Index, Minneapolis, All Items,
   1957-59 = 100.

[3] Incomes here have also been converted to 1957-59 dollars using the procedures described in the preceding footnote.

CHART 6.02

**Median Income by Year of Marriage for Those Married More
and Those Married Less Than Median
Number of Years—Grandparent and Parent Generations***

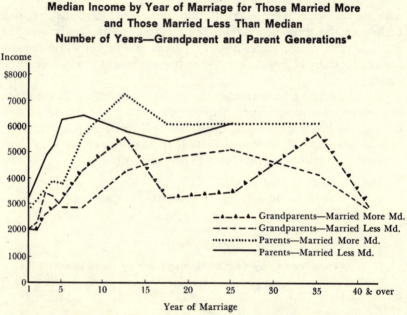

* Constant Dollar—1957-1959. Consumer Price Index, Minneapolis, All Items, 1957-59 = 100.

much more variable when the two cohorts are shown separately. The younger married cohort conforms to the classical picture, but the older cohort has experienced the depression of the thirties much more drastically than the younger cohort, only to recover even more convincingly during World War II. It does not conform to the parabola.

2. The younger cohort in each generation made more progress in the first years of marriage than the older.

3. All cohorts make most of the upward movement they are going to make in the first fifteen years of marriage—thereafter they level off or actually experience declines.

These income curves should have implications for other types of economic activity of these generational cohorts. The dramatic life span changes in monthly rental value of dwelling (Chart 5.07) and in residential tenure status (Chart 5.06) for the parent and the child generations may reflect their relative income position at the time. This can be verified by noting the correspondence between the curves for income (Chart 6.01) and for percent home owners (Chart 5.06) by year of marriage. Many other achievements in the families' careers may be affected by these income fluctuations, as we shall note later.

Changes in financial holdings. Another expression of a family's financial career is the changing pattern of investment of any surpluses.

In Table 6.02 the changing pattern of investing surpluses in liquid assets is shown for the family life span by generation. The great majority of the grandparent generation had no margin set aside in any form until the *third* decade of marriage. Until that time savings was virtually the only form of investment employed, and even at the peak only 57 percent had some savings. The grandparent generation lagged all generations in savings. Thirty-seven percent of this cohort have not

TABLE 6.02
History of Liquid Assets Acquisitions by Generation*

Pattern / Liquid Assets	Year of Marriage										
	1 %	2 %	3 %	4 %	5 %	6-10 %	11-15 %	16-20 %	21-30 %	31-40 %	41+ %
Grandparents											
None (1)	88	86	83	82	79	64	54	54	47	34	28
Savings Only (2)	11	12	14	13	15	20	28	26	24	22	30
Stocks (3)						2			1	1	1
Govt. Bonds (4)				1	2	10	10	9		16	4
Savings, Stock (5)							1		2	1	2
Savings & Bonds (6)	1	2	1	2	2	3	5	6	11	19	27
All Three (7-8)			2	1	1	1	2	5	4	7	7
Totals	100	100	100	100	100	100	100	100	100	100	100
Number of families	94	94	94	94	94	94	94	93	93	91	89
Parents											
None (1)	73	70	68	67	63	36	27	21	15	17	
Savings Only (2)	21	24	27	25	25	19	11	20	29	28	
Stocks (3)	1	1	1				1	2	4	3	
Govt. Bonds (4)			1	1	3	14	16	12	6	3	
Savings, Stock (5)					1	1		1	6	10	
Savings & Bonds (6)	3	2	2	5	7	28	43	32	36	28	
All Three (7-8)	1	1	1	1	1	2	3	13	4	10	
Totals	100	100	100	100	100	100	100	101	100	100	
Number of families	98	98	97	97	97	97	94	92	85	29	
Children											
None (1)	31	30	22	26	23	15	22	50			
Savings Only (2)	42	38	40	41	44	48	33				
Stocks (3)		2	1								
Govt. Bonds (4)	6	5	6	4	3	4	11	50			
Savings, Stock (5)	2	3	5	5	7	9					
Savings & Bonds (6)	18	21	24	23	23	15	22				
All Three (7-8)	1	1	2	1		9	11				
Totals	100	100	100	100	100	100	100	100			
Number of families	102	97	85	74	61	46	9	2			

* Percents may not add to 100 due to rounding.

yet opened a savings account, and the median year the grandparents opened a savings account was 13.7.

The parent generation shows the greatest propensity to distribute their liquid assets in all forms of investment. In Table 6.02 they shift to a majority having some savings and/or government bonds in the last half of the *first* decade of marriage, despite the fact that these were depression years. Twenty-five percent had some savings in the first year of marriage, and in the second half of the first decade almost half had added government bonds. By the *third* decade of marriage when 50 percent of the grandparents had no form of investments as yet, only 16 percent of the parent generation were saving none of their current income.

The child generation, despite its younger age at marriage and its shorter interval between completing school and marriage, starts marriage in the first year with 70 percent having savings and/or bonds. The proportion without liquid holdings declines still further over the first five years to 23 percent. By the second half of the first decade this had declined to 15 percent. In this latter period 26 percent of the child generation had moved to multiple types of assets. Compared with the patterns of its predecessors, the child generation shows remarkable movement toward investments in the first years of marriage.

In analyzing the reasons for saving given by respondents, the child generation offers family advancement, educational and style of consumption type reasons much more than the other generations (56 percent compared with 34 percent for parents and 27 percent for grandparents). The older generations are more likely to save for retirement and for emergencies. As to deciding how much to save, all generations were predominantly "sporadic savers," but the child generation was three times as likely to be involved in "self-imposed regular" savings plans.

Government bonds were the second most popular form of liquid investment and appear in the majority of the portfolios of the two older generations at some time in the marriage (71 percent of grandparents, 83 percent of parents, but only 37 percent of children). The median year for picking up the first government bonds was 24.3 years for grandparents, 10.5 years for parents, and the first year of marriage for the child generation. (These years correspond roughly to the various World War government bond drives.) Seventy percent of those who bought bonds in the child generation did so in the first year—many received them as gifts.

Stocks and corporate bonds are infrequently present and are picked up late in marriage. Twenty percent of parents have made such investments compared to 17 percent of grandparents and 16 percent of the child generation.

In this picture of liquid assets acquired over the life span, we have not collected data about the dollar amounts set aside in each of these categories. We do get, however, an impression of acceleration in number of categories utilized as each generation has aged, and a picture of marked increase in participation year for year as one moves from the oldest to the youngest generation. If continued at its present rate of acquisition, the child generation should easily surpass the parent generation in the spread of its assets for investment purposes.

The propensity to spread holdings into multiple combinations is caught in Chart 6.03 which shows the child generation more diversified from the beginning of marriage. The parent generation begins to diversify slowly but makes marked strides in the second half of the first decade of marriage. In contrast, the grandparents remain tied to single savings type accounts until late, waiting until the third decade before launching into multiple type investments. Of the three generations, the child generation appears ahead in its program of diversification of holdings.

Life insurance and retirement provisions. The essence of long-term financial planning is caught in the acquisition of life insurance and provisions for retirement. To structure one's future by premium payments to assure income maintenance for the family after the death of the breadwinner or after his retirement is prudential planning in an advanced form. The earlier a generation makes these acquisitions, the more forward looking they may be said to be in their planning.

Table 6.03 has been prepared to compare the three-generational cohorts by year of marriage on the acquisition of life insurance and retirement provisions. It is quite apparent that the oldest generation was slowest of all to make such provisions and the child generation is in this sense the most planful.

Grandparents began marriage with 71 percent unprotected by life insurance and without having made any provisions for retirement. Not until 6-10 years after marriage, long after children have arrived, does the majority, 57 percent, have at least one life insurance policy. Even at the close of the family life span (44+ years married), 31 percent of this generation is still uncovered by life insurance.

Retirement provisions including Social Security, company or union

CHART 6.03

Percent of Families with Multiple Liquid Assets (Stocks, Bonds, or Savings) by Year of Marriage and by Generation

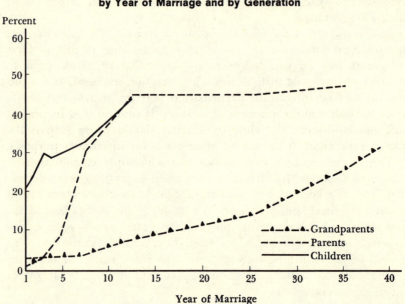

Year of Marriage

plans, annuities, and other investments are almost absent from this generation's career pattern. They begin in number only in the third decade of marriage when children are being launched, when 24 percent report some retirement provision, and reach a peak in the last years (44 and over) of 33 percent of all families.

The parent generation begins more auspiciously, with 50 percent having no life insurance at marriage compared to 71 percent for grandparents. The first policy is picked up the second year of marriage by the majority of parents, and only 10 percent had not obtained such coverage by the third decade of marriage whereas 23 percent were still uncovered among the grandparents at that stage of their career.

Retirement provisions were also more rapidly acquired. The most rapid acquisition was in the second half of the first decade when Social Security went into effect, with 26 percent showing coverage in that period, rising to 51 percent in the third decade of marriage, twice the grandparent coverage at that stage.

The child generation starts marriage with only 17 percent not covered with life insurance, and this declines to 5 percent by the

TABLE 6.03

History of Acquisitions of Life and Retirement Insurances*

Types of Insurance in Financial Portfolio	Year of Marriage										
	1 %	2 %	3 %	4 %	5 %	6-10 %	11-15 %	16-20 %	21-30 %	31-40 %	41+ %
Grandparents											
None (1)	71	65	57	56	50	40	39	33	23	24	31
Life Insurance (2)	26	31	37	38	44	53	49	53	53	46	36
Retirement Prov. (3)	1	2	2	2	2	2	5	4	6	7	9
Both (4)	2	2	3	3	4	4	6	10	18	23	24
Totals	100	100	100	100	100	100	100	100	100	100	100
Number of families	94	94	94	94	94	94	94	93	93	91	89
Parents											
None (1)	50	43	40	35	35	25	20	15	10	14	
Life Insurance (2)	39	45	46	46	44	49	47	43	39	48	
Retirement Prov. (3)	5	5	5	6	6	5	4	5	7	3	
Both (4)	6	7	8	12	14	21	29	36	44	34	
Totals	100	100	99	100	100	100	100	100	100	99	
Number of families	98	98	97	97	97	97	94	92	90	29	
Children											
None (1)	17	13	8	5	5	4					
Life Insurance (2)	51	53	53	54	51	39	33	50			
Retirement Prov. (3)	6	2	2	3	2	2		50			
Both (4)	26	32	36	38	43	54	67				
Totals	100	100	100	100	101	100	100	100			
Number of families	102	97	85	74	61	46	9	2			

* Percents don't always total 100 due to rounding

fifth year of marriage. Retirement provisions are not as widespread, but 32 percent are covered the first year, which is three times the parental coverage and eleven times the grandparental coverage at marriage. By the second half of the first decade more than half the child generation (56 percent) have developed at least one provision for retirement.

CHART 6.04

**Percentage Having Both Life Insurance and Retirement Provisions
by Year of Marriage and by Generation**

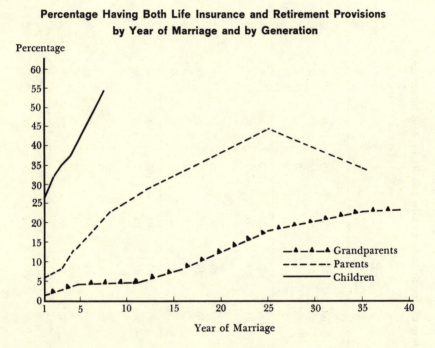

Year for year the child generation leads its predecessors in its structuring of the future through retirement provisions and life insurance. This is especially apparent when the proportion of the cohort having both life insurance and retirement is compared in the early years of marriage (see Chart 6.04). The child generation begins with 26 percent covered by both compared with 6 percent for the parents and 2 percent of the grandparents. By the 6-10 years married stage, 54 percent have both insurance and retirement plans working for them compared with 21 percent of the parents and 4 percent of the grandparents. The differences over the life span are already dramatic but promise to diverge even more as the child generation ages.

Shifting now to the number of policies ever owned and the number currently active, the more mature cohorts would be expected to have some advantage over the child generation. The average parent family, for example, has owned in the course of its life span 3.15 policies, the average child generation family 2.00 policies, and the grandparent families only 1.20 policies. The number of policies which are still active by generation follows the same pattern. Parents average 2.50 policies, children 1.33, and grandparents only 0.26. The range of number of policies now active is also greatest for the parent generation (none to 8 or more for parents; none to 7 for children; none to 3 for grandparents). From these data it would appear that grandparents have been not only less inclined to acquire life insurance protection over the life span, but they have dropped more of their policies than the other generations, since the currently active policies amount to only one-fifth (0.26/1.20) of those once carried compared to four-fifths (2.50/3.15) for parents and two-thirds (1.33/2.00) for the child generation.

There is also a greater propensity for the child generation to acquire life insurance on the wife early in the marriage, since over half had obtained such a coverage in the first year of marriage compared to a median for the parents of 2.5 years married and 14 years married for the grandparents. Fifty-four percent of the latter have never taken out coverage on the wife whereas the two younger generations leave only 30 percent (parents) and 35 percent (children) without coverage.

Analysis of types of coverage shows the child generation more diversified in the types of policies acquired with substantial representation in six types of plans, parents in five types, and grandparents in three types. Eighty-five percent of the grandparents' coverage was in straight life contracts, 73 percent of parents were so narrowly limited, and only 53 percent of children put all their faith in this type of coverage. The child generation used combinations of term insurance and straight life (family plan policies) as well as combinations of straight life with group insurance and with endowment policies as well as other combinations much more frequently than the other generations. All this, one might think, may only reflect the greater variety of plans available to the younger generation as it began to lay out its program of hedging against the future. Actually, the older generations have had access to such a variety of plans for an even longer period of time. It is, we think, more a matter of timing than a propensity to plan or to acquire quantities of policies. The child generation started earlier in its acquisitions, has spread its risks more elaborately among types of plans, and has more frequently included both family heads than did the preceding generations. Although it is behind the parent generation in sheer number of policies ever owned, it is ahead for the years of marriage which are comparable for the two generations and may well be expected to surpass parents within the next decade.

Very much the same picture is available in analyzing the provisions made by the three generations for retirement. The parent generation leads in the number of families that have made some provision for retirement, in the number of retirement provisions per family, and in the spread of types of retirement plans. It is in the timing of taking out retirement options that the child generation leads the cohorts, since 72 percent of those with plans took them out in the first year of marriage compared with 28 percent of the parents and only 14 percent of the grandparent generation.

The first retirement plan was taken out in the first year of marriage for the median child generation family, in the 11th year for the parent generation, and in the 28th year for the grandparent generation, suggesting earlier concern for this distant exigency by the younger than by the older generations.

TABLE 6.04

Percentage Distribution of Types of Present Retirement Provisions by Generation

	Grandparent %	Parent %	Child %
None	48.89	32.6	54.89
Insurance only	0.0	5.10	5.88
Savings only	1.06	1.02	0.0
Investments only	2.13	3.06	1.96
Company or Union Plan only	12.76	23.5	25.49
Social Security only	26.60	11.22	3.92
Social Security + Insurance	1.06	2.04	0.98
Social Security + Savings	2.13	1.02	0.0
Social Security + Company or Union Plan	5.31	20.40	6.86
Total	100.0	100.0	100.0
Number of families	94	98	102

In number of provisions for retirement per family, the parent generation leads with 1.14, followed by the child generation with 0.72 per family, and 0.66 per family for grandparents.

Table 6.04 presents an array of types of retirement provisions by generation which are currently held. It is immediately apparent that the proportion of families with no retirement provisions at all is smaller for the two oldest cohorts than for the youngest, which is just beginning its life span. The spread in types of plans is greatest in the parent generation, which also has a higher proportion of combinations of plans, 23 percent with social security combined with other plans, virtually three times that achieved in either of the other generations. The child generation leads in company or union plan coverage and is lowest in total reliance on Social Security, where the grandparent generation is concentrated. A cursory examination of Table 6.04 suggests the grandparents are least adequately distributed in retirement plans and the parent generation best. In time the child generation may be expected, even so, to surpass both older generations because of the earlier timing of its acquisitions and its relatively good position this early in its career.

Budgeting patterns by generation. It was thought that an index of the planning tendencies by the three-generational cohorts might be the extent to which they budgeted their expenditures in advance. Before asking about the presence or absence of budgeting over the family's career, the respondents were asked what budgeting meant to them. The answers are classified in Table 6.05, where it is apparent that there are rather marked differences in the meaning of budgeting to the generations. The older generations are less acquainted with the term than the child generation, almost two-thirds of the grandparents not being able to define it. Among those who do define it, the propensity among grandparents is to see it as a way of accounting for expenditures rather than a system of forward planning. The child generation is most articulate in defining the term and has more of its families (50.7 percent) defining it as a plan for estimating expenditures in advance, a forward planning system. Nevertheless, 30 percent of this more educated generation perceive budgeting as an accounting system only.

The actual use made of budgeting increases by generation but remains fairly constant over the life span, see Chart 6.05. At marriage, grandparents did not know how to budget and haven't learned over time. Parents are somewhat better informed but show little movement upward. The child generation greatly outdistances the other two in frequency of use, between 40 and 50 percent of families employing the method. This finding is interesting since we have already shown qualitative differences in favor of this generation in

CHART 6.05

Percent Budgeting by Year of Marriage and by Generation

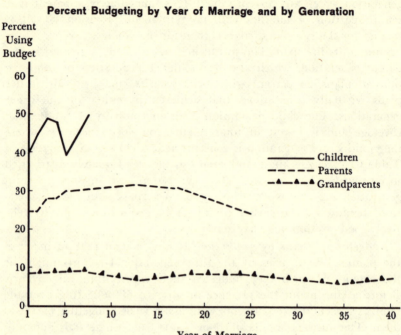

Year of Marriage

TABLE 6.05

Percentage Distribution of Meaning of the Term Budgeting by Generation

Categories of Meanings	Grandparents %	Parents %	Children %
Don't know meaning	64.0	36.3	19.2
Accounting System			
A way to live within your income	9.9	7.3	4.0
A way to keep track of money	7.7	11.4	11.0
A way to see bills are paid	4.4	3.0	15.1
Forward Planning			
A plan for distributing income	6.6	21.0	26.4
A way of estimating expenses and setting specific amounts aside	7.7	21.0	24.3
Total	100.0	100.0	100.0
Number of families responding	91	96	99

Table 6.05, where the children demonstrate a more planful view of the budgeting process.

It has been asserted that many families which begin marriage with the budgeting pattern give it up as the issues of how much should be allocated to various categories of expenditure are settled. Chart 6.05 suggests an altogether different pattern—one of steady but modest use by the grandparents, steady use by a substantial proportion of the parent generation, and a high and variable but not decreasing use over its short life span by the child generation.

Financial outlook. Before concluding this discussion of financial career patterns, which has included changes in the financial portfolio of each generation as well as the budgeting patterns since marriage, we should devote some attention to the definition the three generations make of their current financial situation. It would appear to be a consequence of their financial careers to date.

Earlier we provided (Table 2.08) a distribution of replies about the adequacy of family income by generation. The grandparents, especially, defined their income as deficient; 28 percent checked that they "do without many needed things" whereas only 4.7 percent of parents and 1.2 percent of children felt so deprived. The bulk of the child generation (76 percent) checked that they "Have the things we need and a few of the extras" compared with 61 percent of the parents and only 30.5 percent of grandparents. But parents lead (28.4 percent) in the most flush categories of having enough "for any extras we want" and enough "for extras and still have money left over to save or invest" compared with 18 percent for both the grandparents and the grandchild generation. These are definitions of income adequacy by the families themselves, which may be more relevant to their patterns of expenditure and savings than the absolute amounts of income available to them.

Two questions were asked at the end of the year of the study which are relevant to financial outlook: "Do you think your financial situation is better, about the same, or worse, than at the beginning of our visits?" and "What income do you anticipate next year?" By contrasting present income with anticipated income we can get a somewhat factual bit of evidence about financial outlook. We have arranged the answers to these two questions in such a way that they tell us whether or not the families see themselves in a declining, a status quo or an improving financial situation (see Table 6.06).

Certainly the year of the study was not perceived as a bad one by most families regardless of generation. The older generations tended

TABLE 6.06

Percentage Distribution of Data on Financial Outlook by Generation

	Grandparents %	Parents %	Children %
Is Financial Situation:			
1. Better than at the beginning of visits?	15.0	41.0	62.0
2. About the same?	72.1	47.0	27.5
3. Worse than at the beginning of visits?	12.9	12.0	10.5
Is Anticipated Income:			
1. Higher than present income?	15.3	25.8	32.3
2. About the same?	62.4	43.0	34.4
3. Less than present income?	22.4	31.0	33.3
Total	100.0	100.0	100.0

to see less change in their situation than the child generation. Grandparents see themselves predominantly as the same, parents divide almost equally between no change and an improved situation, and the married children see themselves predominantly as better off. This is more or less in line with the more objective expression of the financial situation caught in answers to the second question. When the two ways of expressing outlook are compared the income differences for the three generations as between the two years shows much less factual basis for optimism, especially for the parent and married child generations. The child generation sees itself on the march, planning, acquiring, and upgrading its living accommodations, and maybe able to continue to do so. Its income base for this upgrading, however, is not proving sufficient by itself to permit this acceleration in advancement. It will have to be accounted for in better management, and a greater willingness to incur deficits by more skillful use of credit.

Changes in Financial Holdings During Year of Study

A number of types of financial holdings have been included in the observations undertaken during the year of study ranging from liquid assets (savings accounts, government bonds, stocks, and/or corporate bonds), long-run assets (retirement provisions, business and property investments), property and personal protection insurances (auto liability and collision insurances, auto fire and theft insurances,

TABLE 6.07

Changes in Financial Holdings During the Year of Study by Type of Assets and by Generation

Types of Holdings	Grandparents				Parents				Children			
	Decrease in		Increase in		Decrease in		Increase in		Decrease in		Increase in	
	f	%	f	%	f	%	f	%	f	%	f	%
Liquid Assets	12	50.0	14	54.0	10	47.5	55	63.0	13	39.4	44	39.3
Long-Run Assets	2	8.3	2	7.7	3	14.5	9	10.3	3	9.2	10	8.9
Property and Personal Protection Devices	10	41.7	10	38.3	8	38.0	19	21.7	16	48.4	34	30.4
Liquid and Long-Run Assets	0		0		0		2	2.3	0		5	4.4
Liquid Assets and Protection Devices	0		0		0		0		1	3.0	17	15.2
Long-Run Assets and Protection Devices	0		0		0		2	2.3	0		1	.9
All Three Holdings	0		0		0		0		0		1	.9
Total Changes	24	100.0	26	100.0	21	100.0	87	100.0	33	100.0	112	100.0

house fire insurance, house content fire insurance, liability insurance, mortgage insurance, health insurance, life insurance, accident insurance, accident insurance, and social security insurance).

We show first in Table 6.07 the changes which occurred in these various types of holdings during the twelve months of observation. From the numbers of decreases and increases by types, the grandparent generation is the one cohort to make very nearly as many decreases as increases. The other two generations were prominently building up their holdings rather than decreasing them. There were altogether almost four times as many increases as decreases registered in the parent and child generations.

Decreases occurred prominently in the same clusters of liquid assets and property and personal protection insurances where increases occurred. Except for the child generation, the protection devices were less likely to be decreased than the liquid assets accounts. Additions are especially heavy in these two clusters taken singly and in combination for the child generation. The parent generation shows more activity than the other two in the manipulation of the long-run assets of retirement provisions, business and property investments.

Frequency of plans made and actions taken. A second table depicts the volume of plans made and the number of changes made in the

TABLE 6.08

Number of Plans for Changes in the Financial Holdings and Changes over Year of Study by Generation

Generation	Plans	Actions	Ratio of Plans/Changes
Grandparent Generation	96	54	1.78
Per Family (N = 100)	.96	.54	
Parent Generation	233	122	1.91
Per Family (N = 105)	2.22	1.16	
Child Generation	312	173	1.80
Per Family (N = 107)	2.92	1.62	

family's financial holdings during the year of study, see Table 6.08. In sheer quantity of plans enunciated and in actions taken, the child generation far outdistances the older generations. The parent generation follows, and the grandparents are least active on both counts. All three generations were much greater in plans made than in actions executed. With the much greater volume of plans and of actions in the child generation, is not this group overreaching itself? It will be edifying to discover if, despite its high volume of plans and actions, the percentage of plans fulfilled and the percentage of actions preplanned is as high for this generation as for its elders.

TABLE 6.09

Types of Plans Made for Changes in Financial Holdings and Rate of Fulfillment by Generation

Types of Plans	Grandparents			Parents			Children		
	f	%	Ratio	f	%	Ratio	f	%	Ratio
Immediate Plans	40	42		93	40		119	38	
Longer Plans	14	15		29	12		37	12	
Indefinite Plans	42	44		111	48		156	50	
All Plans	96	101		233	100		312	100	
Planning Completion Ratios									
$\dfrac{\text{Immediate Plans Fulfilled}}{\text{Immediate Plans}}$			.45			.42			.39
$\dfrac{\text{Longer Plans Fulfilled}}{\text{Longer Plans}}$			.21			.24			.14
$\dfrac{\text{Indefinite Plans Fulfilled}}{\text{Indefinite Plans}}$			.10			.25			.23
$\dfrac{\text{Total Plans Fulfilled}}{\text{Total Plans}}$			.26			.32			.28

Types of plans and extent of plan fulfillment. In Table 6.09 the types of financial plans are shown as well as their rate of fulfillment by generation. All three generations divide about equally between indefinite and definite plans (combining immediate and longer plans together as definite). The grandparent generation appears slightly more inclined to definite plans of short horizon than the other two generations. Plan fulfillment is not high for any generation, but immediate type plans are most likely to be fulfilled, as was true in job changes, residential moves, and renovating changes noted in earlier chapters. The rate of fulfillment, however, is much lower in financial plans (involving deferred expenditures) than in more direct actions such as job changes or residential moves. Indefinite plans have especially low probabilities of being carried out in the financial holdings area compared with job changes. Looking at plan fulfillment by generation, we do not find the child generation significantly lower than the less active older generations except in the "longer run"

TABLE 6.10

Ratios of Types of Actions to Types of Plans in Financial Holdings by Generation

Ratios	Grandparents	Parents	Children
Unplanned Actions / All Actions	.54	.39	.50
Planned Actions / Unplanned Actions	.86	1.54	1.01
Definite Planned Actions / All Actions	.39	.38	.29
Indefinite Planned Actions / All Actions	.07	.23	.21

type plans, which constituted only a fraction of its plans. Given the quantity of plans articulated, 312 plans, the rate of fulfillment was midway between the plan fulfillment ratios of the other two generations, a rather enviable achievement.

Using the number of actions taken, decreases as well as increases in the family's portfolio, we see in Table 6.10 that unplanned actions constituted roughly half of all actions. The parent generation was most and the grandparents least circumspect in preplanning actions, since the ratio of unplanned to planned actions showed parents with 1.54 planned to one unplanned action whereas for grandparents the number of unplanned actions outnumbered planned actions 100 to 86.

From this analysis it would appear that high risk taking, in the number of actions taken, is not clearly related either favorably or unfavorably to preplanning of actions, since the lowest risk takers (the grandparents) ranked lowest in preplanning actions and the highest risk takers ranked in the middle. It was the moderate parent generation which was most circumspect of the three in preplanning its changes in financial holdings.

CHAPTER VII

Acquisition of the Family's Durable Goods Inventory

FROM THE STANDPOINT of family members, acquisitions of durable equipment do not occur in isolation from each other but are highly interdependent. What are being acquired are not unrelated items but parts of an *"inventory,"* an organized set of means for performing the whole range of household functions. Before a particular piece of equipment is acquired, usually the function it fulfills was performed by other means, although perhaps not as effectively. In the complex of habits by which each family organizes the behavior of its members, each alteration in its equipment thus has repercussions not only for the household budget but for its pattern of living. When each acquisition is regarded as an addition to the household inventory, the preceding content of this inventory can be recognized as an influential condition of both the nature and timing of successive acquisitions.

Inventories at the Beginning of the Study

There are several standpoints from which it is useful to view the household inventory of durables as a whole. It would be useful to know the value of the total inventory relative to the income and assets of the family, so as to distinguish those families which emphasize expenditure on their homes from those whose household represents only minimal means for performing necessary functions. In this study, however, it was not possible to account in dollar terms for the value of inventories. Instead the effort has been to consider qualitatively the kinds of durables present or absent, both individually and as a systematic accumulation over the years of marriage. From this selected standpoint, the household inventory is construed as the product of the history, circumstances and characteristic pattern of values of the family. When the associations between the various shapes of this constellation and the various backgrounds have been fully explored, it should be possible to look at the current inventory of any given household and infer a great deal from it about the family's style of living.

In looking at the household's array of equipment as an organized whole, and at the process by which each item is added, it immediately becomes evident that acquisitions occur by various means. "Purchase new" is only one of several modes or channels of acquisition. Research which confines itself to purchasing behavior and ignores other modes of acquisition (such as gifts, hand-me-downs, loans and rentals) does so to the detriment of understanding. To purchase an item new for cash may best be thought of as an ideal which families move toward at varying rates, graduating through previous modes in differing sequences. Becoming a purchaser is a lengthy process. In this light, to explain the process of becoming a purchaser can be seen essentially to require a longitudinal account of the behavior of each household.

From recognition that families acquire their inventories of household equipment over considerable periods of time and through diverse and changing channels, it is not far to the conclusion that where each stands in this process is one of the characteristics which differentiate families at any moment in time. To the extent that this process of acquisition follows an orderly sequence, common to large numbers of households, it can potentially serve as the basis for predicting other changes in family development.

One of the common sense hypotheses which we encountered in advance of this study was that each family from its formation onward would keep adding durable items to its household inventory as it moved through its life cycle. This would keep growing until some kind of ceiling or plateau was reached late in life. Size of inventory would be correlated, therefore, with age. This common sense hypothesis is not, however, supported by the data from this study when we aggregate the actual distribution of possessions among the three generations (See Table 7.01).

A selection of 24 durables—mostly appliances, but including a few other major home furnishings—was utilized as an index of the total inventory. Presence or absence of each durable in the home was noted at the first interview with the family. Possession was found to vary according to item, from 1 to 99 percent of households within generations possessing particular items. Out of the 21 possible items possessed, the average (mean) grandparent household enjoyed roughly 10.4; the average parent household enjoyed 13; and the average child household, 12. As will be seen at the foot of Table 7.01, this pattern can also be stated in terms of what proportion of all items owned by all generations is owned by each; grandparents possess least, parents, most, with children intermediate, but the differences among means are not great.

While there was considerable dispersion in possession of items above the average, only 5 percent of the families were found (in a tabulation not shown) to possess fewer than nine items, and these were mostly grandparents. At the other end of the scale, 5 percent possessed 19 or more of the durables enumerated.

In understanding these results, it may be noted that the grandparent generation includes many quite aged couples. On the other hand, it must also be noted that the child generation includes many very young couples. The spread of ages within each generation, moreover, makes it quite evident that relative quantity of possessions is not a function of age alone. It may be supposed that lower incomes at both ends of the family life cycle help explain higher possession by parents. Later findings below will exhibit the particular influence of income differences and changes on inventory acquisitions. Meanwhile the influence of generation itself, as a factor different from age, can be illuminated as differences are noted in possession of individual items within the list of 24 making up the inventory index.

A second common sense hypothesis about household possessions that seems inconsistent with the facts displayed in this study is that nearly every family will acquire necessities first and luxuries later. What appears to be true, instead, is that definitions of which items are necessities and which are luxuries differ among the generations. In seeking to ascertain what kinds of order might prevail in the distribution of durable possessions among the three generations, the list of 24 items was first segregated into time-saving, time-filling, and comfort-providing equipment. Then the time-savers were tentatively arrayed by saturation rank in necessity (majority possess) and luxury (minority possess) categories in order to facilitate inspection for clues. Whether time-fillers and comfort-providers are luxuries or necessities is left open. As exhibited in Table 7.01, the acceptance of some of the newer appliances among the child generation runs far ahead of that among their parents and grandparents, especially the latter. The exception, which may be significant despite the small numbers, is with

TABLE 7.01

Numbers of Households Possessing Specific Durables by Generations

Item	Grand		Parent		Child		Total	
	N	%	N	%	N	%	N	%
Time-Saving Necessities								
Range—electric	24	25	25	26	26	27	75	26
Range—gas	74	76	76	78	72	74	222	76
Range—total	98	101	101	104	98	101	297	102
Refrigerator	95	98	97	100	95	98	287	99
Washing Machine	82	85	93	96	88	91	263	90
Vacuum cleaner	77	79	92	95	73	75	242	83
Sewing machine	80	82	88	91	62	64	230	79
Electric coffee maker	38	39	58	60	67	69	163	56
Time-Saving Luxuries								
Electric frypan	30	31	46	47	44	45	120	38
Food freezer	21	22	41	42	27	28	89	31
Clothes dryer—electric	6	6	12	12	19	20	37	13
Clothes dryer—gas	4	4	19	20	27	28	50	17
Clothes dryer—total	10	10	31	32	46	47	87	30
Garbage disposer	3	3	11	11	5	5	19	7
Dishwasher	1	1	4	4	5	5	10	3
Time-fillers								
Radio	89	92	90	93	93	96	272	93
Television set	84	87	96	99	90	93	270	93
Musical instrument	22	23	38	39	26	27	86	30
Record player	7	7	36	37	27	28	70	24
Hi-fi equipment	3	3	12	12	14	14	29	10
Comfort providers								
Floor covering—carpet	62	64	74	76	68	70	204	70
Floor covering—other	39	40	26	27	38	39	103	35
Sofa	87	90	95	98	94	97	276	95
Dining room table	74	76	81	84	54	56	209	72
Electric blanket	11	11	16	16	7	7	34	12
Air conditioner	3	3	10	10	1	1	15	5
Total	1016		1236		1123		3374	
Percent of total by each generation		30%		37%		33%		100%
Average Number of items possessed by each generation		10.4		13.0		12.0		

regard to electric blankets and air conditioners; physical comfort may be of greater value to grandparents than time-saving or even time-filling. The converse appears true for the more traditional items. Sewing machines and clothes dryers clearly represent extremes of traditional and novel products respectively, but to rank all 24 products on a scale from traditional to novel has not been attempted. It appears now, however, to deserve further research.

Modes of Acquisition. Seven different modes of acquisition of durables were discerned, as shown in Table 7.02. While "purchase new for cash" was the most frequent mode of acquisition, it accounted for only 39 per cent of all the items enumerated.

TABLE 7.02

Numbers and Proportions of Families Possessing
Present Inventory Items by Mode of Acquisition and by Generation

Mode of Acq. of Items	Grand		Parent		Child		Total	
	N	%	N	%	N	%	N	%
New cash	457	45	551	44	308	28	1316	39
New credit	138	14	323	26	237	21	698	21
Gift	198	19	145	12	228	20	571	17
Used cash	159	16	135	11	115	10	409	12
Used credit	4	0	11	1	18	2	33	1
Furnished by Landlord	49	5	62	5	134	12	245	7
Brought to Marriage	11	1	9	1	82	7	102	3
Total	1016	100%	1236	100%	1122	100%	3374	100%

As might be expected of families at the earliest stages of the family life cycle, the child generation acquired most often by gift—20 percent of the durables listed in their impressively large inventories. More items in their inventories were also furnished by the landlord or brought to the marriage by one of the partners than was true for the two earlier generations.

On the other hand, it is interesting to note that the parent generation has acquired somewhat more of its inventories by "purchase new for credit" than have the children to date, and much more than the grandparents. Less frequent use of credit differentiates the grandparents sharply from the two younger generations.

Another distinction of the grandparents is their higher rate of acquisition of used items. That purchase of second-hand durables, like payment in cash, may be a sign of traditionalism is also hinted at by the low frequency of second-hand acquisitions among the children. They might have been expected to start equipping their households by relying heavily on second-hand furnishings but they did not.

Only a negligible number of second-hand items ("hand-me-downs") acquired as gifts were reported; virtually all gifts were new, so the used gifts were simply included within the gift category. No instances at all were reported of renting or borrowing the enumerated durables by any of the families. These three minor modes of acquisition might turn up more frequently if closely scrutinized in other samples, however, which would lengthen to ten the list of modes by which household durables are acquired. It is the utilization of these numerous modes of acquisition which enables the child generation especially (only 28 percent of whose acquisitions were bought new for cash) to possess an inventory comparable in size to that of their parents within very few years after marriage.

Ignoring momentarily the differences among generations, some strong contrasts between particular products and particular modes of acquisition can be discerned in Table 7.03. Some of the salient relationships are well-known, such as the fact that electric coffeemakers, frypans and blankets are favorite gift items. But it may be less expected to find that what young people bring to marriage nowadays are not hope chests filled with housekeeping necessities, but predominantly time-filling entertainment devices.

The use of credit shows no appreciable relation to whether items acquired are luxuries or necessities, and only a weak association with their expensiveness. On the other hand, it may be noted that items fairly often purchased on credit are not given very often as gifts. It may also be noted that in general, and possibly for a similar reason, those items most often received as gifts are less often acquired second-hand. Scanning closely the list for those items most frequently obtained used, the more salient are recognizably the less novel: ranges, refrigerators, sewing machines, musical instruments and dining room tables. It may also be noted that the more costly "big ticket" items are more often acquired second-hand, as are installed items like ranges and carpeting, which are often purchased from the previous tenant.

More detailed analysis by generation sheds some light on what contrasting trends may be glimpsed among the principal modes of acquisition. It appears that the use of credit is growing, and most strongly among younger families, even though more actual items were added to the present inventories of parents through purchase on

TABLE 7.03

Numbers and Proportions of Families Possessing Inventory Items, by Mode of Acquisition, All Families

Item	New Cash N	New Cash %	New Credit N	New Credit %	Gift N	Gift %	Used Cash & Credit N	Used Cash & Credit %	Furnished N	Furnished %	Brought N	Brought %	Total N	Total %
Time-Saving Necessities:														100
Range—electric	33	44	15	20	4	5	15	20	8	11	—	0	75	
Range—gas	85	38	45	20	21	10	44	20	26	12	1	0	222	
Refrigerator	103	36	81	28	26	9	55	19	20	7	2	1	287	
Washing machine	98	37	97	37	20	8	31	12	16	6	1	0	263	
Vacuum cleaner	117	48	57	24	32	13	26	11	8	3	2	1	242	
Sewing machine	74	32	48	21	38	17	44	19	7	3	19	8	230	
Coffeemaker	33	20	3	2	106	65	1	1	18	11	2	1	163	
Time-Saving Luxuries:														
Electric frypan	38	32	—	0	69	57	—	0	12	10	1	1	120	
Food freezer	33	37	23	26	9	10	17	19	7	8	—	0	89	
Clothes dryer—electric	17	46	12	32	1	3	5	13	1	3	1	3	37	
Clothes dryer—gas	13	26	26	52	3	6	3	6	5	10	—	0	50	
Garbage disposer	13	69	1	5	0	0	—	0	5	26	—	0	19	
Dishwasher	3	30	3	30	0	0	1	10	3	30	—	0	10	
Time-Fillers:														
Radio	117	43	14	5	66	24	26	10	20	7	29	11	272	
Television	100	37	87	31	40	15	29	10	10	4	7	3	270	
Music Instrument	25	29	10	12	8	9	23	27	2	2	18	21	86	
Record player	34	49	5	7	15	21	5	7	4	6	7	10	70	
Hi-fi equipment	15	52	7	24	3	10	1	4	—	0	3	10	29	
Comfort providers:														
Floor covering—carpeting	89	44	47	23	17	8	22	11	29	14	—	0	204	
Floor covering—other	62	60	8	8	17	16	2	2	13	13	1	1	103	
Sofa	121	44	74	27	30	11	34	12	15	5	2	1	276	
Dining-room table	76	36	31	15	26	13	57	27	13	6	6	3	209	
Electric blanket	9	26	4	12	20	59	—	0	1	3	—	0	34	
Air conditioner	8	57	3	21	0	0	1	7	2	15	—	0	14	
Total	1316		698		571		442		245		102		3374	

credit, so far, than to the inventories of the child generation. Also grandparents proportionately most frequently acquired current inventory items second-hand. Acquisition on credit may be taking the place of acquisition second-hand.

It may very well be that credit would be found used more often for luxuries than for necessities, as these are defined by each generation. Then the lack of any difference in frequency of use of credit as between luxuries and necessities defined in general would be understandable: many items considered luxuries by grandparents are considered necessities by their grandchildren who use credit more often to buy them.

Acquisition by Gifts. One of the modes of acquisition, gift giving, included enough cases and shows a clear enough pattern to be broken down product by product to show generational contrasts. This was done in Table 7.04 by computing a ratio between the frequency with which the product had been given to grandparents and to children in this sample. Only in record players did gifts to parents exceed the flow to grandparents and children. This flow of gifts predominantly to the oldest and youngest generation was anticipated by the findings on interkin transfers reported in an earlier chapter.

Electric blankets led the list of gifts directed mainly toward the oldest generation, followed in order by television sets, radios, musical instruments, ranges and dining room tables. The actual numbers of television sets and radios given to grandparents, a quarter and a third respectively of all those they own, are especially impressive.

Time fillers and comfort providers seem to be the general categories most often conceived as gifts for the grandparents. The presence of ranges and dining room tables in the list may be there largely through default, since on a relative basis, due to their typical housing arrangements, the married children have no dining rooms requiring tables, and their ranges (and refrigerators) are especially often furnished by their landlords.

Of those products which tend strongly to be directed as gifts toward the child generation (grandparent/child ratio .5 or .6) the proportions of their acquisitions from this source are striking (see Table 7.05). Gifts to the child generation are very much of the setting-up-housekeeping variety, in contrast to the time-fillers and comfort providers which predominate in gift-giving to grandparents. This is further support for our earlier findings from interkin exchanges that they are functional and symbiotic, since the direction of gift giving is toward the needful generations and focussed on their level of need.

Acquisitions Since Marriage: Historical Findings

The key observation in all historical comparisons of inventory acquisitions by the three generations is *acceleration*. Parents have

TABLE 7.04

Percentages of Families Possessing Items in Current Inventories Acquired by Gift by Generation

Item	Grandparents %	Parents %	Children %	G/C Ratio
Time-Saving Necessities:				
Range—electric	2	1	1	2.
Range—gas	9	4	8	1.1
Range—total	11	5	9	1.2
Refrigerator	10	3	13	.8
Washing machine	6	3	11	.5
Vacuum cleaner	9	6	17	.5
Sewing machine	9	14	15	.6
Electric coffeemaker	28	32	49	.6
Time-Saving Luxuries:				
Electric frypan	19	24	29	.6
Food freezer	3	2	4	.7
Clothes dryer—electric	—	—	1	—
Clothes dryer—gas	—	1	2	—
Clothes dryer—total	—	1	3	—
Garbage disposer	—	—	—	—
Dishwasher	—	—	—	—
Time-Fillers:				
Radio	37	12	19	2.
Television	26	4	11	2.3
Musical instrument	4	1	3	1.3
Record player	—	10	5	—
Hi-fi equipment	1	2	—	—
Comfort Providers:				
Floor covering—carpet	4	5	8	.5
Floor covering—other	6	2	9	.7
Sofa	9	7	14	.6
Dining room table	12	5	9	1.2
Electric blanket	8	9	3	2.7
Air conditioner	—	—	—	—

equipped their households faster than grandparents; children have acquired faster than parents.

Some acceleration might reasonably have been expected, but the actual rate, when displayed in terms of duration of marriage at first acquisition, is startling. Table 7.06 shows how soon after marriage each of the generations acquired the durables it possessed at the outset of the study. If the median item acquired is taken as charac-

TABLE 7.05

**Proportions of Current Inventory Acquired
by Gift-Child Generation**

Product	Number Owned	Number by Gift	Percent by Gift
Washing machine	88	11	12
Vacuum cleaner	73	17	23
Sewing machine	62	15	24
Coffee maker	67	48	72
Electric frypan	44	28	64
Floor carpeting	68	8	12
Sofa	94	14	15

teristic except for the more novel or luxury items, characteristically the original acquisitions were made during the first year for the child generations, in the third decade for the parents, and in fourth or fifth decade for the grandparents.

There is some question, nonetheless, just how far the average duration of ownership can be generalized in a cohort of families still engaged in acquiring. If some not yet possessing acquire later, would that not raise this median? It would for those particular families, of course, but it would not for a comparable new sample drawn later; in fact, assuming acceleration continues, this particular median would in future samples drop slightly further. Meanwhile, the contrast among the three generations in how soon after marriage they acquired the items would remain obvious. The rate of acceleration, in other words, might be calculated differently, but the fact of acceleration is unquestionable.

Table 7.07 identifies the typical inventory for each generation based on the ranking according to the point when 50% of the generation had acquired the constituent items. It will be noted that the order of acquisition, so defined, is not the same for each generation, despite the overlap among the three lists of items.

Sewing machine for example, descends from first to fifth to ninth ordinal position in the typical sequence of acquisition within succeeding generations; dining table, from third to sixth to eleventh item acquired. Meanwhile, washer and vacuum cleaner become progressively more urgently acquired, relatively, to the other items. These historical changes in order of acquisition do not severely qualify the general finding of acceleration among the generations in rate of inventory acquisition; there is no item, no matter how traditional,

TABLE 7.06

**Median Duration of Marriage in Years
at Original Acquisition of Items,
by Generation, Possessors Only**

	Grandparents Years	Parents Years	Children Years
Time-Saving Necessities			
Range—electric	37	13	1
Range—gas	23	1	1
Refrigerator	24	2	1
Washing machine	24	4	1
Vacuum cleaner	32	12	2
Sewing machine	18	5	2
Electric coffeemaker	41	24	1
Time-Saving Luxuries			
Electric frypan	41	26	1
Food freezer	41	23	4
Clothes dryer—electric	41	24	4
Clothes dryer—gas	41	23	5
Garbage disposer	41	25	1
Dishwasher	41	25	3
Time-Fillers			
Radio	29	8	1
Television set	41	21	2
Musical instrument	18	11	1
Record player	21	20	4
Hi-fi equipment	32	25	4
Comfort providers			
Floor covering—carpet	26	7	1
Floor covering—other	28	3	1
Sofa	26	2	1
Dining room table	20	5	1
Electric blanket	41	26	1
Air conditioners	41	22	4
Median duration of marriage	52	27	5

which any generation acquired on the average sooner after marriage than did the succeeding generation. It seems very likely that the order of acquisition of durables by families is a valid index of the priorities they assign to the various items in their inventories and thus of the values they attach to them.

A second question can be raised about the medians used in Table 7.06: are the contrasts among the three generations entirely due to

TABLE 7.07

**Typical Inventory Possessed by Each Generation
Ranked by Average Order of Acquisition**

Grandparents	Parents	Children
Sewing machine	Range (gas)	Range (gas)
Range	Refrigerator	Refrigerator
Dining table	Sofa	Washer
Refrigerator	Washer	Radio
Washer	Sewing machine	Sofa
Sofa	Dining table	Vacuum cleaner
Radio	Radio	Television
Carpeting	Vacuum cleaner	Carpeting
Vacuum cleaner	Carpeting	Sewing machine
Television	Television	Coffeemaker
. . . .	Coffeemaker	Dining table
. . . .	Musical instrument	Electric frypan
. . . .	Electric frypan	. . . .

acceleration of acquisition, or at least partly to the fact that certain appliances only became available some years after parents and grandparents married? In some part, obviously, yes. But the acceleration is evident even for those items such as sewing machines, musical instruments, floor coverings and furniture which were available long before the oldest grandparents were born. Moreover, among the young; given an equal period of availability, the pattern of acceleration is undiminished. Nonetheless, it will be worthwhile to examine further the fact that, for all three generations, most of their accumulation of household durables has occurred since World War II.

Trends in Size of Inventory for each Generation. As mentioned above, little dispersion of the size of the household inventory occurs below the average number of durables possessed by each generation, but there is wide dispersion in the numbers possessed above the average. This observation supports the concept of a "floor" or "standard package" of items regarded as necessary for housekeeping. The basic required set, somewhat larger for the parents, was acquired much faster by the children, and the order in which it was acquired differs in some respects among the generations. Very nearly the same items, however, were found to make up the set. Although the average inventory of the children was smaller than that of the parents at the outset of the study, all the evidence at hand indicates that it will soon surpass that of the parents. In other words, the size of the basic inventory has grown from one generation to the next.

CHART 7.01

Size of Inventory by Year of Marriage and Generation

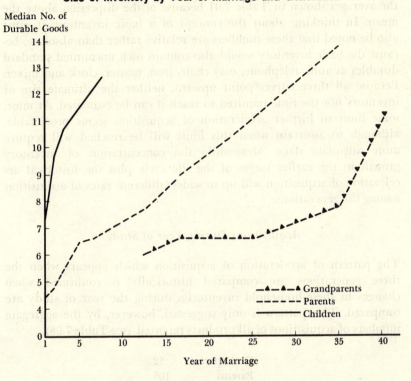

Median No. of Durable Goods

Year of Marriage

▲—▲—▲ Grandparents
‑‑‑‑‑‑ Parents
——— Children

As in all things, growth of the basic inventory must eventually slow down; it certainly cannot indefinitely accelerate. Is there any sign as yet that this is occurring? At any given time in any given household, it appears that the family possesses all the items it can manage to acquire, that it is pressing against various current limits to further acquisition. These limits, as will be seen below, are primarily financial and residential. As family size diminishes late in the life cycle, acquisitions slow down but do not cease. And while older couples are also slower to adopt novel products, many continue to do so. So with the historical upgrading of income, occupation and education, and with the usual improvement of housing situations over the life cycle, environmental constraints on ultimate size of inventory are progressively if unevenly being lifted in all generations. The floor is rising, and no ceiling is in sight.

Chart 7.01 traces the steady rise of the median size of inventory in each generation over those portions of their marital careers which are feasible to compare. The terminal medians shown are higher than the averages shown in Table 7.01 because of the dispersion above the mean. In thinking about the concept of a basic inventory, it must also be noted that these numbers are relative rather than absolute, because the basic inventory would also contain such uncounted standard durables as auto, telephone, easy chair, iron, toaster, clock and mixer. Because all three curves point upward, neither the ultimate size of inventory nor the time required to reach it can be estimated. At most, some limit to further acceleration of acquisition seems predictable, although to ascertain when this limit will be reached will require more adequate data. Meanwhile the concentration of inventory growth in the earlier stages of the life cycle plus the historical acceleration of acquisition add up to widely different rates of acquisition among the generations.

Acquisitions During Year of Study

The pattern of acceleration of acquisition which appears when the three generations are compared historically is confirmed when changes in their household inventories during the year of study are compared. This pattern is only suggested, however, by the aggregate numbers of acquisitions of all products reported (see Table 7.08).

Grandparents	52
Parents	106
Children	132
Total	290

It will be recalled from Table 7.01 that in terms of total items possessed at the outset of the study, parents led (1236 items), followed closely by the married children (1122 items), with grandparents trailing both by quite a margin (1016 items). Aggregate acquisitions during the year can be shown as a proportion of aggregate possessions at the outset, within each generation:

Grandparents	$52 \div 1016 =$	5 percent
Parents	$106 \div 1236 =$	9 percent
Children	$132 \div 1122 =$	12 percent

These percentages do not exaggerate the contrasts among rates of acquisition of the three generations, but more accurately state them.

By themselves, however, they still offer no confirmation of any acceleration, as it could be supposed that merely being in an earlier stage of the family life cycle is sufficient to account for a higher rate. Inventory growth rates for comparable periods of the marital career have to be taken into account. The above percentages might be entitled "inventory activity rates," but they cannot properly be called "inventory growth rates," because the inventory changes enumerated include not only original acquisitions but also replacements (and duplicates—additional units of the same item).

TABLE 7.08

Numbers of Families Making Inventory Acquisitions of Enumerated Durables During the Year of Study, by Generation

	Grandparents	*Parents*	*Children*
Time-Saving Necessities			
Range—electric	—	3	4
Range—gas	5	2	6
Refrigerator	7	5	9
Washing machine	2	8	10
Vacuum cleaner	1	4	11
Sewing machine	1	3	7
Electric coffeemaker	2	6	2
Time-Saving Luxuries			
Electric frypan	5	13	6
Food freezer	—	1	6
Clothes dryer—electric	—	2	3
Clothes dryer—gas	3	4	4
Garbage disposer	—	1	2
Dishwasher	1	—	3
Time-Fillers			
Radio	2	14	3
Television	3	14	12
Musical instrument	1	2	2
Record player	—	1	4
Hi-fi equipment	1	5	3
Comfort Providers			
Floor covering—carpet	3	4	11
Floor covering—other	3	3	4
Sofa, etc.	4	5	8
Dining room table	1	2	9
Electric blanket	5	3	1
Air conditioner	2	1	2
Total	52	106	132

The proportions of original acquisitions among the total made during the year were:

Grandparents	33 percent
Parents	37 percent
Children	42 percent

These differences are not as great as might have been expected, probably due to both acceleration and the fact that accumulation of larger inventories is still going on in all three generations.

If the numbers of original acquisitions added to household inventories during the year of the study are divided by the total numbers they possessed at the outset of the study, the following annual growth rates result:

Grandparents	$17 \div 1016 = 1.7$ percent
Parents	$39 \div 1236 = 3$ percent
Children	$56 \div 1122 = 5$ percent

Modes of Acquisition During Year of Study. The current utilization of the auxiliary modes of acquisition among the three generations for the year of study is assessed by aggregating the data for all the durables in Table 7.09.

As already observed in comparing modes of acquisition over the life span, grandparents are less able to pay cash now than they were earlier in their careers. But instead of utilizing credit, they turn more heavily to sources of second-hand items. Perhaps this reflects expectations of only a brief and uncertain future ahead, perhaps their economic weakness, perhaps their traditional orientation, perhaps all

TABLE 7.09

Numbers and Proportions of Families Making Acquisitions During Year of Study by Mode of Acquisition and Generation

Mode	Grandparents		Parents		Children		Total	
	N	%	N	%	N	%	N	%
New, cash	16	31	65	61	60	46	141	49
New, credit	9	17	15	14	41	31	65	22
Used, cash and credit	16	31	6	6	19	14	41	14
Gift, new and used	11	21	19	18	12	9	42	14
Furnished	—	—	1	1	—		1	1
Total	52	100	106	100	132	100	290	100

three. What was said earlier about "hand-me-ups" is sufficiently emphasized by these figures on current receipts of gifts to suggest that in future research new and used gifts should be carefully distinguished.

The most interesting feature of the modes of acquisition utilized currently by the parent generation is the high proportion of gifts, well above that of children and almost equal to that of grandparents. This rise contrasts with the low proportion of gifts in their previous household inventories. Whereas gifts earlier appeared to flow from parents toward children and grandparents, apparently during the study year the parents were beginning to receive more and more gifts from their children. This may be in reciprocity for other helps given by parents to children if we interpret the earlier data about married children conforming to the reciprocity norm in inter-kin exchanges more than the other two generations. Interest in this matter led to a listing of the nature of the 19 gifts received during the year by the parents:

1 gas range
1 clothes washer
3 coffee makers
7 electric frypans
5 radios
1 television set
1 electric blanket

Except for the first two, these could very well be silver wedding anniversary gifts. Could it be that wedding anniversaries eventually lead to a greater total of gifts than do weddings?

The modes of recent acquisition utilized by the married children, as contrasted with the ways they acquired their previous inventories, show the effects of their rapidly increasing economic capacity (see Table 7.02). Purchase new for cash, and purchase new for credit, have both risen, the utilization of credit now surpassing that of parents. Meanwhile dependence on gifts and furnished items dwindles whereas reliance on used items stays about the same.

Planning and Plan Fulfillment During Year of Study

The volume of purchase plans expressed to the interviewers over the period of the study and the actual purchases undertaken appear in Table 7.10, below. In marked contrast with residential moves (Table 5.03) where all three generations expressed more intentions to move

TABLE 7.10

**Number of Purchase Plans and Purchases
over Year of Study by Generation**

Generation	Plans	Purchases	Ratio of Plans/ Purchases
Grandparent	29	53	0.55
Per Family (N = 100)	0.29	0.53	
Parent	101	118	0.86
Per Family (N = 105)	0.97	1.12	
Child	206	148	1.39
Per Family (N = 107)	1.92	1.38	
Total	336	319	1.05

than did so, it would appear that purchase plans are less frequently made than purchases themselves. The married child generation is the only one of the three that actually expressed more plans than undertook purchases. This greater propensity to verbalize its wants into plans by the child generation is twice as great as that of the parent generation and seven times that of the grandparent generation.

Looking at the ratio of plans expressed to purchases undertaken, the parent generation appears to have the two more in balance. To be certain of this point we should examine the types of plans enunciated and their rates of fulfillment by generation.

Types of Durable Goods Purchased by Types of Plans. Utilizing the same durable goods types that were presented in previous sections (i.e., timesaving necessities, time-saving luxuries, time fillers, and comfort providers), we notice from Tables 7.11 - 7.12 that each durable goods type presents a different volume, horizon, and definiteness ratio for plans.

Grouping the three generations to examine the relative volume of plans, we notice that the 291 families planned to purchase 107 time-saving necessities. The children planned for slightly less than two-thirds of these expected purchases, the parents another one-fourth, while the 97 grandparent families articulated only about one-twelfth of the total number of plans to purchase time-saving necessities.

Planned changes in the inventory of comfort-providing items show the second highest volume of expected purchases. The child generation plans to account for 60 percent of the changes, the parents 30 percent, and the grandparents 10 percent. It is interesting

TABLE 7.11

Number and Types of Plans by Durable Goods Types

Time-Saving Necessities

Generation	Immediate N	%	Longer Run N	%	Indefinite N	%	Total N	%
Children	15	23	20	31	30	46	65	100
Parents	.. 5	19	4	15	18	67	27	100
Grandparents					15	100	15	100
Total	20		24		63		107	

Comfort Providers

Generation	Immediate N	%	Longer Run N	%	Indefinite N	%	Total N	%
Children	13	24	17	30	26	46	56	100
Parents	8	31	9	35	9	35	26	100
Grandparents	1	13	4	50	3	38	8	100
Total	22		30		38		90	

Time-Saving Luxuries

Generation	Immediate N	%	Longer Run N	%	Indefinite N	%	Total N	%
Children	10	33	7	33	14	45	31	100
Parents	4	24	2	12	11	65	17	100
Grandparents	1	100					1	100
Total	15		9		25		49	

Time Fillers

Generation	Immediate N	%	Longer Run N	%	Indefinite N	%	Total N	%
Children	9	29	10	32	12	39	31	100
Parents	6	50	1	8	5	42	12	100
Grandparents			1	33	2	67	3	100
Total	15		12		19		46	

that the children, who are just beginning their inventory accumulation, plan to acquire the largest number of comfort-providing items.

The plans to acquire time-saving luxury and time filler items together present an interesting puzzle. In both areas the child generation plans to complete three-fourths of the purchases. Interest is

TABLE 7.12

Selected Ratios by Generation by Durable Goods Type

	Definite	*Immediate*	*Definite*	*Plans*
	Indefinite	*Longer Run*	*Total*	*Actions*
Time-Saving Necessities	.69	.83	.38	1.15
Children	1.16	.75	.53	1.35
Parents	.50	1.25	.33	.84
Grandparents	.00	.00	.00	.83
Time-Saving Luxuries	.96	1.66	.47	.90
Children	1.22	1.42	.54	1.29
Parents	.54	2.00	.35	.80
Grandparents	.00	1.00	1.00	.11
Time Fillers	1.42	1.21	.58	.65
Children	1.58	.90	.61	1.10
Parents	1.40	6.00	.58	.33
Grandparents	.50	.00	.33	.50
Comfort Providers	1.36	.73	.57	1.28
Children	1.16	.76	.53	1.60
Parents	1.88	.88	.65	1.44
Grandparents	1.66	.25	.62	.44
Durable Goods—Total	1.01	.95	.50	1.02
Children	1.23	.87	.55	1.35
Parents	.90	1.43	.44	.82
Grandparents	.35	.40	.25	.52

further stimulated when we recognize that almost all of the grand-parent generation and a substantial proportion of the parents are retired and have the free time to "fill." The children, on the other hand, are just beginning their occupational careers and have con-siderably less time to spend utilizing the time filler items they plan to acquire. The high proportion of the time-saving luxuries the child generation plans to acquire may be used to vacate time so they may consume their leisure items.

Using the ratio of plans to actions as an indicator of "unplanful-ness," we notice that the three generations combined perform fairly well (Table 7.12). They have roughly the same number of plans as actions. The generational differences, however, are illuminating. The child generation planned to acquire about 35 percent more durable goods than they actually did. This types them as "much talk and less action." The parent generation, however, planned to purchase only 82 percent of the items they actually did acquire, while the grandparent generation planned to purchase 52 percent of the items they acquired. This gives a picture of the parents and grandparents as "impulse" purchasers, with the child generation as "plan postponers."

In the planning for the purchase of comfort provider items, we notice the three generations "overplanned" by 29 percent. The children, as we would expect, were the number one "overplanners"— by 60 percent. The parent generation planned to purchase 44 percent more comfort providers than they actually acquired, while the grandparents only had 44 percent as many plans as purchases.

In planning for the acquisition of time-saving necessity items, the child generation planned for 35 percent more purchases than they completed, while the parents and grandparents had 16 percent more actions than plans.

In planning for time-saving luxuries and time-filler items, the child generation again overestimates its "acquisitive power," while the parents and grandparents both underestimate the number of purchases they expected to make. The generational differences are larger for time fillers than for time-saving luxuries.

Over-all, the parents and grandparents exhibit impulsive behavior in the purchase of time-saving necessities, time-saving luxuries, and time-filler items, while the children are "poor planners," characterized by more plans than acquisitions for all four types of durable goods.

Types of Purchase Plans and Plan Fulfillment. The payoff in analyzing the characteristics of purchase plans is to discover what types carry over most consistently into purchases. Table 7.13 has been prepared to provide this test by generation.

Looking at total purchase plans fulfilled divided by total plans expressed, it is clear that a minority of plans end up with the consumer completing the plan by entering the store and making the purchase, if we take the period of a year as long enough to test the viability of purchase plans. The grandparent generation which makes the fewest plans is most likely to carry through with them.

By type of plan, definite plans are clearly superior to indefinite plans in fulfillment for all three generations. Among definite plans, those which are immediate with horizons of three months or less, are roughly three times more likely to be fulfilled than longer range plans.

An alternative way of viewing consumption activity is to focus on the planning which precedes a purchase. This approach has the actual purchase as the focus rather than the plan. Instead of analyzing how many and which types of plans result in a purchase, we

TABLE 7.13

Plan Fulfillment Ratios for Types of Durable Goods Purchase Plans by Generation

Ratio of Plans Fulfilled to Purchase Plans	Generation		
	Grandparent	Parent	Married Child
Immediate Plans Fulfilled Immediate Plans	1.00	0.59	0.68
Longer Run Plans Fulfilled Longer Run Plans	0.40	0.19	0.22
Definite Plans Fulfilled Definite Plans	0.50	0.42	0.39
Indefinite Plans Fulfilled Indefinite Plans	0.36	0.08	0.15
Total Plans Fulfilled Total Plans	0.39	0.25	0.27

will look at the quality of planning which precedes a purchase using total purchases as our base figure (see Table 7.14).

At the top of the table we are reminded of the propensity to express plans as compared with the volume of purchases made. The married child generation is the only group which made more plans than purchases, undoubtedly an expression of its greater needs. Of the total purchases made, the parent generation was the lowest in preceding its purchases with a purchase plan (only 22% of its purchases

TABLE 7.14

Types of Purchase Plans Which Precede Purchases of Durable Goods by Generation

Ratios	Grandparent	Parent	Married Child
Plans/Purchases	0.67	0.87	1.37
Planned Purchases/Purchases	0.26	0.22	0.39
Immediate Purchase Plans/Purchases	0.02	0.15	0.20
Longer Run Purchase Plans/Purchases	0.05	0.03	0.08
Indefinite Purchase Plans/Purchases	0.19	0.03	0.10
Planned Purchases/Unplanned Purchases	0.35	0.28	0.63

were planned purchases.). The child generation, in contrast, planned almost forty per cent of its purchases.

When we compare the specificity of the purchase plans that did precede purchases, we note that most of the purchase plans are definite rather than indefinite as to the time for the proposed purchase. The grandparent generation is an exception in having more indefinite than definite plans.

Within the definite plans, those with immediate short run horizons of three months or less are much more likely to appear linked with actual purchases in all except the grandparent generation. Only a negligible proportion of the purchases were preceded by a longer run purchase plan, less than ten per cent for any generation. In preplanning their purchases it would appear that the couples of the married child generation look better than their predecessors, not only because of the high propensity to express purchase plans, but also because of the higher proportion of immediate short run horizons which have greater likelihood of being carried out.

Changes in Inventory and in Other Areas of Economic Activity During the Year of Study

We turn at this moment to the analysis of contingency relationships between actions taken by the family in one area of activity and actions taken in purchasing durable goods during the year of the study. Is there any confirmation of our contention that changes in family composition, in jobs, in financial situation, or in residential location are interlinked with each other and with the acquisition of durable goods? Because the grandparents undertook too few changes in these several contingency areas we have focussed our attention in the analysis on the two more active younger generations. Table 7.15 has been prepared to elucidate these relationships. The table exhibits the *incidence* of effect—the proportions of families, among those experiencing the same kinds of change, which acquired one or more durables in the same or next interval.

Since acquisitions include replacements as well as additions to household inventories, they might be expected to prove more sensitive to changes in contingencies than inventory size might be. Except with respect to moving, however, any direct relationship that exists between acquisitions of durable goods and changes in contingent variables is weak and irregular. The only really powerful precipitant of durables purchasing as disclosed in these data is change of residence, particularly in the child generation. In this generation, about a third of the acquisitions are made by families who changed residences. In the parent generation, while movers likewise buy at high frequencies and rates, so few families moved that moving can account for only a small part of the acquiring that occurs. Remodeling accounts for more, due to its frequency, even though it is a weaker influence when it occurs. In the child generation, remodeling is both less frequent and weaker as an influence than among parents.

TABLE 7.15

Average Numbers of Durables Acquired by Parents and Children During Same and Subsequent Planning Intervals as Contingencies Changed During Year of Study

(based on 97 cases in each generation, NA's omitted)

Type of change in contingency	Parents		Children	
	Same interval	Next interval	Same interval	Next interval
Household size				
Added member	.53	.40	.34	.50
No change, or decrease	.36	.23	.49	.32
Occupation				
Husband/wife changed or started job	.47	.17	.64	.21
No change	.35	.25	.44	.35
Moving dwelling				
Moved	.57	.80	1.30	.37
No change	.36	.23	.36	.34
Remodeling dwelling				
Remodeled	.61	.27	.52	.21
No change	.39	.24	.48	.36
Financial situation	*(Year as a whole)*		*(Year as a whole)*	
Better off	1.19		1.36	
No change	1.15		1.30	
Worse off	.83		1.81	

There are, to be sure, suggestions in these tables of minor relationships which, if verified, could prove of significance. The addition of adults to the household, occurring most often in the parent generation, may have more effect on acquisitions than the addition of babies (after the first), which is the most common addition to households in the child generation. It may also be that the coming of a baby has an immediately depressing effect on acquisitions followed by a stimulating effect, since the child generation is generally a little harder pressed financially than the parents.

Likewise with regard to job changes, the distributions in parent and child generations suggest that job changes have an immediately stimulating but a later depressing effect on acquisitions. It is almost idle to ask whether family size changes or job changes have more effect on acquisitions of durables, since neither have very much. Such differences that do appear, however, seem to show a somewhat greater effect from family size changes.

Although the cases of leaving the labor force are few in the two youngest generations, they did occur among both husbands and wives and were often accompanied by acquisitions of durables in the same or subsequent intervals (tabulation not shown). In three of the four possible comparisons, these acquisitions were more frequent in families where husband or wife quit work than in families where no job changes occurred. The numbers are too small to be significant but nonetheless suggest that, particularly in the child generation, the exit of wives from the labor force to have children or the exit of husbands to return to school may be more stimulating than depressing to acquisitions. It is evident that more research with more adequate data will be needed with husband's and wife's employment being treated separately to pin down decisively the timing of these ambiguous effects.

The association between changes in the overall financial situation and acquisition appear regular and logical in the parent generation: those better off acquire more, those worse off less, with those finding themselves in about the same situation during the year falling in the middle. When we look at the child generation, however, those better off and about the same show no significant difference, while those worse off acquired the most durables. This could be purely a result of unreliability of judgment by respondents of the overall financial situation. On the other hand, recalling that a frequent reason given for feeling worse off financially was an increase in debts, it may not be unreasonable that some young people feel worse off because they have bought numerous durables on credit, even though the economists might argue that they have thereby increased their assets by an equal amount.

The influence of residential moves on acquisition of durables is more direct and powerful than any other contingency studied, but residential moves do not simply occur randomly and spontaneously. Instead they appear to be precipitated by other events which make a family's erstwhile dwelling no longer suitable, either in adequacy or location. Both the timing and nature of the residential moves made appear to derive from such major contingencies as increases in household size or changes of job by husband or wife. Thus, although changes in family composition and in occupation do not appear to influence acquisition of durables in a strong, direct manner, it is probable that they do so indirectly, through their influence on residential moves.

Because of the rarity of such events and the limits of the sample, it is not possible to display all these intercontingencies simultaneously. In Table 7.16, however, the distribution is laid out to take maximum advantage of the longitudinal design of the study. Not only is the association of family size change with acquisition visible in the child generation, but also the fact that change in family size more often comes before moving than after moving. With respect to changes

TABLE 7.16

Changes in Household Size and Job Occurring in Same Year as Changes of Residency, by Interval

(Based on 97 cases in each generation, NA's omitted)

Household change	Parents Moves				Children Moves		
	I (4)	II (1)	III (2)		I (13)	II (11)	III (9)
I (6)	9	1	—	(15)	—	3	1
II (4)	1	—	1	(13)	—	3	2
III (5)	—	—	—	(7)	1	—	1
(15)	3	1	1	(35)	1	6	4

4 household-related moves out of
7 moves = 57%
4 out of 15 household changes tie to
moves (27%)

11 household-related moves out
of 33 moves = 33%
11 out of 35 household changes
tie to moves (31%)

Job changes
(quitting work excluded)

I (6)	1	—	—	(17)	7	3	4
II (6)	1	—	1	(11)	2	3	1
III (7)	—	—	—	(11)	1	1	2
(19)	2	—	1	(39)	10	7	7

3 job-related moves out of 7 moves = 43%.
3 out of 19 job changes tie to moves (16%)

24 job-related moves out of
33 moves = 73%
24 out of 39 job changes tie
to moves (62%)

of the husband's job, the same is clearly true in the child generation and appears probably true in the parent generation, i.e., job change leads to house change. As the appended percentages also show, change of family size and job account for substantial proportions of the residential movement which occurs in both generations.

In closing this section on linkages between areas of economic activity and durable goods acquisitions, the prominent part played by residential moving suggests one further specification. We have selected the data from the married child generation for this analysis because of the greater number of residential moves and the higher activity in durable goods acquisitions.

We can consider each family interval of four months for the 95 complete cases of the Child Generation giving, with three intervals during the year per family, a total of 285 family-intervals, which will be the unit of analysis here. This limits somewhat the effects of moving on purchasing. Since the average interval is about four months in length, and if on the average people moved at the midpoint of the interval, we are considering the effects of moving on purchasing in a period of two months subsequent to the move, on the average.

We can divide the family-intervals into three groups: those involving a move to a rented residence, those involving a move to an owned residence, and those not involving a move. For each of these groups we have counted the total number of purchases of the twenty-four household durables made during the same family-interval. The results are shown in Table 7.17.

TABLE 7.17

Numbers of Purchases of Twenty-Four Durables for Movers and Non-Movers, within Family-Intervals, Child Generation

Type of Move During Family-Interval	Number of Purchases	Per cent of All Purchases	Number of Family-Intervals	Average Number of Purchases per Family-Interval
Move to Owned Residence	33	25%	20	1.7
Move to Rented Residence	14	11%	16	.9
Total Movers	47	36%	36	1.3
Total Non-Movers	84	64%	249	.3
All Family-Intervals	131	100%	285	.5

Overall, there are 131 purchases of the twenty-four durables during the 285 family-intervals, for an average of something less than .5
purchases per family-interval. The intervals with residential moves
accounted for 47 or 36% of the purchases, with an average of 1.3 purchases per family-interval as against .3 for the family-intervals not
involving moves.

When the moves are divided into moves to rented and moves to
owned housing, we find that the 20 family-intervals involving moves
to owned quarters included 33 purchases, or 25% of all purchases
made by the child generation, for an average of 1.7 purchases per
family-interval. The 16 family-intervals involving moves to rented
quarters included 14 purchases, or 11% of the total number, for an
average of .9 purchases per family-interval.

Thus we see that the periods of moving involved, on the average,
four times as many purchases of these durables as did the periods
of non-moving. But within the intervals of moving, the moves to
owned residences involved twice as many purchases, on the average,
as those to rented residences.

Another and somewhat overlapping way to look at the moves is in
terms of the type of dwelling moved to, whether detached or multi-
unit, furnished or not furnished. It happens that of the 36 moves
made by the child generation families only a very few were moves to
furnished quarters, so we are limited to unfurnished apartments and
houses. Table 7.18 shows how durables purchasing relates to these
types of moves.

TABLE 7.18

**Number of Purchases of Twenty-Four Durables for Movers and Non-Movers,
within Family-Intervals, by Type of Dwelling: Child Generation**

	Number of Purchases	Number of Family-Intervals	Average Number of Purchases per Family-Interval
Move to Detached House	32	18	1.8
Move to Multi-Unit House (including double)	7	11	.6
Non-Movers			.3

We see that the intervals in which families moved to detached
houses involved an average of 1.8 purchases, six times as many as for
the family-intervals not involving moving. The moves to multi-unit

houses involved an average of .6 purchases, about one-third as many
as for the moves to detached houses and about twice as many as for
the non-moves.

Summary

In this chapter we have examined the fifth area of decision-making,
the acquisition of the family's durable goods inventory, in some
depth. The chapter design has involved appraisal of the size and
quality of the inventories at the beginning of the study, an analysis of
the historical sequences in acquisitions over the families' life spans, a
description of the pattern of acquisition followed during the year of
study, and closed with a consideration of the linkages of changes in
the inventory over the year with changes in other areas of economic
activity. The chief findings are listed below in line with these major
divisions of the chapter:

Inventories at the Beginning of the Study

1. There is no steadily mounting size of inventory among families
    as they age.
2. Possession of novel items tends to be higher among children,
    lower among grandparents, with parents intermediate rather
    than highest as on more traditional items.
3. Modes of acquisition of their durables differ among the genera-
    tions, as do products differ in modes of acquisition.
4. Durables given as gifts differ in whether they tend to flow pre-
    dominantly toward the oldest or the youngest generation.

Acquisitions Since Marriage: Historical Findings

1. The speed of acquisition of the family inventory from marriage
    onward is greater for each successive generation.
2. The typical sequential order in which families acquire specific
    durables has changed historically.
3. No limit to further growth of the average household inventory
    appears to be emerging within any generation.

Acquisitions During Year of Study

1. Inventories of the children will take more time to surpass those
    of their parents than it took for the parents' to surpass the grand-
    parents'.
2. As the child generation moves toward purchasing new for cash

or credit, the other two generations move toward auxiliary modes of acquisition—parents toward receipt of gifts and grandparents toward used items.

3. Of the three generations, the child generation does the most forward planning of purchases, and the grandparent generation the least.

4. When planning, the largest number of purchase plans were for time saving necessities and comfort providers, while fewer plans were for time fillers and time-saving luxury items.

5. The plans to purchase time fillers and comfort providers are definite as to time of expected purchase, while the plans to purchase time-saving luxuries and time-saving necessities are indefinite as to the time proposed for acquisition.

6. Definite plans are carried into action more frequently than indefinite plans by all generations. Among definite plans, those which are of short horizons are more likely to be fulfilled than longer run plans.

Linkage of Changes in Inventory with Changes in Other Areas of Economic Activity

1. Viewed within the three planning intervals comprising the year of the study, the contingency showing the strongest, most consistent and direct influence on acquisitions of durable goods is residential moving.

2. Changes in family composition and in occupation are of direct influence on residential moving, thus influencing the acquisition of durables indirectly, if not directly.

3. Families who move to owned residences buy more than those who move to rented residences.

4. Families who move to detached houses buy three times as many durables as families who move to multi-unit houses, who in turn buy twice as many durables as those who do not move.

CHAPTER VIII

The Intercontingency of Planning Careers

FOR SEVERAL CHAPTERS we have been examing the performance of families by areas of economic activity, looking at one area at a time for each chapter. We now turn to an overview of the career patterns of the three generations when the several areas of activity are viewed together as interdependent and interrelated contingencies.

We have, first of all, observed from previous chapters remarkable upgrading from grandparent to grandchild generation in all spheres of family development: occupational status, home ownership, housing amenities, income, education, and the acquisition of durable goods. There has not only been upgrading but an acceleration in this process from generation to generation.

A number of questions to which we address ourselves in this chapter involve the extent of interplay between these areas. Are some areas more interdependent than others? What areas do we judge are dominant, that is, which areas precipitate changes and which accommodate to changes in other areas. Is the interdependence among areas closer in the child than in the parent generation?

To begin our analysis let us examine the extent to which families appear to have synchronized their residential moves with changes in family composition and/or changes in job. We can exploit our historical career data for this purpose. To what extent do residential moves occur in the same time periods, year by year over the marriage, as do the adding of or launching of children, or as do changes in job by the husband?

Synchronization of Residential Moves, Family Composition Changes, and Job Changes

If our theory about family development is sound, namely that families change their quarters as their family space needs change, we would expect residential moves to occur heavily in the early childbearing years of marriage when children are being added, relatively less during the childrearing years after the family has been closed, and somewhat more again in the launching years as the family adjusts to declining space needs. Job changes would also be expected to precipitate residential moves, to be nearer one's work location, to be nearer the neighborhoods of one's work-mates, and to be housed at a level commensurate with one's occupational position.

Family composition changes and residential moves. In analyzing the interrelationship of changes in family size and residential moves by specified time periods, it is apparent that families can take one of four courses: (1) make no changes in residential location or in family composition, (2) make one or more residential changes but no family composition changes, (3) make a family composition change without a change in residence, or (4) make both a family composition change and one or more residence moves. Chart 8.01 depicts the percentage of category four type actions for each of several time periods since the beginning of marriage for each generation. This percentage is calculated by dividing the number of families that synchronized residential moves with family composition changes by the total number of families reporting residential moves in the specified time period. In the time periods after the first five years of marriage, it should be noted that the time span of each period increases to five years until the third decade of marriage, when it shifts to ten years. There is, therefore, given our method of calculating, a five to ten times greater chance of synchronized moves in the longer time priods.

For most families, the first child is born not in the first but in the second year of marriage (see Chart 2.01). The first year is also not a period of high residential mobility, roughly 80 percent of all generations remaining in place during the first year of marriage. Nevertheless, of those couples that did move in the first year, an appreciable proportion combined the move with a shift to parenthood (15 percent of the child generation, 23 percent of parents, and 25 percent of grandparents). This is substantially higher than the proportion of families in which couples became parents without a residential move.

It is in the second year of marriage that most of the couples in the study became parents for the first time (56 percent of both grandparent and parents cohorts and 61 percent of the married child generation). It is also in this second year that the synchronization of family change and residence changes appears highest of the early years of marriage. All three generations run high; between 27 and 32 per-

CHART 8.01

Percentage of All Families Whose Moves Were Synchronized with Changes in Family Size—by Generation and by Duration of Marriage

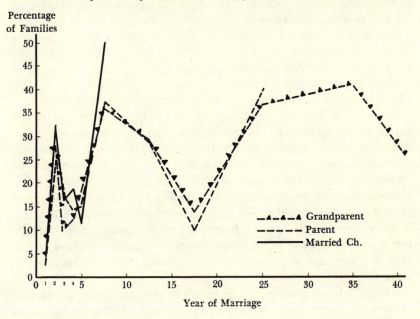

Year of Marriage

cent of all families combine residence and family composition changes. This may tell us something about the nature of the housing accommodations of the newly married, that so many must move to find room for a baby.

The third year is a bit late for the first child and too early for the second, so fewer children are born in the third year of marriage. Nevertheless, families to whom they were born were also more likely to move than other families.

The second child born to the grandparent and married child generation cohorts came on the average in the fourth year of marriage, arriving in the fifth year for the parent generation (see Chart 2.01). The proportion of residence moves synchronized with family size change increases for the grandparent generation but decreases for the parent generation, as might be expected. In general, the responsiveness of all three cohorts is much lower in the proportion who move following the second child than the first. *The shift to parenthood for the first time requires more changes in the living quarters than the shift from a one-child to a two-child family and therefore is less likely to precipitate a residential move.*

By the fifth year of marriage the relationship between family composition change and residence movement appears to have attenuated for the two younger cohorts. For the first time, in the fifth year of marriage the proportion of families which add a child without making a residence move is higher for both of these cohorts than the families who synchronized the two changes. Nevertheless, looking at each of the five years, these two career variables are interrelated for at least two of the three generations beyond that expected by chance.

As we move into the second half of the first decade of marriage the curves go up, to be sure, but the size of the time span has increased roughly five times for each family. If we had been able to continue our per year analysis, the attenuation between residence and accessions of children probably would have become more pronounced. Shifting to time spans of five years, we note a continuation of the downward trend of responsiveness for the two older cohorts which remain. There is little evidence of marked residence changes occurring in the launching years in response to decreased needs for space, yet there is also little evidence that non-synchronized residence moves are undertaken more frequently than expected by chance during these later years of marriage. In the grandparent generation, especially, the proportion of families combining residence moves with family composition changes exceeds families in which residence movement occurs without a family composition change in every time period from the third year of marriage onward.

Comparing the three generations over the period covered, there are suggestions from Chart 8.01 that the child generation is probably the most responsive to the pressure of family size on residence spaces. Beginning in the second year of marriage it leads the three generations in the proportion of its families which moved when family additions were made. The overpowering impression, however, is not the difference but the similarity among the generations. The three cohorts make a marked shift in the second year to the assumption of parenthood status, many apparently picking up sufficient space that moving again for the second child is not necessary. Subsequent children appear even less likely to precipitate residences moves. Synchronization of residence moves in the launching years, 21-40 years, is not as likely to occur as in the early years of adding members, although there are increases greater than expected by chance.

Job changes and residential mobility. Job changes do not appear to have precipitated as many residence changes for grandparents as for

the younger generations. Chart 8.02 depicts the percentage of all
families whose residence moves in any given period were accompanied
by a change in occupation. Comparing the responsiveness of the
generations to job changes as against family composition changes
(compare Chart 8.01 and Chart 8.02) it would appear that job
changes count for less than family composition changes for the two
older generations, and at a number of points this would be true
also for the child generation. This latter group changes residence,
changes jobs, and adds children in the same years, it would appear.
The second, third, fourth, and sixth to tenth years find high activity
in all three areas.

Comparing the three generations over the period covered, the child
generation is again somewhat the most responsive residentially to the
contingency of a job change, just as it was to a family composition
change. The grandparent generation's residential movements appear to
operate independently of job mobility, but actually the low synchronization percentage is more a function of low residential and low occupational mobility than of independence. Among the families who

CHART 8.02

**Percentage of Families Whose Moves Were Synchronized with Changes
in Occupation by Generation and by Duration of Marriage**

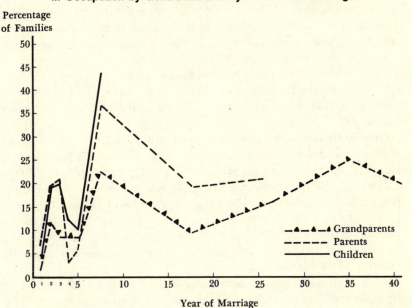

did move, the percentage which had job changes was always higher in the grandparent generation than movers who did not. The parent generation is highly variable in not being able to move with job changes during the fourth and fifth years of marriage, when for them the economic crises may have been quite acute. The pickup shown in the later years of marriage for this generation suggests that it is not as impervious as the grandparent cohort to the impact of this contingency variable.

We may be justified in concluding from this analysis that family composition more than job changes link up with residential mobility, especially in the early years of the family's life cycle. The interplay of these three activities is most erratically represented by the parent generation, most insensitively represented by the grandparent generation, and most dynamically shown by the actions of the child generation, in which high proportions of changes in all three areas occur simultaneously.

Changes in Four Areas of Activity and Acquisitions of Durable Goods

A pronounced tendency for changes in the durable goods inventory to be associated with residential moves of different types during the year of the study was noted in the previous chapter; see Tables 7.16, 7.17, 7.18. It was also noted that changes in family composition and in occupation were of direct influence on residential moving during the year of the study, suggesting that these activities had an indirect influence, if not a direct influence, on durable goods purchasing.

In this chapter we have already confirmed the dependence of residential mobility on family composition and occupational changes over the life span. It remains to discover how changes in these several areas of activity affect the growth in the durable goods inventory over time.

We select changes in family size, occupational status, residence and income to correlate with acquisitions of durable goods for the first five years of marriage for the parent and child generations to ascertain the degree of interdependence here. Do increments in each of these independent variables actually cause increments in household inventories? Are there not many families who experience rises in family size, occupational status, residential amenities and income but do not increase their household inventories? Table 8.01 provides a partial answer to these questions.

What this table displays are the results of a laborious analysis of the historical data on changes in each of four areas of activity and the

TABLE 8.01

**Coefficients of Correlation Between Changes in Four Areas of Activity
and Acquisitions of Durables During Each of First Five Years of Marriage,
with Parent and Child Generations**

Year of Marriage

Contingency	*Second*	*Third*	*Fourth*	*Fifth*
	Parent			
Increase in family size	—.52	—.28	.06	.28
Change of job by husband	—.07	—.31	.45	—.23
Residential move	.15	.27	.19	.36
Increase in income	.33	—.08	.04	—.24
	Children			
Increase in family size	.41	.20	.22	—.13
Change of job by husband	.27	.29	.15	—.08
Residential move	.44	.37	.81	.31
Increase in income	—.39	—.03	.02	.05

inventory of durables from the beginning of marriage in the parent
and child generations. Durables acquisitions by the grandparent generation were too infrequent for analysis. Changes in these four areas of
economic activity were found to be highly concentrated in the first
five years of marriage. Fortunately, the historical events of this period
had been gathered in one-year intervals for the first five years. Moreover, since only half the families in the child generation had been
married this long, these first five years were as many as could be
validly compared between the parent and child generation.

Increases were identified by comparing the ordinal numbers of
children, jobs, dwellings, and dollars of estimated income that had
been recorded for each successive interval. This meant, of course, that
no changes could be shown for the first year, but only between the
first and second, second and third, etc. Only increases (upward
changes) were counted for purposes of this analysis.

Questions can be raised whether the use of intervals a year in
length is not too crude, whether mere concurrence within the same
year adequately measures correlation, and whether respondents'
(especially parents') memories of these events are sufficiently reliable
to be taken seriously. If strong correlation exists, however, it should
appear in any given year and be consistent from year to year.

The strongest and most consistent pattern of correlation that appears
is that between residential moves and increases in size of household

inventory, moderately in the parent generation and fairly strongly in the child generation. The same type of finding was reported in Chapter 7 for changes occurring together during the year of the study. These two variables of moving and acquiring are apparently closely intertwined, not only historically from parent to child generation but currently.

Family size changes show fairly consistent and positive relations to durable goods acquisitions for the second through the fourth year, suggesting that the first two children precipitate acquisitions of durables, but the third child (arriving in the 5th year) depresses the propensity to make added purchases. The negative correlations in the parent generation may be interpreted in conjunction with the data from Chart 2.01 which show a very long interval between marriage and birth of the second child for the depression oriented parent generation. If *children were born* to this (the parent) generation in the first years of marriage, they *depressed* rather than *encouraged* acquisition of durable goods, whereas in this generation if an *increase in income* occurred, acquisitions of goods would increase. In general, however, durable goods purchases were more insensitive to income changes than to any of the other areas of activity.

Interdependence of planning careers by areas of activity has been confirmed from these several analyses suggesting (1) that residence changes are affected strongly by changes in family composition and moderately by changes in the husband's occupation, especially in the first years of marriage, (2) that this interdependence is least marked in the grandparent generation and most apparent in the child generation, (3) that durable goods acquisitions over the first five years of marriage are most affected by residential mobility and least consistently by increases in income, and (4) that, in general, changes in family composition and in occupation probably affect changes in the inventory of durable goods indirectly, rather than directly, through residential changes. An exception occurs in the child generation, where there is a pronounced direct interdependence among all three areas of activity.

Achievements Patterns over the Life Span

We turn now to an exposition of our findings on the relative achievements over the life span of the generations. To what extent do families which over the marriage lead their generation in one area of activity also lead in the other activities being studied? Does the timing of marriage earlier than the average for the generation handicap achievements in the various areas of activity examined?

To make these comparisons, we have classified families by their performance over the life span as *leaders, on schedule,* or *laggers.* A family may be classified as *leading* at a given point in the life span if it is in the upper tercile, *on schedule* if in the middle tercile, and *lagging* if in the lower tercile of its generation. Couples have been designated as predominantly leading, predominantly on schedule, or predominantly lagging based on the number of periods in which they led, were on schedule, or lagged over the marriage span.

Table 8.02 provides an aggregate picture of the comparative performance of the three generations for four areas of economic activity: income level and occupational level, size of residence and acquisition of durable goods.

When we look at the most consistent families in their performance over the marriage span, there is more of a tendency for the married child generation to be predominantly leading (21.1%) in performance than the other two generations. No generation seems to be consistently in the middle tercile of on schedule families. It is as if there is little tendency to dead level conformity to the Jones. (If the Jones are average people, they don't inspire their peers to live either "up to" or

TABLE 8.02

Percentage Distribution of Families by Their Performance over the Marriage Span Aggregated for Four Areas of Economic Activity (Income, Occupational Level, Size of Residence and Size of Durable Goods Inventory) by Generation

Predominance over the Marriage Span (3 or more areas) of:	Grandparents %	Parents %	Children %
Leading	15.2	19.0	21.1
On Schedule	6.1	1.9	8.3
Lagging	22.2	12.4	10.1
Evenly Divided over Marriage Span between			
Leading and on Schedule	3.0	9.5	11.9
Leading and Lagging	9.1	13.3	1.8
On Schedule and Lagging	14.1	1.3	9.2
Highly Inconsistent in Performance			
Leading in two areas, others divided	9.1	14.3	12.8
On Schedule in two areas, others divided	9.1	8.6	11.9
Lagging in two areas, others divided	12.1	20.0	12.8
Total	100.0	100.0	100.0
N	99	105	109

"down to" them.) There is more consistency in lagging in three or more areas than in being on schedule, and the consistent grandparent generation families are particularly likely to be predominantly lagging (22%).

Even in the evenly divided performances, the grandparents tend to be found in the categories where lagging in two areas is characteristic (14.1% and 9.1%), and the married child generation appears in the leading-on schedule combination (11.9%). The parent generation is not noted for its consistency of high or low performance over the marriage span, but resembles more the married child generation in its performance than the grandparent generation, since it is more consistently leading than lagging. (See categories under "Highly Inconsistent in Performance" in Table 8.02).

Among the most erratic of the families where high performance in two areas was achieved at the cost of lowered performance in others, or low performance in two areas was compensated by higher achievements in the other areas, we find the parent generation more frequently represented; nearly half the parent generation families falls in this style of performance ($14.6 + 8.6 + 20.0 = 42.9\%$).

From Table 8.02, in sum, we have discovered the performance of the three generations to be characterized by three distinct styles of achievement over the marriage span: the married child generation families tend to be more consistently leading in all four areas, the grandparent generation tends toward consistent lagging in performance, and the middle generation is found to be inconsistent in performance from area to area as if compensatory gains and losses were built into their achievements over the life span.

A specification of some interest in explaining the differences among the three generations may be the differential impact of timing the marriage. Table 8.03 cross classifies the performance categories of predominantly leading, predominantly on schedule, and predominantly lagging by generation by whether the couples married earlier or later than average for their generation. It is apparent that the timing of marriage more prudently (marrying later) is found associated with leading one's generation in economic achievements in the married child generation (51% of late marriers are leading). Early marriers, in contrast, are predominantly laggers or on schedule. The phenomenon is not so marked in the parent generation where the most frequent style of performance of the "late marriers" is to be on schedule over the life span (42.6%) and the "early marriers" to be lagging. The grandparent generation reverses this pattern, suggesting that these "late marriers" were poorer than other members of their cohort and therefore are found predominantly in the lagging category over the life span (50%). In sum, the timing of marriage later than the median appears to have presented advantages to two of the three generations, more especially to the married child generation, but for the grandparent generation, the relationships appear reversed. We shall see later in this chapter other evidences of the differences in achievements between the grandparent generation and its successors.

Interrelations of Achievement Among Areas of Activity

Having classified the achievements over the marriage span for each family on each of several areas as leading, on schedule, or lagging compared with others in the generation, we are prepared to ascertain whether leading or lagging in one area is contingent upon leading or lagging in other areas. We have cross-classified the achievement designations for two areas at a time to answer this question.

Family size and income. Does adding children faster depend on increasing income faster than the average for the generation? Only in the grandparent generation does this appear to be true. In the

TABLE 8.03

Percentage Distribution of Families by Generation and by Duration of Marriage Aggregated for Performance over the Marriage Span on Four Areas of Economic Activity (Income, Occupational Level, Size of Residence and Size of Durable Goods Inventory)

	Grandparent		Parent		Child	
	Married Later	*Married Earlier*	*Married Later*	*Married Earlier*	*Married Later*	*Married Earlier*
Achievement Categories	%	%	%	%	%	%
Predominantly Leading (14-20)	22.7	23.6	31.9	31.0	50.9	30.0
Predominantly On Schedule (9-13)	27.3	32.7	42.6	32.8	21.8	36.0
Predominantly Lagging (0-8)	50.0	43.6	25.5	36.2	21.1	34.0
Total	100	100	100	100	100	100
N	44	55	47	58	57	50

grandparent generation, among the "early marrieds", 72% of those leading in income over the marriage span also were leaders in family size. Similarly, among families lagging in income over the marriage, 42% lagged in family size. (Table not shown).

Family size and durable goods acquisitions. The issue of the relation of family size and durable goods acquisitions has been debated. There appears to be a slight negative relation between size of household and durable goods acquisitions in the two younger generations as if leading in acquiring children is at the expense of durable goods acquisitions. The two phenomena appear quite independent in the grandparent generation. (Table not shown).

Income and durable goods. If the acquisition of durable goods is a function of disposable income, then achievement over the marriage span should be interrelated for these two areas. When we aggregate the three generations there is a small, but positive, relation between leading in income and leading in durable goods acquisitions over the life span (see Table 8.04). Forty-four percent of the leaders in income level were leaders in durable goods acquisitions, on the one hand, and 47.5 percent of the families predominantly lagging in income level lagged their generation also in acquiring durable goods. The relationship approaches the 5% level of statistical significance.

Occupational level and durable goods. The same kind of inter-dependence should appear between occupational level and the acquisition of durable goods. Examination of Table 8.05 reveals that the relationship is curvilinear rather than linear. Nearly fifty percent of the leaders in occupational level also were leaders in durable goods acquisitions, but fifty percent of the families that were in the middle group of "on schedule" in occupational advancement lagged

TABLE 8.04

Percentage Distribution of Families (All Generations) by Achievement over the Life Span on Durable Goods Acquisitions by Income

Durable Goods Acquisitions

Income Level	Lagging		On Schedule		Leading		Total	
	f	%	f	%	f	%	f	%
Leading	41	33.3	35	50.7	60	50.4	136	43.7
On Schedule	31	25.2	13	18.8	24	20.2	68	21.9
Lagging	51	41.5	21	30.4	35	29.4	107	34.4
Total	123	100	69	100	119	100	311	100

TABLE 8.05

Percentage Distribution of Families (All Generations) by Achievement over the Life Span on Durable Goods Acquisitions by Occupational Level

Durable Goods Acquisitions

Occupation Level	Lagging		On Schedule		Leading		Total	
	f	%	f	%	f	%	f	%
Leading	32	26.0	20	29.0	46	38.7	98	31.5
On Schedule	54	43.9	25	36.2	29	24.4	108	34.7
Lagging	37	30.1	24	34.8	44	37.0	105	33.8
Total	123	100	69	100	119	100	311	100

in durable goods and, suprisingly, forty-two percent of those lagging in occupational advancement led in the purchase of durable goods over the life span. The relationships are statistically significant at the 5 percent level.

Size of residence, in contrast with the level of income and level of occupational achievement, is unrelated to durable goods acquisitions when aggregated for all generations. Similarly, size of residence is not a function of income level over the life span.

Size of residence and occupational level. The only achievement variable with which size of residence appears to relate is with occupational level. Lagging in size of residence does appear to be associated with lagging in occupational level when all three generations are aggregated (see Table 8.06). Leading in residence size is disproportionately found associated with families on schedule in occupational achievements (48% of this median occupational group of families led their cohort in size of residence over the life span.)

Occupational level and level of income. The closest interdependence of any of the life span achievement measures is between occupational level and income (see Table 8.07). Almost 60 percent of leaders in income level over the life span are also found leading in occupational advancement, and better than forty percent of laggers in income are behind schedule in their occupational advancement. This is but a validation of the higher esteem accorded to occupations of the white collar and professional levels over the blue collar categories in the amount of income earned by these categories over the life span. It will be of interest to see which of these two variables best predicts durable goods acquisitions and size of residence over the life span when the other is held constant by cross-classification.

TABLE 8.06

Percentage Distribution of Families (All Generations) by Achievement over the Life Span in Occupation Level and Size of Residence

Occupational Level

Size of Residence	Lagging		On Schedule		Leading		Total	
	f	*%*	*f*	*%*	*f*	*%*	*f*	*%*
Leading	33	31.4	52	48.1	39	39.8	124	39.9
On Schedule	31	29.5	32	29.6	31	31.6	94	30.2
Lagging	41	39.0	24	22.2	28	28.6	93	29.9
Total	105	100	108	100	98	100	311	100

TABLE 8.07

Percentage Distribution of Families (All Generations) by Achievement over the Life Span on Occupational Level and Level of Income

Occupational Level

Income Level	Lagging		On Schedule		Leading		Total	
	f	*%*	*f*	*%*	*f*	*%*	*f*	*%*
Leading	37	35.2	43	39.8	56	57.1	136	43.7
On Schedule	23	21.9	27	25.0	18	18.4	68	21.9
Lagging	45	42.9	38	35.2	24	24.5	107	34.4
Total	105	100	108	100	98	100	311	100

Durable goods, income and occupational level. The highest percentage of families leading in durable goods acquisitions is found, of course, among families leading in both income level and occupational level (See Table 8.08), but nearly as high a proportion is found among lagging families occupationally where income level was leading (51.8% vs. 48.6%). Similarly, the highest proportion of laggers in durable goods acquisitions are found where income level is lagging, even when occupational level was leading or on schedule. We conclude that income level rather than occupational level is the longitudinal factor most important in accounting for high durable goods acquisitions.

From these several analyses of the interdependence among achievement variables over the life span it is apparent that achievements are more frequently interdependent than independent, but that the relationships are not necessarily always linear. More careful specification in later studies will be required with larger samples to confirm the relations here adduced.

TABLE 8.08

Durable Goods Acquisition Level by Income and Occupation Level over the Life Span (All Generations)

	Income Level										
	Lagging			On Schedule			Leading			Total	
	Occupation Level			Occupation Level			Occupation Level				
Durable Goods Acquisition	Lag %	On Sched %	Lead %	Lag %	On Sched %	Lead %	Lag %	On Sched %	Lead %	N	%
Leading	37.8	21.0	41.7	39.1	29.6	38.9	48.6	30.2	51.8	119	38.3
On Schedule	24.4	18.4	12.5	21.7	18.5	16.7	21.6	30.2	25.0	69	22.2
Lagging	37.8	60.6	45.8	39.1	51.8	44.4	29.8	39.6	23.2	123	39.5
Total	100	100	100	100	100	100	100	100	100	311	100
N	45	38	24	23	27	18	37	43	56		

Congruence of Achievements in Income and Durable Goods

As a final analysis of the interdependence of performance in areas of economic activity, we turn to the two closely allied areas of income level and durable goods acquisitions. In this instance we ask the number of years that each family is leading both in income and in durable goods, on schedule in both, or lagging in both. We relate this figure which we call the total years of congruence to the total years married. For example, Case 2004 of the parent generation had been married 30 years and had been leading in both income and durable goods for 21 years and on schedule in both for one year for a total of 22 years of congruence. This family's level of congruence was 22/30 or 73%.

There are, of course, families with high congruence and families with no congruence at all. Table 8.09 presents the distribution of families for the parent and child generations for those married earlier than average and those married later than the average.

There is manifestly more congruence over the life span between the two economic areas of income level and durable goods in the married child generation than in the parent generation as seen in the medians for the two groups (48% for the married child and only 27% for the parent generation). The interdependence shows up at both extremes of the scale—more parent generation families with no congruence at all (no time period in which performance in income corresponded with performance in durable goods purchases) and more child generation families with very high congruence.

Comparing the effect of timing of marriage on congruence the interdependence appears highest in the early marrieds of the child generation where the median congruence in performance over the life span was 63%. No other cohort approximates that level of congruence. Within the parent generation, the two cohorts are not too different in their congruence levels. The differences appear to be more a function of generation than of timing of marriage.

TABLE 8.09

Percentage Congruence in Achievement over the Marriage Span on Income and Durable Goods Acquisitions by Generation and by Duration of Marriage

Percent Congruence	Parent Generation			Child Generation		
	Married Earlier Than Median	Married Later Than Median	Total Sample	Married Earlier Than Median	Married Later Than Median	Total Sample
	%	%	%	%	%	%
No Congruence	32.8	25.5	29.5	14.0	26.3	20.6
1–29	20.6	25.6	22.6	8.0	157.	14.0
30–59	29.3	23.4	27.6	24.0	29.8	27.1
60–89	12.0	17.0	14.4	34.0	14.1	23.4
90–100	5.1	8.5	6.7	18.0	12.3	14.9
Total	100.0	100.0	100.0	100.0	100.0	100.0
Number of Families	58	47	105	50	57	107
Median Congruence	25%	29%	27%	63%	36%	48%

Interdependence of Achievement Careers

As we conclude this discussion of the interplay of planning careers, we have attempted to summarize in one large multi-layered contingency matrix the interdependence of achievements of families within four areas of activities over their life span. We have aggregated the three generations for this analysis but are prepared where indicated to specify what the contribution of each generation is to each of the cells of the matrix. The matrix is labelled Table 8.10 and is designed to record the propensity of leading and lagging over the marriage span in one area of economic activity to be associated with leading and lagging in the other three areas studied. Table 8.10 helps us answer these questions: Are there any families at all, which have led in all four areas of achievement, in income level, occupational advancement, residence size and size of durable goods inventory over the marriage span? Will the younger generations be more represented than the oldest generation in this multiple achievement syndrome?

First of all, it is noteworthy that there is relatively little concentration along the diagonal from the upper left hand corner where the preponderantly lagging families in all four activities would be found down to the middle section where the preponderantly on schedule families would be located, to the lower right hand corner where the predominantly leading families would be found.

The clustering of family career types appears to be pulled away from the diagonal into the predominantly leading on income level sector on the right and even in the leading in durable goods sector on the extreme right where more cells with high frequency are found. A second row of high frequency cells is found in the leading in size of residence—on schedule in occupation combination which in three career types was combined with lagging in durable goods acquisitions.

There are also a number of empty cells located near the center of the matrix, suggesting unlikely career types. Being on schedule in durable goods, income level and size of residence is especially unlikely. Indeed, of the empty cells, being on schedule in two or more areas was characteristic of six of the seven empty cells. The reason for this deviation from the "middle of the road" in achievement is not at all clear, since the distribution on each of these achievement variables were trichotomized before being cross-classified into the matrix.

In Table 8.11 we have assembled into ten career types the most common combinations of achievements among the 312 families. Type I, the most frequent career type, with fourteen families (predominantly found among child and parent generations), is a joining of leading on income, residence size, and durable goods acquisitions and leading in occupational advancement. Quite similar is the pattern of still eleven other families (many of whom were of the grandparent generation) of being on schedule in residence size, leading in income, in acquisition of durables and in occupational advance-

TABLE 8.10

Contingency Matrix of Career Types Cross-Classifying Performance over the Life Span on Income, Durable Goods, (All Generations) Size of Residence and Occupational Level

		Income								
		Lagging Durable Goods			On Schedule Durable Goods			Leading Durable Goods		
		Lag	On Sched.	Lead	Lag	On Sched.	Lead	Lag	On Sched.	Lead
Residence Lagging	Occupation Lagging	6	4	6	1	3	4	6	4	7
	On Schedule	6	2	1	3	1	1	4	1	5
	Leading	4	3	3	3	1	1	5	4	4
Residence On Schedule	Occupation Lagging	5	4	5	5	0	4	4	0	4
	On Schedule	8	2	4	3	0	0	4	7	4
	Leading	4	0	3	3	0	3	2	5	11
Residence Leading	Occupation Lagging	6	3	6	3	2	1	1	4	7
	On Schedule	9	3	3	8	4	7	9	5	4
	Leading	3	0	4	2	2	3	6	5	14

ment. These two patterns have in common both high income and the heavy investment of that income into the visible status symbols of residence and its furnishings by professional families.

A most interesting combination of achievements is Career Type III which is quite frequent, namely, nine families who lag in income and in durable goods acquisitions while leading in residence size and being on schedule in occupational level. They might be termed house-poor white collar employees. At a certain level of income, investment in housing may be at the expense of furnishings and equipment.

TABLE 8.11

Distribution of Families Among the Ten Most Frequent Career Types
(Source: Table 8.10)

Career Types	All Generations f	Grandparent f	Parent f	Child f
Lead Income, Lead Durables, Lead Residence, Lead Occupation	14	1	6	7
Lead Income, Lead Durables, On Schedule Residence, Lead Occupation	11	5	2	4
Lag Income, Lag Durables, Lead Residence, On Schedule Occupation	9	2	4	3
Lead Income, Lag Durables, Lead Residence, On Schedule Occupation	9	2	4	3
On Schedule Income, Lag Durables, Lead Residence, On Schedule Occupation	8	2	1	5
Lag Income, Lag Durables, On Schedule Residence, On Schedule Occupation	8	4	0	4
Lead Income, Lead Durables, Lag Residence, Lag Occupation	7	5	2	0
On Schedule Income, Lead Durables, Lead Residence, On Schedule Occupation	7	1	3	3
Lead Income, On Schedule Durables, On Schedule Residence, On Schedule Occupation	7	3	0	4
Lead Income, Lead Durables, Lead Residence, Lag Occupation	7	2	3	2
Total	87	27	25	35

Each of the other career types listed tends to demonstrate the interdependence of income and durable goods performance, whereas in very few types are residence size and occupational level uniformly linked in the same way to the other performing variables. It is particularly clear that residence size and durable goods acquisitions appear to vary independently of one another.

When the propensity of the generations to appear in the frequently repeated career types is scanned, the married child generation is highest in multiple leadership in Type I or Type II careers. The parent generation is the most random and the child generation most likely to show some interdependence in performance over its life span. A total of 35 families of this youngest generation is found in the ten modal career types listed in Table 8.11 compared to only 25 for the parent generation. We advance the interpretation that this is further evidence of the tendency to consistency in behavior in the married child generation. This finding is consonant with the more careful planning and more rational choice making observed among the child generation families compared with their parents and grandparents over the period of the study itself.

Summary

This chapter on the interdependence of planning careers opened with three questions: Are some areas of economic activity more interdependent than others? What areas do we judge are dominant, that is, precipitate changes, and what areas accommodate to changes in other areas? Is the interdependence among areas higher in the child generation than in the parent or grandparent generation? Findings are presented which bear upon all three of these questions, but they are made up of sequences of different types and levels. A first order of proof is drawn from the extent to which change in one area of economic activity in any one year is associated with a change in another area of activity. A second order of proof looks at the extent to which leading or lagging one's generation in performance over the marriage span in one area of activity is associated with leading or lagging in performance in other areas of activity.

Interdependence of planning careers by areas of economic activity has been confirmed at the level of synchronization versus randomness of changes as follows: (1) Residence changes are affected strongly by changes in family composition and moderately by changes in the husband's occupation, especially in the first years of marriage; (2) This interdependence is least marked in the grandparent generation and most apparent in the child generation; (3) Durable goods acquisitions over the first five years of marriage are most affected by residential mobility and least consistently by increases in income; and (4) In general, changes in family composition and in occupation affect changes in the inventory of durable goods indirectly, rather than directly, through the residential changes which they precipitate. Within the child generation, there is a pronounced direct interdependence among all three areas of activity.

At the level of lagging and leading one's generation over the life span, three distinct styles of achievement have been discovered in assessing the performance of the three generations on income level, occupational level, size of residence and size of durable goods inventory: The married child generation families tend to be more consistently leading in all four areas, the grandparent generation tends toward consistent lagging in performance, and the middle parent generation shows inconsistency in performance from area to area as if compensatory gains and losses had been built into their achievements over the life span.

A third analysis has involved ascertaining whether leading or lagging in one area over the life span is *contingent* upon leading or lagging in other areas. We discovered such a relationship between income level and family size (for grandparents only), and for income level and durable goods inventory size, and occupational level and income (all generations). Increasing income faster than average for the generation was associated with increasing the size of the family and the size of the family's inventory of durables, for example. No such relation was found between income level and size of residence, although house size did appear contingent upon rate of occupational advancement. When rate of advancement in income and occupational level are both juxtaposed with increases in durable goods acquisitions over the marriage span, degree of movement in income level proves to be the dominant explanation of the longitudinal data.

A finer examination of the interrelation of income level and size of durable goods inventory by generation shows the interdependence highest in the "early marriers" of the child generation and lowest in the "early marriers" of the parent generation. The historical circumstance of marrying during the depression for the parent generation and marrying under conditions of relative affluence by the married child generation may account for the differences in degree of interdependence between these variables for these two generations.

Analysis of the career types created by the juxtaposition of performance in four areas in a multi-layered contingency matrix has provided evidence that multiple leading in several areas is most characteristic, multiple lagging is next, and multiple performances on schedule are least likely to occur. Of the ten career types characterizing the career patterns of most families, the Type I career, involving leading in all four areas on income level, occupational level, size of residence and size of durable goods inventory, encompassed the largest number of families. Income level and durable goods inventory size were most prominently featured as interdependent in the high frequency career types.

Among the generations, the married child generation is both the most likely to show multiple leading in three or more areas, but is also most likely to be congruent and interdependent in achievement over its more limited life span. The parent generation is both the most erratic and the most random in its performance, that is, it is most frequently found among the career types in which leading in one area is accomplished at the expense of lagging in other areas.

PART TWO

EXPLANATIONS OF FAMILY CONSUMERSHIP PLANNING AND ACTION

CHAPTER IX

Correlates of Family Consumership

THE CONSUMPTION CYCLE may be conceptualized in four major phases beginning with the identification of unmet needs in the form of plans (Phase 1), an intervening process of decision-making in choosing the best course of action (Phase 2), followed by an action of purchase and consumption (Phase 3), ending with an evaluation of the adequacy of the action as satisfying or dissatisfying (Phase 4).

The consumption cycle may be arrested at almost any point by failure to carry through to the next phase. Fortunately, in this study relatively few families failed to have sufficient plans and actions to be given a score on their consumership for each phase.[1] Thus over the year's period of observation, families have been classified on their consumership as high or low on plans (Phase 1); high or low on the thoroughness of their search for information, consultation, and weighing of consequences in the decision-process (Phase 2); and high or low on the number of actions carried out, high or low on the number of actions preceded by a plan, or of plans fulfilled (Phase 3). Families have also been classified with respect to Phase 4 as high or low on the way they evaluated the outcome of the entire process which permits us in a separate chapter to assess the consequences of consumership in each of the antecedent phases.

In the discussion which follows, these phases will be looked at

---

[1] Only in the grandparent generation do we have any families (23 families) who went through the year without either plans or actions. The characteristics of the twenty-three non-planning, non-acting grandparents are of some interest. They are older chronologically, have no children at home, have had a higher life income and the wife is not now working. The non-planning group is more prudential and fatalistic in outlook, but also more optimistic. As a type of family organization, the non-acting families are more frequently husband dominant with high marital agreement and high marital integration.

separately. We may well expect that high consumership in some phases may be achieved at the expense of consumership in other phases. We will find ourselves searching for the optimum combination of achievements by phases as we close this discussion. This is quite different from the theoretically oriented assumption that high volume of plans combines with high scores on efficiency in decision-making, which in turn combines with high volume of actions and of pre-planned actions.

The exposition procedure to be employed minimizes the presentation of tables because of the enormous number of antecedent variables assessed and the repetition which would be required for each of the three phases of the consumption cycle. At the end of the discussion of each phase one summary statistical table is presented which shows at the zero order level the amount, direction and significance of the correlation between each antecedent variable and the consumership variable of that phase for all generations. Under a second caption the table will show separately for each generation the direction of the correlation if statistically significant, and whether or not the correlation is curvilinear. The generations are abbreviated to G_1 for the grandparent generation, G_2 for the parent generation and G_3 for the married child generation. Statistical significance at the 5% level or higher is shown as "s" and below that as "ns."

Correlates of Needs-Identification (Phase 1)

We would expect developmentally that the family's unmet needs would be highest in the child generation, next highest in the parent generation and lowest in the grandparent generation, needs being associated with expanding family size. This is precisely what we find when we use as our indicator volume of plans reported over the twelve months of observation. The volume of planning increases from 2.3 plans per family among the grandparents, to 4.6 for the parents to 6.4 per family in the married child generation. Moreover, within generations the younger marrieds and the younger ages tended to make more plans, making the developmental explanation important even for small age ranges.

In terms of life-time income, high planners have had lower life-time income in all three generations, as one might expect from younger marrieds ($r = -.254$). When life income is cross-classified by years married in the parent generation, the highest volume of plans is in the younger married but high life-time income group (61.5% High

Plans) and the lowest volume of plans in the older married high life-income group, an interaction effect. In the child generation the original negative relation between high life-time income and volume of plans remains when years married is held constant, suggesting that life-time income is the more important variable (See Table 9.01).

In rather striking contrast to life-time income which cumulates almost like a developmental variable, the relation of needs identification and current income is positive ($r = .18$) when the generations are merged. Examination by generations separately demonstrates that this positive relation, an incentive to articulate plans, is true for the older but not the married child generation where current income, if high, suppresses volume of planning. Indeed when we combine low current income and large family size in the child generation, we maximize the number of plans enunciated over the year's period.

TABLE 9.01

Volume of Plans by Life Time Income and Years Married for Parent and Married Child Generation

	Parent Generation						Child Generation					
	Years Married						Years Married					
	High		Low				High		Low			
	Life Income		Life Income		Total		Life Income		Life Income		Total	
	High %	Low %	High %	Low %	N	%	High %	Low %	High %	Low %	N	%
Volume of Plans												
High	38.7	56.5	61.5	58.6	50	52.0	40.0	71.4	40.0	51.0	49	47.6
Low	61.3	46.5	38.5	41.4	46	48.0	60.0	28.6	60.0	49.0	54	52.4
Total	100	100	100	100		100	100	100	100	100		100
N	31	23	13	29	96		40	7	5	51	103	

Large family size makes for high volume of plans in both the grandparent and the child generation but is negative in the parent generation. (See Summary Statistical Table for Phase 1, Table 9.02). When families in the parent generation are divided by stage of the family cycle (a developmental variable which divides the generation into the families with children still at home and families with children launched) the younger unlaunched families had most plans, suggesting size and stage of development affect volume of plans differently. When cross-classified, the *small* pre-launched families were most likely to be high in plans (60% High Plans) compared with the large pre-launched (49%) or the launched (47.6%). Family size, then, works differently in the middle generation from the other two in which size is favorable to plan articulation. This latter relation holds up even when cross-classified by income. In the grandparent generation large size and high income interact to produce 75% high plans compared to 38% high plans for high income and low family size.

So far, the effects of the developmental and constraints variables have been to decrease the volume of plans in the first case and to increase them in the second for all generations. What differences do we get when the indicators of social abilities and competences are employed? We would expect in general that the ability to identify needs would be higher for the higher educated but that their unmet needs, as yet, would be fewer.

Competences

Only in the grandparent generation is years of education positively related to volume of plans for both husband and wife. In the child and parent generations the husband's education is negatively related to high volume of plans. The more educated are more circumspect in enunciating plans or have fewer needs to identify (see Summary Statistical Table for Phase 1, Table 9.02).

Value Orientations

It has been suggested that many of the foregoing variables of generation, age, income, and education are linked to behavior through the value orientations held. Are the older generations less likely to enunciate plans because they are more fatalistic, prudential, pessimistic, and traditional in their orientations to life? We know from an earlier discussion in Chapter 2, that the generations vary on these values but are not entirely clear about how they relate to consumership.

In general, high plans (identification of needs) are more frequent among those scoring low on fatalism, prudence, developmentalism and high on optimism. Exceptions are noteworthy in the child generation where prudence is positively related to volume of plans (Is it more prudent to express plans in this generation just beginning its cycle with many unmet needs than in the older generations?) and in the parent generation where high optimism is associated with *low* rather than *high* volume of plans. Does developmental stage oper-

TABLE 9.02

Summary Statistical Table Phase 1, Correlations Between Volume of Plans and Hypothesized Explanatory Variables by Generation

Class of Explanatory Variables	Direction and Significance of Correlation All Generations	Direction of Relation by Generation		
		G1	G2	G3
Developmental	"*r*"			
Generation	— .32 s	—	—	—
Age of Husband	— .36 s	neg.	neg.	neg.
Years Married	— .35 s	neg.	neg.	neg.
Incentives and Constraints				
Life-Time Income	— .24 s	neg.	neg.	neg.
Current Income	.18 s	pos.	pos.	neg.
Current Family Size	.08 ns	pos.	neg.	pos.
Social Competences				
Education (Husband)	.24 s	pos.	neg.	ns
Education (Wife)	—	pos.	pos.	neg.
Occupation (Husband)	— .08 ns	pos.	pos.	neg.
Value Orientations				
Developmentalism-Traditionalism Score	.19 s	pos.	ns	neg.
Fatalistic-Manipulative	— .19 s	neg.	neg.	ns
Prudential-Impulsivity	— .10 ns	neg.	neg.	pos.
Optimism-Pessimism	.06 ns	pos.	neg.	pos.
Future Time Orientation	.05 ns	neg.	pos.	ns
Restrictiveness of Family Organization				
Authoritarian-Equalitarian Family	— .03 ns	neg.	pos.	pos.
Sex Role Conventionality	—	curvilinear	neg.	neg.
Social Participation (Wife)	.06 ns	pos.	ns	pos.
Wife Working Gainfully	—	ns	pos.	pos.
Marital Organization				
Marital Integration	— .24 s	neg.	neg.	ns
Marital Agreement	— .24 s	neg.	ns	pos.
Communication	+ .17 s	pos.	ns	pos.

ate to make outlook and behavior different in the launching period than earlier or later?

Restrictiveness of Family Organization

The structural properties of families may be irrelevant to the identification of needs in volume of plans, but we advance the hypothesis that restrictive and rigid family structures in decision-making, role allocation, and restrictions on participation of wife in the labor force and in outside activities will be negatively related to consumership. Whether this will extend to volume of plans expressed remains to be seen.

Volume of plans appears higher in the two younger generations in authoritarian families where conventionality of roles is low and where the wife is active socially and gainfully employed. This outcome is as hypothesized for consumership generally. In the grandparent generation however, it should be noted that it is the equalitarian family which is the most active in needs identification.

Marital Organization

A different order of family organization is caught in the measures of marital felicity and solidarity. Here we have measures of communication, affection, agreement and integration which in general should be positively related to consumership. Examination of the tabulations of these variables against volume of needs identified shows more negative than positive relationships. In the child generation high marital communication and high marital agreement are positively related to high plans. But for both older generations marital integration is negatively related to plans expressed. It would seem plausible that the married child generation requires a certain amount of communication and agreement between spouses to function effectively because their consumption patterns are in flux. Just to bring needs to light requires much discussion in a new family. In the older generations it is the couples who are dissatisfied with marriage who are high in unmet needs, and these are consequently reported as plans. A theory of progressive disenchantment and disengagement over the life span is needed to explain the differences between the youngest and the two older generations on these variables.[2]

Summary

The largest differences in volume of plans are found in the developmental categories of generation, years married, and age of spouses. Stimulants and constraints such as family size, life-time income, and deficiencies in social competence represented by low education also have marked positive effects on articulating needs. Less clear, although in many cases not less significant statistically, (see Table 9.02), are the impacts of value orientations, types of family

---

[2] See work by Peter Pineo on this theory and its implications, "Disenchantment in the Later Years of Married Life," in *Marriage and Family Living*, 23 (1961), pp. 3-11.

organization, and extent of marital cohesion which operate differently depending upon the generation studied.

Correlates of Rationality in Decision-Making (Phase 2)

We now enter the discussion of the second phase of the consumption cycle, namely the process of choosing and deciding on the appropriate actions to be taken in implementing the plan expressed in the first phase. To a limited extent a family's success in decision-making is related to the level of its activities in the first phase, the number of needs to be met (volume of plans), and the type and quality of the plans expressed. Sheer volume of planning, however, is not as related to rationality in decision-making ($r = 0.09$) as is the type of plan, whether it is definite as to time ($r = 0.22$) and whether it is short-run in horizon, to be carried out within the next three months ($r = 0.14$). The extent of rationality utilized in decision-making is thus affected by the prior number and types of plans expressed.

A word may be in order to specify the indicators of rationality in decision-making. For every action taken, the respondent was asked to show what he had done before taking action to assure the best outcome possible. These activities have been scaled into a score which ranges from zero to eight. The frequency of activity can be determined from the way in which the items array themselves on the scale in Chart 9.01. The lower the score the fewer the activities the family participated in preceding the taking of an action. From Chart 9.01 we observe that the activity which preceded all but a few of the actions was projection of short-run satisfaction. Following this, in order of frequency, were: (1) discussion within the family, (2) satisfaction weighed among the alternatives the family proposes, (3) satisfaction projected into the more distant future, and (4) costs weighed among alternatives. Most actions were presumably taken on the information the family members were able to provide. Fewer families actually went to the trouble of seeking alternatives, fewer yet had a set family policy, while the last item to scale, or the item the fewest families answered positively, was (5) information seeking outside of the immediate family. From this array it appears that the family first utilizes its immediate members as sources of information, evaluates costs, and projects the outcome of the alternatives they propose. Only as a last step, does the family leave the home to seek alternatives. This, then, is a descriptive presentation of the way the items arranged themselves on our operational indicator of rationality. It does not, however, describe the relative performance of the families during the year. For this purpose we must shift to Chart 9.02.

CHART 9.01

The Scaling of Rationality into Scale Types

A	B	C	D	E	F	G	H	
Confer outside of family.	Family policy	Alternative seeking	Costs weighed among alternatives.	Satisfaction projected over long run	Satisfaction weighed among alternatives	Confer within family	Satisfaction projected over short run	SCALE SCORE
+	+	+	+	+	+	+	+	8
−	+	+	+	+	+	+	+	7
−	−	+	+	+	+	+	+	6
−	−	−	+	+	+	+	+	5
−	−	−	−	+	+	+	+	4
−	−	−	−	−	+	+	+	3
−	−	−	−	−	−	+	+	2
−	−	−	−	−	−	−	+	1
−	−	−	−	−	−	−	−	0

From the distribution of scores presented by generation in Chart 9.02, it appears that a substantial number of actions actually force the family to go beyond its immediate members for evidence in making a decision to purchase or to move, for example. This is the case for almost one-fourth of all the plans the three generations completed. The child generation in particular is more active in seeking outside information; 31 percent of all its actions were preceded by first using all eight methods of obtaining information and evaluating solutions. Parents and grandparents were less active in this respect since only 16 percent and 19 percent of their respective actions carried them to all sources of information. As far as utilizing only the information the family could provide, the child generation ended its evidence-seeking with its immediate family on one-half of its actions, the parents on two-thirds, and the grandparents on about 70 percent of their actions. This means that the child generation is the most likely to seek alternatives outside of the family, to have a family policy to cover given situations, and to discuss their impending actions outside of the immediate family. The grandparents, in contrast, are less likely to seek alternatives and to project expected satisfaction.

We may speculate that the reason the child generation is the more active is that it is in the process of formulating its consumption habits while the parents and grandparents have an accumulation of agreements and of past experiences to draw upon. In summary, it appears that although families in general consider outside sources as the last resort, many actions are actually preceded by discussion and alternative seeking outside of the immediate family.

With this background about the operational indicator of rationality in decision-making in this second phase of the cycle and the discussion of the variable achievements of the three generations in decision-making, let us examine the major correlates of rationality drawing from our framework of developmental variables, incentives and constraints, value orientations, and family organization properties.

CHART 9.02.

Distribution of Scale Types by Generation

Scale Scores	Actions by Children		Actions by Parents		Actions by Grandparents	
	N	%	N	%	N	%
8	112	31	42	16	19	19
7	65	18	46	18	10	10
6	60	16	50	19	13	13
5	33	9	28	11	8	8
4	25	7	29	11	15	15
3	28	8	26	10	8	8
2	19	5	19	7	7	7
1	11	3	9	4	5	5
0	14	4	9	4	13	13
	367	100	257	100	99	99
Reproducibility:		90%		88.9%		87.4%
Mean Score:		5.88		5.17		4.61

Developmental

We don't have the same case for anticipating higher achievement in the second phase from our younger respondents that we made for the identification of needs in Phase 1. Rationality in decision-making may be expected to relate more to the social competences provided by education and occupational experience, and to a family's participation in settings where the problem solving approaches are characteristic. Developmentally we might expect age to be negatively related to rationality because of the lesser exposure to educational and occupational settings stressing rationality.

We have already noted that the child generation ranks highest, the parent generation next, and the grandparent generation lowest in their scores on rationality in decision-making. Within the generations, years married appears negative but not linear in its relation to rationality in decision-making. Among the parents, those married longest (31-40 years) have the lowest score, but those in the middle category (26-30 years married) are highest. In the child generation the older group (5-15 years married) are both high and low in their performance while the very young marrieds, largely childless, are in the middle rationality scores. Age of wife, however, is positively related to rationality of decision-making in all generations. These differences argue for examining rationality in decision-making by age at marriage. When we do this for the child generation we find about what we would expect, that couples where the husbands were above average age at marriage (one might infer they had been more rational in timing the marriage) are also highest in rationality scores over the year's observation. This is the only generation where we could legitimately expect such a correlation, since age at marriage would lose its power as the generations move further along the life span.

Incentives and Constraints

There are humanitarian if not theoretical reasons to suppose that low income or large family size should stimulate rationality in decision-making, since such families have fewer disposable resources to expend thoughtlessly or impulsively. The findings with respect to life-time income ($r = -.11$) suggest this may be the case, but the reverse is true for current income ($r = 0.11$). The findings on family size offer little comfort, since the smaller the family the more rational the decision processes. This is especially clear within the child generation. In sum, in this area of incentives and constraints we see the very factors which encouraged high identifying of consumer needs associated with lowered rationality in decision-making. *Large family size and low income account for unmet needs in families while depressing the careful rational decision-making required to meet those needs.*

Social Competences

The best explanation of consumership in this second phase would be the possession of educational and occupational competences. Education of husband is positively related to rationality ($r = .21$) when all three generations are merged. Looked at singly, the grandparent generation is negative and the younger generations positive on this variable. Education of wife is negatively related in the grandparent and parent generation but shows up as positive in the child generation. When education of husband is cross-classified by education of wife, some interesting results are obtained. In the grandparent generation and the parent generation the lowest rationality is found among the couples where both spouses have high education, and the highest rationality where both spouses are poorly educated. In these generations greater education may have enabled them to formulate policies and rules short circuiting the many components of decision-making that give high scores. In the child generation the opposite relation obtains, with high rationality located in families where both spouses have high education.

Supporting this general thesis are the findings that high education of husband combined with high life-time income is associated with low rationality in the grandparent generation, whereas families of low education and high life-time income are very high in rationality. The deviant high education-low life-time income group of families in the two older generations makes middle rationality scores. In the child generation, however, high education remains associated with high rationality even when life-time income is held constant, and the lowest rationality is found in the deviant low education-high life-time income set of families.

Occupational differences between blue collar and white collar workers give a net advantage to white collar workers, especially in the married child generation. Moreover, in the two younger generations, families in which the wife is gainfully employed lead those families where wife remains at home in rationality in marked fashion. This holds up even when educational differences are held constant.

Although the differences in occupational level show less impact than expected, the major thesis that educational and occupational competences are associated with rationality in decision-making is confirmed.

Value Orientations

The bridge between value orientations and rationality of decision-making should be easy to establish if one's outlook on the world, time, and human nature motivates one's intellectual pursuits. We have chosen three dimensions to test this in the optimism-pessimism, prudential-impulsivity, and future vs. present and past orientation scales from Brim's Cognitive Values Scales. In addition we have drawn from a scale of ideologies about child and parents called the Developmental-Traditional Score for a fourth dimension.

Optimism is positively related to rationality when the three generations are merged but appears negatively related within the child generation. Future time orientation is negatively related when all generations are merged but is positive in the child generation. Prudential views are positive in both the younger generations but are negligibly related when the generations are merged. Subscription to developmentalism as an ideology is positively associated with education which we have already found to be predictive of rationality. It shows up however, as only slightly positive in the grandparent generation and negatively related in both younger generations.

When education of wife is taken into account a number of differences among the generations appear. In the two older generations the lowest rationality is found in the deviant group with high education and low developmentalism, the educated group we would not have suspected of traditionalist orientations (64.7% for grandparents and 45% for parents respectively). The highest rationality in these older generations is found among the bonafide traditionalists, women of low education – low developmentalism orientations (45% for grandparents and 56.2% for parents). In the child generation, in contrast, the formerly negative relations between developmentalism and rationality largely disappear with education held constant, suggesting education to be the more powerful influence on rationality in this generation.

Restrictiveness of Family Organization

The theory for determining relationships in this cluster of factors is not yet firmly established. The direction expected would be one of greater rationality among the less rigid family types: the equalitarian, non-conventional, non-specialized, with high scores on wife's social participation. The correlations are not significant when all three generations are merged, with the exception of social participation, where the correlation is opposite to the direction hypothesized. In the child generation equalitarian authority patterns are positively associated with rationality in decision-making ($r = 0.18$). The division of sex roles, although not significantly related statistically, are in the expected direction of low conventionality and low specialization being associated with rationality in decisions reached. The flexibility in family organization suggested by wife working gainfully is associated positively with rationality in decision-making in the two younger generations, and remains positive in these generations when education of wife is held constant. With a few noteworthy exceptions in sum, rationality is greater for the less rigid family types.

TABLE 9.03

Summary Statistical Table Phase 2, Correlations Between
Rationality in Decision-Making Score and Explanatory Variables by Generation

Class of Explanatory Variables	Direction and Significance of Correlation All Generations	Direction of Relation by Generation		
		G1	G2	G3
Developmental				
Generation	— .23 s	..	..	..
Age of Husband	.28 s	neg.	curvi-linear	pos.
Age of Wife	.25 s	pos.	pos.	pos.
Years Married	— .28 s	pos.	curvi-linear	curvi-linear
Age at Marriage of Husband	..	..	..	pos.
Incentives and Constraints				
Life-Time Income	— .11 s	curvi-linear	curvi-linear	curvi-linear
Current Income	.11 s	neg.	curvi-linear	ns
Family Size	— .11 s	ns	curvi-linear	neg.
Social Competences				
Education (Husband)	.21 s	neg.	pos.	pos.
Education (Wife)		neg.	neg.	pos. ns
Occupational Status (Husband)	.02 ns	pos.	curvi-linear	pos.
People vs. Things Oriented Occupation (Husband)		..	pos.	neg.
Index of Social Position	.02 ns	pos.	curvi-linear	pos.
Value Orientations				
Developmentalism-Traditionalism Score	— .11 s	pos.	neg.	neg.
Optimism-Pessimism	.16 s	ns	pos.	neg.
Prudential-Impulsivity	.01 ns	ns	pos.	pos.
Future vs. Past Time Orientation	— .10 ns	neg.	neg.	ns
Fatalism-Manipulative Score	..	pos.	neg.	ns
Restrictiveness of Family Organization				
Authoritarian-Equalitarian Family	.00 ns	ns	pos.	r = — .18
Sex Role Conventionality	..	pos.	curvi-linear	neg.
Wife Working Gainfully	..	neg.	pos.	pos.
Role Specialization vs. Role Sharing	..	pos.	pos.	pos.
Social Participation	— .11 s	ns	ns	neg.

Class of Explanatory Variables	Direction and Significance of Correlation All Generations	Direction of Relation by Generation		
		G1	G2	G3
Marital Organization				
Marital Integration	.06 ns	neg.	neg.	curvi-linear
Marital Agreement	— .15 s	ns	neg.	neg.
Harmony-Conflict	.03 ns	neg.	curvi-linear	pos.
Communication Between Spouses	.19 s	neg.	pos.	pos.
Hostility-Indifferent-Affectionate (Husband)		curvi-linear	curvi-linear	neg.
Hostility-Indifferent-Affectionate (Wife)		curvi-linear	curvi-linear	neg.
Antecedent Consumership Variables				
Volume of Plans	.09 ns			
Percent of Plans Definite	.22 s			
Percent of Plans with Short Horizons	.14 s			

Marital Organization

Family development theory suggests that rationality in decision-making should be associated with good marital communication, high marital agreement and integration as well as absence of conflict and hostility between spouses.

Communication between spouses does appear to be significantly associated positively for two of the three generations with rationality in decision-making. The measures of integration, agreement, and affection are however, negatively related to consumership, as if good marriage adjustment were associated with more relaxed and less circumspect searching for information, conferring, and taking into account long-run and short-run consequences. Is it possible that couples possessing high cohesion and high consensus don't bother with preliminaries but proceed directly to take action, feeling they know one another's wishes well enough, or can risk a bad purchase without threatening the marriage? Pluralistic ignorance may also be higher in cohesive marriages which would, of course, be associated with lowered rationality in decision-making.

Summary

Rationality in decision-making is best predicted in this study by the kinds of plans preceding the decision process, the developmental variables of generation, years married, and age of spouses. The best single explanation for rationality in decisions, however, is to be found in the amount of educational exposure in school, especially of the husband, and the exposure of the wife to the occupational world through gainful employment. Insights are obtained from the contradictory impact of life-time income, current income and family size, and the several value orientations which affect the generations differently. Family and marital organization is also less uniform in its impact on rationality except for marital communication which should be added to the developmental and social competence variables as an important antecedent of efficiency in decision-making.

Correlates of Planfulness of Actions Taken (Phase 3)

We are now at the point in the consumption cycle where the impact of needs articulated (Phase 1) in the form of number of plans, and the quality of the decision-making process (Phase 2) should be reflected in the volume and planfulness of the actions taken (Phase 3). In a society as affluent as our own we might expect that high volume of plans will be associated with a high volume of actions. We also expect that high specificity of plans, namely, a high proportion of short-run plans (three months or less) and high rationality of decision-making will be positively related to the fulfillment of plans.

We begin with an assessment of the interrelation of these various antecedent expressions of consumership with the volume and planfulness of actions. The number of plans made is significantly and positively correlated with volume of actions taken during the year $(r = 0.30)$ and even more so with the proxy variable we are using for planfulness, the proportion of actions preceded by a plan $(r = 0.37)$. Volume of actions is also anticipated by the rationality of decision score $(r = 0.31)$ and by the specificity of planning, the proportion of plans of short horizon $(r = 0.24)$. Planfulness (Percent of Actions Preceded by Plan) is predicted well by both the measure of specificity of planning $(r = 0.34)$ and by the rationality of decision score $(r = 0.36)$. Thus, in this third phase of the consumption process, volume and planfulness of actions are affected positively by their antecedents: the identification of needs (Volume of Plans), the rationality of decisions made, and by short run specific plans rather than indefinite or longer run plans. So far in the process, the sequences fit together in reasonably compatible fashion.

In the discussion which follows we will seek to compare the impact of the several independent variables which we have used for the explanation of the first two phases on the two expressions of consumership which are salient in this third phase of the consumption process, the volume of actions and the planfulness of those actions.

Developmental Factors

The volume and planfulness of actions vary by generation as expected. The grandparent generation is lowest in volume of actions, averaging 1.8 per family, followed by the parent generation with 3.8 and the child generation with 5.0 per family. The propensity to take risks and carry plans into actions appears greatest in the needy youngest generation. Planfulness (Proportion of Actions Preceded by a Plan), is also highest for the child generation (51% of actions are preplanned) and about the same for the two older generations (G_1 44.2%; G_2 45.2%).

Even within the generations the ages of spouses and the number of years married were negatively related to risk taking and planfulness, suggesting a common depressant of age and marital duration. Age at marriage similarly appears negatively related to risk taking in all generations. The relationship is especially marked in the child generation, where it persists even when present age and income are held constant. The older the husband was at marriage the lower his volume of actions during the study year. However, in this youngest generation the pre-planning of actions is positively related to age at marriage.

A more interesting test of the impact of time married on planfulness is to link it with life-time income which is also negative in its impact on planfulness. The grandparent generation is much less planful when life income is higher than average and years married lower than average (high income per years married), and higher than expected in pre-planned actions when life-time income is lower and years married high. The same relation appears in the parent generation with respect to high planfulness which is found disproportionately in the high years married-low life-time income group. The same impact is not apparent in the child generation.

Incentives and Constraints

None of the relationships in this set of variables are very marked, and when examined by generation the impact is quite variable. Cur-

rent income is negatively related to planfulness in the parent generation but positively related in the oldest and youngest generation.
Family size is negatively related to planfulness in both the parent and
child generation. When family size is run, holding income constant,
the negative relations remain, indeed they are exacerbated. Parent
generation families with large families and low incomes are least
planful (47% of them are low in pre-planned actions). Small families
with low income, however, have the largest number of pre-planned
actions. In the child generation the paradox occurs in even purer
form. The highest pre-planning of actions occurs among small families with high incomes and poorest pre-planning among large families with low incomes. This runs entirely contrary to the best interests of the families and requires further study.

The paradox of the income-family size impact on planfulness should
be pursued by noting the effect of other variables known to be correlated with income and with family size. Wife working is one of
these variables. If there are dependents at home, the mother is less
free to work gainfully and family income will be lower, accordingly,
than if she worked. Examination of the impact of income when gainful employment of the wife is held constant merits our attention. In
the parent generation where the zero order relation of income to planfulness was negative, and of wife working to planfulness was positive,
the negative relation of income to planfulness is even higher among
families where the wife works, see Table 9.04. Fifty percent of *low
income* families where wife works are in the high planful group (51-
100% of actions pre-planned) whereas forty-two percent of the *high income* families with wife working are in the group (0-29% of actions
pre-planned) which undertake actions with little advance planning.
For families with wives at home, the negative impact of income
on planning disappears, with the modal patterning being middle
group planfulness. It is in this latter group where a large family size
would-have been more likely to keep the mother at home.

In the child generation where the impact of income is positive
on planfulness, the presence of a working wife increases planfulness
among the high income families and her staying at home decreases
planfulness among the low income families. Thus a syndrome of explanations for planfulness emerges: small families, wife working and
high income.

Social Competences

Both volume and planfulness of actions are modestly predicted by
years of schooling completed by both spouses in each of the two

younger generations. (See Statistical Summary Table, Phase 3, Table 9.06). When all three generations are merged, education of husband is significantly correlated with both consumership variables. The Index of Social Position and occupation of husband, however, are not good predictors of planfulness.

TABLE 9.04

Planfulness in Parent Generation by Employment of Wife and Family Income

Percent of Actions Pre-Planned	Wife Working Income		Wife at Home Income		Total
	High %	Low %	High %	Low %	%
High (51%-100%)	26.3	50.0	25.9	21.0	30.1
Middle (30%-50%)	31.6	33.3	33.3	44.4	34.9
Low (0%-29%)	42.1	16.7	16.7	29.6	34.9
Total	100	100	100	100	100
N	19	18	27	19	83

Value Orientations

When the three generations are taken together, only one of the value orientations, Fatalism-Manipulativeness appears significantly related to planfulness ($r = -.13$) and none are related to volume of actions taken (see Statistical Summary Table 9.06).

When the generations are viewed separately, families in all three generations holding developmental conceptions about parenthood and childhood are more likely to pre-plan actions, although less likely to be high risk takers. When the education of the wife is held constant, developmentalism continues to be positively related to planfulness in the grandparent and child generation, whereas in the parent generation it practically disappears.

Among the value orientations expected to show a relation to planfulness were Fatalism which we expected to be negatively related, Prudence which we expected to be positive, Optimism which we expected to be positive, and Future Time Orientation for which we anticipated positive relations. As the summary table shows, the generations varied markedly in the extent to which these relations actually were obtained. The value orientations predict poorly the behavioral variables of risk-taking and pre-planned actions.

Restrictiveness of Family Organization

The measures of restrictiveness of family organization which anticipate best volume and planfulness of actions are: (1) sex role conventionality which is negatively related, (2) social participation of wife which is positively related, and (3) wife working gainfully which is positively related except in the grandparent generation. Authoritarian family patterns tend to be negatively related to planfulness but are not uniformly so.

Restrictiveness of family organization as a syndrome of conventionality of sex roles such as cloistering of wife at home, no social participation, wife not working, and authoritarian decision-making patterns, appears negatively related to planfulness in the parent and child generations. The grandparent generation, in contrast, reverses the field with respect to wife not working and authoritarianism, with these latter patterns appearing positively related to planfulness.

Marital Organization

We would theoretically expect a higher volume of actions and higher planfulness among families in which there was high marital agreement, marital integration, lack of conflict and good marital communication. When all three generations are merged, the correlations on most counts are either non-significant (see Summary Statistical Table, Table 9.06) or negative, contrary to expectations.

When examined separately by generation, marital integration is negatively related to risk taking and planfulness in the two older generations but is positively related to planfulness in the child generation. The hint that marital integration may change in its impact on planfulness over the life cycle from positive in the early years of marriage to negative is corroborated in an analysis of the differential impact within the child generation by years married (see Table 9.05). For couples married less than the median years, high marital integration—high planfulness, and low integration—low planfulness are associated, whereas in the couples married more than the median number of years, the association changes direction toward a negative relation.

Knowing from the data in Table 9.05 that marital integration is positively related to planfulness in the first years of marriage and changes to negative among the more "seasoned" couples of the child generation, with continuation of this relationship in the parent and grandparent generation, we must alter our hypothesis about marital integration and planfulness.

TABLE 9.05

Planfulness by Years Married and Marital Integration (Child Generation)

	Years Married			
	High		Low	
	Marital Integration		Marital Integration	
	High	Low	High	Low
	%	%	%	%
Percent of Pre Planned Actions				
High	54.2	69.2	60.0	37.0
Low	45.8	30.8	40.0	63.0
Total	100.00	100.00	100.00	100.00
N	24	13	20	27

Let us speculate a bit about the form the new hypothesis should take. As a marriage begins, the couples have much to learn about each other. Facing the necessity of planning together they begin through discussion to achieve marital consensus (one of the components of marital integration). As the marriage seasons, the couples having the highest consensus have less need to articulate a plan before taking action because they have at hand long term policies on which actions are based. Thus, high marital integration will appear increasingly associated with low pre-planning of actions, and low marital integration will be associated with the necessity to pre-plan because the couples dare not risk taking action without having first made out a plan.

Some support for this interpretation is found in the negative relation between marital agreement and planfulness in the seasoned parent generation contrasted with the positive relation found in the child generation. Communication, on the other hand, appears positively related to planfulness in the two older generations and negatively related in the child generation. When, however, years married is held constant within the child generation, it is in the older couples of this generation that high communication is associated with high planfulness. Thus communication changes direction from negative to positive in its relation to planfulness as the couples become older and remains slightly positive for each successive generation. Why this should be so is not clear if the relationship of marital integration and marital agreement to planfulness is negative over time for the reasons we have listed. High communication does not seem to be the property of

TABLE 9.06

Summary Statistical Table Phase 3, Correlations Between Explanatory Variables and Both Volume of Action and Preplanning of Actions by Generation

Class of Explanatory Variable	Direction and Significance of "r", All Generations		Direction of Relation by Generation			
	Volume of Actions	Percent Pre-Planned Actions		G1	G2	G3
Antecedent Consumership Variables						
Volume of Plans	.30 s	.37 s	VA	pos.	pos.	pos.
			PPA	pos.	pos.	pos.
Percent of Plans Short-Run	.24 s	.34 s	VA	—	neg.	pos.
			PPA	—	pos.	curvilinear
Rationality of Decision Process	.31 s	.36 s	VA	curvilinear	neg.	curvilinear
			PPA	curvilinear	pos.	pos.
Volume of Actions	——	.23 s	PPA	pos.	pos.	pos.
Developmental						
Generation	—.18 s	—.12 s				
Age of Husband	—.36 s	—.16 s	VA	neg.	neg.	neg.
			PPA	ns	curvilinear	pos.
Age of Wife	.——	——	VA	neg.	neg.	neg.
			PPA	ns	curvilinear	curvilinear
Years Married	—.21 s	—.13 s	VA	ns	ns	neg.
			PPA	ns	neg.	neg.
Age at Marriage	——	——	VA	neg.	neg.	neg.
			PPA	neg.	neg.	pos.
Incentives and Constraints						
Life-Time Income	—.13 s	—.07 ns	PPA	neg.	curvilinear	neg.
Current Income	.13 s	.09 ns	VA	pos.	neg.	neg.
			PPA	ns	neg.	pos.
Current Family Size	—.04 ns	.04 ns	VA	pos.	neg.	neg.
			PPA	—	neg.	curvilinear
Social Competences						
Education Husband)	.15 s	.16 s	VA	ns	neg.	pos.
			PPA	ns	pos.	pos.

Class of Explanatory Variable	Direction and Significance of "r", All Generations		Direction of Relation by Generation			
	Volume of Actions	Percent Pre-Planned Actions		G1	G2	G3
Education (Wife)			VA	ns	pos.	pos.
			PPA	ns	pos.	pos.
Occupation	.04 ns	.04 ns	VA	pos.	neg.	ns
			PPA	pos.	ns	curvi-linear
Index of Social Position	.05 ns	.00 ns	VA	neg.	neg.	neg.
			PPA	pos.	curvi-linear	curvi-linear
Devel.-Traditionalism Score	.09 ns	.07 ns	VA	pos.	neg.	neg.
			PPA	Pos.	pos.	pos.
Fatalistic-Manipulative	—.04 ns	—.13 s	VA	neg.	ns	ns
			PPA	pos.	neg.	curvi-linear
Prudential-Impulsivity	.08 ns	—.07 ns	VA	pos.	neg.	pos.
			PPA	ns	ns	pos.
Optimism-Pessimism	.05 ns	—.03 ns	VA	neg.	neg.	pos.
			PPA	ns	neg.	ns
Future-Time Orientation	.07 ns	.00 ns	VA	pos.	ns	pos.
			PPA	ns	curvi-linear	neg.
Restrictiveness of Family Organization Husband Dominance-Equalitarian Wife Dominance	.12 s	—.09 ns	VA	pos.	neg.	neg.
			PPA	pos.	neg.	pos.
Authoritarian-Equalitarian	.04 ns	.00 ns	VA	neg.	pos.	neg.
			PPA	pos.	neg.	neg.
Sex Role Conventionality	——	——	VA	neg.	neg.	neg.
			PPA	neg.	neg.	ns
Restrictiveness of Family Organization Social Participation (Wife)	—.11 s	—.06 ns	VA	pos.	neg.	pos.
			PPA	Pos.	pos.	pos.
Wife Working Gainfully	——	——	VA	pos.	ns	pos.
			PPA	neg.	pos.	pos.
Marital Organization Marital Integration	—.17 s	—.10 s	VA	ns	neg.	neg.
			PPA	neg.	neg.	pos.
Marital Agreement	—.15 s	.08 ns	VA	neg.	ns	neg.
			PPA	ns	neg.	pos.

Class of Explanatory Variable	Direction and Significance of "r", All Generations		Direction of Relation by Generation		
	Volume of Actions	Percent Pre-Planned Actions		G1	G2	G3
Harmony-Conflcit	.05 ns	—.05 ns	VA	ns	pos.	neg.
			PPA	neg.	curvi-linear	pos.
Communication	—.09 ns	.00 ns	VA	pos.	ns	neg.
			PPA	pos.	pos.	neg.

Key: VA = Volume of Actions
      PPA = Percent Pre-planned Actions

planful couples who are well integrated in the first years of marriage but is achieved later when marital integration has become negatively correlated with planfulness. This paradox begs for further research and interpretation.

Consumership Types

In the preceding discussion we have taken as our chief indicators of consumership in Phase 3 *volume of actions* and the *degree of pre-planning of actions*. We could just as well have used the proportion of plans fulfilled as our indicator. Although proportion of plans fulfilled and proportion of actions pre-planned are highly interrelated, they are by no means identical, see Table 9.07. In the child generation the high volume of plans and actions increases the likelihood of nonfulfillment and of unplanned actions so that we see in Table 9.07 a large number of families that are high in the proportion of plans fulfilled and at the same time are in the middle or low categories in proportion of actions pre-planned—altogether 47% are deviants in this respect. The two indicators of planfulness depart from different baselines; proportion of plans fulfilled uses plans as its denominator whereas proportion of actions preplanned use actions as its base. We propose to join these two indicators to form an empirical typology of consumership. The first criterion, *Percentage of Plans Fulfilled,* and the second criterion, *Percentage of Actions Pre-planned* are joined in a coordinate system running from zero to 100 on two axes. Four quadrants are created by dichotomizing the dimensions (see Chart 9.03).

TABLE 9.07

Percent of Actions Preplanned by Generation and Percent of Plans Fulfilled

Generation

	Parent % *Plans Fulfilled*						*Child* % *Plans Fulfilled*				
	High		*Middle*		*Low*		*High*		*Middle*		*Low*

Percent of Actions Preplanned

	f	%	f	%	f	%	f	%	f	%	f	%
High	14	48.3	10	34.5	2	5.7	17	53.1	13	36.1	3	8.3
Middle	11	37.9	16	55.2	6	17.1	10	31.3	13	36.1	12	33.3
Low	4	13.8	3	10.3	27	77.1	5	15.6	10	27.8	21	58.3
TOTAL	29	100	29	100	35	100	32	100	36	100	36	100

Each quadrant represents a different grouping of families sharing common consumership achievements, occupying what Lazarsfeld and Barton have called "common property space."[3] Using medians for dividing the two dimensions of planfulness we distribute the families into four quadrants, below the median and above the median on proportion of actions preplanned. The first quadrant represents those families which are above the median on both dimensions, families exhibiting "High Consumership."

The third quadrant identifies those families which were below the median on both plans fulfilled and pre-planned actions, families typifying "Low Consumership."

"High fulfillers with many unplanned actions" are isolated in the second quadrant, above the median in plan fulfillment but below in pre-planning their actions. They are hybrids which we have termed "Unplanned Actors."

Quadrant four also defines a hybrid type, the "Fruitless Planners," resembling the ineffective planners in plan fulfillment while emulating the high consumers in their pre-planning of actions.

We thus have two "pure types" of consumption patterns and two "mixed types." The analysis of each type on a similar set of measures should enable us to refine our conceptualization of phase three of the consumption cycle.

[3] Allen H. Barton, "The Concept of Property Space in Social Research," in Paul Lazarsfeld and Morris Rosenberg, eds. *The Language of Social Research* (Chicago: Free Press, 1955), pp. 40-54.

CHART 9.03

A Typology of Consumership Expressed in Property Space

Percent of Plans Fulfilled	100%	*High Plan Fulfillment but Many Unplanned Actions*	*High Consumership*

Percent of Plans Fulfilled   100%

	High Plan Fulfillment but Many Unplanned Actions	*High Consumership*
	All Generations: 43 families (15.8%)	*All Generations:* 76 families (27.8%)
	Grandparent 5 (6.5%)	Grandparent 19 (24.7%)
	Parent 17 (18.3%)	Parent 29 (31.2%)
	Child 21 (20.2%)	Child 28 (26.9%)
	a) Low percent of actions preplanned	a) High percent of actions preplanned
	b) High percent of plans fulfilled	b) High percent of plans fulfilled

50%

	Low Consumership	*Much Fruitless Planning but Few Unplanned Actions*
	All Generations: 102 families(37.0%)	*All Generations:* 53 families (19.4%)
	Grandparent 38 (49.4%)	Grandparent 15 (19.5%)
	Parent 34 (36.6%)	Parent 13 (14.0%)
	Child 30 (28.8%)	Child 25 (24.0%)
	a) Low percent of actions preplanned	a) Low percent of plans fulfilled
	b) Low percent of plans fulfilled	b) High percent of actions preplanned

0   50%   100%

Percent of Actions Preceded by a Plan

In sheer numbers the 102 pure type low consumership families outnumber the rest, compared with 76 high consumership families and 96 hybrids (43 of one type and 53 of the other). The distribution of types by generation is even more varied with grandparents being disproportionately found in the pure low consumership group, the parent generation in the high consumership group and the unplanned actor group, while the child generation is somewhat more frequently found in the two deviant hybrid types of fruitless planners and unplanned actors. These differences by generation could have been predicted only in part by the greater propensity of the child

generation to verbalize plans (thereby risking lower plan fulfillment) and to undertake actions (thereby taking action without a
prior plan). The concentration of the grandparent generation in the
low consumership type and of the parent generation in the high
consumership group was not anticipated by their performance in
previous phases of the consumption process. In this respect something
new has been added in this empirical typology. Let us turn to an
examination of the impact of the explanatory variables on the distribution of families by these constructed consumership types. For
most analyses, the generations have been merged to give sufficient
cases for reliability.

Developmental

The several variables involving years married, age of spouses, and
stage of life cycle are so highly correlated with generation that we
see little which goes beyond generation differences in these variables.
When age of husband is calculated within generations by consumership type, however, there is some tendency for the high consumership
type to be older, especially in the child generation. Age at marriage
shows a similar propensity to be higher for the high consumership
types for both the parent and the child generations (see Chart 9.04).

Incentives and Constraints

Planfulness represented by the consumership types is associated
with current family income but not entirely as expected. Families
with the lowest income are found in the low consumership quadrant,
even when the analysis is run for the two younger generations alone
(see Chart 9.04). There may be what has been termed secondary poverty[4] here. High consumership families are next and the Fruitless
Planner group boasts the largest income. Family size reflects needs
indirectly. Note that large size appears associated with low consumership, ("And the poor have children") with high consumership found
in the middle size category. The smallest families are found among
the unplanned actors with many actions unplanned.

Social Competences

More directly related to the consumership typology should be the
indicators of social competence, education and occupation. With all
generations merged education of wife appears positively related to

---

[4] Secondary poverty refers to a low level of living due to faulty management of
resources rather than to inadequate income.

CHART 9.04

Characteristics of Consumership Types
(Merger of Parent and Child Generations)

Unplanned Actors (n = 43)		High Consumership (n = 76)
9.7	Md. Years Married	23.5
21.9	Average Age at Marriage	23.7
3.7	Md. Family Size	3.7
3.63	Md. ISP	3.57
$5,730.00	Md. Family Income	$4,870.00
11.9	Md. Years of Education of Wife	12.0
8.2	Md. Developmentalism Score	8.9
5.50	Rationality of Decision Score	5.50
4.71	Mean Durable Goods Inventory Rank (P & C only)	5.23
66.0	Percent Satisfaction with Actions Taken	60.0

Low Consumership (n = 102)		Fruitless Planners (n = 53)
27.5	Median Years Married	16.0
23.6	Average Age at Marriage	23.0
3.4	Md. Family Size	4.0
3.60	Md. ISP	3.53
$4,360.00	Md. Family Income	$5,830.00
10.4	Md. Years of Education of Wife	11.3
7.7	Median Developmentalism Score	8.4
5.80	Rationality of Decision Score	5.40
4.02	Mean Durable Goods Inventory Rank (P & C only)	4.79
83.0	Percent Satisfaction with Actions Taken	76.0

high consumership (see Chart 9.04). The education of wife increases from the low consumership quadrant to the high quadrant with the deviant types falling in between. Occupation of husband likewise shows positive relations to consumership with white collar workers found in the successful high consumership group. We summarize the impact of these two variables on consumership in the Index of Social Position which shows a somewhat higher rank as we move from low consumership to high consumership (see Chart 9.04). The regularity of these variables in identifying the consumership types is presumptive of a theoretical linkage of some import.

Value Orientations

It has been our contention that the life conditions and social competences are linked to consumership through the value orientations and skills of family organization shared by the social class categories. We have not been able to corroborate these relations uniformly well in the preceding analyses.

The Developmental-Traditional Conceptions of Parenthood constitutes a value orientation that has proved significant in predicting previous indicators of consumership. We find it again successful in that the pure high consumership type has the highest median developmentalism score (8.9) and the pure low consumership type the lowest (7.7). Can this be explained by the contribution of education of wife, since we know developmentalism is associated with education? Holding constant education of wife (see Table 9.08) the same relation appears with high consumership where developmentalism is high. As for low education – low developmentalism families, fifty one percent of the cases in this extreme are all of the pure low consumership type. Again the deviant types fall in between.

TABLE 9.08

**Consumership Types by Education of Wife and Developmentalism
Three Generations Merged**

	Education of Wife					
	High		Low			
	Developmentalism		Developmentalism			
Consumership	High	Low	High	Low	Total	
Types	%	%	%	%	*f*	%
Low Consumership						
Low Plans Fulfilled						
Low Actions Preplanned	33.0	35.1	36.1	51.0	96	37.5
Fruitless Planners						
Low Plans Fulfilled						
High Actions Preplanned	17.9	22.8	19.4	17.6	49	19.1
Unplanned Actors						
High Plans Fulfilled						
Low Actions Preplanned	15.2	12.3	11.1	21.6	39	15.2
High Consumership						
High Plans Fulfilled						
High Actions Preplanned	33.9	29.8	33.3	9.8	72	28.1
Total	100	100	100	100		100
N	112	57	36	51	256	

The several scores in the Brim Value Orientations Tests show some rationale but are only modestly correlated with consumership types. High Consumership families tend to be more pessimistic, less fatalistic, less future oriented and ever so slightly more prudential than the Low Consumership families. These relations hold even when years married is held constant to dilute the generational influences. Low Consumership families are even more clearly concentrated in categories of low prudence, high optimism, more fatalism and more future orientated. From our theory we would have expected most of these differences but would have expected future orientation and optimism scores to have been reversed.[6]

Restrictiveness of Family Organization

Closer to consumership behavior, theoretically, are the last factors we shall discuss, family and marital organization. We would expect that the rigidities suggested by conventionality in the division of tasks by gender, authoritarian modes of decision-making, and restrictions on the wife's activities in social participation and gainful employment will be negatively related to High Consumership and associated directly with the Low Consumership syndrome.

Sex Role Conventionality is found predominantly among families of low consumership (51%) and only rarely found among high consumership families (20%) whereas the latter families are characterized by "some crossing" of the sex lines or by actual reversals of sex roles (51.7%). This relationship of rigidity of sex roles to low consumership doesn't disappear even when the interrelationships between wife working and the division of labor in the home are taken into account. This is shown in Table 9.09 where the three variables are cross classified. From the distribution of the cases the importance of role conventionality in differentiating between high and low consumership types is shown to be greater than the effects of whether or not the wife is working gainfully.

Patterns of decision-making also differentiate among consumership types well, both from self-reported data and from the observations of interviewers. Both sets of data agree that equalitarian types are more likely to be found among high consumership families and that

---

[6] Brim points out, however, that this scale of Optimism-Pessimism appears to elicit the "whistle in the dark" mechanism so that those who are most insecure and dependent obtain high optimism scores which may explain why we have obtained high optimism scores among the less competent consumers in this analysis.

authoritarian decision-making was found more among low consumership families.[7]

It remains to be seen whether the remaining two indicators of restrictiveness in family organization are also predictive of low consumership. An earlier cross-classification (Table 9.04) has suggested that gainful employment of wife is positively associated with high pre-planned actions. More wife working families are in the high consumership group and more wife-at-home families are found in the low consumership group. The deviant types divide between the unplanned actors in the wife-working group and the fruitless planners in the wife-at-home group. If the wife is working then, more purchases and other actions without planning occur (Unplanned Actors), whereas the Fruitless Planners represent wives-at-home who plan but can't carry through on plans, possibly wishful planning. Social participation is only slightly related to high consumership, but nonparticipation is clearly centered in the low consumership families.

TABLE 9.09

Consumership Types by Role Conventionality and Employment of Wife
Three Generations Merged

| | Role Stereotype | | | | | |
| | High | | Low | | | |
Consumership Types	W. Working %	W. Home %	W. Working %	W. Home %	Total f	%
Low Consumership	75.0	70.0	43.2	53.0	78	55.3
High Consumership	25.0	30.0	56.8	47.0	63	44.7
Total	100	100	100	100		100
N	8	30	37	66	141	

$$X^2 = 6.81$$
$$.05 > P < .10$$

On a zero-order level each of the hypothesized relationships have been corroborated in direction although not tested for statistical

[7] From the interviewers' ratings the low consumership group was heavily wife-dominated in decision-making. In other studies it has been shown that wife dominance in decision-making is most characteristic of working class families. This finding is also congruent with the thesis that low consumership is found disproportionately in the working class.

significance. Low consumership families are characterized by restrictiveness of family organization which we have elsewhere termed familistic.[8] The net effect of three of these factors, role conventionality, authority patterns, and employment of wife on the distribution of families within the two "pure consumership types" is shown below:

TABLE 9.10

Percentage Distribution of High Consumership Families by Familistic-Restrictiveness Types

Familistic Types	Percent High Consumership	n
Conventional-Authoritarian-Wife At Home	22	9
Conventional-Authoritarian-Wife Working	00	1
Conventional-Equalitarian-Wife At Home	33	21
Conventional-Equalitarian-Wife Working	29	7
Role Crossing-Authoritarian-Wife At Home	43	14
Role Crossing-Equalitarian-Wife At Home	48	52
Role Crossing-Authoritarian-Wife At Home	67	6
Role Crossing-Equalitarian-Wife Working	55	31
All Families	45%	141

Although this is by no means a perfect distribution, still the cumulative negative effect of restrictiveness of family organization on the proportion of families demonstrating high consumership is impressive.

Marital Organization

We have already found marital integration and agreement negatively related to other indicators of consumership except within the child generation and have offered an interpretation of this paradox. We can expect empirically, therefore, somewhat similar relations in the interplay between High Consumership and marital happiness indicators, although this runs contrary to our *a priori* hypotheses.

With all three generations merged marital integration is low for High Consumership and high for Low Consumership families. When marital integration is related to the consumership types, taking into account years married, the negative relation with High Consumership remains only for the families in the older duration of marriage

[8] See familistic typology discussion in Reuben Hill, *et al., The Family and Population Control* (Chapel Hill, University of North Carolina Press, 1959), pp. 203-217.

group (see Table 9.11). Indeed, when newly married (less than 5 years) couples of the Child Generation are examined (Table 9.12), Low Marital Integration is found disproportionately in the Low Consumership and Unplanned Actor families, supporting our thesis of the interrelation of these variables in the early years.

TABLE 9.11

Consumership Types by Years Married and Marital Integration Three Generations Merged

	Years Married					
	High		Low			
	Integration		Integration			
Consumership	High	Low	High	Low		Total
Types	%	%	%	%	f	%
Low Consumership						
Low Plans Fulfilled						
Low Actions Preplanned	33.3	18.8	29.5	28.6	54	28.3
Fruitless Planners						
Low Plans Fulfilled						
High Actions Preplanned	19.0	25.0	31.1	16.1	44	23.0
Unplanned Actors						
High Plans Fulfilled						
Low Actions Preplanned	19.0	9.4	13.1	19.6	30	15.7
High Consumership						
High Plans Fulfilled						
High Actions Preplanned	28.6	46.9	26.2	35.7	63	33.0
Total	100	100	100	100		100
N	42	32	61	56	191	

With this increasing support for our earlier interpretation that marital integration is positively related to consumership in the early years of marriage and that it only later becomes negative, let us examine the other measures of marital organization, notably, marital communication and marital agreement. We find marital agreement, like marital integration, slightly negative to high consumership, whereas marital communication is barely positive. With the differences among generations on these matters merged there is considerable masking of relationships here. One interpretation might be that marital communication is important for achieving high consumership primarily in those families where marital agreement is low (as in younger families) and would be less important in families where marital agreement is high. This appears to be the case in our study as Table 9.13 below demonstrates. High communication is concentrated among High Consumership families (although only slightly more than among low consumership families) when marital agreement is low, but is distributed quite randomly among consumership types when marital agreement is high. Combining these findings with the earlier finding that planfulness is helped along early in the marital career by marital integration but shifts direction midway in the child generation, we can advance now the theory that marital integration is in circular relation with communication and consumership in which the direction of the relation changes over time as a repertory of agreements and problem solutions are built. For those families which succeed (high scores on marital integration in the later years) less planning is required before acting (some of our low consumership families), for families which remain fluid and change in their interests and desires (caught as lower on marital agreement and integration) the consumption process continues to demand communication and planning (our high consumership families) even in the later years of marriage. This interpretation seems to account for the contradictions between the empirical findings and the original hypotheses advanced.

TABLE 9.12

Consumership Types by Years Married and Marital Integration Child Generation

Consumership Types	Integration		Integration		Total	
	High %	Low %	High %	Low %	f	%
Low Consumership	29.2	15.4	30.0	37.0	25	29.8
Fruitless Planners	41.7	23.1	35.0	11.1	23	27.4
Unplanned Actors	16.7	15.4	10.0	25.9	15	17.9
High Consumership	12.5	46.2	25.0	25.9	21	25.0
Total	100	100	100	100		100
N	24	13	20	27	84	

Continuity in Planfulness and Consumership

We have been ever sensitive to the large differences by generations in our analyses of the explanations of consumership. Generational differences have been shown to reflect maturational (age) differences,

TABLE 9.13

**Consumership Types by Marital Agreement and Communication (Self-Rated)
Three Generations Merged**

Consumership Types	Agreement					
	High		Low			
	Communication		Communication		Total	
	High %	Low %	High %	Low %	f	%
Low Consumership						
Low Plans Fulfilled						
Low Actions Preplanned	26.3	30.6	34.4	30.9	64	31.1
Fruitless Planners						
Low Plans Fulfilled						
High Actions Preplanned	26.3	19.4	14.1	26.5	44	21.4
Unplanned Actors						
High Plans Fulfilled						
Low Actions Preplanned	18.4	22.2	15.6	13.2	34	16.5
High Consumership						
High Plans Fulfilled						
High Actions Preplanned	28.9	27.8	35.9	29.4	64	31.1
Total	100	100	100	100		100
N	38	36	64	68	206	

developmental (stage in family development, duration of marriage, family size) differences, and a broad cluster of social class (education, occupation, and income) differences. Comparing the generations permits us to assess empirically and observe social change and continuity in family behavior. In an earlier chapter we showed that discontinuity from generation to generation was high in education, in occupation, in income level, and in ideologies held about parenthood and childhood. Continuity from generation to generation was most marked in religious affiliation where shifts were minimal.

In this chapter we can assess the extent of continuity in planfulness and consumership with two measures, the proportion of plans enunciated during the year which are fulfilled and the typology of consumership which divides families into four groups according to their achievements in plan fulfillment and pre-planned actions. High continuity constitutes similarity in consumership for all three generations of the same family line, moderate continuity constitutes similarity between any two generations of the same family line (Grandparent-parent, parent-child, or Grandparent-child), and discontinuity represents no similarity among the generations.

James Morgan in a recent study of low income families has advanced the thesis that poverty patterns are transmitted from generation to generation.[9] Students of the multi-problem family have similarly asserted that crisis-proneness and secondary poverty run in families. Will low planfulness show continuity in the generational line? Will high planfulness be transmitted as well, or is this more frequently achieved by improved education and occupational mobility? Based on the empirical studies and social change theory we would expect low planfulness and low consumership to be more continuous within the family line than high planfulness and high consumership achievements.

Table 9.14 provides the first test of the extent of continuity in planfulness behavior within the same family line.[10] Although the numbers are small, high continuity three generations deep is found associated with high planfulness (% of plans fulfilled over the year) more than expected by chance. Moderate continuity, two generation similarities, are found in middle performing and low performing families. The third column in Table 9.14 shows the distribution of planfulness among those families in the three generation lineages of two generation continuity that broke the chain of continuity by deviating from the pattern followed by the other two generations. There is more of a tendency for these deviant families to be low in percent of plans fulfilled. In these lineages of moderate continuity of two generation depth only there is less likelihood of high than low plan fulfillment being transmitted from generation to generation. Lineages in which there was no continuity at all were evenly distributed among all planfulness levels. In the face of these data we might tentatively conclude that "good management patterns" are more frequently transmitted from generation to generation than poor management practices when the transmission is three generations in depth, but in two generation continuity low planfulness is even more likely to persevere.

The test by consumership types, however, would be even more rigorous because it permits the four behavioral expressions of plan-

[9] James Morgan, Martin David, Wilbur J. Cohen, and Harvey E. Brazer, *Income and Welfare in the United States* (New York: McGraw-Hill, 1962), see especially discussion, "Transmission of Poverty between Generations," pp. 206-212.
[10] All families where the family line over three generations was broken by refusals or non-response on the items in question have been eliminated for this analysis.

TABLE 9.14

Planfulness by Generational Continuity-Discontinuity
Three Generations Merged

Planfulness	High (3 generation continuity)	Moderate (2 generation continuity)	(Deviant Families)	Discontinuous (All generations differed)		Total	
				f	%	*f*	%
% of Plans Fulfilled	%	%	%				
High	50.0	23.8	26.2	14	33.3	57	29.7
Middle	12.5	38.1	31.0	14	33.3	62	32.3
Low	37.5	38.1	42.9	14	33.3	73	38.0
Total	100	100	100	42	100	192	100
N	24	84	42				

fulness to be examined for transmissibility. Table 9.15 shows that low consumership (low plans fulfilled and low actions preplanned) is more likely to persist over three generations than any other behavior pattern. Nine of the fifteen families in three generation lines, having similar consumership behavior, were of this indiscriminate planning, impulsive acting-without-planning type. High consumership is, nevertheless, more likely to be continuous than non-continuous since thirty-four of fifty-nine (58%) high consumership families were continuous over two or more generations. Analysis of the two generation linkages in high consumership show them to be disproportionately parent-child generation transmissions which was also true of the two generation continuities in educational level and ideologies about parenthood.[11] Looking at the consumership properties of the deviant families in column three whose deviation made their lineages "two generation continuity lineages only" we note higher than expected "Unplanned Actors" with high plans fulfilled and low actions pre-planned. Indeed, discontinuity was most characteristic also of the Unplanned Actor type family lines which follows from the large amount of impulsive acting in this set of families.

There are many implications for social action in these findings of generational continuity-discontinuity in consumership. If family lines can be counted upon to transmit the extremes of consumership, programs of consumer education might focus on low consumership families, knowing that if successful in breaking the poverty pattern link-

---

[11] See Chapter II, pp. 29-58.

TABLE 9.15

**Consumership Types by Generational Continuity-Discontinuity
Three Generations Merged**

Consumership Types	High (3 generation continuity) %	Moderate (2 generation continuity) %	Discontinuous (Deviant Families) %	(All generations differed) %	Total f	Total %
Low Consumership Low Plans Fulfilled Low Actions Preplanned	60.0	32.5	42.5	30.3	72	35.8
Fruitless Planners Low Plans Fulfilled High Actions Preplanned	20.0	22.5	12.5	25.8	43	21.4
Unplanned Actors High Plans Fulfilled Low Actions Preplanned	—	2.5	30.0	19.7	27	13.4
High Consumership High Plans Fulfilled High Actions Preplanned	20.0	42.5	15.0	24.2	59	29.4
Total	100	100	100	100		100
N	15	80	40	66	201	

age, good management patterns may be transmitted in subsequent generations.

Evaluation of the Consistency of the Explanatory Variables

Before concluding this chapter we should take a look back at the consistency with which the several classes of explanatory variables account for variation in consumership over the first three phases of the consumption process. For this purpose Table 9.16 has been prepared to show the predominant direction of the relationship observed between each of the explanatory variables and each of the measures of consumership employed over the three phases of the consumption

TABLE 9.16

Summary of Consistency of Explanatory Variables over the Consumption Span Predominant Direction of Relation Observed

Class of Explanatory Variables	Phase 1 Number of Plans	Phase 2 Rationality of Decision-Making	Phase 3 Percent of Pre-Planned Actions	Consistency of Direction Score
Developmental				
Generation	negative	negative	negative-curvilinear	3 negatives
Age of Husband	negative	inconsistent	inconsistent	0
Age of Wife	negative	positive	curvilinear	0
Years Married	negative	curvilinear	negative	2 negatives
Incentives and Constraints				
Life-Time Income	negative	curvilinear	negative	2 negatives
Current Income	positive	inconsistent	inconsistent	0
Current Family Size	positive, ns	inconsistent	negative	0
Social Competences				
Education of Husband	inconsistent	positive	positive	2 positives
Education of Wife	positive	negative	positive	2 positives
Occupational Status	positive	positive	inconsistent	2 positives
Index of Social Position	—	positive	curvilinear	0
Value Orientations				
Developmentalism-Traditionalism	inconsistent	negative	positive	0
Optimism-Pessimism	positive	inconsistent	inconsistent	0
Prudential-Impulsivity	negative	positive	inconsistent	0
Fatalism-Manipulative	negative	inconsistent	inconsistent	0
Future Time Orientation	inconsistent	negative	inconsistent	0

Table 9.16 (Continued)

Class of Explanatory Variables	Phase 1 Number of Plans	Phase 2 Rationality of Decision-Making	Phase 3 Percent of Pre-Planned Actions	Consistency of Direction Score
Restrictiveness of Family Organization				
Authoritarian-Equalitarian Family	positive	inconsistent	negative	0
Sex Role Conventionality	negative	inconsistent	negative	2 negatives
Social Participation of Wife	positive	inconsistent	positive	2 positives
Wife Working Gainfully	positive	positive	positive	3 positives
Marital Organization				
Marital Integration	negative	inconsistent	negative	2 negatives
Marital Agreement	inconsistent	negative	inconsistent	0
Marital Communication	positive	positive	positive	3 positives
Total Inconsistents	4	9	8	
Antecedent Consumership Variables				
Number of Plans	—	ns	positive	0
Specificity of Plans	positive	positive	positive	3 positives
Rationality of Decision-Making	positive, ns	—	positive	2 positives
Number of Actions	positive	positive	positive	3 positives
Percent of Plans Fulfilled	positive	positive	positive	3 positives
Percent of Pre-Planned Actions	positive	positive	—	2 positives
High Consumership-Low Consumership Types	—	positive	—	0

cycle covered in this chapter. Positive, negative, or curvilinear relations are listed when true for two or more of the generations. Otherwise the designation "inconsistent" has been entered.

The most striking consistency is found in the persistent negative relations of generation, duration of marriage, life-time income, conventionality of sex roles and marital integration to consumership. The most consistently positive relations are those of social participation and gainful employment of the wife.

The explanatory variables which have had the same relationship most consistently to consumership over the entire span of the consumption process are seen in Table 9.16 as follows:

Generation among the Developmental Variables, always negative.
Life-time income among the Incentives, usually negative.
Education of husband and education of wife among the Social Competence variables, usually positive.
Wife working gainfully, among the Family Organization variables, always positive.
Marital communication, among the Marital Organization variables, always positive.

These variables are not all high in the variance they account for in consumership, but they are unusually consistent in direction. Taken as a class the clusters of variables most consistent in direction are the Social Competence variables of social class and the Restrictiveness of Family Organization variables of power structure and role allocation structure. These two classes barely outstrip the Incentives and Constraints class in impact but far exceed the Value Orientations and Marital Organization classes, which are cluttered with many inconsistencies both internally from generation to generation and when viewed over the different phases of consumption.

Looking at the phases of consumption comparatively for a moment, the best predicted by the variables listed is Phase 1, Needs Identification, since it has the fewest inconsistencies in direction by generation. Phase 2, Rationality of Decision-Making is heaviest in inconsistencies and picks them up especially in the Family Organization variables, whereas Phase 3, Percent of Pre-Planned Actions, finds most of the Value Orientation variables ambiguous in their effects on planfulness by generation.

To simplify by summarizing what has proved to be a most complicated problem, we have found that there are factors which related predictably to consumership whether it be at the early stage of needs identification, choosing and deciding on a course of action or taking action planfully. The successful family conforming to the yardstick of excellence measured by the criteria of the three phases of consumption is characteristically:

1. Of the married child generation
2. Of higher education, both husband and wife
3. Of higher occupational and social class status
4. Flexible in role allocation with much sex role crossing
5. Families where wife is gainfully employed
6. Families where wife has high social participation
7. Of lower marital integration
8. Of high marital communication

Finally we note substantial consistency in relationships among the generations between each of the several indicators of consumership employed in this chapter (see Table 9.16). The relations are almost invariably positive for all generations suggesting that the phases of the consumption process we have conceptualized are tightly interlinked empirically. We turn in the next chapter to an examination of the payoff in satisfaction of high consumership over the first three phases of the consumption cycle, knowing there may be surprises in store for us from this confrontation.

CHAPTER X

The Payoff of Consumership: Satisfaction With The Outcome of Decisions Made

WE NOW ENTER the final payoff phase of the consumption process in which the means chosen are evaluated against the needs they were expected to meet. The criterion variable is of a different order qualitatively from those utilized to assess consumership in the three preceding consumption phases. It is more attitudinal than behavioral, highly subjective and if sensitively measured might be expected to vary more from family to family than the other consumership indicators we have employed. It resembles closely the economist's concept of "utility," the differential valuing of consumption outcomes.

We have constructed satisfaction-with-outcome scores from the answers to two questions with respect to every decision made and action taken during the year of study: (1) If you could start over again would you make the same decision (with respect to a given plan)? (2) If you could turn the item purchased back, or push a button and be back, (in your old residence, for example) would you do it?

James Morgan[1] has suggested that such expressions of satisfaction with decisions made may be generated through diverse channels which should be specified before drawing firm conclusions about the correlates of satisfaction. He notes a marked tendency, once the decision has been made, to rationalize it as the only possible and reasonable decision to have made.

We must report that families in all three generations are predominantly affirmative about most of their decisions and most of the actions taken. Regrets and recriminations are not widespread. The child generation is most critical with only two-thirds in the "High Satisfaction With Outcome" category. The two older generations were more

---

[1] Personal communication, March 28, 1963.

affirming (Parent Generation 77% high satisfaction, Grandparent Generation 75%). Most families reported they would do nothing to alter the decisions made nor to repudiate the actions taken over the twelve month period even if it were possible to do so.

We recognize with Morgan that such high frequency of unqualified affirmation may carry heavy components of self-justification for many of the actions evaluated. Our indicator may be telling us more about the distribution of the propensity to rationalize past actions than it does about the actual gratifications experienced in the consumption process. Having forewarned the reader, we turn to an analysis of the correlates of satisfaction with actions taken in the discussion which follows.

Consumership and Satisfaction with Outcomes

Among the antecedent measures of consumership are the number of plans articulated (an index of needs identified), specificity of plans (proportion of plans specific as to time to be carried out), rationality of decision-making score, proportion of plans fulfilled, and proportion of actions preplanned. The size and direction of correlations between these indicators of consumership and the measure of consumer satisfaction (see Table 10.07) tell us that there are both some strong links and some disjunctions between the antecedent phases of consumption and this final evaluative phase. The needs indicator is negatively related in all three generations to satisfaction.[2] Time specificity of planning is significantly correlated but the coefficient is low enough to suggest that indefinite plans and even unplanned actions may evoke a certain quantum of satisfaction for some families.

The consumership expression which best predicts satisfaction with the actions during the year is the rationality of decision-making score, our operationalization of the economist's concept of "rationality" which has usually been treated as an assumption in the economist's studies of consumption behavior. The correlation of 0.74 between the scores on rationality in decision-making and satisfaction provides a partial empirical confirmation of the economist's assumption that

---

[2] In a multiple regression analysis of thirty-two variables against the criterion variable of satisfaction moreover, number of plans shows up as *negatively related* to satisfaction, that is, high needs identification is associated with high dissatisfaction with outcome. High risk taking caught in the quantity of actions taken is also negatively associated with satisfaction. See Reuben Hill, "Judgment and Consumership in the Management of Family Resources," *Sociology and Social Research*, Vol. 47, No. 4 (June 1963), pp. 446-461.

rationality acts to increase satisfaction, more effectively joining ends and means, as compared with the situation in which irrationality and impulsive action characterize the decision-process. A comparison of the way these two variables interact can be made for each of the three generations (see Chart 10.01). Note that the largest absolute difference in rationality of decision score as we move from high satisfaction to low satisfaction occurs in the grandparent generation, even though its overall mean score is the lowest of the generations. The second largest difference occurs in the child generation where we also observe the highest mean "rationality score." It is perhaps noteworthy that the two generations which achieve highest payoff from rationality are also experiencing the greatest financial constraints. The parent generation with more disposable income suffers less from the consequences of impulsive purchasing.

The findings about the interrelations between evidence of pre-planning actions and satisfaction are difficult to interpret. Instead of the expected positive relationship pre-planning of actions is negatively related with consumer satisfaction for all three generations. Not only do those families which carry their plans into action most frequently appear to be dissatisfied with the outcome of their decisions, but families which have been most frequently impulsive in moving or

CHART 10.01

Pictoral Representation of Interrelation of Rationality
and Consumer Satisfaction by Generation

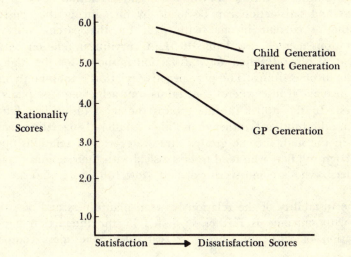

purchasing without prior plans congregate in the high satisfaction categories. Classifying families by Consumership Types (described earlier) by degree of plan-fulfillment and pre-planning actions demonstrates clearly the negative relation of pre-planning to satisfaction —dissatisfaction.

	% Dissatisfied	No. of Families
Low Consumership (Low Plans Fulfilled, Low Actions Preplanned)	17.5%	64
Fruitless Planners (Low Plans Fulfilled, High Actions Preplanned)	23.7%	38
Unplanned Actors (High Plans Fulfilled, Low Actions Preplanned)	34.2%	38
High Consumership (High Plans Fulfilled, High Actions Preplanned)	40.4%	57
Total	28.4%	197

Do we have in the negative interplay of the behavioral variable of planfulness and the attitudinal variable of satisfaction suggestions of reaction formation? The more planful, the higher the standards of performance demanded and therefore, the more critical of the results; the more impulsive, the more halo effects in evaluating the results?

Examination of the stability of the negative relation between planfulness and satisfaction can be made by introducing the constraint variable of current income with data for the parent and child generations merged; see Table 10.01. A curvilinear relation between percent of plans fulfilled and satisfaction is shown for the high and middle income groups. The pure negative relation is found only in the low income group where constraints on achieving its plans are greatest. In the upper income groups the most dissatisfied families are "middle fulfillers" rather than "high fulfillers," suggesting that we have in the high income groups three categories of relations operating: High fulfillers who tend to be satisfied with their actions, "middle fulfillers" who are most critical, and "low fulfillers," who are least critical.

The instability of the relation between planfulness and dissatisfaction with outcome is further suggested by the interaction between education of wife and these two variables. The most competent

TABLE 10.01

**Satisfaction with Outcome by Family Income and Percent of Plans Fulfilled
Parent and Child Generation Merged**

Satisfaction with Outcome	High Income % Plans Fulfilled			Middle Income % Plans Fulfilled			Low Income % Plans Fulfilled			Total
	High %	Middle %	Low %	High %	Middle %	Low %	High %	Middle %	Low %	%
High Satisfaction	75.0	55.6	92.8	81.0	65.4	86.9	57.1	55.0	81.2	71.6
Low Satisfaction	25.0	44.4	7.1	19.0	34.6	13.0	42.9	45.0	18.8	28.4
Total	100	100	100	100	100	100	100	100	100	100
N	12	18	14	21	26	23	28	20	32	194

$$X^2 = 16.69 \quad P < .05$$

	Percent Dissatisfied with Outcome
High Wife Education—High Pre-Planned Actions	42%
High Wife Education—Middle Pre-planned Actions	23%
High Wife Education—Low Pre-planned Actions	12%
Low Wife Education—High Pre-planned Actions	27%
Low Wife Education—Middle Pre-planned Actions	33%
Low Wife Education—Low Pre-planned Actions	37%
All Families	29%

families should be the high education-high pre-planned action group who are the most critical of their actions (42%), but the next most critical is the least competent, low education-low pre-planned action group. The least critical of all appears to be the high education-low pre-planned group which resembles our high income-low plan fulfillment group which in Table 10.01 is least critical of its actions. Satisfaction with outcome is apparently multi-dimensional rather than uni-dimensional and therefore, may be expected to vary with the social class, economic constraints, and competence categories in which families are located. If this be true, we will need to interpret the zero-order correlates of satisfaction with the greatest of care and should not be disturbed if some of the factors shown to be associated with consumership for the first three phases of the consumption process do less well in predicting satisfaction with the outcomes of consumption. We turn now to the task of identifying other correlates of consumer satisfaction.

Developmental Measures and Satisfaction

We noted earlier that the propensity to be satisfied with consumer actions taken during the year was highest in the grandparent generation and lowest in the child generation. When the generations are merged and satisfaction is examined by age of husband it is only the couples in the very youngest age group (ages 20-25) who are critical in significantly large numbers (38% dissatisfaction) while the eighty year olders are significantly more satisfied than expected by chance (85% satisfaction).[3] When we remember that almost all of our previous indicators of consumership have been negatively related to age, we suspect that satisfaction is surely drawn from a different universe of discourse.

Examining satisfaction by duration of marriage becomes meaningful when life time income is included. When life time income is higher than average, satisfaction with actions taken tends to be high for all durations of marriage except the newlyweds (1-4 years) for whom 40% dissatisfaction is recorded. In the lower than average life time income group, high satisfaction is only found in the 16-25 years married and the Golden Anniversary couples (51 years and over). In general, the younger the marriage, the more dissatisfaction and if of low life time income, dissatisfactions expressed are especially marked.

Incentives and Constraints

We might expect satisfaction with outcome to be affected negatively by family size and to be positively affected by income. For families having children still at home family size is, however, positively related to satisfaction in the two younger generations. Income, too, encourages satisfaction. Table 10.02 demonstrates that income is the more important variable since satisfaction remains high if income is high, even when family size is small. When income is low, dissatisfaction is highest for medium size families. Where per capita income would be lowest, namely in large families of low life time income, satisfaction is the highest of the low income groups—an unlikely result if all families were using the same standards to evaluate the consumption process, which they are not.

---

[3] The same findings hold by age of wife.

TABLE 10.02

Satisfaction with Outcome by Life Time Income and Size of Family
Parent and Child Generations Merged

Satisfaction with Outcome	High Life Time Income Family Size			Low Life Time Income Family Size			Total	
	Large %	Med. %	Small %	Large %	Med. %	Small %	f	%
High Satisfaction	80.8	76.9	75.0	74.3	52.9	67.6	139	71.3
Low Satisfaction	19.1	23.1	25.0	25.7	47.1	32.4	56	28.7
Total	100	100	100	100	100	100		100
N	47	26	16	35	34	37	195	

$$X^2 = 8.56$$
$$.10 < P < .20$$

Social Competences

We would expect satisfaction to be favorably affected by education of spouses, by occupational status and by social class, although the discovery above that dissatisfaction is greatest for the youngest age groups should modify the impact of education.

Our findings show that satisfaction by education of wife, is higher for the better educated in each generation. By education of husband, the parent generation alone shows a positive relation. When the education of husband and wife are run together against satisfaction, the wife's education seems most important in the grandparent and child generations since regardless of the husband's education, if the wife's education is low, dissatisfaction is marked. The deviant families where husband had higher or lower education •than his wife were not deviant in evaluating their consumption patterns.

As occupational status improves, so does satisfaction for both parent and child generations. When income is held constant, however, this relation disappears, since the propensity to be critical of actions taken is great only for the lowest income and occupation category.

The Index of Social Position which utilizes education, occupation, and area of residence as social class indicators, predicts satisfaction positively for each of the generations. The higher the class, the greater the satisfaction. Merging the parent and child generations and holding life time income constant, some interesting findings emerge. (see Table 10.03). Upper class families show high satisfaction whether

TABLE 10.03

**Satisfaction with Outcome by Life-Time Income and Index of Social Class
Position Parent and Child Generations Merged**

Satisfaction with Outcome	High Life Time Income Index of Social Position			Low Life Time Income Index of Social Position			Total	
	Upper %	Middle %	Lower %	Upper %	Middle %	Lower %	F	%
High Satisfaction	86.9	78.4	66.7	76.9	64.6	60.7	139	71.3
Low Satisfaction	13.0	21.6	33.3	23.1	35.4	39.3	56	28.7
Total	100	100	100	100	100	100		100
N	23	51	15	13	65	28	195	

$$X^2 = 7.34$$
$$.10 < P < .20$$

income is high or low, while lower class families are prone to dissatisfaction under these same conditions. Middle class families, in contrast, present a happy countenance about actions taken when their life time income has been high and a sour one when income has been low. Satisfaction is the first consumership variable we have used that proves very responsive to social class influences, a fact which further emphasizes its unique properties.

Value Orientations

Of the several measures of value orientations, we would expect optimism and developmentalism to be positively, and fatalism and future time orientation to be negatively, related to satisfaction with actions.

Developmentalism is positively related to satisfaction in the parent generation, negatively related in the grandparent generation and randomly related in the child generation. Optimism, on the other hand, is positively related to satisfaction in the two younger generations and negatively related in the grandparent group.

Fatalism, as expected, is negatively related to satisfaction in two of three generations and randomly distributed in the child generation. The relation does not hold up, however, when education, occupational status, or social class position are held constant. These latter are apparently more influential than the value orientations held in affecting satisfaction.

Time orientation varies in curious ways with consumer satisfaction since the future oriented in the older generations are more prone

toward satisfaction, whereas the future oriented in the child generation are more prone to dissatisfaction. Merging the three generations
and running time orientation by duration of marriage, some interesting findings emerge; see Table 10.04. The newly weds with many
unmet needs are prone to dissatisfaction whether future oriented or
not. The 5-15 years married, if future oriented are prone to be
critical of actions taken, whereas the group just ten years further
along (16-25 years married) whether or not future oriented are
highly satisfied. In the 26-40 years married when most children have
been launched from the home, non-future oriented (with short horizons) are especially dissatisfied compared with future oriented. The
relation shifts in the next cohort back to a negative relation between
future orientation and satisfaction and ends with future orientation
over-shadowed by age in encouraging high satisfaction. The developmental time span has played tricks on the relation of the time
orientation variables to satisfaction, producing relations which we
are better able to describe than explain.

Restrictiveness of Family Organization

Any rigidities in family organization might be expected to lower the
effectiveness of family consumership and therefore increase the dissatisfaction with decisions made and actions taken. We would,
therefore, expect lowered satisfaction among families characterized by
authoritarian decision-making patterns, wife or husband dominance
as against equality in marital relations, conventional sex role al-
locations, and so on.

Authority patterns tend to have the expected impacts upon satisfaction, the more authoritarian the more dissatisfied. Wife dominance
is associated in all generations with high dissatisfaction. Wife dominance, of course, may be linked with wife working which is also
negatively related to satisfaction scores. In Table 10.05 we see that the
most dissatisfaction is found among Wife dominant and Husband
dominant families where the wife works. Only in Equalitarian families where the wife is at home do we have high frequency of satisfaction scores.

Role conventionality unexpectedly appears positively rather than
negatively related to satisfaction in all generations (The first time it
has been positively related to any consumership variable). Dissatisfaction is highest in families of flexible role organization where there are
role reversals, whereas satisfaction is highest where the sex roles are
strictly observed. These relationships, moreover, are maintained

TABLE 10.04

Satisfaction with Outcome by Years Married and Future Time Orientation Scores Three Generations Merged

Years Married

Satisfaction with Outcome	51+ Future Time Orient.		41-50 Future Time Orient.		26-40 Future Time Orient.		16-25 Future Time Orient.		5-15 Future Time Orient.		1-4 Future Time Orient.		TOTAL	
	Hi %	Lo %	Hi %	Lo %	Hi %	Lo %	Hi %	Lo %	Hi %	Lo %	Hi %	Lo %	%	%
High Satisfaction	100	79.2	70.0	77.8	81.0	69.0	89.5	76.5	62.5	80.0	60.6	65.0	186	73.8
Low Satisfaction	00	20.8	30.0	22.2	19.0	31.0	10.5	23.5	37.5	20.0	39.4	35.0	66	26.2
TOTAL	100	100	100	100	100	100	100	100	100	100	100	100	100	
N	7	24	10	18	21	29	19	17	24	30	33	20	252	

TABLE 10.05

Satisfaction with Outcome by Dominance Pattern and Employment of Wife Parent and Child Generations Merged

	Dominance Pattern												Total	
	Husband Dominant				Equalitarian				Wife Dominant					
	Wife Working				Wife Working				Wife Working					
	Yes		No		Yes		No		Yes		No			
Satisfaction with Outcome	f	%	f	%	f	%	f	%	f	%	f	%	f	%
High Satisfaction	7	53.8	34	73.9	18	69.2	41	82.0	8	47.1	15	71.4	123	71.1
Low Satisfaction	6	46.2	12	26.1	8	30.8	9	18.0	9	52.9	6	28.6	50	28.9
Total	13	100	46	100	26	100	50	100	17	100	21	100	173	100

when specified by duration of marriage. High satisfaction is characteristic of families with role segregation in the youngest marital cohort (1-4 years married) and in each successive cohort except one (26-40 years married) and, vice-versa, role sharing and exchanging is associated with the propensity to be critical of consumer actions in every cohort except one (16-25 years married). These findings are suggestive of a syndrome associated with satisfaction-dissatisfaction which we will underline as we conclude this analysis.

Social participation and gainful employment of the wife are also indicators of flexibility in family organization since they legitimize a richer role content for the position of wife and mother. Both of these indicators are negatively related to satisfaction for all three generations. Families in the child generation where the wife works are very high in expressed dissatisfaction (57% dissatisfied compared to 33% for this generation as a whole). Moreover, this relation is maintained when education of wife is held constant.

Summarizing the correlates of consumer satisfaction-dissatisfaction we find some evidence that internal incoherence in family organization is associated with dissatisfaction: Wife working, social participation, and exchangeability of roles hang together but the fourth correlate, authoritarian patterns of decision-making, doesn't fit with the first three. However, finding that it is in the wife working group that both wife dominance and husband dominance as authoritarian patterns are most associated with dissatisfaction makes some theoretical sense. The converse syndrome associated with high satisfaction also contains some incongruity: Wife at home, no social participation, strict conformity to the conventions of sex role allocation, yet characterized by equalitarian authority patterns. Except for the equalitarian decision-making patterns this syndrome fits the traditional familistic norm.

Marital Organization

Analysis of the interrelations of types of marital organization and satisfaction suggests that they are independent rather than interdependent dimensions. Marital integration, marital consensus, and marital agreement show negligible and capricious relations to satisfaction. Marital communication is slightly positive for two of the three generations but when these generations are merged shows changing effects by duration of marriage. Dissatisfaction predominates regardless of communication for newly weds, but communication and satisfaction shift to a positive relation during the child bearing years (5-15 years married) becoming negatively related in the middle years (16-25 years married) when couples may communicate highly only over dissatisfactions. Thereafter for older couples communication is once again positively related to satisfaction.

Continuity Within Lineages

One final analysis seems warranted—does satisfaction tend to run in family lines? Will the propensity to be happy with the outcome of actions taken be found more frequently in all three generations of a family line, in two generation linkages or will it be relatively discontinuous? Table 10.06 records the results showing dissatisfaction more frequently associated with intergenerational discontinuity. The critical stance vis-a-vis consumption outcome is, to be sure, exceptional anyway, constituting only about one fourth of the families, but it could have been concentrated within family lines, in three genera-

TABLE 10.6

Satisfaction with Outcome by Generational Continuity-Discontinuity
Three Generations Merged

Satisfaction with Outcome	Continuity							
	High		Moderate				Total	
	(3 generation continuity)		(2 generation continuity)		(Deviant families)			
	f	%	f	%	f	%	f	%
High Satisfaction	69	92.0	50	75.8	8	24.2	127	77.0
Low Satisfaction	6	8.0	16	24.2	25	75.8	47	27.0
Total	75	100	66	100	33	100	174	100

tion lineages or at least in two generation combinations. However, this is not the case. It is rather the majority pattern of high satisfaction which shows up in three generation linkages (92% of these linkages are high satisfaction). Low satisfaction by contrast is found in lineages where the three generations deviate each from the other (76% of these families are dissatisfied with the outcome of their actions). We can not account for the variance in satisfaction, therefore, by social inheritance. Dissatisfaction with the outcome of consumption actions is clearly not transmitted by family lines but must be otherwise explained. The propensity to be highly satisfied tends to be more similar for all three generations of a lineage than for two generations only and seemingly is more transmissible than dissatisfaction proneness.

Summary

In some respects the last phase of the consumption process is anticlimactic since the drama of consumership is found in the doing, that is, in planning, deciding, and acting, only to arrive at the end of the process with retrospective evaluations of the results. Success in the earlier phases does not necessarily guarantee a high score in the evaluative phase although developmental theory suggests it might be expected to do so, if the measure were uncontaminated by such other considerations as general dissatisfaction with life situations, on the one hand, or rationalization and self-justification on the other.

In quick summary (see Table 10.07) we have found favorable evaluation of outcome of actions associated most highly with one of the antecedent measures of consumership, rationality of decision-making, confirming empirically the close tie asserted by economists between "rationality" and "utility." Other behavioral measures of planfulness such as risk taking and pre-planning of actions appear to be more frequently negatively than positively related to high satisfaction with actions taken. However, specification by income and by

TABLE 10.07

Summary Statistical Table (Phase 4)

Correlations Between Satisfaction with Outcome of the Consumption Process Hypothesized Explanatory Variables by Generation

Class of Explanatory Variable	Direction and Significance of Correlation All Generations	Direction of Relation by Generation		
	"r"	G_1	G_2	G_3
Antecedent Consumership Variable				
Volume of Plans		neg.	neg.	neg.
Percent of Time Specific Plans	0.18 s	—	—	—
Rationality of Decision-Making Score	0.74 s	pos.	curv.	pos.
Volume of Actions	− 0.31 s	neg.	neg.	neg.
Percent of Plan Fulfillment	—	neg.	neg.	neg.
Percent of Pre-Planned Actions	− 0.36 s	neg.	curv.	neg.
High Consumership–Low Consumership Types	—	ns	neg.	neg.
	"r"	G_1	G_2	G_3

	Direction and Significance of Correlation All Generations	Direction of Relation By Generation		
Developmental				
Generation	0.16 s	—	—	—
Age of Husband	0.21 s	pos.	ns	pos.
Age of Wife	—	neg.	curv.	pos.
Age at Marriage	—	ns	ns	ns
Years Married	0.20 s	pos.	neg.	pos.
Incentives and Constraints				
Life-Time Income	—	pos.	pos.	pos.
Current Income	—	pos.	pos.	pos.
Family Size	—	ns	pos.	pos.
Social Competences				
Education of Husband	0.18 s	ns	pos.	neg.
Education of Wife	—	pos.	pos.	pos.
Occupational Status (Husband)	0.03 ns	pos.	pos.	pos.
Index of Social Position	—	pos.	pos.	pos.
Value Orientations				
Developmentalism–Traditionalism Score	—	neg.	pos.	ns
Optimism–Pessimism	0.05 ns	neg.	pos.	pos.
Future Time Orientation	0.19 s	ns	pos.	neg.
Fatalism–Manipulation	— 0.07 ns	neg.	neg.	ns
Prudence–Impulsiveness	0.03 ns	neg.	pos.	pos.
Restrictiveness of Family Organization				
Authoritarian–Equalitarian	—	pos.	neg.	neg.
Husband Dominance–Equal.– Wife Dom.	— .01 ns	curv.	pos.	curv.
Sex Role Conventionality vs. E Role Reversals	—	pos.	pos.	pos.
Social Participation (Wife)	— 0.10 ns	neg.	neg.	neg.
Wife Working	—	neg.	neg.	neg.
Marital Organization				
Marital Integration	—	ns	ns	ns
Marital Consensus	— .02 ns	ns	neg.	neg.
Marital Agreement	—	neg.	pos.	pos.
Marital Communication	0.15 s	pos.	neg.	pos.

education suggests that the negative relationship may be due in large part to reaction formation and rationalization among the low income and low education sectors of the sample, where low plan fulfillment is accompanied by high satisfaction. In the better educated classes the relation of plan fulfillment to satisfaction tends to be positive, which is more in line with good consumership theory.

There are also family properties associated with favorable evualation of the consumption process, the direction of which was not always accurately predicted by family development theory:

1. Satisfaction is positively related to age of spouses and to duration of marriage. Even large family size is positively associated with satisfaction. When the effects of income are factored out, age is positively related to satisfaction only at the upper and lower extremes of the age scale and the influence of family size wanes.

2. Satisfaction is especially sensitive to social class variations, which override the influences of income. Both educational level and occupational status are positively related to satisfaction.

3. The various attitudinal measures of value orientations are capriciously related to satisfaction, especially when duration of marriage is left uncontrolled.

4. Satisfaction is firmly predicted by a syndrome of family organization type variables: Wife at home, no social participation, strict observance of sex role differences, and equalitarian decision-making patterns. With exception of the last named, these are all traditional familistic patterns. Marital communication too is positively related, but is the only marital organization variable to be more than randomly related to satisfaction.

5. Finally, continuity over three generations is more frequently observed among families of high than low satisfaction. Dissatisfied families are concentrated among lineages which are dissimilar in their evaluations of actions taken.

There have been many reversals of direction from the theoretically expected in the correlates of consumer satisfaction in this three generation study. The more circumspect the pre-planning, the more vulnerable to dissatisfaction despite high rationality in making choices. The more active, needful, risk taking youngest generation was especially dissatisfaction prone. Duration of marriage, advanced education, white collar occupations and higher social class are all indicators of alignment with established institutions and are predictive of favorable evaluation of the consumption process. Traditional familistic patterns also predict high satisfactions. Is the finding, finally that high satisfaction runs in family lines whereas the propensity to be critical is itself discontinuous, a deviant pattern? Satisfaction with consumption outcomes, in sum, seems to be part of a conformity syndrome of familism, and close intergenerational linkages at one level, and of integration into the model setting educated and middle classes at another level. Dissatisfaction with outcomes may reflect some alienation and non-conformity. It begins as a deviant pattern expressed most frequently by the socially marginal marriages of short duration, by families of flexible organization manned by gainfully employed socially active wives and upward mobile husbands whose alignment as yet with the establishment appears tenuous. These characterizations begin to suggest that improvement in consumership in the early phases of the consumption process may be promoted as much by a critical stance with respect to the actions taken as by an affirming stance. Clearly the phases of consumption are interdependent rather than linked in determinant-consequence chains. To specify the quality of feedback that would be most likely to stimulate improved consumership will require further study using some of the above findings as the basis of hypotheses to be tested.

CHAPTER XI

A Comparison of the Characteristic Patterns of Consumership and their Correlates by Generation

FROM THE DISCUSSION in the preceding chapter, it is apparent that the families of each generation experienced the several phases of the consumption process in distinctive fashion. The married child generation, near the beginning of its family cycle and the grandparent generation, approaching the end of its family life span were farthest apart in their consumption behavior over the year of observation. The parent generation more typically fell in between these two extremes.

When the achievements of the three generations are compared for each phase of the consumption process, a consistent pattern is discernible for three of the four phases (See Table 11.01). In Phase I, needs-identification, almost half (48%) of the total sample made five or more plans, while slightly over half (52%) reported four or fewer plans.[1] However, a comparison of the generations shows that 72% of the child generation had five or more plans, and 90% of the grandparent generation had four or fewer plans, with the parent generation splitting about evenly. Rationality of decision making, Phase 2 of the consumption process, also reveals this same pattern for the three generations. With the total sample divided into three equal groups according to their rationality scores, we would expect by chance that one-third of each generation would fall in each of the three groups. We find that 48% of the grandparent generation scored low on rationality, 41% of the parent generation were of moderate rationality, while 44% of the child generation were highly rational.

In Phase 3, planfulness, half the total sample preplanned 50% or

---

[1] If generation was not related to achievement in consumption, one would expect that each generation would resemble the total sample.

more of their actions, a quarter preplanned 10-49%, and the last
25% of the sample preplanned less than 10% of their actions. However,
48% of the grandparent generation preplanned less than 10% of their
actions, while 29%, slightly more than expected, of the parent generation preplanned 10-49% of their actions, and 57% of the child generation preplanned over half their actions. Phase 4 of the consumption
process looks slightly different from the earlier three phases, since
72% of the merged three generations were completely satisfied with
their actions, with only 28% at all dissatisfied. Looking at satisfaction
by generations, we find the grandparent generation divided up as
expected, and the parent generation slightly more satisfied than
expected. The child generation, however, showed more dissatisfaction
than would be expected—33% of this generation was dissatisfied with
their actions.

TABLE 11.01

Achievements of the Three Generations

	Grandparent %	Parent %	Child %	Total %
Number of plans				
5-29	10.4	52.0	72.1	48.0
1-4	89.6	48.0	27.9	52.0
$\chi^2 = 68.47$ P $= .001$				
Rationality Score				
600-800	29.0	23.9	43.7	33.1
450-599	22.6	41.3	33.0	33.5
0-449	48.4	34.8	23.3	33.5
$\chi^2 = 16.36$ P $= .01$				
Percent of Actions Preplanned				
50-100	44.2	45.2	57.0	47.1
10-49	7.8	29.0	41.9	26.3
0-9	48.1	25.8	12.9	26.6
$\chi^2 =$ P $= .001$				
Percent Satisfaction				
100	74.6	77.2	66.3	72.3
0-99	25.4	22.8	33.7	27.7
$\chi^2 = 2.88$ P $= .30$				

Thus it can be seen that the child generation had a modal pattern
of high needs, high rationality, and high preplanning, with somewhat more dissatisfaction than in the other generations. In contrast,
the grandparent generation demonstrated low needs, low rationality,

low preplanning, and high satisfaction. The parent generation fell between the other two, with a middling amount of plans, middle rationality, middle preplanning of actions and high satisfaction.

To highlight the differences between the generations in their reactions to the several phases of the consumption process we are taking the characteristic performance of each generation and are noting what family properties are associated with this behavior. We will ask of the grandparent generation what is associated with low needs (low plans), low pre-planning of actions, for example, whereas for the married child generation we will ask what is associated with high needs and high preplanning of actions. The result will be a delineation of the similarities and differences in the factors associated with the typical modes of consumption by generation.

The Grandparent Generation

The grandparent generation has experienced the various phases of the consumption process differently from the younger generations. Having fewer needs they have made fewer plans, fewer decisions, fewer actions, and have experienced fewer frustrations with the untoward consequences of actions, hence have expressed high satisfaction with the few actions taken.

The modal consumption patterns for families in the grandparent generation are associated with properties which we shall attempt to identify in this discussion. We begin with a discussion of the factors associated with low needs followed by the identification of factors associated with low rationality in decision-making. We will continue with a discussion of the characteristics associated with low planfulness (low proportion of pre-planned actions) and will conclude with the picture of the concomitants of high satisfaction with outcomes. These characteristics are summarized in Table 11.02.

Low Needs. The families in the most extreme group (not shown in Table 11.02) which had neither plans nor actions (numbering twenty-three families) were very similar to those with the lowest number of plans. The syndrome is one of extremely aged couples married longer than their peers, living alone without dependents, with higher life-time and current income. The spouses have lower than average education, and are retired. The family organization is characterized by restrictiveness, disengagement from outside contacts, no social participation and wife not working gainfully, conventional division of sex roles, and a wife dominant authority system. The

TABLE 11.02

Characteristics Associated with the Modal Patterns of the Grandparent Generation by Phases of Consumption

Class of Factor	Phase 1 Low Needs	Phase 2 Low Rationality Scores	Phase 3 Low Preplanning Scores	Phase 4 High Satisfaction
1. Developmental	Older, Married longer, Children launched	Married shorter time, Children launched	Older wives, but married younger	Older husbands, younger wives, older marrieds
2. Incentives and Constraints	Higher Life Income, High Current Income	High Life Income and High education of husband, High Current Income	High Life Income, Low Current Income	High Life Income, High Current Income
3. Social Competences	Low education of spouses, Retired, —	High education of spouses, Retired, Lower Class	Lower education of husbands, Retired, Lower class	High education of spouses, Employed fulltime, Upper class
4. Family Organization	Authoritarian, wife dominant, No social participation, Conventional sex roles	— — — —, Role crossing	Authoritarian, wife dominant, — — — —, Conventional sex roles, Wife working	Authoritarian, husband dominant, No social participation, Conventional sex roles, Wife at home
5. Marital Climate	High marital integration, High marital agreement, — — — —, — — — —	High marital integration, High harmony, Low communication, Future Oriented	High integration, High harmony, Low communication, Future oriented	— — — —, Low marital agreement, High communication, — — — —
6. Value Orientations	Fatalistic, Prudent, Pessimistic, Traditional beliefs re. parenthood.	Manipulative, Prudent, — — — —, Traditional beliefs	Manipulative, Prudent, Optimistic, Traditional beliefs	Manipulative, Impulsive, Pessimistic, Traditional

marital climate is good with high marital agreement and high marital integration. The value orientations are caught by a cluster of fatalism, prudence, pessimism, and traditional conceptions of parenthood.

Low Rationality in Decision-Making. A somewhat different picture is associated with low rationality (the modal pattern of this generation in the second phase of the consumption process). The low rationals are younger than average, have higher education, are more flexible in sex role allocation with some role crossing and show low communication. Otherwise they tend to parallel the syndrome associated with low needs detailed above.

Low Planfulness. The grandparent generation was divided in its planfulness with almost half preplanning none of their actions and a quarter preplanning all of their actions. We are selecting only the most striking of the modalities in choosing the low preplanning group to characterize the grandparent generation. Associated with low preplanning are many of the same properties listed for low rationality, younger marriages, retired, high marital integration and low communication. Low preplanning differs in being characterized by low education of wife, low current income, wife working, and a more conventional allocation of sex roles. The values orientations are characterized by optimism, future time orientation, manipulativeness and prudence which if consistent would have argued for higher rather than lower preplanning. Only the presence of traditionalism in beliefs about parenthood and childhood would have been predicted by our theory.

High Satisfaction with Outcome. The grandparent generation is very nearly the highest of the generations in the proportion of its families expressing high satisfaction with actions taken during the year (75%). We have, therefore, regarded "high satisfaction" as its modal pattern. Associated with high satisfaction are properties which differ in many respects from those associated with low needs, low rationality and low pre-planning of actions.

From the standpoint of stage of the life span, high satisfaction is associated in this generation with older husbands, older marriages and high lifetime income—essentially the same syndrome found among the low needs families. In terms of competences, however, high satisfaction is associated with high education, with continued employment of the husband and with location in the upper class which differs almost at every point from the low needs, low rationality and low preplanning families.

In the language of family organization, high satisfaction does resemble the low needs and low preplanning families, since the pattern is one of restrictiveness in family organization: authoritarian decision-making, conventionality of sex role allocation, no social participation and wife not gainfully employed.

Turning to marital climate, high satisfaction presents a syndrome, namely, low marital agreement accompanied by high communication, which is quite different from the pattern associated with low rationality and low preplanning of actions. In value orientations the only common feature appears to be the acceptance of traditional conceptions of parenthood and childhood, a common denominator of the modalities of all four phases of consumption.

Joining the Modalities. The overriding impression in examining Table 11.02 is that the different performance modes for each consumption phase draw upon different properties of the families. Is it possible that there are no families which share what we have typified as characteristic performance for every phase of consumption? If there are such families, what properties do they have in common?

We employed the principle of case grouping to sort out the families which were both low on needs (low plans), low on rationality scores in decision-making, low on pre-planning actions, and yet high on satisfaction. We found a total of five families which shared this combination of consumption performances. In Table 11.03 we present their case profiles.

Developmentally these five cases are more frequently younger married (41-50 years), husbands are in the next highest age bracket, 71-80 years of age, and there are no children at home. The couples are primarily of high life time and high current income levels. The spouses have better than average education for their generation and they are of middle class or better with husbands all in retirement. Organizationally the couple is equalitarian or wife dominant with flexible assignment of sex roles. The marital climate is not clearly favorable with low marital agreement combined with average to high communication. The value orientations are more frequently to the future than to the present or past, manipulative, prudent, optimistic, and developmental rather than to their counterparts.

This set of profiles for the grandparents was anticipated only in part in the changing clusters for each of the phases of consumption shown in table 11.02. It is, however, a set of concrete profiles in which we can have more confidence than in the synthetic patterns of Table 11.02 since it is found in actual cases. The general picture is one of reasonably well off older couples without dependents, of middle class social status, and better than average education with low

TABLE 11.03

Profiles of Five Cases Sharing the Modalities of All Four Phases of Consumption of the Grandparent Generation

Class of Variable	Case # 1016	Case # 1026	Case # 1033	Case # 1060	Case # 1112
1. Developmental	Husb. over 81 Married 51-60 yrs. launched	Husband 71-80 Married 41-50 yrs. launched	Husband 71-80 Married 41-50 yers. launched	Husband 71-80 Married 51-60 yrs. launched	Husband 71-80 Married 41-50 yrs. launched
2. Incentives and Constraints	low life income low current income	high life income high current income	high life income high current income	high life income high current income	very high life income high current income
3. Social Competences	somewhat high educ. of spouses retired lower class (4)	somewhat high educ. of spouses professional upper class (2)	somewhat high educ. of spouses retired middle class	somewhat high educ. of spouses retired middle class	superior educ. of husband high educ. of wife retired upper class (1)
4. Family Organization	Non-Eq (Matri) Wife dom. (int.) role spec. role reversal wife working	Equalitarian Equal (int.) No soc. part (w) role sharing role crossing wife working	Non-Eq. (Matri) Equal (int.) No soc. part (w) role spec. Conv. sex roles wife home	Non-Eq. (Patri.) —— —— Soc. Part (w) role sharing —— —— —— ——	Equalitarian Equal (int.) No soc. part (w) role sharing role crossing wife home
5. Marital Climate	—— —— —— —— —— —— —— ——	high integration average communication "low" agreement	low integration very high communication "low" agreement	—— —— —— —— —— —— —— ——	low integration high communication "low" agreement
6. Value Orientations	present oriented manipulative impulsive pessimistic developmental	future oriented manipulative prudent optimistic developmental	future oriented *very* manipulative prudent optimistic *very* developmental	future oriented manipulative impulsive pessimistic traditional	present oriented very manipulative prudent pessimistic traditional

marital agreement but high communication combined with flexible type family organization whose needs are low, whose actions are not preplanned or rationally decided upon but who are easily satisfied with the decisions they have made.

The Parent Generation

The parent generation has appeared closer to the married child generation than to the grandparents on many measures we have employed in earlier chapters. This is again the case with respect to the performance on various phases of the consumption process. The parent generation had more plans expressed than the grandparent generation (4.3 compared with 2.3 per family for the grandparents). It does not reach the level of the 6.4 plans per family of the child generation. Ideally we should list the parent generation as having "middle needs" but our analyses throughout on the proxy variable, "number of plans", has been divided into only two classes, "high volume of plans" and "low volume of plans". We have, therefore, selected "high needs" as the characteristic performance for this generation because it is more frequently high than low in volume of plans. On the two intervening variables of rationality in decision-making and pre-planning of actions, we are able to place the parent generation in the middle group. On the evaluative phase measure, satisfaction with outcome, the parent generation will be characterized as "high satisfaction" since it leads the generations in this respect. The interrelations of the factors associated with these four modalities in the parent generation appear in Table 11.04.

High Needs. Families having high needs in the parent generation are still rearing children, the youngest marrieds (under 25 years), with heads 31-50 years of age. They have a lower life income than average but high current income per family member. The family is white collar, wife possessing high education, but husband of less than average education. The wife is working, making for role reversals in the home and tends to be dominant in decision-making. The couples are not highly integrated as a married pair and hold values of manipulativeness, impulsivity, pessimism and developmental conceptions of parenthood, a progressive cluster of values.

Middle Rationality Pattern. Whereas almost half of the grandparent families had rationality scale scores in the lowest tercile, and 44% of the child generation families were found in the highest tercile, the parent generation congregated in the middle tercile (41%).

TABLE 11.04

Characteristics Associated with the Modal Patterns of the Parent Generation by Phases of Consumption

Class of Factor	Phase 1 High Needs	Phase 2 Middle Rationality	Phase 3 Middle Pre-Planning	Phase 4 High Satisfaction
1. Developmental	Younger couples, 31-50 Youngest marriages, under 25 Children at home	Younger couples, 31-50 Youngest marriages, under 25 Children at home	Younger couples, 31-50 Youngest marriages, under 25 Children at home	Middle aged, 46-20 Youngest marriages, under 25 Children at home
2. Incentives and Constraints	Lower life income High current income Small 1 child family	Lower life income Low current income Large family, 2 or more children	High life income High current income Small 1 child family	High life income High current income Large family, 2 or more children
3. Social Competences	High educ. wife Low educ. husband White collar occup.	High educ. wife and husband White collar occup. Middle class	High educ. wife High ed./high income of husband Upper class	High educ. wife and husband White collar occup. Upper class
4. Family Organization	Wife dominant Role reversals Wife working	Wife dominant Role sharing Role reversals Wife at home	Wife dominant Role reversals Wife at home No soc. participation	Husband dominant Conventional roles Wife at home No soc. part.
5. Marital Climate	Low marital integration	High marital integration High harmony High affection Low communication	Low marital integration Low mar. agreement Low communication	High marital integration High mar. agreement Low communication
6. Value Orientation	Manipulativeness Impulsivity Pessimism Developmentalism	Manipulativeness Prudence Future oriented Traditionalism	Manipulativeness Prudence Future oriented Pessimism Developmentalism	Manipulativeness Prudence Future oriented Optimism Developmentalism

This leads us to consider what accounts for their middle rationality position.

The middle scorers are youngest married of the generation (under 25 years), have two or more children still at home, lower than average life time income and a current income low enough to suggest some pressure of population on resources. The family is clearly middle class, of higher than average education, and of white collar occupations. Organizationally there is flexibility with much role sharing and role reversing as well as equalitarian (leaning to wife dominant) type power relations. The marital climate is positive: high integration, harmony and communication. The value orientations are oriented to the future, manipulative, and prudent, but with traditonal beliefs about childhood and parenthood.

The similarity between the families of this generation representing high needs and middle rationality families is not high. They are both younger families, of modest lifetime incomes, and with children still unlaunched. It is in family organization, marital climate and value orientations where there are high divergences between the two groups.

Middle Preplanned Actions. Middle achievers in the parent generation have been married under 25 years, are under 50 years of age with one child still at home, but have high life time and high current income. This is a peculiarly favorable situation compared with our middle rationality scorers who were experiencing population pressures. This is an upper class group of high education, occupation, and income. The family organization is relatively restrictive with the exception of some reversing of roles. Power relations are in the wife's hands. There is no social participation by the wife and she is not gainfully employed. The marital atmosphere is characterized by low marital agreement, low integration and low communication. Value orientations are future oriented, manipulative, prudential, pessimistic, and developmental.

This set of families resembles quite closely the middle rationality group in some respects but its marital and family properties are much less coherent.

High Satisfaction. High satisfieds are found among the younger marrieds (under 25 years) but the spouses are in their middle forties (46-50). They have two or more children still at home, have had a high life time income and enjoy a high income currently. These highly satisfied parent generation families are well educated, white collar, and upper class with a family organization of relative rigidity—husband dominant, wife cloistered with no social participation or gainful employment and with high conformity to conventional sex roles. The couples are characterized by low communication, high marital integration and marital agreement. Value orientations are to the future, to manipulative views, to optimism and to developmental views about parenthood and childhood.

This syndrome is similar to the symptoms associated with middle rationality and planfulness in developmental stage, in social competences, and freedom from financial constraints, but in family organization the pattern diverges significantly.

It is noteworthy that the syndrome associated with high satisfaction in the parent generation compares closely with the cluster of factors found linked with high satisfaction in the grandparent generation. High income, high education of spouses, upper class background, and restrictive family organization (authoritarian, conventional sex roles, no social participation or employment of wife) make up the common core for both high satisfaction groups.

Joining the Modalities. As in our discussion of the grandparent generation, we find that the performance modes for the several consumption phases draw upon somewhat different properties of the families. Employing the principle of case grouping we sort out the families of the parent generation which are both high on needs (high volume of plans), middle on rationality scores, middle on preplanning actions, and high on satisfaction with outcome. We found a total of seven families which shared this combination of consumption performances. Their case profiles are presented in Table 11.05.

The seven families as a group are still engaged in childbearing with two or more unlaunched dependents. Low life time income but high current income suggest families somewhat behind schedule in their material achievements. A differential education between spouses with husband high and wife low is combined with white collar occupations and upper or middle class social status. The family organization is equalitarian (as reported by the wives) and equally divided between wife dominant and equalitarian (as reported by the interviewers). There is both role sharing and role crossing. The wife is not gainfully employed and there is variable social participation by the wife. With respect to marital climate there is no clear pattern of marital integration, communication or agreement although the interviewers do report high harmony between spouses in the joint interviews. In value orientations, the seven cases tend to be future oriented and manipulative but to vary on the other orientations.

TABLE 11.05

Profiles of Seven Cases Sharing the Modalities of All Four Phases of Consumption of the Parent Generation

	Case # 2005	Case # 2027	Case # 2042	Case # 2045	Case # 2052	Case # 2079	Case # 2100
1. Developmental	Husband 31-40 younger	Husband 51-55 older	Husband 51-55 older	Husband 41-45 younger	Husband 46-50 younger	Husband 61-70 older	Husband 41-45 younger
	Younger marr. 16-20	Older marr. 31-35	Older marr. 31-35	Older marr. 26-30	Younger marr. 21-25	Older marr. 26-30	Younger marr. 21-25
	Pre-launched	Pre-launched	Pre-launched	Launched	Pre-launched	Pre-launched	Pre-launched
2. Incentives and Constraints	Lo life income	Hi life income	Lo life income	Lo life income	Lo life income	Hi life income	Lo life income
	Lo current inc.	Lo current inc.	Hi current inc.	Lo current inc.	Hi current inc.	Hi current inc.	Hi current inc.
	3 ch. home (hi)	2 ch. home (hi)	3 ch. home (hi)	No ch. home (lo)	1 ch. home (mid)	2 ch. home (hi)	1 ch. home (mid)
3. Social Competances	Ed. husb. lo wife hi	Ed. husb. hi wife lo	Ed. husb. lo wife hi	Ed. husb. hi wife lo	Superior ed. of both spouses	Ed. husb. hi wife lo	Both spouses lo ed.
	Blue collar	White collar	Blue collar	White collar	White collar	White collar	Blue collar
	Middle class	Middle class	Middle class	Upper class (2)	Upper class (1)	Upper class (2)	Lower class (4)
4. Family Organization	Equalitarian	Equalitarian	Patriarchal	Equalitarian	Equalitarian	Equalitarian	Equalitarian
	Wife dom. (int)	Wife dom. (int)	Equal (int)	Husb. dom. (int)	Equal (int)	Equal (int)	Wife dom. (int)
	Much soc. part.	Much soc. part.	Some soc. part.	No soc. part.	Some soc. part.	No soc. part.	No soc. part.
	Role sharing	Role sharing	Role spec.	Role spec.	Role spec.	Role sharing	Role sharing
	Role reversals	Role crossing	Role crossing	Role reversal	Role conventional	Role crossing	Role crossing
	Wife working	Wife home	Wife home	Wife home	Wife home	Wife home	– – – –
5. Marital Climate	Hi integration	Hi integration	Hi integration	Hi integration	Lo integration	Lo integration	Lo integration
	Hi communication	Lo communication	Lo communication	Hi communication	Lo communication	Hi communication	Lo communication
	Lo agreement	Hi agreement	Lo agreement	Hi agreement	Lo agreement	Hi agreement	Lo agreement
	Harmony	Harmony	Harmony	Harmony	Harmony	Harmony	Harmony
6. Value Orientations	Future oriented	Past oriented	Future oriented	Future oriented	Future oriented	Future oriented	Present oriented
	Manipulative	Manipulative	Manipulative	Fatalistic	Manipulative	Manipulative	Fatalistic
	Impulsive	Prudent	Impulsive	Prudent	Prudent	Prudent (very)	Impulsive
	Pessimistic	Pessimistic	Optimistic	Optimistic	Pessimistic	Optimistic	Optimistic
	Traditional	Developmental	Traditional	Developmental	Developmental	Developmental	Traditional

There are a number of similarities but also a number of differences between the patterns identified in Table 11.04 for each phase of consumption separately and those epitomized by the seven cases whose profiles appear in Table 11.05. Our seven cases have been married longer, have had lower life time incomes, and appear to be more equalitarian in decision-making. The families are more pressed by needs than the typical grandparent generation because they still have children at home, a low life-time income but high current income. The occupational level, educational level of husband and class level, all suggest families striving to catch up.

The families show a flexible family organization in decision-making, role sharing, and role crossing. The consumership patterns of high plans and high satisfaction combined with middle rationality and middle preplanning of actions are consonant with the family properties here listed.

The Married Child Generation

The families of the married child generation are particularly vigorous and active with high needs, high rationality of decisons, high preplanning of actions, but much more prone to dissatisfaction with actions taken. The interrelations of these consumership patterns and the properties associated with them are summarized in Table 11.06.

High Needs. High needs are associated with youngest couples, lower income, large families of two or more children with low per capita income. Socially these families are lower class, blue collar and of more modest education. Organizationally the family is flexible (role reversals, equalitarian relations, wife working gainfully and participating socially). The marital climate is harmonious with high agreement and high communication. Value orientations are to prudence, optimism and traditional beliefs about children.

High needs in the child generation at the beginning of its cycle are located in a different sector of the population than in the parent generation. In the parent generation, families with many plans were comfortable white collar units with high disposable incomes and small families whereas in the child generation the plans expressed are by blue collar families of low incomes and large families. Flexibility of family organization is common to both generations but the marital climate is much more favorable in the child generation.

High Rationality Pattern. Associated with high rationality in the

TABLE 11.06

Characteristics Associated with the Modal Patterns of the Married Child Generation by Phases of Consumption

Class of Factor	Phase 1 High Needs	Phase 2 High Rationality	Phase 3 High Pre-Planning	Phase 4 Low Satisfaction
1. Developmental	Younger husb., under 25	Older couples, 26-40 Older married, 5-20 yr. Later age at marriage	Older couples Younger married, 1-4 yr. Later age at marriage	Younger couples, under 25 Younger married, 1-4 yr.
2. Incentives and Constraints	Lower life income Low current income Large family, 2 or more children Lowest per capita inc.	High life income Small family, 1 child	High current income Medium family, 2 children	Low life income Low current income Medium family, 2 children
3. Social Competences	Low ed. of wife Blue collar occup.	High ed. of both White collar occup. Upper and mid. class	High ed. of wife Low ed. of husb. Blue collar occup. Lower mid. class	Low ed. of wife Blue collar occup. Lower class
4. Family Organization	Equalitarian Role reversals Wife working Some soc. participation	Equalitarian Role reversals Wife working No soc. part.	Equalitarian Wife working Some soc. part.	Wife dominant Role crossing Wife working Some soc. part.
5. Marital Climate	High mar. agreement High communication	Low mar. agreement Low integration Low communication	High mar. agreement High integration Low communication	Low mar. agreement Low communication
6. Value Orientation	Prudent Optimistic Traditional	Future oriented Prudent Pessimistic Traditional Fatalistic	Present oriented Prudent Developmental Fatalistic	Future oriented Pessimistic Impulsive

child generation are a number of properties summarized in Table 11.06:

— Older couples, married longer, marrying at later age
— Higher life income, small family of one child
— Upper and middle classes, high education, white collar occupation
— Flexible family organization
— Low marital agreement, low integration and low communication
— Future oriented, fatalistic, prudent, pessimistic, trational beliefs

There are similarities with the middle scorers on rationality among the parent generation with respect to social class and the social competences of education and occupation as well as the flexibility of family organization and marital climate. Differences appear in the developmental variables of duration of marriage and age of spouses. Actually the older marriages of the child generation are closer in duration to the younger marriages of the parent generation which suggests we may have here an "age for maximum rationality" appearing.

High Preplanning of Actions. In the child generation high preplanning is associated with still another cluster of characteristics:

— Older couples, older age at marriage, but more recently married (1-4 years)
— High current income, two child family and expanding
— Lower middle class, blue collar, lower education of husband, but high education of wife
— Flexible family organization, equalitarian decision-making, wife working gainfully, but no social participation by wife
— High marital agreement, harmony and integration, but low communication
— Fatalistic, prudent, present oriented, and developmental in beliefs.

This is a much less coherent cluster than the high rationality syndrome and has some internal contradictions built into it. The child generation's high preplanners are less endowed with social position and education, and with life time income than the parent generation middle scoring families. The characteristic flexibility of family organization and generally favorable marital climate joins with the now familiar property of low communication to provide a pattern similar to that of the parent generation middle scoring couples.

Low Satisfaction. Only in the child generation is there a significant cluster of families critically dissatisfied with decisions and actions. The families in this generation which were most dissatisfied had properties listed in some detail in Table 11.06.

— Youngest marrieds (1-4 years), wives under 20, husbands under 25
— Low life-time income, low current income and 1 child family
— Lower class, blue collar, low education of wife
— Wife centered but flexible family organization, wife working, role crossing, some social participation
— Low marital agreement and low communications
— Impulsive, future oriented and pessimistic

This modal group of child generation families is closely related to only one other modality of this generation; namely the families with "high needs" who expressed many plans. Both groups are young, of low income, low education, lower class, and of flexible family organization differing primarily in marital climate and value orientations. There may be something in this commonality which causes families to plan for more than they can fulfill and then to be dissatisfied with the actions they undertake.

Joining the Modalities. Utilizing the same principles of case grouping we have employed in the older two generations we have sorted out the families of the married child generation which are both high on needs (high volume of plans), high on rationality scores, high on preplanning actions, and low on satisfaction with outcome. We found a total of five families which shared this combination of consumption performances. The greatest attrition occurred in trying to combine high rationality families with low satisfaction families, since the correlation between these two expressions is negative and marked. The case profiles for the five families are presented in Table 11.07.

The couples tend to be relatively recently married and are in the expansive child bearing phase of the life cycle with great pressure of population on resources. The couples have had lower life time incomes but thanks to gainfully employed wives they have high current incomes. The couples are predominantly of low education, blue collar groups yet middle class of social class status. They are equalitarian in decision-making, with much role crossing and the wife is active socially. The marital climate data are lacking on two of the five cases but tends to be one of low marital agreements and low communication. Value orientations are variable except for time orientation which tends to be future oriented.

The properties of this set of five cases are those of high strivers, couples both in a hurry and under pressure. They have high needs, are apparently quite circumspect in preplanning their actions and in their style of rational decision-making yet they are dissatisfied with the results. They bring to this consumership pattern a flexible family

TABLE 11.07

Profiles of Five Cases Sharing the Modalities of All Four Phases of Consumption of the Child Generation

	Case # 3007	Case # 3021	Case # 3031	Case # 3062	Case # 3065
1. Developmental	Husband 21-25 younger Marr. 1-4 younger Expanding	Husband 26-30 older Marr. 5-10 older Expanding	Husband 26-30 older Marr. 1-4 younger Expanding	Husband 21-25 younger Marr. 1-4 younger Childless	Husband 21-25 younger Marr. 1-4 younger Expanding
2. Incentives and Constraints	Low life income Low current inc. 1 child (lo)	High life income High current inc. 3 children (hi)	Low life income High current inc. 2 children (med)	Low life income High current inc. Childless (lo)	Low life income High current inc. 3 children (hi)
3. Social Competences	Ed.—husb. hi wife lo Blue collar Middle class	Ed.—both spouses lo White collar Middle class	Ed.—both spouses lo Blue collar Middle class	Ed.—husb. hi wife lo Blue collar Middle class	Ed.—both spouses lo White collar Middle class
4. Family Organization	Equalitarian Wife dom. (int) No soc. part. (w) Roll spec. Role reversal Wife working	Equalitarian — — — *Much* soc. part. Role spec. Role crossing —	Equalitarian Equal. (int) Some soc. part. Role sharing Role crossing Wife home	Equalitarian Equal. (int) No soc. part. Role sharing Role crossing Wife working	Equalitarian Husb. dom. (int) Some soc. part. Role spec. Role crossing Wife working
5. Marital Climate	"lo" integration hi communication lo agreement	— — — — — — — — —	"hi" integration very lo comm. very lo agreement	— — — — — — — — —	"hi" integration lo communication lo agreement
6. Value Orientations	Future oriented Manipulative Impulsive Optimistic Traditional	Hi future oriented Fatalistic Prudent Pessimistic Traditional	Hi fut. oriented Manipulative Prudent Pessimistic Traditional	Present oriented Fatalistic Prudent Optimistic Developmental	Future oriented Fatalistic Impulsive Pessimistic Developmental

organization, a peppery marital climate of low agreement and communication, and an indifferent set of social competences in lower than average education. With an expanding family, 1-3 children and the wife working, the atmosphere is fairly pressured much of the time.

This is a rather marked departure from the picture we have obtained in looking at the child generation as a whole in comparison with the preceding generations, and in looking at the patterns for each of the phases of the consumption process separately in Table 9.16. The principle of case grouping has provided us with cases which illuminate the analysis and make possible corrections of the easy generalizations we arrived at from viewing the patterns associated with the phases of consumption separately.

CHAPTER XII

Linkage of Planning Career
Achievements and Consumership

IN THIS CHAPTER we bring together the two major sets of dependent variable data of the study; namely, the longitudinal measures of achievement over the life span of the families, and the several measures of consumership derived from panel type observations of the family's planning and decision making over a twelve months period. We seek to answer the question of how well a family's consumership over a specified period of time can be predicted by its cumulative career performance over its life's span to date.

The chapter opens with a discussion of the correlates of planning career achievements and of inter-area consistency in achievement as a prelude to the analysis of the linkage of these career variables with family consumership.

Quantification of career achievements into cumulative scores. In an earlier chapter, it may be remembered, the families were examined in terms of their propensity to lead, to be on schedule, or to lag their generation in four career areas: income level, durable goods acquisitions, residence size and occupational level. Combinations of career achievements were created from these data ranging from families which led in all four careers over the life span down to families which lagged their generations in all four careers. In order to treat these data quantitatively we have ascribed numerical scores to overall performance in each of these careers:[1]

---

[1] In order to deal with all families of each generation comparably in this analysis, the scores are computed for the performances on each variable over the median years married—thus couples married less than the median years for their generation are comparable with those married more than the median years since both are scored for the first half of the median family's marriage span.

Leading one's generation in one career over the life span = 5 points
On schedule in one career over the life span = 3 points
Lagging one's generation in one career over the life span = 0 points

Possible combinations of careers and their distribution by generation may now be teased out from Table 8.10 giving the following range of career achievement scores:

	Grandparents	*Parents*	*Children*	*Total*
Leading in four careers, 20 points	1	6	7	14
Leading in three, on schedule in one, 18 pts.	10	5	8	23
Leading in two, on schedule in two, 16 pts.	3	10	13	26
Leading in three, lagging in one, 15 pts.	4	9	8	21
Leading in one, on schedule in three, 14 pts.	3	2	6	11
Leading in two, on schedule in one, lagging in one, 13 pts.	9	15	14	38
On schedule in four, 12 pts.	0	0	0	0
Leading in one, on schedule in two, lagging in one, 11 pts.	9	9	13	31
Leading in two, lagging in two, 10 pts.	9	14	2	25
On schedule in three, lagging in one, 9 pts.	3	0	3	6
Leading in one, on schedule in one, lagging in two, 8 pts.	12	21	14	47
On schedule in two, lagging in three 6 pts.	14	1	10	25
Leading in one, lagging in three, 5 pts.	12	7	3	22
On schedule in one, lagging in three, 3 pts.	7	5	4	16
Lagging in four, 0 pts.	3	1	2	6
Total	.. 99	105	107	311

It would appear from the above distributions that outstanding performance in one career is most often achieved at the expense of achievement in other careers. The modal combination of achievements represented by 47 families is one which brings a score of 8 points, combining leading in one area, on schedule in two and lagging in two. Next most frequent are the scores of 13 and 11 where leading in one or more areas is also matched with lagging and being on schedule in one or more areas. In general this pattern of checkered performance holds for all three generations, *leading* occuring in one area at the expense of lower achievement scores in other areas.

In subsequent analyses for this chapter the phenomenon of achievement over the life span will utilize the score for each family as the means of summarizing career data over the life span. The distribution of achievement scores by generation is found in Table 12.01 which shows the married child generation highest in achievement over its shorter life span with a median score of 13.1 compared with the parents's 11.3 and the grandparent generation's 10.2. The modal pattern for the high scoring married child generation is in the predominantly leading categories (16-18 points) with the parent generation clustering just below them in the three middle intervals of 7-9, 10-12 and 13-15 points. The grandparent generation in contrast is heavily represented in the predominantly lagging category of 4-6 points.

TABLE 12.01

Percentage Distribution of Life-Span Achievement Scores by Generation

Achievement Scores	Grandparent Generation		Parent Generation		Married Child Generation		Total	
	f	%	f	%	f	%	f	%
0 – 3	5	5.1	3	2.9	3	2.8	11	
4 – 6	26	26.3	9	8.6	18	16.8	53	
7 – 9	17	17.1	26	24.8	10	9.3	53	
10 – 12	21	21.2	23	22.0	21	19.5	65	
13 – 15	20	20.2	27	25.6	24	22.5	71	
16 – 18	8	8.1	12	11.4	25	23.3	45	
19 – 20	2	2.0	5	4.8	6	5.6	13	
Total	99	100.0	105	100.0	107	100.0	311	
Median	10.2		11.3		13.1			

A possible check on the validity of this method of scoring families is to run the achievement scores developed above against the families' own subjective estimate of how nearly they have attained their family goals. The two older generations were asked a question designed to elicit this judgement: "Looking back over your marriage how close would you say you've come in realizing your desires for your family?" The replies were coded as "Almost none, about half of them, all of them, and over achieved." The married child generation was asked the extent to which they were behind schedule, on schedule or ahead of schedule in achieving their goals. Table 12.02 provides evidence of the degree of correspondence between these two ways of appraising progress over the life span. In both of the younger generations the families which see themselves as over-achieving have higher average achievement scores. In the grandparent generation the relationship is reversed. There is, moreover, some tendency for those in the middle group who see themselves as "having achieved most of their goals" to appear in their achievement scores as "laggards over the life span". The families in the older generations which see themselves as having reached few of their goals have highly variable achievement scores. It is in this category of the grandparent generation who see themselves retrospectively as least successful that the correspondence between subjective judgments about family accomplishments and the objective career scores is lowest. Further research is surely indicated to illuminate this finding.

Correlates of Career Achievements

We turn now to a discussion of the factors associated with leading and lagging one's generation over the life span, which we have operationalized into career achievement scores. We look first at indicators of developmental differences, second at the impact of family size pressures, third at indicators of social class, fourth at the influence of value orientations, fifth at types of family structure, and finally at indicators of marital climate. At the conclusion of this presentation indicating the direction and the significance of the relationship of each of these several factors to career achievement for each generation.

Developmental Differences. The propensity to lead one's generation in the four areas of level of income, level of occupation, size of residence and size of inventory of durable goods is related to the *timing of marriage,* the age at marriage of husband and the age at marriage of wife. *Later age at marriage* of the husband, especially, is associated with the propensity to lead in achievements over the life span—we show this relationship in Table 12.03 in which data for all three generations are aggregated. Specified by generation, the relationship is most marked in the married child generation, present in the parent generation, but weakest in the grandparent generation.

Paul Glick[2] has already shown that couples marrying when husband

---

[2] Paul C. Glick, *AMERICAN FAMILIES* (New York: Wiley, 1957) pp. 119-120.

TABLE 12.02

Achievement Patterns by Generation and Evaluation of Progress

Evaluation of Progress

Achievement Scores	Grandparent					Parent					Child				
	Under Achieved	Most Goals Achieved	Over Achieved	Total		Under Achieved	Most Goals Achieved	Over Achieved	Total		Under Achieved	Most Goals Achieved	Over Achieved	Total	
	%	%	%	N	%	%	%	%	N	%	%	%	%	N	%
High	42.9	37.8	38.5	28	38.9	26.1	31.1	41.2	27	31.8	15.4	36.0	43.8	34	35.8
Middle	35.7	24.4	30.8	20	27.8	39.1	33.3	35.3	30	35.3	30.8	34.0	21.9	28	29.5
Low	21.4	37.8	30.8	24	33.3	34.8	35.6	23.5	28	32.9	53.8	30.0	34.4	33	34.7
Total	100	100	100	72	100	100	100	100	85	100	100	100	100	95	100
Mean	11.0	9.7	10.1			10.5	10.7	12.1			9.23	12.05	12.1		

TABLE 12.03

Achievement Scores by Age of Husband and Wife at Marriage
Three Generations Merged

Achievement Scores		Husband's Age at Marriage		Wife's Age at Marriage	
		High %	Low %	High %	Low %
High		44.3	22.2	40.1	27.0
Middle		25.3	39.2	27.6	36.5
Low		30.4	38.6	32.2	36.5
	Total	100	100	100	100
	N	158	153	152	159

is under 25 have markedly lower incomes at marriage than couples marrying when the husband is between 25-29. He sees this as a consequence of the late marrying husband having been in the labor force for a longer period of time, or having remained in school long enough to enter the labor force at a higher salary. We are producing evidence here that there is not only a tendency for later marriers to start ahead of their marital cohort in income, but to remain ahead in four significant areas of economic activity over the marriage span. Moreover, since this is more characteristic of the married child generation than of the older generation, we might advance the hypothesis that the timing of marriage is more important today than it once was in establishing later career achievement pattern of couples.

Children as Burden or Incentives to Achievement. From an earlier chapter, Chapter III, we know that the timing of marriage is not unrelated to the number of children ever born to couples. Since age at marriage is negatively related to the number of children ever born, and we have discovered above that age at marriage is negatively related to career achievement scores over the life span, we hypothesize that number of children ever born will not be an incentive but will be a constraint on career achievement. This proves to be the case with the two younger generations where the predominantly lagging group (low achievement scores) had the largest families and the high achievers had the smallest number of children. Forty-one percent of the parent generation's large size families (four or more children) were in the lagging group (averaging 4.5 points) as against 23 percent in the predominantly leading category (averaging 17 points). Similar findings obtained for the married child generation which has not been bearing children long enough to have closed its families. Here 41 percent of the large families (3 or more children) are found in the lagging category in achievement compared with 30 percent of the small families. In the grandparent generation, which undoubtedly did not practice family planning, the relationships are, if anything, reversed, with large family size (5 or more children) associated with high achievement scores and small family size with low achievement scores. In an agrarian situation to be sure, the larger the family size the greater the number of potential farm hands, and therefore, the higher the income level and the size of residence, but not the occupational level. We are puzzled by these contradictory findings for the oldest as against the youngest generations, but the conclusion we must come to is that in contemporary families children are apparently more of a burden and constraint on family career achievements than an incentive to leading out in this respect.

Social Class. Since occupational level is reflected in the advancement and retardation in occupational level over the life span in the career achievement scores, we are limited to educational level of husband and wife as indicators of social class. It is, nevertheless, interesting to note that the Index of Social Position which takes into account *present* occupational position plus educational achievement, and adequacy of neighborhood lived in, predicts remarkably the career achievement category in which families fall. This might better be seen as a validity test of the Index of Social Position than as an explanation of career achievement, see Table 12.04. Note that Upper and upper Middle Class families (listed in the table as Upper) are disproportionately in the high achievement group which led their generation over the life span in all three generations. Similarly, Lower Class families are disproportionately in the lagging group for all three generations. Middle Class families are more variable, tending in the grandparents generation to be more frequently leaders in achievement, but being predominantly "on schedule" in the other two generations.

Years of schooling completed may be more properly treated as a possible explanatory variable in accounting for the variance in achievement scores. Because level of education of husband and wife are associated with life long achievement scores in all three generations we have aggregated the findings for all three generations (see Table 12.05). Clearly amount of schooling obtained affects life span achievements in the areas of economic activity studied.

Value Orientations. When examined against the value orientations professed by families some inconsistencies and reversals appeared by

TABLE 12.04

Percentage Distribution of Achievement Scores by Generation and by Social Class Position

Achievement Scores	Grandparent Index of Social Position				Parent Index of Social Position				Child Index of Social Position			
	Upper Class %	Middle Class %	Lower Class %	Total %	Upper Class %	Middle Class %	Lower Class %	Total %	Upper Class %	Middle Class %	Lower Class %	Total %
High	75.0	40.7	12.5	34.3	53.8	35.7	4.5	31.4	64.0	30.4	15.4	34.6
Middle	12.5	28.8	43.8	32.3	23.1	37.1	22.7	32.4	16.0	37.5	34.6	31.8
Low	12.5	30.5	43.8	33.3	23.1	27.1	72.7	36.2	20.0	32.1	50.0	33.6
Total	100	100	100	100	100	100	100	100	100	100	100	100
N	8	59	32	99	13	70	22	105	25	56	26	107

TABLE 12.05

**Achievement Patterns by Education of Husband
Three Generations Merged**

Achievement Scores	Education of Husband		
	High %	Low %	Total %
High	43.8	26.0	33.4
Middle	30.0	33.7	32.2
Low	26.2	40.3	34.4
Total	100	100	100

generation, but in general the high achievers carried the expected values associated with their performance over the life span (for summary relationships see Table 12.06). For example, as expected, high achievers tended to be low on fatalism, high on prudentiality, more pessimistic than optimistic, and to be future rather than past oriented. It is interesting that the high achievers tend to be developmental rather than traditional in their conceptions of childhood and parenthood. The lagging low achievers were quite variable in their orientations, and definite only in their optimism and their present time orientation. Middle achievers, "predominantly on schedule", resemble more high achievers than low achievers in their value orientations. None of these differences are statistically significant but all of them conform to our *a priori* hypotheses about the relations expected between values held and career performance.

Family Organization. With respect to family organization our hypothesis is that flexibility in family organization should make for higher achievements over the life span. To test this we should ideally have been able to collect data about family organization for the same period as we have for the career achievements in income and occupational level and in size of residence and of durable goods inventory. Unfortunately, we have measures only for the year of the study and will be making the doubtful assumption that these measures are representative of past family patterns. Our measures deal with the centralization versus the diffusion of power in decision-making, the degree of specialization versus sharing of household duties, and the extent to which the wife is cloistered or actively participating in community affairs. Power centralization in the wife or the husband appears associated with low achievement scores in all three generations, whereas equalitarian decision-making is associated with high

TABLE 12.06

Summary Statistical Table Correlates of Achievement Patterns

Class of Explanatory Variable	Direction of Relation by Generation		
	G_1	G_2	G_3
Developmental			
Age of Marriage (Husband)	Non-significant	Positive	Positive
Age at Marriage (Wife)	Non-significant	Positive	Positive
Incentives or Constraints			
Number of Children Ever Born	Positive	Negative	Negative
Social Class Position			
Education of Wife	Positive	Positive	Positive
Education of Husband	Positive	Positive	Positive
Index of Social Position	Positive	Positive	Positive
Value Orientations			
Fatalistic-Manipulative	Negative	Non-significant	Negative
Future vs. Past Orientation	Non-significant	Positive	Positive
Optimism-Pessimism	Negative	Negative	Non-significant
Prudential-Impulsivity	Negative	Positive	Positive
Developmental-Traditional	Non-significant	Positive	Non-significant
Family Organization			
Equalitarian vs. authoritarian (Interviewer rating)	Positive	Positive	Curvilinear
Role Specialization	Positive	Negative	Negative
Social Participation of Wife	Positive	Positive	Non-significant
Marital Climate			
Marital Communication	Non-significant	Non-significant	Negative
Marital Companionship (Interviewer rated)	Positive	Positive	Positive
Marital Integration	Negative	Positive	Positive

achievement in two of the three generations. Role specialization, the phenomenon of rigid division of labor in the household tasks, is associated with low achievement scores in two of the three generations. Similarly high social participation of the wife in community activities appears to be associated in two of the three generations with high achievement scores. Thus, on all three indicators of flexibility in family organization the hypothesis appears upheld for at least two of the three generations. The relationships do not, however, appear to be statistically reliable (see Table 12.06).

Marital Climate. With respect to marital climates we have hypothesized that the more communicable, better integrated couples, and those in agreement on the basic issues of marriage would have made higher career achievement scores than less endowed couples. Here again we should have had longitudinal measures of the phenomenon of marital climate to relate to the longitudinal measures of achievement in economic activities. Our findings are somewhat puzzling to interpret and may suggest that measures of marital climate obtained today may be more a consequence than an antecedent of career achievements.

With few exceptions we find no significant relationships between our measures of marital climate and career achievements. Moreover, there is great variation by generation in the direction and significance of the relationships (see Table 12.06). With respect to communication, high communication is negatively related to career achievement in the child generation and randomly distributed in the other two generations. This finding suggests that we have a reversible proposition in which lagging over one's life span must make for greater conflict between spouses producing in turn higher communication.

Companionship scores (from ratings by the interviewers) appear positively related to career achievements in all three generations (not significant statistically). Marital integration, combining indicators of marital consensus and of role tension, appears positively but modestly related to career achievements in two generations and negatively related in the grandparent generation. In overall assessment our hypotheses with respect to marital climate have failed of confirmation.

In examination of the summary statistical table we may now conclude that issues of optimum timing of the marriage and the number of children in the family appear more predictive of career achievement patterns than the value orientations held, the types of family organization and marital climates found. The educational backgrounds and other indicators of social class must at least be considered in any program of long term family development. The secret of getting ahead needs to take into account both the resources and competences transmitted from generation to generation, the form of family organization developed for making good decisions about timing the marriage and the bearing of children, since these seem to be predictive of achievement patterns over the life span.

Intergeneration continuity and achievement scores. Before closing this discussion of career achievement scores we should utilize the intergenerational design of our study to ascertain the extent of continuity of leading, being on schedule, and lagging in achievement within the same family lines. Does the propensity to lead or to lag over the life span run in families?

Table 12.07 has been prepared to specify the extent of continuity ranging from "no continuity", that is, all three families in the family line are substantially different in their achievement scores over the life span, to two generation continuity where grandparent and parent or parent and married child are similar, to three generation continuity where all three demonstrate essentially the same propensity to lead, to be on schedule or to lag in career achievements.

First of all, there does appear to be substantial continuity of achievement levels from generation to generation. In only seventeen (20%) of eighty-seven lineages (three generations of the same family line) on which we have complete records was there no continuity at all, leaving 80% where there is either two generation continuity or three generation continuity.

When Table 12.07 is examined for the extent of continuity by achievement score levels we note that complete three generation continuity is much more likely to be found for high achievement patterns than for "on schedule" or lagging patterns: forty-one percent for high achievers compared with twenty-nine percent each for the lesser achievements. Affluent career patterns appear to be transmitted more faithfully over three generations than poverty patterns. Lagging one's generation, by contrast appears to be a phenomenon of parent-married child transmission with almost half (46.7%) of the parent-child transmissions being low in achievement scores. Middle achievers, predominantly families which have been about average for their generation in achievement appear to be clustered in the grandparent to parent continuity group dominating this latter type of transmission (45% of cases).

Lineage type and achievement scores. Still another way to utilize the intergenerational design of the study to explicate career patterns has been conceptualized by Aldous and applied to these data.[1] She has identified four three generation lineage types; Type I a pure male patrilineage, grandfather-father-son, of which there are fifteen in our sample; Type II, a cross-sex but predominantly male lineage, grand-

---

[1] Joan Aldous and Reuben Hill, "Social Cohesion, Lineage Type and Intergenerational Transmission", *Social Forces* 43 (May, 1965) pp. 471-482.

TABLE 12.07

Extent of Continuity in Achievement Scores

	Partial Continuity			Complete Continuity	No Continuity	Total
	Grandparent to Parent	*Parent to Child*	*Grandparent to Child*	*Grandparent-parent-child*		
Achievement	%	%	%	%	%	%
High	30.0	33.3	38.9	41.2	31.7	34.5
Middle	45.0	20.0	22.2	29.4	34.6	31.8
Low	25.0	46.7	38.9	29.4	33.7	33.7
Total	100	100	100	100	100	100
Number and percent of three generation lineages.	23.0	17.2	20.7	19.5	19.5	100

father-father-daughter, of which there are twenty-one in the sample; Type III, a pure matrilineage, grandmother-mother-daughter, of which there are thirty-one in the study; and Type IV, a cross-sex but predominantly female lineage, grandmother-mother-son, of which there are twenty in the study. Aldous has hypothesized that the cohesion of the pure lineages would be higher than the cross-sex lineages, thus making for greater continuity in these lines and that for certain expressive patterns the female lineages would be more likely to transmit successfully than the predominantly male lines. Male or predominantly male lineages would be expected to transmit instrumental patterns such as occupational and income levels more successfully than female lineages.

In the present analysis we ask which of the lineage types is most likely to be associated with high, middle and low achievement scores. Because of its greater cohesion we hypothesize that the all female lineage, Type III, should be ranked highest followed by the all male lineage, Type I. Next in order would be the predominantly male cross-sex lineage, Type II, ending with the Type IV cross sex lineage. Our reason for the ranking of the types following Type III invokes the principle that the achievement patterns being scored are all instrumental patterns more likely to fall within the province of the male heads of the household and that achievement motivation may be, therefore, greater in the male and predominantly male lineages. Table 12.08 provides a partial test of our hypothesis.

TABLE 12.08

**Median Achievement Scores by Generations for Members
of Four Lineage Types**

	N	Grandparent Generation		Parent Generation		Married Child Generation	
		Median	Rank	Median	Rank	Median	Rank
Type I, Grandfather-father-son, Pure patrilineage	15	8.5	4	11.5	2	15.3	1
Type II, Grandfather-father-daughter, predominantly male, cross sex lineage	21	8.9	3	11.3	3	12.5	3
Type III, Grandmother-mother-daughter, pure matrilineage	31	10.8	1	13.0	1	11.8	4
Type IV, Grandmother-mother-son, predominantly female cross-sex lineage	20	10.0	2	10.3	4	14.0	2

Although the varability is not great among the several lineage types there is some edge in favor of Type III, the all female lineage, for two of the three generations, ranking first for both the grandparent and the parent generation. Second in importance is the all male Type I lineage which is ranked first by the married child generation and second by the parent generation. The next ranks are less clear although all three generations agree that Type II, the predominantly male cross sex lineage is third. Only in the parent generation is the hypothesized rank order maintained perfectly. Nevertheless, we should regard our hypothesis as at least partially supported—pure lineages characterized ostensibly by greater cohesiveness were somewhat more successful in transmitting higher achievement patterns than cross-sex lineages.

A finer discrimination of the power of lineage types to differentiate in transmitting high as against low achievement patterns can be tested by examining the degree of continuity for each lineage type with respect to the three levels of achievement scores, as we have attempted to do in Table 12.09.

We would hypothesize that the Type III all female lineage, would show the greatest degree of continuity in high achievement scores, both because of its greater cohesion and because of its performance in the previous table with higher achievement scores in two of the three generations. We would expect Type I to be second only to Type III for the same reasons, anticipating somewhat less cohesion in all

TABLE 12.09

Extent of Continuity of Achievement Patterns by Lineage Types

Achievement Scores	Lineage Type I Degree of Continuity			Total		Lineage Type II Degree of Continuity			Total		Lineage Type III Degree of Continuity			Total		Lineage Type IV Degree of Continuity			Total	
	Complete %	Partial %	None %	f	%	Complete %	Partial %	None %	f	%	Complete %	Partial %	None %	f	%	Complete %	Partial %	None %	f	%
High	50.0	40.0	26.3			14.3	16.7	55.6			83.3	38.9	25.6			—	38.5	28.6		
Middle	—	30.0	42.1			57.1	50.0	16.7			—	22.2	35.9			50.0	23.1	39.3		
Low	50.0	30.0	31.6			28.6	33.3	27.8			16.7	38.9	38.5			50.0	38.5	32.1		
Total	100.	100.	100.			100.	100.	100.			100.	100.	100.			100.	100.	100.		
Number and Percentage of Lineages	13.3	66.7	20.0	15	33.3	57.1	33.3	9.5	21	19.4	19.4	58.1	22.6	31	22.6	10.0	65.0	25.0	20	25.0

Grand Total: f = 20, % = 100

male than all female lineages, and somewhat lower achievement scores to be transmitted. We would anticipate that the cross-sex lineages would be lowest of all in continuity and that their achievement scores would be lower than the pure lineages.

Let us attempt to read Table 12.09 with these considerations in mind. Type III is not the most successful of the four types in the proportion of its lineages with complete continuity [read the bottom row to see the proportion of each lineage type that is characterized by complete, partial (two generation transmissions), and no continuity]. It is second to Type II, the predominantly male cross-sex lineage, which also is lowest in lineages with no continuity at all (only 9.5%). By contrast the lineage type with the greatest proportion of no continuity is Type IV, with a fourth of its families dissimilar in their achievement patterns.

Yet the real question we are searching for is which lineage type will be both high in continuity, and high in the transmission of high achievement patterns—this is certainly the Type III, pure matrilineage, which is highest in transmitting high achievement patterns where there was complete continuity (83.3% of three generation transmissions were high achievement) and very high in transmitting high achievement patterns when there was partial, two generation transmissions (39% of two generation transmissions were high achievement). Second to Type III in this respect is Type I, the pure patrilineage, which although the number of families involved is small in this lineage, transmitted 50% high achievement patterns in its three generation transmissions, and 40% in its partial, or two generation transmissions. Transmission of "on schedule" patterns, or middle achievement scores, was most likely to be done with complete continuity or partial continuity by Type II, the predominantly male cross-sex lineage, which was highest of the lineage types in complete or partial continuity of all types of achievement patterns. The Aldous type hypotheses have been largely supported.

To summarize the findings of this section on intergeneration continuity, lineage types and achievement scores, we might recapitulate briefly. Continuity from generation to generation is more frequent than discontinuity in achievement scores. Complete three generation continuity is most likely to be found among high achieving families whereas middle achievement and low achievement is at most a two generation transmission phenomenon. When achievement scores are examined by lineage types, pure female and pure male lineages (Types I and III) have higher achievement scores than combinations of cross-sex lineages. Furthermore, these so-called pure lineages perform better in transmitting high achievement patterns with complete continuity (three generation transmissions) and partial continuity (two generation transmission). A theoretical rationale for the rank order of performance of four lineage types was provided and partially confirmed in these findings; namely, that Type III, the all female lineage, grandmother-mother-daughter, would be most effective, because of its greater cohesiveness and success in socializing its descendents; that Type I, the all male lineage, grandfather-father-son, would be next most effective, second only because mothers are closer to daughters than fathers to sons; that Type II, the predominantly male cross-sex lineage, grandfather-father-daughter, would be third, invoking a principle second only to cohesion, the instrumental nature of the patterns being transmitted which would give an advantage to predominantly male lineages, leaving the Type IV predominantly female cross-sex lineage last in the achieving order.

We close this analysis with a renewed appreciation of the importance of issues usually absent from sociological analyses; namely, the cumulative career type variables such as intergenerational transmissions and transfers which represent an extension of the notion of career backward into the culture stream of the past. We will return to this discovery in the last chapter on implications for family development theory.

Distribution of Consistency in Career Achievement Types by Generation

	Total	Grandparent	Parent	Child
Type I, Consistently High Achievers (Achievement Scores 14-20, Inconsistency Scores 0-6)	99	23	33	43
Type II, Consistently Middle Achievers (Achievement Scores 9-13, Inconsistency Scores 0-6)	53	16	16	21
Type III, Consistently Low Achievers (Achievement Scores 0-8, Inconsistency Scores 0-6)	73	34	17	22
Type IV, Inconsistent, High Achievers (Achievement Scores 10-14, Inconsistency Scores 7-8)	47	12	21	14
Type V, Inconsistent, Low Achievers (Achievement Scores 4-9, Inconsistency Scores 7-8)	39	14	18	7
Total	311	99	105	107

Correlates of Consistency in Achievement

To sharpen up the concept of career achievement used in this chapter we would like to impose the concept of consistency-inconsistency in achievement. Many of the families in the middle achieving group may be inconsistent achievers, leading in one career, on schedule in a second, and lagging on two others, whereas other families in the same achievement score range may be consistently "on schedule" performers. To sort out the phenomenon of inconsistency in performance we have calculated an inconsistency score[1] for each family and have used it to produce a typology of Consistency in Career Achievements involving five types whose distribution is presented by generation on p. 291.

These five types of families are more homogeneous types than the three-fold categories based on achievement scores alone. They reflect not only achievement over time but consistency in career style. It remains to be seen whether or not the new types predict consumership over a year's period better than the less specified quantitative achievement scores.

---

[1] Quantification of inconsistency in achievement was undertaken by treating the distance between "leading in a career" and "on schedule in a career" as a one step deviation, the distance between "on schedule" and lagging as a one step deviation, and the distance between "leading" and "lagging," in a career as a two step deviation. A family's inconsistency score would, therefore, be the sum of the step deviations represented by inter-area differences in performance over the life span. For example, if a family, over its life span led in income level, lagged in durable goods, lagged in occupation level and was predominantly on schedule in residence size we would calculate the inconsistency score as follows:

Led in income level but lagged in durable goods	2 step deviations
Led in income level but lagged in occupation	2 step deviations
Led in income level but on schedule in residence size	1 step deviation
Lagged in durable goods vs. lagged in occupation	0 step deviation
Lagged in durable goods but on schedule in residence size	1 step deviation
Lagged in occupation level but on schedule in residence size	1 step deviation
Total score, equals sum	7

When all families are arrayed by their inconsistency scores it is clear that inconsistency is more widespread among families than consistency:

Inconsistency Scores	Percent All Generations
0-2	6.7
3-4	28.6
5-6	36.9
7-8	27.8

Let us now examine briefly the distinctive backgrounds and properties of the five Consistency in Achievement Types. From the frequency of the types within the generations shown above, it is apparent once again that the married child generation leads in both consistency and achievement in dominating the Type I, Consistently High Achievers. The Type III, Consistently Low Achievers, are found most frequently among the grandparent generation. The heterogeneous inconsistent types, both Types IV and V, are led by the parent generation suggesting this generation has been spottiest in its achievements, leading when it does in one area at the expense of lagging in other areas.

A summary table has been prepared (Table 12.10) which shows the properties of families and the ordered typology of Consistency in Achievement aggregated for all three generations.

TABLE 12.10

Summary Statistical Table Correlates of Consistency in Achievement Types

Class of Explanatory Variables	Direction of Association, All Generations
Timing of Marriage	
Age at Marriage (Husband)	Positive
Age at Marriage (Wife)	Positive
Children As Incentives or Constraints	
Number of Children Ever Born	Negative
Social Class	
Education of Husband	Positive
Education of Wife	Positive
Index of Social Position	Positive
Value Orientation	
Fatalistic-Manipulative	Negative
Future vs. Past Orientation	Positive
Optimism-Pessimism	Not significant
Prudential-Impulsivity	Positive
Developmentalism-Traditionalism Score	Positive
Flexibility of Family Organization	
Equalitarian Family vs. Husband or Wife Dominance (Interviewer Rating)	Positive
Role Specialization	Not significant
Social Participation of Wife	Positive
Marital Climate	
Marital Companionship (Interviewer Rating)	Positive
Marital Communication	Not significant
Marital Integration	Not significant

The effect of sharpening the summary measure of achievement over the life span in four areas by introducing the dimension of consistency from area to area increases the relationship between high achievement and certain background items but does not change basically the findings with respect to the properties of high vs. low achievement families. We obtain from examining our individual tables on each of the background factors (not shown) few distinctive properties for Types IV and V, the inconsistently high and inconsistently low achievement types.

Type I, Consistently High Achievement, has many distinctive properties, only a few of which it shares with its inconsistent counterpart, Type IV, Inconsistently High Achievement families. Both types are found with greater than average education of spouses, and with equalitarian patterns of decision-making. They differ in age at marriage, Type I married when husband was older than average for the cohort, Type IV when the husband was younger, than average. Type IV appears distinctive in only one area, that of low role specialization with husband and wife sharing many tasks together. Type I leads all types by contrast in its superior social class position, high social participation, high companionship in marriage, and the cluster of value orientations which constitutes its outlook on the world: Non-fatalistic, prudential, future oriented, and developmental in its views about parenthood.

Type V, Inconsistently Low Achievement, is disproportionately found among families of low education and lower social class as are Type III Consistently Low Achievement families. They differ in the consistently low Type III having disproportionately large families, being more past oriented, more husband dominated, more specialized in role allocation, lower in social participation and marrying at an earlier age whereas the more inconsistently low achievement Type V is not distinctively different from the rest of the sample on these matters.

In comparing the two summary tables 12.06 and 12.10 we see that the same attributes appear associated with Consistency in High Achievement types as with high achievement scores. The direction of association, wherever it is significant, is invariably the same. We are thus, not justified in analyzing separately the impact of consistency of achievement upon the consumership variable.

Predictability of Consumership

With the evidence in hand from the analyses of the correlates of career achievement and consistency in achievement that many of the same factors explain career achievement over the life span as explained consumership in its various phases in earlier chapters we are ready to test the interrelationship of these two sets of data directly. We are asking one major question: Does leading or lagging one's generation in four career areas over the life span predict consumership performance over the twelve months of the study?

Four phases of consumption provide possible measures of consumership: Needs-Identification Phase (Volume of Plans), Rationality in Decision-Making (Rationality Score), Planfulness (percent of Pre-Planned Actions), and Satisfaction with Outcome (Satisfaction Score). (See Chapter 9 for full description of these phases).

Needs-Identification Phase. In Table 12.11 the volume of plans

TABLE 12.11

Volume of Plans by Achievement Scores
Three Generations Merged

	Achievement Scores			
Volume of *Plans*	*High* %	*Middle* %	*Low* %	*Total* %
8 – 26	37.6	27.4	18.1	27.7
4 – 7	29.0	35.8	31.9	32.3
0 – 3	33.3	36.8	50.0	40.1
Total	100.	100.	100.	100.

and career achievement scores for all three generations have been aggregated to demonstrate the positive relationship between career achievement scores and volume of plans. The propensity to lead one's generation over the life's span anticipates reasonably well the volume of plans articulated for the sample as a whole. The greater the career achievement scores the greater the volume of plans articulated during the year of the study—thus the phenomenon of identifying needs which require plans appears associated with leading rather than lagging one's generation over the life's span. The relationship does not hold up, however, for each of the generations as it appears to do for all three generations merged.

Rationality in Choice-Making Phase. The relationship between life time achievement scores and the consumership variable of rationality in the choice-making phase appears to be positive but curvilinear (see Table 12.12). High achievers are more likely to be circumspect in conforming to the rationality procedures caught in the Rationality Scale of consulting with experts, weighing long term con-

TABLE 12.12

Rationality in Decision-Making by Achievement Scores
Three Generations Merged

Rationality Scores	Achievement Scores			
	High %	Middle %	Low %	Total %
High	38.5	24.1	36.6	33.2
Middle	30.8	41.0	31.7	34.4
Low	30.8	34.9	31.7	32.4
Total	100.	100.	100.	100.

sequences and taking into account costs and satisfactions than middle achievers who predominate in the middle and low rationality scores. But low achievers who have been lagging their generation were also more frequently rational in their choice-making procedures during the year of the study. We may have a conversion phenomenon in which high achievement families (leaders over the life span) have long used rational procedures, one of the reasons they are leaders, but the low achievers (lagging over the life span) are new converts to consumership procedures. This will bear further study.

Planfulness of Actions Taken Phase. Career achievement scores do not predict pre-planning of actions in striking fashion, but the direction is in general positive, if not linear. Table 12.13 shows high achievement scores associated more than expected with high preplanning of actions, but middle achievement scores (families predominantly on schedule over the life span) appear more frequently in the company of low preplanning of actions than the low achievement score families. This relationship is not dissimilar to that noted

TABLE 12.13

Percent Pre-Planning by Achievement Scores
Three Generations Merged

Percent Preplanning	Achievement Scores			
	High %	Middle %	Low %	Total %
High	32.0	26.4	28.0	28.9
Middle	26.8	29.9	37.6	31.4
Low	41.2	43.7	34.4	39.7
Total	100.	100.	100.	100.

between career achievement scores and consumership in the rationality of choice-making phase. High achievers are high consumership scorers in both, middle achievers are also low consumership scorers in both. Laggards in achievement, however, are found in the middle range of preplanning of actions rather than high. We may draw some comfort that there is any relationship at all between these scores which cover performance over such widely disparate time spans.

Satisfaction with Outcome Phase. This phase has been the most dubiously measured of the four. First of all, the number of families dissatisfied are few. Second, there has appeared in earlier analyses a tendency for families to rationalize their decisions favorably after the fact on the one hand or to be more critical if they have been careful in choice making and pre-planning, thus making for a negative relationship between preplanning of actions and degree of satisfaction with outcome.

Examination of Table 12.14 relating career achievement scores to satisfaction with outcome of the decisions undertaken during the year reveals a greater relationship than anticipated. High achievement over the life span is disproportionately found in the high

TABLE 12.14

Satisfaction with Outcome by Achievement Scores
Three Generations Merged

	Achievement Scores			
Degree of Satisfaction	High %	Middle %	Low %	Total %
High	84.0	66.3	67.1	72.3
Low	16.0	36.1	32.9	27.7
Total	100.	100.	100.	100.

satisfaction set of families (84% of families) whereas middle achievement and low achievement scores are disproportionately located among families of low satisfaction scores. By generation, the married child generation is most faithfully predicted in this final phase of the consumption process.

Summary

This chapter has brought together the two major sets of data we have been trying to explicate in this study; namely, the longitudinal measure of achievement over the life span of all families, and the several measures of consumership derived from observation of the four phases of the consumption process as families have planned and carried out plans over a twelve months period.

The chapter opened with a discussion of the correlates of planning career achievements and of inter-area consistency in achievement. Career achievement scores for each family ranging from 0-20 were calculated by ascribing points for leading, being on schedule and lagging one's generation in each of four areas of economic activity over the life span: Income level, durable goods acquisitions, size of residence and occupational level. Inter-area consistency scores were also devised ranging from 0-8 for each family based on the similarity-dissimilarity of achievement over the life span for each of four areas of activity. From these two sets of scores five Consistency in Career Achievement Types were derived: Type I, Consistently High Achievers; Type II, Consistently Middle Achievers; Type III, Consistently Low Achievers; Type IV, Inconsistent High Achievers; and Type V, Inconsistent Low Achievers.

By generation Career Achievement Scores were Highest for the Married Child Generation (13.1), next highest for the Parent Generation (11.3), and lowest for the Grandparent Generation (10.2). Inter-area inconsistency scores were lowest for the Married Child Generation (5.8) and highest for the Parent Generation (6.7). This accounted for the greater concentration of the Married Child Generation in Type I, Consistently High Achievers (44% of all families in this type), and of a concentration of Grandparents in Type III, Consistently Low Achievers (47% of all families). The Parent Generation with its high inconsistency scores was disproportionate found in Types IV and V, the inconsistently high and inconsistently low achievement families (45% and 46% of families in these types respectively).

The major correlates of career achievement scores were found to be Age at Marriage (Positive), Number of Children Ever Born (negative), Education of Spouses (Positive), and Social Class Position (Positive); Fatalism (Negative), Future Orientation (Positive), Prudentiality (Positive); Equalitarian Decision-making (Positive), Role Specialization (Negative), Social Participation of Wife (Positive). Companionship in Marriage (Positive); and Marital Integration (Positive). These same factors also appeared associated in the same direction with the Consistency in Career Achievement Types.

Examination of the extent of intergenerational continuity of career achievement scores produced several interesting generalizations: 1) Continuity from generation to generation was more frequent than discontinuity in career achievement scores. 2) Patterns of affluence were more likely to be transmitted intact than poverty patterns, that is, complete three generation continuity was most likely to be found among higher career achievement families, whereas middle achievement and low achievement were at most a two generation transmission phenomenon. 3) When achievement scores were examined by lineage types, pure female and pure male lineages had higher achievement scores than combinations of cross-sex lineages. Furthermore, these so-called pure lineages performed better in transmitting high achievement patterns with complete continuity (three generation transmission) and partial continuity (two generation transmissions) and were lowest in discontinuity of transmission.

The chapter closed with an examination of the linkage between the longitudinal career achievement scores and the several measures of consumership derived from panel type observations during the 12 months of the study. This section sought to answer the question: Does leading or lagging one's generation in four career areas over the life span predict consumership performance over a 12 months period?

When one considers the disparity in historical time periods covered by the two sets of measures for each of the three generations (three sets of life spans for the longitudinal career achievement data and a common 12 months period in 1958-59 for the consumership measures) the level of prediction achieved in Table 12.11-12.14 appears to be remarkably high. Career achievement scores predicted the Needs-Identification Phase (Volume of Plans) best— the relationship was positive and linear. The Rationality in Decision-Making Phase (Rationality Score) was partially predicted since the relationship was positive and curvilinear—High Career Achievement Scores were located in High Rationality Score families but the least rational families were not Low Achievers, but Middle Achievers. Similarly in the Planfulness of Actions Phase, Preplanning of Actions was highest for High Career Achievers, but Middle Achievers were lowest in pre-planning actions and Low Achievers appeared high—another curvilinear relationship. Finally, Satisfaction with Outcome appeared effectively predicted by Career Achievement Scores—High Career Achievement being associated firmly with High Satisfaction with decisions made over the study period. It would appear that despite the disparity in historical time periods covered that career achievement type measures do provide a set of predictors of some usefulness in anticipating the consumership behaviors of families as they move forward over time.

PART THREE

IMPLICATIONS OF FINDINGS

IT NOW BECOMES OUR TASK to examine the implications of the several hundred discrete findings of this longitudinal study of families for their contributions to the growing body of theory about the family and for their utility in devising programs of training in family life education and consumer education.

In mining the findings for their theoretical contributions we will not be engaged in constructing grand theory, although some day a theoretician may venture to link up the macro changes in society with the micro changes in family organization as families form and pursue careers over their life spans. We have set for ourselves the lesser task of distilling from the findings in the several preceding chapters a few miniature or partial theories. These theories will be phrased at a higher order of generalization than the several empirically based propositions from which each theory has been generated, but they will remain at the level of the middle range because we will not generalize beyond the level of families, to other groups or to the society. These miniature theories will pertain to family behavior and even more narrowly on occasion to the economic behavior of families.

It is our intention, in turn, to derive from these several miniature theories a more informative general theory dealing with the central issues encountered by families in the management of their careers; namely, the issues of relations with kin and the synchronization of time, money and talent as resources.

The closing chapter provides an opportunity to spell out the ways the several findings of this study can be put to use in upgrading the performance of families over their careers. The clientele for a program of training would be families encountering problems of career management at critical points in the life span. Some attention will be given to designing adult socialization programs for couples to help them master the patterns of time and resource management practiced by the most successful of the families in this study as an alternative to having families serve as socialization agencies for training their own children in the skills of time and money management.

CHAPTER XIII

Implications for a Theory of Family Development and Family Consumership

IN THE SEVERAL PRECEDING CHAPTERS there have been many discoveries not anticipated by the theoretical model of hypothesized interrelationships depicted in Chart 1.02. Yet, the family development framework which provided the key concepts and many of the propositions to be tested has offered a scope of inquiry large enough to encompass these several discoveries. We would hope to use these findings to sharpen and improve the framework for further development.

To date the family development framework has been largely silent about the transactional patterns between the family and its vertical kin in three generation depth and the intersecting of the family careers of these three generations over time. The framework has also tended to assume similar stages of development for each generational cohort, treating as residual the issue of continuity and change from generation to generation. The findings from this study can be used to correct these deficits in the framework.

The first cluster of miniature theories to be constructed are derived from the many empirical generalizations about interdependence among the generations and about generalizational similarities and differences which the intergenerational design of this study has generated.

Interdependence of the Generations and the Modified Extended Family Network

The intergenerationally linked sample design has enabled the collection of data for the first time in the history of family research about interfamily transactions in three generation depth with respondents from each generation reporting on their own behavior and demarcating their own networks of transaction. A number of essentially descriptive propositions consonant with earlier findings of interkin transactions in two generation depth are presented below upon which to base a more encompassing miniature theory about interdependence among the generations:

1. Endorsement of the norms of kinship obligations and kin contact increases from oldest to youngest generation.
2. The vertical kinship network of three generations is turned to predominantly for giving and receiving help in time of trouble compared with the horizontal network of siblings and cousins, the peer network of friends and neighbors, and helping agencies.
3. Intergenerational sharing of activities, visiting and help exchanges are *three generations in depth* with most frequent activity occurring between adjacent generations, empirically supporting the presence of a functioning extended family network which deserves the term *modified extended family* rather than *classical extended* because of the limited number of functions performed.
4. The middle or parent generation in a modified extended family network of three generations serves as the "kinkeeping" lineage bridge across the generations, being most involved with its adjacent generations both in intergenerational contacts and in help exchanges.
5. In a modified extended family network of three generations each generation turns to the network for help in solving problems it can't solve itself: the oldest generation for problems of illness and household management; the middle generation for emotional gratification; and the youngest generation for problems of child care and economic assistance.
6. In help exchanges the balance between giving and receiving within the intergenerational network is sufficiently asymmetrical that invidious statuses are created with the oldest generation in a *dependent status* (receiving more than giving), the parent generation in a *patron status* (giving more than receiving) and the youngest generation in a *reciprocator status* (high both in giving and receiving).
7. *Dependency*, characterized by receiving help without giving, is associated with infrequent visiting with kin and minimal participation in activities with kinsmen whereas *self reliance* characterized by non-reciprocated giving appears to be positively associated with high kinship interaction. Full reciprocity of giving and receiving appears randomly associated with cultivation of kinship contacts.

From these seven empirically based propositions a picture emerges of a symbiotic functioning modified extended family network three generations in depth characterized by much boundary crossing and interdependence based upon a wide range of help exchanges. A miniature theory built from these propositions should attempt to specify the conditions for maintaining the viability of such a modified extended family network.

Miniature Theory #1

Given normative support for the maintenance of kinship obligations and preference to utilize immediate vertical kin over other sources of help, three generation lineages develop networks of interdependence based upon a wide range of help exchanges and frequent kin contacts that approximate modified extended families in their symbiotic functioning. The viability of these networks is advanced by the heavy involvement of the middle generation as the lineage bridge initiating more activity and giving more help both up and down the generation ladder than it receives and by means of this kin-keeping activity moderating the strains occasioned by nonreciprocity in giving and receiving within the network.

Change Versus Continuity from Generation to Generation

Six empirical propositions encompass the major findings about change as against continuity from generation to generation:

1. When the statuses of families are examined there is a marked tendency for upgrading to occur from generation to generation of the same family line with respect to educational level, occupational level, and income category, whereas certain patterns symbolic of kinship solidarity such as religious affiliation and residential location tend to be similar from generation to generation.
2. With respect to value orientations about child rearing and family behavior patterns over three generations, the phenomenon of discontinuity is more pronounced than continuity. There appears to be much innovating and creating of new patterns, especially between the first and second generations where the differences in educational achievements is also greatest for the three generations.
3. When the achievements of the three generations for the first years of marriage and the achievements for the two older generations through the middle years are compared on several dimensions of performance the impression is one of acceleration of achievement from generation to generation (on measures of occupational level, income, labor force participation of wife, home ownership, housing amenities, durable goods acquisitions and the number of items in the financial portfolio of insurances and investments).

4. There is, however, more of a tendency toward continuity than discontinuity from generation to generation in the patterns of high and low consumership (preplanning actions and fulfillment of plans). Low consumership tends to be transmitted three generations in depth, whereas high consumership is more frequently a two generation transfer, specifically from the parent to the married child generation. If family lines can be counted upon to transmit the extremes of consumership, programs of consumer education might focus on low consumership families, knowing that if successful in breaking the poverty pattern linkage, good management patterns may be transmitted to subsequent generations.

5. When the families of each generation are classified as predominantly leaders, on schedule, or laggards of their generation in career achievements over the life span, there is a marked tendency toward continuity rather than discontinuity for all three patterns of achievement. Continuity three generations in depth was most characteristic for high achievers over the life span, continuity two generations in depth was reported for low achievers (parent to married child generations) and for middle achievers (grandparent to parent generation).

6. In an examination of types of family lines most likely to have three generation continuity of high career achievement scores it was discovered that the hypothesized most highly cohesive (as indicated by same-sex linkages) female lineage (grandmother-daughter-granddaughter) led the lineage types followed by the next most solidary male lineage (grandfather-son grandson) with the two less cohesive cross-sex lineages showing lowest continuity of all.

A miniature theory encompassing these substance bound propositions might be stated as follows:

Miniature Theory #2

Under conditions of rapid social change characterized by higher levels of education, greater range of occupational choice, and greater options for residential location, the bonds of solidarity and interdependence which would normally make for intergenerational continuity do so selectively rather than uniformly. Such bonds tolerate and even encourage upgrading and innovation from generation to generation with respect to economic and educational achievements as instrumental to ends common to all generations while maintaining continuity with respect to the expressive patterns of religion and residence proximity. This selective upgrading in instrumental competence has the effect of bringing about change in consumership patterns in one generation followed by continuity of the new pattern into the third generation. Where higher continuity of behavior three generations in depth occurs it is predicated on the expressive functioning of same-sex linked lineage types of high cohesion and interdependence.

Orderliness of Family Development over the Life Span

At the heart of this study of family development over the generations are the issues of timing of crucial life decisions over the life span, of time scheduling of activities and the synchronization of the family's reproductive, residential, occupational and acquisitional careers in the process of getting ahead in life. Is there some order to the sequences of events which all families encounter which our charts of achievements of three generations from early marriage onward have made explicit? How does the timing of marriage, childbearing, and of closing the family affect decisions of family heads in making residential moves, purchasing a home, acquiring durable goods, or undertaking long-term investments? Does each succeeding generation follow the same curves of rapid accumulation in the early years, leveling off in acquisitions in the middle years and withdrawing entirely from the market in the later years?

In preceding chapters we have presented an abundance of descriptive data on the careers over the life span of the two older generations and on the first ten years of marriage for the youngest generation. It should be remembered that the generations began marriage under radically different historical circumstances: the average grandparent was married in 1907 well before World War I, the next generation married in 1931 under the influence of the depression, and the youngest generation married in 1953 under conditions of increasing prosperity. The empirical propositions which follow reflect some of the most interesting theoretical findings about timing and life cycle management.

The timing of crucial life decisions and life cycle management.

1. Age at entering marriage for men has declined for each succeeding generation, whereas years of schooling has increased sharply for the same period of time lengthening in effect the adolescent period of dependence for men. Thus, for each succeeding generation the husband enters marriage with less time in the labor force in which to have accumulated the wherewithal to support a family.

2. The timing of the birth of the first child at roughly twenty months is similar for the three generations suggesting early parenthood as a

common goal, but differences of some magnitude separate the generations with respect to subsequent births and closing of the family with the
parent generation elongating spaces between births more than the other
two generations.

3. The grandparent generation closed its family at five children after
   15 years of childbearing. The parent generation closed at 3.5 children
   after ten years of childbearing. The youngest generation has not had
   time to complete its childbearing but appears to be bunching its children
   to date into a shorter time span than its predecessors.

4. The timing of launching children into jobs and marriage occurred later
   and extended over a longer period of time for the grandparent than for
   the middle generation with the result that the parent generation entered
   the post-parental period after 25 years of marriage, almost nine years
   earlier than its predecessor (in the 34th year of marriage).

5. Home ownership typically was achieved both by the grandparent and
   the married child generation in the fifth year of marriage, five years
   ahead of the middle generation.

6. Timing the entry, departure, and the reentry of the wife into the labor
   force differs sharply for each of the generations. Fewer than ten per cent
   of the wives of the grandparent generation were working gainfully until
   the postparental period when 20% have entered the work force. In the
   parent generation, 20% were already employed at marriage, about half
   dropping out for the childbearing period but within the first ten years
   of marriage this loss has been recovered and by the third decade 50% were
   in the labor force declining to 30% in the fourth decade of marriage. 60
   per cent of wives in the youngest generation were employed at marriage
   dropping to 25 percent during the first years of the childbearing period
   but reentering quickly to reach 40 per cent employed by the tenth year
   anniversary.

7. Timing the acquisition of life insurance policies differs sharply for the
   generations. The average grandparent waited until ten years after
   marriage when more than half of his children had been born before
   taking out his first life insurance policy, moreover at the close of the life
   span more than a fourth of this generation were still unprotected. The
   average parent generation family picked up its first policy in the second
   year of marriage and only 10 per cent were still unprotected by the third
   decade of marriage. Only 17 per cent of the married child generation
   didn't have life insurance upon entering marriage and this declined to
   five per cent by the fifth year of marriage. Year for year the child generation leads its predecessors in its structuring of the future through life
   insurance and retirement provisions.

8. The timing of job changes over the life span differs substantially among
   the generations. The grandparent generation made its first job change
   only in the seventh year of marriage and ended the life span with no
   more than four occupational changes. The parent and youngest gen-

eration both made their first job changes in the second year of marriage and were much more mobile thereafter with 40 per cent of the married child generation in its fourth or higher ordinal job by the end of the first decade.

9. The speed of acquisition of the family's durable goods inventory from marriage onward is greater for each successive generation with children entering marriage with a larger inventory than their grandparents had acquired after 30 years of marriage and larger than their parents reached after more than ten years of marriage. The rate of acquisition thereafter for the married child generation is so great that in five years of acquisition they have overtaken their parents' acquisitions of 25 years of marriage. The typical sequential order in which families acquire specific durables has also changed historically from generation to generation due in part to the range of alternatives available.

10. The timing of residential changes are remarkably similar for the three generations in the first years of marriage with 12-24 per cent moving the first year and 42-50 per cent moving in the second year of marriage and thereafter the number moving each year declining at about the same rate for all generations.

11. The generations varied in their appraisals of the degree to which they had achieved goals or were on schedule in this quest. With lower initial aspirations, 72 per cent of the respondents in the grandparent generation felt they had achieved all goals, 20 per cent half and half, six per cent said they had underachieved. With substantially higher goals, 63 per cent of the parent generation had achieved all goals, 31 per cent half and half, and six per cent had underachieved. With the highest aspirations of all the married child generation was most optimistic; 34 per cent seeing themselves ahead of schedule, 53 per cent on schedule, and 13 per cent agreeing they were behind schedule.

The foregoing eleven empirical statements have in common the issue of timing of one or more actions over the life span and the phenomenon of variability in synchronization for three generational cohorts. To construct a miniature theory from these several statements requires attention to both of these dimensions. Faced with similar problems of family formation, family maintenance and protection, under different historical circumstances, how similarly did the generations schedule themselves in making decisions to act upon these problems? Do the generations appear to have different strategies for shaping their careers over time?

Miniature Theory #3

The timing of one's marriage, the number and spacing of children, the changes of jobs by the husband and the wife's entry or reentry into the labor force, the timing of acquisitions of homes and durables, of life insurance and investments, all reflect attempts at life cycle management to achieve long-term goals *unattainable on phase* without some such structuring of the future. The three generational cohorts bring different career strategies to bear in scheduling the several sequences which make up the family's career although there are remarkable similarities in the timing of certain crucial decisions. The distinctive strategies of each generation are specified below:

1. *The career strategies of the grandparent generation appear to have involved settling for most modest goals, a more cautious development of resources, and a less achievemental oriented occupational career, lagging the succeeding generations year by year from early marriage onward.*

    The grandparent generation entered marriage at a later age and, lacking knowledge and competence in family planning methods, bore more children at closer intervals over a longer period of time than its generational successor. At the mercy of an unplanned economy and limited occupational opportunities, this generation shifted jobs infrequently while remaining in the blue collar class, acquired home and adequate amenities only after children were launched. Unprotected by life insurance over most of its career and prevented from building a nest egg for retirement after launching children because of the economic depression, this generation launched its children into marriage later and over a longer period of time with altogether a longer period of childbearing, childrearing and leave taking. Educational aspirations for its children were lowest of the generations with most of its children over achieving these goals.

2. *The career strategy of the parent generation appears to have been most prudent in its family planning and development of resources.* Having high educational aspirations for its children, over half setting college education as the goal, and having high housing aspirations, *the middle generation has had a strategy of controlling spacing and number of children, high occupational mobility, delayed home ownership, but early acquisition of protective life insurances and retirement provisions to achieve a high level of life cycle management.*

    This generation entered marriage during the Great Depression at a prudent age for marriage, spaced children farthest apart and closed their families early with the smallest total number of children, augmented the family income by the early reentry of the wife into the labor force to take advantage of war-born opportunities for employment. Deferred from military service because of age and family responsibilities, the breadwinner upgraded his occupational position by shifting jobs frequently. Home ownership was postponed latest of the generations whereas children were launched nine years earlier, thus enabling this generation to be in a position to be helpful financially to both grandparent and married child generations.

3. *The married child generation's career strategy shows the most forward planning of any generation acquiring more rapidly than its predecessors both life insurance and retirement provisions and being most precocious in its timing of home ownership.* It leads all the generations in its acquisitions and economic achievements year by year over its shorter life span although it is also the most extended in its utilization of credit. *Its strategy of life cycle management is a combination of risk taking in the volume of its durable goods and automobile acquisitions and of prudential hedging in its heavy investments in protective insurances and retirement plans.*

Couples of the married child generation entered marriage youngest at slightly more modest jobs than their parents when they married, but with more than half its wives working and expecting to remain in the labor force. Although they have the highest aspirations for their children, they have spaced them closest together of the generations, and have expectations of a larger family size than their parents. The close spacing may cause this generation to be badly off-phase later in the life span compared with their parents since their closer spaced children will be in college and getting married within a short period bringing a pile-up of expenses which occur in educating and marrying off children. The child generation may gain enough margin to survive this error in life cycle management, however, since it leads the generations year by year in its acquisitions of housing amenities and durable goods, in its occupational advancement, and in its rapidly advancing income level.

Intercontingency of Family Careers.

Three theoretical issues converge in the examination of the intercontingency of family performances over the life span. To what extent do families synchronize changes in one area in any given year with changes in other areas of activity, for example undertaking residential moves or durable goods acquisitions contingent with changes in family composition, and/or changes in occupation? To what extent are some areas of activity dominant or accommodating to changes in other areas? To what extent is leading one's generation in achievement in one area linked with leading in other areas? The empirical propositions on these three issues follow:

1. Residence changes are affected strongly by changes in family composition and moderately by changes in the husband's occupation, especially in the first years of marriage.
2. The interdependence over the life span of family composition, occupational and residential mobility is least marked in the grandparent genera-

tion, most apparent in the more responsive married child generation, and is most erratic in the middle parent generation.

3. The inventory of durable goods acquisitions over the first five years is most affected by residential mobility and least consistency by increases in income.

4. Changes in family compositon and in occupation appear to affect changes in the durable goods inventory indirectly, that is, through their impact on residential changes, although for the married child generation there is a pronounced direct interdependence within all three areas of activity.

5. Leading, lagging, or being on schedule in one area of economic activity over the marriage span tends to be selectively associated with comparable performances with respect to other areas of activity with income level, occupational level, and size of durable goods inventory all tending to be intercontingent.

6. Far from living up to or down to the conforming on-schedule Jones, the most consistent career patterning is to go beyond the Jones of one's generation in all four areas of economic performance; income level, occupational level, size of residence, and size of durable goods inventory.

7. Congruency between level of achievement in income and durable goods acquisitions year by year over the marriage span is highest for "early marrieds" in the child generation and lowest for "early marrieds" in the parent generation.

8. Among the generations, the married child is both the most likely to show multiple leading in three or more areas, but is also most likely to be congruent and interdependent in achievement over its more limited life span. The grandparent generation is most likely to show multiple lagging in three or more areas. The parent generation is both the most erratic and the most random in its performance.

9. Marrying later than the average is markedly associated in the married child generation with leading one's generation, and although early marriage makes for lagging in all areas for both the parent and child generations—no such differences appear in the grandparent generation.

Miniature Theory #4

Given the historical changes which have occurred in the society and the economy over the time span encompassed by the overlapping life cycles of the three generations the phenomenon of increasing intercontingency of family careers may be theorized as an increasing responsiveness of the generations to an increasingly bureaucratized, rationalized, and technologized economy and polity. Families are increasingly able to synchronize their several career activities because the economy and polity are more predictably "fine tuned" to maintain a high level of prosperity and a favorable climate for family consumption.

Two phenomena at the family level reflect the decreasing capriciousness of the political economy and the rising prosperity of the period. There is both an accelerated upgrading in all spheres of economic activity from the oldest to the youngest generation and achievements from generation to generation. Let us assert the components of this theory in the form of interlinked generalizations.

Given an increasingly rationalized and bureaucratized political economy differential changes in family planning and career management follow from the degree to which the generations have been beneficiaries of these changes:

1. Family development over the life span shows not only upgrading in performance from the oldest to the youngest generation in all spheres of economic activity but there is an acceleration in this process from generation to generation.
2. Associated with this accelerated upgrading by generation is increasing synchronization of changes in family space needs with residential moves, and in turn more responsiveness to residential mobility in undertaking acquisition of needed durable goods by the youngest generation as compared with the older generations for the early years of the marriage span.
3. Over the entire marriage span the family's several career achievements are generationally increasingly intercontingent, with income and occupational levels most interdependent, income level and size of durable goods inventory next most linked, and size of residence most independent of the other areas of achievement.
4. These intercontingencies of family careers are also expressed in the phenomenon of families multi-leading, or multi-lagging the families of their generation in all four of these careers, with the married child generation most frequently the multiple leader in three or more careers.
5. The timing of marriage has increasing impacts on the interdependence and congruence of economic career achievements over the generations. In the grandparent generation age at marriage is unimportant in predicting multiple leading in achievements but beginning in the parent generation early marriers are more likely to be laggards in achievements. In the youngest generation timing of the marriage decision has a double impact, that is, the early marrieds are handicapped and the late marriers are markedly superior in leading their generations over the marriage span in all four areas of economic activity.

We theorize, therefore, that the acceleration in upgrading in economic achievements from generation to generation reflects a decreasingly capricious economy and the possibility at the family level of an increasing interdependence among career achievements.

Beginning with a relatively nonresponsive grandparent generation which benefited almost not at all from the new political economy over its biography, caught in the constraints of a low range of income, narrowly restricted occupational alternatives, and limited housing and durable goods alternatives, it was followed, in turn, by an erratic and relatively inconsistent middle generation which got off to a slow start in the depression of the thirties and compensated by leading in selected areas of achievement at the expenses of lagging in others. Both of these generations compared poorly in performance and synchronization of career achievements with the youngest generation whose entire marriage span has been beneficiary of the managed economy with its multiple alternatives and rising affluence.

Properties and Social Contexts of Families of High Career Achievements Over the Life Span

A number of empirical propositions have been generated by arraying the data about the social and economic contexts of career achievements over the life span. What are the properties of families which succeeded best in management of their resources over the life cycle? The empirical propositions reflect the relative influence of age at marriage, family size pressures, social class contexts, family value orientations, and types of family structure.

1. Age at marriage of both spouses but especially of husband is associated positively with later career achievements over the family span. The relationship is most marked in the married child generation, present in the parent, and weakest in the grandparent generation.
2. Age at marriage is associated positively with income at marriage and negatively with eventual number of children in the family.
3. Family size is negatively associated with multiple leading in four areas of economic activity in the two youngest generations and positively associated in the grandparent generation.
4. Education of spouses is positively related to career achievements over the marriage span for all generations.
5. Value orientations of high achievers over the life span tend to be future oriented, prudential, pessimistic, and manipulative rather than present or past oriented, impulsive, optimistic, or fatalistic.
6. Flexibility in family structure characterized by equalitarian decision-making, role integration, and high social participation of wife appear associated with high career achievements over the marriage span.
7. There are weak but positive associations between marital companionship and marital integration on the one hand and multiple leading in career achievements on the other for the two younger generations.

Miniature Theory #5

A number of developmental properties group together as necessary if not sufficient antecedents of high economic achievement over the life span; namely, late marriage, limited offspring, high education, labor force participation of wife, and a flexible form of family organization. Each of these properties is increasingly necessary as we shift from an agrarian to an urban industrial society.

Leading one's generation in several areas of economic activity is powerfully facilitated by remaining in school long enough to enter the labor force at a higher salary, postponing marriage until schooling is completed and one has had some labor force experience, and limiting offspring to a small number. Such couples tend to have a head start not only in income and the economic bargaining power of a good education but have a form of family organization and marital climate developed for making good decisions required for the timing of home and durable goods acquisitions which are at the heart of life cycle management.

Family Development Patterns and Consumership

Five miniature theories have been adduced to this point about the lawfulness of change and continuity, and degrees of interdependences from generation to generation, as well as the orderliness of family development careers within the generations. There remain a number of empirical propositions to be arrayed about the linkages between the family's timing of actions in its career, or the family's stage of development, or the family's various career achievements and its consumership at a later point in time. To what extent can a family's developmental history be used to explain and predict the several phases of its consumption cycle, i.e., its identification of unmet needs as plans to expend resources, its rationality of choice making, and its preplanning of actions?

The several propositions arrayed below covering these issues are less descriptive and more explanational than previous propositions, and the miniature theory to be constructed from them should encompass these several explanations.

Developmental Properties and Consumership

1. The identification of unmet needs in the form of number of plans to expend resources increases within the married child generation as number of children increases, but decreases thereafter over the marriage span from

child to grandparent generation and within generation by age of spouses and duration of marriage.

2. Size of family and current income interact as per capita income to increase the volume of unmet needs expressed in both the married child and grandparent generation.

3. Timing the marriage within the married child generations showed late marriers with low income most depressed in volume of plans and early marriers with high life time income highest in plans. In the parent generation farther along in the life cycle the relationship of timing of marriage and life time income to volume of plans is reversed with lowest volume among early marriers with high life time income, and the highest volume of plans among late marriers of high life time income.

4. Rationality in decision-making and preplanning of actions are highest at the beginning of the marriage span and decline thereafter with the addition of children and the aging of parents, reaching the lowest point with the oldest couples of the grandparent generation.

5. Timing the marriage later is a matter of indifference to the grandparent generation but stimulates preplanning of actions for the parent generation and is positively related to both rationality of decision-making and preplanning of actions in the married child generation, suggesting more selective and prudential consumership among late marrieds.

6. Size of family and current income interact as per capita income to decrease rationality of decisions and preplanning in both the parent and child generations.

There are cruel paradoxes emergent in the propositons about family life cycle changes and consumership patterns. The number of unmet needs in families increases with the addition of children under conditions of low income but these are the same conditions which depress consumership patterns of rationality of decision-making and preplanning family actions. Moreover, over the family life cycle families do not appear to improve but to deteriorate in their consumership patterns which leave many families in a state of continuous secondary poverty.

Miniature Theory #6

Family consumership viewed developmentally over the marriage span is not so much a profile of growth and increased competence as of regression and deterioration. The youngest generation representing the beginning of the family life cycle is the most competent of the generations in consumership, with the parent generation, farther into the cycle, less effective in consumership and the grandparent generation at the end of the developmental cycle clearly the least competent. Age of spouses interacts with number and age composition of children and with lags in income to increase the level of unmet needs but to depress the planfulness and rationality of decision-making required for optimum resource management. Poor life cycle management represented by couples precociously marrying earlier than others in their generation with less education, lower initial income, and earlier childbearing makes for poorer consumership performance through the early years and into the middle years of marriage compared with "late marriers" of the same generations. We theorize that such couples lack the minimum economic cushion to be able to preplan expenditures and make a rational choice of strategies.

Life Span Achievement and Family Consumership

The propositions to be constructed here are drawn from juxtaposing the families' longitudinal achievements in four areas of economic activity (income level, adequacy of residence, size of durable goods inventory and occupational level) with their consumership performance over the twelve months of the study. To what extent does a family's career over the life span predict its subsequent consumership behavior?

1. The higher the life span achievement scores the higher the volume of plans articulated during the year of study.
2. High rationality of decision-making scores are found disproportionately both in multi-leading and multi-lagging families whereas on-schedule families have lower rationality scores.
3. Planfulness scores are highest for families of high life span achievements but the lowest scores are found among on-schedule achievers, whereas multi-lagging families tend to be middle run preplanners.

Miniature Theory #7

Leading in economic achievements over a family's history is predictive of high subsequent consumership performance. Leading one's generation in resource management creates an appetite for planning and provides the economic margin required for rationality of choice making and preplanning of expenditures. Lagging one's generation and being on schedule in economic achievement over the life span are indicative of less competence in resource management and represent less homogeneous and less predictable families with quite varied consumership performances. We theorize that achievements or lack of achievements over the life span may be less faithful indicators of consumer competence than of life styles of differential achievement orientation. "On schedule" type families may be viewed as less achievement oriented than the multiple leading families and less depressed economically than the multiple lagging families thus lacking the value orientation to achieve on the one hand and the economic pressures on the other to achieve high consumership.

Time-Bound Properties and Family Consumership

This discussion of the theoretical implications of findings would be incomplete without reference to the several non-developmental properties associated with family consumership. The rudimentary model presented in Chapter I linked a family's goals, value orientations, and aspirations to an understanding of the means required to achieve those goals, together with an effective family organization for taking action as *necessary* for achieving *excellence of performance* of family consumership. The propositions below reflect the limited number of properties found associated with high achievement on two or more phases of family consumership which also tended to be influential for all three generations.

1. The higher the educational level of husband and wife the higher the consumership achievements.
2. The higher the family's occupational status the higher the consumership achievements.
3. The less restrictive the family organization in allowing wife to work gainfully, to participate socially, and the more sharing of family tasks between the spouses, the higher the consumership achievements.
4. The higher the marital communication and the lower the marital integration, the higher the consumership achievements.

Miniature Theory #8

Transcending generation and timing of actions are congeries of properties which facilitate or hinder effective resource management. The guiding theory with respect to consumership of the study has been that effective decision-making is a function of these necessary conditions, high motivation to plan, knowledge of the means of planning and an effective decision-making organization poised to make good choices and take action. We now theorize from our findings that motivations to plan are sufficiently in flux from generation to generation that they appear to be generation bound. However, acquaintance with the means of planning caught in the occupational and educational competencies of families and the types of family problem solving organization and of husband-wife relations most likely to facilitate sharing of information and taking action on a problem do appear closely linked with high consumership at each phase of the consumption process in identifying unmet needs and enunciating them as plans, choosing rationally among alternative actions and preplanning these actions.

Family Consumership and Satisfaction with Outcome

The mechanisms which precipitate change in the patterns of family behavior over time are inadequately understood, as are those which bring about innovation from generation to generation. One such mechanism may be the assessment phenomenon of evaluating the returns from actions taken against the needs they were expected to meet, measured in this study by a satisfaction-with-outcome score for every action undertaken by a family over the twelve months of observation. Several empirical propositions illuminate the unexpected inter-relationships between family consumership patterns and the subjective appraisals by families of actions undertaken.

1. The higher the volume of plans articulated, the greater the dissatisfaction with actions taken for all generations.
2. The higher the rationality of decision-making in choosing among alternative actions, the higher the satisfaction with actions taken for all generations but especially for the grandparent generation.
3. The higher the proportion of actions taken that are preplanned the lower the satisfaction with actions taken. Specifying for constraints imposed by low vs. high income, the use of the halo mechanism is greatest in the low income group where low plan fulfillment is associated with highest satisfaction and middle and high plan fulfillment is associated with low satisfaction with actions taken.
4. Satisfaction with actions taken increases with duration of marriage and from youngest to oldest generation, directly the reverse of high consumership.
5. Dissatisfaction with the outcome of consumption actions is discontinuous from generation to generation. It is rather the majority pattern of high satisfaction which shows up in three generation linkages (92 per cent of these linkages are classified in the high satisfaction categories). Low satisfaction by contrast is found in lineages where the three generations deviate in their evaluation of outcomes each from the other (76 per cent of these families are dissatisfied with the outcome of their action).

Miniature Theory #9

In the continuous cycling of the family consumption process which begins with the identification of unmet needs and continues with a search for information and alternative actions and the process of choosing among these alternatives before taking action, the feedback mechanism of evaluating the wisdom of the choice and the adequacy of the action performs a monitoring function. If critically employed the mechanism facilitates the upgrading of subsequent consumership or if defensively used it can serve as a halo mechanism psychologically masking the deficiencies of those actions which were chosen without prior planning and consultation. Thus, change in family practices may be furthered by critical evaluations (low satisfaction) among the more planful families, whereas less planful families will be spared the full knowledge of the consequences of their impulsive actions by the uncritical halo feedback of rationalization of actions taken (high satisfaction). There may also be associated with the propensity to high satisfaction more continuity of ongoing consumership practices from generation to generation as compared with low satisfaction which tends to make for discontinuity and the possibility of upgrading from generation to generation.

Toward a More General Theory of Family Development and Family Consumership

In the preceding pages, nine miniature theories have been constructed from over sixty empirical propositions drawn directly from the study's chief findings about family development and family consumership. These partial theories are of necessity substance bound and phrased at a level of abstraction only slightly above the empirical statements from which they have been drawn. In the more general theory statement to be developed below, we shall attempt to be more encompassing without departing, however, too far from the substantive issues of life cycle and resource management, of timing the maximum deployment of family resources, including those of the kinship network.

A more general theory of family development and consumership must first of all recognize the overpowering phenomenon of *generation*. This appears as (historical and developmental) generational differences, as generational continuity in intergenerational transfers and transmissions, and as intergenerational exchanges and contacts among vertical kinsmen. No single chapter of this research monograph has been free of the necessity to specify generalizations by generation.

A derivative of the recognition of the phenomenon of generation is the necessity to acknowledge the presence of a modified extended family network within which nuclear family units of the same family line are in symbiotic transaction three generations in depth. The recognition of these networks as resources in depth from which and to which nuclear units draw and contribute is essential for the development of a more informative theory about nuclear family career achievements.

Reconceptualizing family development and family consumership in three generation time depth and in modified extended family network breadth will increase the informative scope of the general theory we are to construct over earlier formulations which have been limited to generalizations about the interplay of *properties of nuclear families and individuals* engaged in economic activities over limited time spans. The nine miniature theories above have already transcended the boundaries of previous theoretical formulations and are destined to provide the basic substance from which to generate a more encompassing general theory.

A Theory of Time and Resource Management

Family development theory may be said to encompass the entire range of family behaviors which are stimulated and constrained by the changing age and sex composition of nuclear or extended families over the family life span. The general theory of time and resource management attempted here focuses on a generous segment of family development but renders residual the orderly changes in the family's internal system, seen especially in the changing role reciprocities of the several positions in the growing family, in favor of whatever orderliness may be found in the family's economic achievements and the transactions of the family with its social network over the life span, with a focus on life cycle and resource management.

Family life cycle management consists of *timing* the *status changes* of the nuclear family in such a way that each of the family's several careers are mutually supportive of the style of life the family is seeking to achieve. Timing includes both the scheduling of rites of passage and the sequential ordering and synchronizing of actions and activities over the family's life span.

Resource management, or *family consumership,* consists of the optimum allocation of energies, information, goods, and expenditures to meet the needs of family members and others within the family's social network. Because families are engaged in realizing both short-run and long-term objectives, forward planning on a long-term basis and preplanning of short-term actions are among the components of optimum resource management.

Nuclear families do not face the issues of timing of career decisions and keeping resources and expenditures in balance in isolation, even in urban settings, but have accessible vertical kinsmen whose counsel and expectations provide norms of conduct and rewards for successful management patterns. In those fortunate modified extended family networks of high solidarity and extensive intra-network transactions, each nuclear generational unit contributes to the network what it can best give and draws on the network for help in solving problems that it can't solve by itself. The middle generation serves as the kin-keeping lineage bridge to maintain contacts and organize intergenerational activities. This bridging generation is in the most strategic position to affect intergenerational transmissions and is, therefore, both the most frequent mediator, if not the actual instigator, of intergenerational change and at the same time the chief liaison for maintaining intergenerational continuity.

Under conditions of rapid economic and social change, each generational cohort encounters at marriage a unique set of historical constraints and incentives which influence the timing of its crucial life decisions, making for marked generational dissimilarities in life cycle career patterns. To some extent each generation is bounded in its career choices by its peculiar biography. The career strategies of life cycle management involving the timing of one's marriage, the number and spacing of children, the changes of jobs by the husband, the wife's entry or reentry into the labor force, and the timing of acquisitions of homes, durables, life insurance and investments are therefore selectively dissimilar for each generation.

Nevertheless, intergenerational continuity three generations in depth occurs with respect to such expressive patterns as religious affiliation and residence location and in many instances of generational upgrading of economic and educational competences there is change in one generation followed by continuity of the new pattern into the third generation. We theorize that the middle generation, as the lineage bridge, is functioning to maintain the cohesion and solidarity which would make possible both continuity in three generation depth and selective discontinuity followed by continuity two generations in depth.

Under conditions of economic growth and increasing predictability of the political economy, successive generations of the same family line experience not only upgrading in performance in all spheres of economic activity but an acceleration in performance from generation to generation. There is better synchronization of changes in family composition requiring improved housing through residential moves, and in turn closer synchronization of residential changes with the acquisition of needed durables by the youngest generation as compared with the older generations for the early years of the marriage span. Indeed, the family's several career achievements are increasingly contingent, success in achieving one status change in phase being increasingly contingent upon successful timing of other career changes. We may theorize that the observed acceleration in upgrading from generation to generation reflects increasing responsiveness by successive generations to this interdependence of career achievements. Among contemporary generational cohorts, for example, the grandparent generation proved relatively non-responsive, constrained as it was by lack of competence in controlling family size, by low range of income, limited occupational alternatives and constricted housing possibilities; the middle generation got off to a slow start in the depths of the economic depression, but was more responsive and planful in child spacing, even though erratic in its synchronization of careers, leading in selected careers at the expense of lagging in others. The youngest generation, whose entire marriage span has been spent under conditions of rising affluence of a managed economy making available multiple options has been the most responsive of the three generations, achieving closest fit among its several career achievements, suggesting the best life cycle planning and management to date.

Good life cycle management reflected in leading one's generation in several areas of economic achievement over the life span is greatly facilitated by circumstances of beginning marriage—how much education the spouses bring to marriage, the income potential at marriage, age of spouses at marriage, and the number and spacing of children early in the marriage. Delaying marriage until education has been completed and both spouses-to-be have had some labor force experience, limiting offspring to a small number, gives couples a headstart not only in income and the economic bargaining power of a good education, but an opportunity to develop the kind of family organization and marital climate for making good collective decisions about the timing of acquisitions of home, durable goods, and protective insurances. Making decisions responsibly early in the marriage keeps open options for better career management over the entire life span.

The same identical syndrome of higher educational and occupational expertise, flexible rather than restrictive family organization, and high marital communication which facilitates good life cycle management is linked with higher consumership, higher volume of planning, greater rationality in choice-making and more preplanning of actions. Indeed, leading in achievements over the life span links up with subsequent consumership performance in much the same way that scholastic achievements in high school predict subsequent college and professional performances. Moderating these *necessary* but *not sufficient* properties associated with both good career management and high consumership are many essentially developmental incentives and constraints to which each successive generation has responded differently, with the married child generation having highest success. Age of spouses interacts with number and age composition of children and with lags in income to increase the level of unmet needs at the same time that these depress the planfulness and rationality of decision-making required for optimum resource management. Thus, without social intervention, families with lowest per capita income and the greatest unmet needs at the beginning of the life cycle are likely not to improve but to deteriorate over time in their consumership patterns leaving them in a continuous state of secondary poverty.

The family consumption cycle fortunately has a potential feedback mechanism, in satisfactions and dissatisfactions experienced, which in evaluating the wisdom of the choices made and the actions undertaken may perform a monitoring function if critically used or serve as a tranquilizer if used defensively.

In contemporary families the feedback mechanism is used most critically by the youngest generation which is also the most likely to preplan its actions. The mechanism appears to be used to discriminate among good and poor decisions since those actions which were undertaken after consultations inside and outside the family and after weighing alternatives (depicting high rationality of decision-making) received high satisfaction scores in all generations. Use of the evaluation mechanism as a tranquilizer to mask the deficiencies of actions chosen on the other hand, appears to be highest in families of low income and low plan fulfillment, precisely where the need for monitoring and negative feedback is greatest. We theorize that the critical use of the feedback mechanism may be instrumental in changing and possibly upgrading family consumership practices since high satisfaction with outcomes appears to be continuous within family lines over three generations, whereas dissatisfaction with action outcomes tends not to persist by family lines but to change from generation to generation, encouraging, thereby, improved consumership patterns in the next generation.

CHAPTER XIV

Applying the Research Findings for Families

THE PERCEPTIVE READER will already have identified many implications of findings for needed changes in family practices, for new programs of training for families, and for necessary modification in local and national policies affecting families. It is our intention in this closing chapter to make explicit the applications which seem indicated, distinguishing between those which are possible for families to undertake without professional help, those which necessitate professional attention, and those which require legislative enactments to facilitate family development. Our objective will be to suggest ways of upgrading families as consumption units. Most of the recent emphasis of social intervention has been on the family as a socialization unit to improve its child care and personality shaping practices. This chapter focusses on the more managerial type practices of family heads in resource use and life cycle management for which there is scanty precedent even in consumer education.

Findings Which Family Heads Can Utilize Directly

Because this three generation study is what Nelson Foote[1] has dubbed "functional research," that is research with which readers can identify because they can see themselves in the findings, an important level of application will be of the self-help variety. Family decision makers should be able to see themselves in the discussions of pre-planning purchases, of help exchanges with kinsmen, and of synchronizing actions in career management.

We would like to begin this discussion of applications by family heads to upgrade the performance of families as problem solving

---

[1] "The Appraisal of Family Research", *MARRIAGE AND FAMILY LIVING*, XIX (February, 1957), pp. 92-99.

groups by drawing from a feedback report by Roy H. Rodgers of our staff to the more than three hundred families who collaborated with us on this project. The report personalizes the research to maximize its functionality for the collaborating readers.

As we told you when we first contacted you, this study has been interested in how families over the generations have met the problems of managing and getting ahead. Because this was our most important interest, each time we visited with you we tried to find out something about what your family was doing in seven different areas of family life: These were (1) the location and characteristics of your home—whether you have moved or were planning to move, (2) the maintenance of your home—whether you had done any remodeling or redecoration and whether you were planning to do any, (3) the acquiring and plans for acquiring various kinds of durable goods and equipment—household appliances, furniture, automobiles, and the like, (4) the occupation of the breadwinners in the family—whether they had changed jobs or intended to change, (5) the makeup of the household—whether you had added or lost any members, either children, relatives who came to live with you, or roomers, (6) the schooling of family members—whether there were plans for changing or going back to school other than the usual changes occurring for children in the public or parochial schools, and (7) your financial status—your savings, investments, and insurance coverage. In addition to finding out what you were doing about these things during the year we visited with you, we also tried to get a complete history on most of these areas since your marriage. Basically, our reason for asking about these things was to find out just how different families made up their minds about what to do about these questions which every family has to answer in one way or another.

As you look around you, in your neighborhood or in your community, we are sure that you know people who seem always to be able to do pretty much what they want to do. Others, however, seem never to get where they want to go. Perhaps you have thought this was just "the breaks" of life. We believe that it is something more than luck. We believe that some people have discovered that there are certain ways of handling their time, their talent and abilities, and their money and possessions—regardless of how much of each of these they may have—in such a way that they do gain the things in life that they want most. Believing this to be true, we wanted to find out what it was about these families that seemed to have all the "good luck" and what it was about the families that seemed to have all the "bad luck" that made them so much different.

What are some of the things we have learned? First of all, we learned that in a typical three- to four-month period most families made changes in at least one of the seven areas studied. These changes could be anything from moving to buying a new washer or refrigerator to painting the kitchen. The married children made more changes than any other generation, averaging about four changes during the period. Grandparents averaged only about one change in the period, with about half of them making no changes at all. The parent generation stood someplace in between, making an average of between two and three changes. This means that *families must cope with changes* in their living conditions whether they would like to do so or not. Since this is true, it seems far better that they learn to do so in the best possible manner.

Secondly, we learned that only about a third of the changes that occurred had been planned in advance—that is, you had been able to tell us on our first visit that you would have moved, for example, by the time we visited with you a second time. In addition, we learned that about one-fourth of all the planned changes which you told us about on our first visit were not carried out by the time we visited you the second time. And the rest of the changes which occurred (about 40 per cent) had not been expected by you at all at the time of our first visit. This means, then, that for the most part, families do not seem to be able to predict as far as three months in advance what they will be doing in these seven areas.

Does this mean that they will be dissatisfied with these changes because they seem to have so little control over them? You tell us that the answer to this question is usually "no". You seem to be as satisfied with the unplanned changes as you are with the planned ones. You are much more likely to be *dissatisfied* with the plans you were unable to carry out.

Family policies and their effect upon planning and control of changes. We learned an interesting thing about these changes. In about 73 per cent of the changes that you had planned, you had what we have chosen to call a "policy" to follow in making the change. Just what is a "family policy"? Well, some of you told us that when you looked for a home you wanted at least a separate bedroom for the boys and one for the girls, in addition to one for the parents. Others spoke of a policy of always redecorating every three years. With regard to purchases, you told us that, "We always buy quality so it will last", or "When it costs too much to repair an item, we replace it with the best one we can get", or "We pay cash to avoid carrying charges and we never buy anything that isn't a bargain". Thus, when you made a change, you had a principle or rule to guide you in making the choice. Interestingly enough, the plans which you failed to fulfill *seemed to have policies only about one-third of the time.* The changes which you made that you hadn't planned to make were covered by a policy far more often—about half the time.

What does this mean? We think that it means that when families sit down in advance and decide just how it is they will go about handling the changes in any particular area of life, they have a better chance of making their plans come about. Even when some unexpected emergency comes up they can handle it because they know how they want to handle it in advance.

Multiple occurrence of changes. Few changes seem to occur alone. That is, when you make one change, this often makes it necessary to make other changes. The important thing to realize is that while the first change is often planned, the other changes are often not planned. For example, it is often true that families plan to redecorate or remodel a part of their home. They fail, however, to plan for the purchases which such changes may make necessary, such as new curtains, rugs, or furnishings which now seem essential to make the job complete. As a matter of fact, purchases of durable goods and household furnishings seem very frequently to be a result of changes in other areas of family living, appearing to indicate that it is fairly common to buy new things when you move, remodel, or redecorate, add or lose members in the household, change jobs, and so forth.

In sum, *when changes occur in more than two areas,* more *unplanned* changes occur, and in addition, more plans are postponed or never get carried out at all. This would appear to mean that families who try to do too many things at one time have less control over what happens than those who try to do only one or two things at a time.

Differential activity and control according to area of activity. Now that we have found that you are usually more satisfied with fulfilled plans than with unfulfilled ones, and that policies seem to help you make decisions, let us look for a minute at where most changes seem to occur.

Most frequently you told us about making changes in the purchase of durable goods and in the realm of financial holdings such as savings, investments, and insurance. You made changes in your household makeup and in the outside services far less often. Another area of great activity in many families is the redecorating and remodeling of their homes.

You can predict best changes in schooling, residence, and finances. Changes in *occupation and purchases of automobiles and durable goods* are more likely to be unplanned. The failure to carry out your plans occurs most often in the areas of redecorating and remodeling. *Financial changes, we find, have policies governing them in over 50 per cent of the cases, indicating that the policy helps families know what is going to happen.* On the other hand, changes in occupation are often completely out of your hands—since they often depend on the needs of the employer rather than on family needs. In this area, too, policies are seldom expressed by families. Changes in durable goods occur so frequently, and as we have seen, are so often linked with other changes, that they quite often cannot be predicted three months in advance. These purchases, however, are made in accordance with a policy over half the time. Policies are also present in redecorating and remodeling more than half the time, indicating that lack of fulfillment may be the result of considerable discussion.

We think we can learn at least three things from this: first, some things are so important and happen so seldom that they demand conscious planning well in advance; second, other things seem to be almost completely out of the control of family members; and thirdly, a number of things, though not planned in advance, nevertheless are under the control of the family because they make the changes in accordance with a policy which they have formed well ahead of time. In summary, then, aside from job changes, which appear to be less controllable, families are able to control their lives through the use of policies, *even when they cannot predict in advance what may happen to them*. The families which have developed policies seem to be most content with their changes.

Effect of generation on changes and control. There is another important fact about this matter of controlling changes in the family. As we pointed out earlier, married children make many more changes than grandparents, with the parents falling someplace in between. The grandparents, however, more often fulfill their plans while at the same time make the most unplanned changes. They are usually satisfied with the outcomes. Parents less often fulfill plans and make many unplanned changes and are nevertheless, the *most* satisfied with what happens. The married children, on the other hand, have more plans and preplan more of their actions than any other generation. At the same time, they are less satisfied with the results.

What can we learn from this? It is true that children are involved in many more changes than any of the other generations. You will remember we said earlier that the more changes that occurred, the less likely it was that there was complete control over them. This may be one of the facts of life for young married people. Life moves especially fast for them and things happen so quickly that they cannot always anticipate what will happen. It appears most important, therefore, for younger people to formulate policies in order to handle this fast pace of living. Our study shows that the married child generation does seem to have more policies than the other generations. Perhaps it is also inevitable with so many things happening that they cannot possibly be satisfied with everything that occurs. Moreover, dissatisfaction with the outcome of actions taken may be used to upgrade future consumer choices.

In this regard, we find some encouraging facts—especially for the younger generation. We find that those families who do the most discussing of plans in advance among themselves, who talk things over with others outside their immediate family, and who do more "shopping around" before they make changes seem to have the most control over changes and seem to be happiest with the decisions they finally make. This probably sounds like "good common sense," yet we find that many families have not learned to do this, and these are the families who seem to obtain fewer of the things they would like to have out of life.

Unmentioned in Rodgers' feedback report to the cooperating families because the relevant data had not yet been analyzed were several findings about the amount of interdependence observed among the nuclear families of the three generations as well as a number of generalizations about career management which family heads might be able to put to work. To what extent does the family helping pattern among the generations aid nuclear families to shape their careers better? Do young couples learn effective methods for making career decisions from their parents? Does the independent couple succeed or suffer in the long run from its refusal to accept material help and advice from parents and grandparents? To what extent is the grandparent generation beneficiary of support from the other two generations, thus equalizing the advantages these have over the oldest generation?

For those families interested in the preservation of their kinship ties the research offers abundant evidence of the normative support for maintaining strong kinship networks. Endorsement of the norms of kinship obligations and kin activities increases from the oldest to the youngest generation in our three generation sample. Behaviorally, the intergenerational sharing of activities, visiting and helping are three generations in depth with most activity (contacts averaging one or more weekly) occurring among adjacent generations. The success or failure of the kinship network leans heavily on the *kinkeeping middle generation* which serves as the *lineage bridge* across the generations, being most involved with its adjacent generations both in intergenerational contacts and in help exchanges. Family heads might well examine their own kin-keeping responsibilities against these findings to prepare for lineage bridging if they are coming into the ages of the middle generation and to be supportive of the kinkeepers if they are not.

There is also good evidence that families engaged in intergenerational help exchanges are evening out the inequities which occur among the generations due to the unequal resources available to them over the marriage span. The middle generation tends to be the advantaged one economically compared to their retired parents and their child burdened children, and gives more to parents and to married children than it receives back from either, thus evening out some of the inequities. Each generation, however, contributes to and draws from the kinship network in terms of its capacities and needs: The oldest generaion in its eighties gives least but, nevertheless, helps economically and provides services downward and receives substantial help with household management and illness. The middle generation gives most in money and services and emotional support and receives heavy inputs of emotional support. The youngest generation provides services in case of illness and household help with much emotional support and receives primarily child care and economic help. Thus, a substantial transfer of money, goods, services, and psychic solace occur in communal fashion, much of it without expectation of reciprocity in kind. The relative headstart that the youngest generation appears to have over its predecessors is probably partly due to these intergenerational transfers. Because strains are introduced among the generations when help appears to move predominantly one way, family heads may find it necessary to modify the usual norms of filial obligation and reciprocity which have legitimized current kinship exchanges with a moratorium from these norms for the newly married until they reach economic maturity and to extend a similar moratorium for the aged after retirement.

From the several research findings about career management problems, the issues of timing of crucial rites of passage appear most relevant for family heads since the issue of timing many actions involves decisions undertaken by young adults in consultation with parents. Parents should note the striking advantages in later economic achievements which couples have in postponing marriage until higher education has been completed, the advantages in having had some occupational experience before marriage for both spouses, and the advantages of timing the number and spacing of children so that they will not all be in college and getting married at the same time. Such couples tend to have a headstart not only in income and economic bargaining power of a good education but also tend to develop an equalitarian form of family organization and a favorable marital climate for making good decisions. Making prudent decisions about these matters of timing, taking into account long-term consequences as well as short-term satisfactions, distinguishes the successful from the unsuccessful in life cycle management.

Implications for Social Policy Changes

There are many determinants of consumership and good career management which appear to be beyond the control of individual families or even local educational and social service agencies. We need to ask how contemporary social policies with respect to education, manpower, and welfare constrain and limit the family as a consumption unit.

The educational level of spouses, for one, appears prominent as a determinant of all indices of consumership and as a significant correlate of the family's economic achievements over the entire life span. The upgrading in education from generation to generation was much less from parent to married child generation than from the grandparent to the parent generation. But, the significance of education in differentiating high from low consumership is not decreasing but increasing from generation to generation. To encourage better consumer practices a policy of low interest loans and scholarships would seem to be indicated to maintain adolescents of both sexes in school and to combine labor force experience with higher education for both sexes before entering marriage. Towards the same end would be a policy encouraging parents to keep their children in school by making costs of higher education tax deductible. This might have the effect also of delaying marriage and child bearing until the young adult children are competent to support a family.

The most effective planners of consumption in the study combined high education of spouses, and gainful employment and high social participation of wife. To make this combination more frequent would require more scholarship aid for women, day care services for preschool children, a wide range of part-time positions for well-educated women, and maternity leave privileges for married women. There might also need to be developed a system of housecleaning services to minimize the housekeeping tasks carried by the employed mother.

On the negative side of consumership is the discovery that precocious marriage and parenthood, large family size, and low income are associated with low consumership on a short-run basis and with lagging one's marital cohort in economic achievements over the entire span under the defeating conditions of secondary poverty. Moreover, these unintended poverty patterns tend to be transmitted from generation to generation unless broken by social intervention. What is needed is a welfare policy which would enable parents to maintain their adolescent children at home and in school through educational allowances or guaranteed annual income accompanied by a program of sex education and marriage education in the schools to encourage delayed marriage and discourage premature parenthood until the adolescents obtain the requisite training and occupational experience to make a good start in marriage.[1]

Of equal import is the discovery that nuclear families are integrated into modified extended family networks three generations in depth. These networks should be recognized publicly as problem solving resources of some moment. Current social policy largely ignores the

---

[1] See further documentation for such a policy in Joan Aldous and Reuben Hill, "Strategies for Breaking the Poverty Cycle", *Social Work* (July, 1969).

presence of functioning three generation networks in favor of the nuclear family unit. Under some welfare laws, to be sure, punitive policies, require that economic resources of kinsmen be exhausted before economic assistance may be given to needy families. Fortunately, perhaps, these policies are largely honored in the breech.[2] What is needed is a policy which rewards intergeneration transfers for educational, professional, and health objectives, recognizing the enormous social gains achieved through these exchanges and supporting a type of modified extended familism which cements intergenerational relationships. This would, in turn, encourage social agencies to treat the kinship network more as a problem solving resource in depth than as a source of problems in boundary maintenance of the basic nuclear family unit.[3]

Needless to say, the findings of this study offer documentation for the importance of maintaining the economy at a high level of activity with high employment levels, accessibility of goods, and fiscal stability. The sluggishness of the economy and the constraints of limited occupational movement for most of the child rearing years of the grandparent generation and the subsequent trauma of the country-wide depression constrained this oldest generation to lifetime careers of limited achievements. By today's standards this generation was never far above the poverty line. The middle generation encountered a sick economy early in its family cycle. It began marriage under the discouraging conditions of the great depression of the thirties which made for a slow start but has reared and launched its children under conditions of war-born prosperity and the new economics of a managed economy. The youngest generation has never known a depressed economy and is the most endowed of the three generations in its career achievements to date. Although the most active in undertaking actions, this generation is also the most planful and the most rational in its consumership. There appears to have been upgrading in consumership from generation to generation coincident with the development of a prosperous and managed economy. It should be noted, however, that a period of uncontrolled inflation could destroy the rationale for rational consumership by encouraging unplanned buying today to avoid the higher prices of tomorrow.

[2] See discussion by Alvin L. Schorr of "Social Security and Filial Responsibility", in his provocative collection of essays, *Exploration in Social Policy*, New York: Basic Books, 1968, pp. 101-123.
[3] See the discussion of this issue in Hope Leichter and William E. Mitchell, *Kinship and Social Casework*, New York: Russell Sage, 1967, pp. 185-263.

Implications for Programs of Adult Socialization in Consumership

In reviewing the several hundred findings of the study and the several miniature theories adduced from them in Chapter XIII, it is apparent that neither changing the economic arrangements of the social system nor informing families of the chief findings would be adequate to bring about some of the key changes indicated. Some training programs of couples by skilled professionals would appear necessary to achieve the competency high consumership requires.

Although training for all occupations was once provided by apprenticeships within the family virtually all occupations today require extra-familial socialization. Even farming and the arts of homemaking, including food preparation and clothing design, which were once taught exclusively within the family require outside adult tutelage to achieve high quality performance. Some such professional programs of training in the aptitudes and values required for family career management and consumership appears necessary to upgrade the performances of family heads as planners, decision makers, and consumers.

The model for the professional service would not be the *therapeutic model*—restoration of the *status quo ante* by remedial therapy, nor the *public health model of prevention* which makes the assumption that health is the absence of disease and, therefore, that the professional task is to prevent disease or malfunctioning. A new *developmental model* is indicated where the emphasis would be on families *realizing* their *potentialities* as instruments for achieving long-term goals through more adroit career management. This is *family development* in the sense of the group transcending itself as it moves through the several crises of transition that mark off the major changes in family composition over the life span.

The stance of the professional worker using the *developmental model* is best exemplified by the master teacher, the play director, or the athletic coach whose approach seeks to stimulate the group to realize its greatest potentialities by increasingly excellent performances.

From the research findings, the helping professional can identify a number of behaviors which, if modified, should result in improved consumership. The conceptual framework and the intergenerational research design have generated data also which suggest alternative strategies for bringing about change. For example, the several stages of the marriage span made explicit by the developmental histories of the three generations, differ so much in the problems encountered that any program of training in consumership should surely be differentiated by critical stages of family development. In such differentiated programs, the three phases of the consumption process, although treated separately analytically in the research, are so interrelated that programs of training should seek to upgrade performance in all three indicators of consumership. At still another level the findings on comparative career achievements of the generations beg that attention be given to the strategies of career management, to the intercontingency of careers over the life cycle, and to the construction of family policies to cover long-term goals and the appropriate means to reach them. Finally, the challenge has also been rendered salient by the study to provide training to family heads in evaluating their consumership achievements. Specific attention should be given in training to insure that assessment serve as a critical feedback monitoring mechanism to upgrade consumership rather than as a defensive mechanism of rationalizing away bad decisions.

Differentiated Programs of Training for Couples by Stage of Development

We propose three stages in the marriage span when professional training programs might have maximum effect: (1) with newly married couples just working out their consumership patterns, (2) with childrearing couples encountering the pressures of numbers on resources and the necessity of eliciting needs of children, and (3) with couples concerned with the social placement of their children in jobs and marriage. An argument could also be made for training couples in the postparental period for entering the retirement status since they face major income management problems with decreased income and mounting medical needs, but we will seek to anticipate some of these issues in the discussion of the third phase. The content of training for each of these stages would necessarily differ markedly since the issues of judgment encountered by couples in these three stages are so different. The findings of the study offer a number of suggesions which we will wish to consider.

A Program for the Newly Married

The couple just recently married is still working out procedures for arriving at decisions as a couple without much guidance from any source. Engaged and newly married couples are left pretty much alone to fend for themselves.[1] Friends, kinsmen, and even parents tend to respect the privacy of the newly married for several weeks after the ceremony. Yet, during this critical transition of getting married (engagement, wedding, and honeymoon), many decisions are made which determine the couple's life style for months to come, such as where they will live, the amenities of the dwelling, the composition of the initial inventory of durable goods as between time savers, time fillers, and comforts, the type of work each spouse will follow, the division of household tasks in the home, and the scheduling of the weekly work and play rhythms. This is a period of maximum learning and emptiest of formal or informal programs of teaching and of training.

What content might be especially appropriate for training the newly marrieds? The research findings about the peculiar problems and competencies needed to achieve high consumership among the couples of the married child generation are especially suggestive for such a program.

From our research findings we know that the most recently married of the child generation (1-4 years married) have the highest volume of plans, and among these, the childless are outranked only by new parents in number of plans. The childless are twice as likely, however, to postpone plans than are child rearing couples, suggesting more indiscriminate planning. The childless newly married are less rational in their decision making and are greater risk takers in the sheer volume of actions undertaken than couples farther along in the life cycle. In acting on plans, the childless fulfill a high proportion of their time specific plans but have low fulfillment of indefinite plans. Moreover, they are less likely to be dissatisfied with decisions made than more seasoned child rearing couples, suggesting some use of the evaluation mechanism as a tranquilizer rationalizing their more impulsive decisions rather than as a critical feedback mechanism. The childless newly married, although lower in absolute income than older couples, have more discretionary income which enables them to undertake more actions without pre-planning.

Still other findings link up marital authority pattern, marital communication, and marital integration with consumership for this early stage of the family cycle. Marital communication and marital integration tend to be lower and wife dominance higher among the

---

[1] See Reuben Hill and Joan Aldous, "Socialization for Marriage and Parenthood" in David Goslin, ed., *Handbook of Socialization Theory and Research,* Chicago: Rand McNally, 1969, pp. 885-951.

newly married than among more seasoned couples. There is, therefore, room for training in marital communication and in role taking to increase indirectly the couple's competence as consumers, since equalitarian relations and communication are positively related to rationality in decision-making and for newlyweds, marital integration is positively related to pre-planning consumer actions.

A training program for newly married couples might profitably focus, therefore, both on improving consumership in the short run and in anticipating the issues of life cycle management in the long run. In the short run, emphasis on greater specificity of plans and on the components of rationality in decision making, particularly in the search for information about alternative problem solutions, would go far towards upgrading the consumership of this age group. In addition, sharpening the assessment function by challenging halo whitewashing of bad decisions and supporting negative feedback would be important for these beginning couples.

On the long-run issues of life cycle management, emphasis in training should be on making long-term goals explicit and formulating policies designed to cover both priorities and time scheduling. Such training would enable this beginning cohort to anticipate the demands of the immediate and intermediate future more effectively. It would be particularly timely to establish policies with respect to number and spacing of children as these affect the later education plans for children.

A corollary program of training would upgrade the couple's internal system of spousal communication and authority allocation in the interest of enabling the couple to make better consumer choices before taking action on them.

In the course of training this newly married cohort to perform at a higher level of competence in decision making and career planning, the trainers should take into account the couple's transactions with their kinsmen since a certain number of plans and actions may be facilitated by decisions made by parents and grandparents. The first years of marriage are both concerned with achieving independence from parents and of maintaining kinship ties in exchanges which are mutually beneficial to the generations involved. A novel training program would recruit not only newly married couples but both sets of parents to examine the issues with which they are all involved, such as subsidies for continued education, for setting up housekeeping or making downpayments on a home for which both sets of parents may be expected to make some contributions.

Training for Child Rearing Families

The most difficult time in the life span for the family to serve as an effective unit of consumption is during the early child rearing period. How can parents know what the needs of infants and young children are which now must be met to make for maximum child growth? Is it sufficient to provide children with food, clothing, and shelter? How much space and what kinds of facilities and equipment are needed to insure physical, mental, and emotional growth of children and how much does one child differ from another in these needs? How soon should parents seek to involve children themselves in choosing their own consumption goods? New parents are singularly lacking in information about these matters and even about where such information can be obtained.

The research findings throw relatively little light on these pressing questions which are so relevant to effective consumership in early parenthood. They do tell us that it is not the childless but the child rearing couples of the married child generation who make the most plans (suggesting high needs) and that the number of plans increases sharply with the first child and declines with each added child, as if parents cut back the volume of plans as their discretionary income decreases. The findings tell us also that residential mobility increases sharply with the addition of the first and remains associated with added children at a declining rate. Marital agreement suffers with added children, but couples do become increasingly communicative and equalitarian in decision making. As consumers, child rearing couples are the most effective in pre-planning their actions, have the highest rationality scores of any cohort in the study, and are the most likely to be dissatisfied with their consumption decisions. Moreover, the more educated the husband in these child rearing couples is, the more likely they are to be dissatisfied, suggesting that they are utilizing dissatisfaction as a monitor to improve their consumership. What isn't known because children were not interviewed is what children would have said about how satisfied they were with given actions taken, i.e., with residential changes and durable goods acquisitions with which they were concerned. In future studies, assessments should be elicited from children as well as parents.

A program of training for child rearing couples should focus on improving communication between children and parents and on greater involvement of children in middle childhood in the generating of plans for consumption actions as well as assessing satisfaction with choices made and actions taken. There might well be included parental training in role taking accuracy with children to further the process of consultation with children as well as encouraging information search among experts in arriving at decisions with respect to the needs of growing children.

Career management issues also beg attention with parents of growing children. Although this is a period in which family consumption is already high, educational plans may require savings now to assure college educations for children. Life insurance and retirement provisions should also have been built into the savings program from the beginning of parenthood but would again be subject to review in any training program examining issues of life cycle management. Is it better policy to sacrifice some short-term consumption now, such as adequate housing and time-filling durables which children value, to assure their education and social placement later, or wait and take these latter costs out of current income at the time children enter college? These are questions of career management on which life insurance underwriters and consumption economists are prepared to provide authoritative data in a program of training.

A Training Program for the Family at Launching Time

There may be some parents who regard the function of social placement as of minor importance and still others who assert that any overt intervention to advance one's adult offspring is undemocratic and nepotistic. Nevertheless, few parents can ignore the responsibilities of doing what they can to give their young adult children a good start if it is in their power to do so. Does consumership for this stage of family development involve such social placement issues and can training by professionals to improve families' performances be provided? What other issues more narrowly focused on the family as a consumption unit are faced at launching time?

We know from our research findings that the launching period for the contemporary parent generation families began with the marriage of the first child in about the twentieth year of marriage and was completed for the majority of families by about the twenty-seventh year of marriage as compared with the grandparent generation families whose children began leave-taking in the twenty-third year and extended their departures into the thirty-fourth year of marriage. Although they now receive a more prolonged education, children are married off earlier and more rapidly today than they were a generation ago.

Other findings about financial aid exchanged between the generations proves conclusively that marrying children off doesn't mean an end to financial outlays to children. Almost half of the married children in this study acknowledged receiving some financial help from parents or grandparents, whereas less than a fifth of the middle generation benefitted from such help from their kinsmen. For those parents now in the launching period, it is apparent that they are giving disproportionately in two directions, to their own aged parents and to their marrying and married children. Fortunately for them, they do have some discretionary income to allocate. The husband is at his peak of earning power and his wife, in many cases, is gainfully employed so that together they are producing the highest income of their earning careers.

But parents also face some problems of career management of their own in this period. There is the unpleasant fact of a limited earning span left to them within which to accumulate a sufficient nest egg for retirement. Parents also face in this period declining needs for residential space (except when children and grandchildren come to visit) and the necessity of stabilizing the acquisitions of durable goods. The need is critical to reappraise family expenditure policies which have been largely oriented to the changing needs of growing children to take into account the couple's own personal and retirement needs. Thus, filial and parental obligations complete with spousal and personal needs, because in the postparental period following launching, preparation for retirement, and pressures for some reduction in the couple's level of living due to reduced income will be issues begging for attention. Training programs for the launching period will, therefore, need to take all of these issues into account.

From the research findings about the consumership of the parent generation at launching time, it would appear that such families are not the most planful of consumers. They are characterized by high needs, middle rationality in decision making, middle performance in preplanning actions, and high satisfaction scores in assessing these actions. This is hardly distinctively high consumership in comparison with the achievements of the child rearing families of the married child generation, although it is substantially better than the record for the retired grandparents. Other behaviors associated with this middle range consumership of the launching families suggest that this may be a more relaxed and less pressured period of family development for the incumbents. Indeed these families see themselves as having a flexible family organization, equalitarian in decision making with much role sharing by spouses, and with role crossing and even role reversals in performing household tasks, even though most wives are not working. The marital climate is pleasant but with variable marital integration and variable levels of marital communication.

A training program devised for families to cope with the issues of launching and postparental living would be a novelty, indeed, and should be regarded as quite experimental. There is room for upgrading the decision-making and preplanning of launching families. Not infrequently they appear to move directly on issues into action taking without preplanning and with a minimum of outside consultation and searching for alternative solutions. It is as if these seasoned couples were operating on the basis of agreements or policies long since worked out. At another level, however, the relatively low agreement on goals registered by this cohort would call this explanation into question. In any event, there is room for improvement in decision-making procedures which a training program might work on, including some attention to a more critical evaluation of actions taken. Beyond this, the new and unique issues of consumership rendered salient by this study do require attention in a training program; namely, improvement in the couple's judgments about their kin-keeping obligations, the extent of financial aid, and how much counseling to offer both the younger and older generations about their own consumer decisions. The middle generation needs a type of training in performing this kin-keeping function for which no program has yet been devised, and in the process of constructing such a program this generation will make contributions to the lore of "practice wisdom" for future generations of helping professionals.

In quick overview, the advantage of undertaking differentiated training programs for families at different stages of family development should now be clear. The issues being faced stage by stage are quite different, the time span perspectives differ, and the typical strengths and errors of consumership vary by stage of development. In assessing the potential contributions of the three differentiated programs, it looks to us as if the highest priority should be assigned to training programs for newly married couples facing the critical transition of "getting married", since so many of the determinants for later success or failure are laid down in the family policies and life styles developed in the first years of marriage. It is as if to win the race in life cycle management, "getting off to a good start" were of equal importance to the strategy of pacing the race thereafter.

Training in Strategies of Career Management vs. Expertise in Short-Run Consumership

We want to focus attention in this section on the competences required to shape a family's several careers over the life span. From our research findings it appears that successful careers are made up of more than a series of rational decisions involving here-and-now issues. They require training that goes beyond short-run consumership! It is also important to anticipate the intercontingency of decisions affecting movement in several careers and to develop a strategy for synchronizing actions to maximize returns from several moves in the same time periods. Wisdom in timing of career changes is an added competence for which training should be instituted.

Documentation for these recommendations is not hard to find. Most of the families studied were incapable of predicting more than a fraction of their actions more than three months in advance. When changes in more than one area occurred, they were inclined to make even less accurate predictions. Changes in areas that were intercontingent, such as family composition, residential location, remodeling, financial changes, job changes, and acquisitions of durable goods were not foreseen as a package even though later events showed that they often occurred in lock-step. Residential location changes were best predicted but not the sequelae of remodeling or redecoration or durable goods acquisitions and financial changes. Moreover, the sequelae were usually less adequately searched for alternatives before taking action, suggesting families were acted upon, rather than initiating the changes autonomously. From examination of the longitudinal data obtained retrospectively, it is clear that leading one's generation in one area was highly associated with leading in several other areas of activity, suggesting intercontingency of these areas over the life span. Moreover, timing of one's marriage later, associated with higher education before entering the labor force, and bearing fewer children were contributors to this successful synchronizing of activities, underlining the importance of timing these crucial life decisions.

Training in the construction of family policies constitutes another aspect of career management. The family policy is a guiding strategy or principle which bridges short-run consumer decisions and the long-run structuring of the future of life cycle management. In Rodgers' discussion earlier in the chapter, the utility of family policies was illustrated. Newly married couples rarely begin marriage with a ready-made set of policies, but do carry over an acquaintance with them from the parental families.

In the interests of economy of discussion time, policies are informally developed in many families which cover the couple's long-term goals and the means they are willing to employ to attain them. Family policies were discovered in this study for the use of credit; for setting aside savings for vacations, children's education, and books over status symbols such as current make cars, modern conspicuous housing and furnishings; for familistic activities with children and kin rather than social climbing, for gift giving to kinsmen and friends, for borrowing, and so on. These policies provided priorities for assessing consumption expenditures both as to what to buy and as to timing of purchases. They appeared to be used by many families as a protection against pressures of sales personnel and the blandishments of the mass media. Like the family budget which evens out the valleys and peaks of expenditures from current income by building up balances from which to draw for annual large ticket items, the family policy structures present consumption in such a way that future needs are prepared for.

Once a couple has developed policies to cover recurring needs and the timing of taking action on longer run goals, the day-to-day consumer decisions are greatly facilitated and many of the eight components in the rationality of decision formula (Table 9.01) can be telescoped with great savings of time and energy. Nevertheless, some decisions involving large expenditures and complex negotiations, such as a change of residential location, change of profession and return to school, even if covered by a prior family policy might still justify taking all eight steps in the rationality of decision formula before arriving at a firm family decision.

It is not entirely clear at this writing whether or not the construction of family policies can be incorporated into professionally-operated training programs, although programs which have included the teaching of family budgeting have been widely adopted in the secondary schools and colleges. The most strategic point in the marriage span for such training to be undertaken, however, would be with newly married couples who are confronting the need for policies most acutely. In working with couples later in the cycle, the emphasis in training should be on reviewing the appropriateness of family policies which had been formulated for an earlier era of family need. It will be remembered from the research findings reported earlier that there was some variability among families in evaluating actions taken, depending on the extent to which they were covered by family policies. There was a marked tendency to be more satisfied with policy-covered than non-covered actions. It may be important with older couples, who are less critical anyway, to ascertain if family policies have the effect of endowing policy covered actions with "rightness" which isn't merited by the objective facts of the case.

Training family heads in the synchronization of consumer actions to achieve maximum returns might profitably draw from the type of management games in which executives are trained to generate alternative strategies for achieving goals involving serveral intersecting and parallel paths. Players would need to distinguish between givens which they cannot change and variables under their control. In the family life cycle management games to be developed, the players would need to role take with other decision-makers in their network such as parents, employers, and others whose decisions would intersect with and modify their own. Scenarios might be created for simulating changes not only within a year's period but over longer time spans to illuminate the critical importance of timing of career changes in getting ahead, such as the timing of marriage, the spacing of births, the assumption of home ownership, and the timing of job changes. The games would make apparent what decisions tended to close off or open up options much later in the family cycle, when the social placement of children and the securing of an independent retirement situation would have high saliency.

Training in Evaluation of Actions

There is probably no dimension of consumership more difficult for family heads to master without professional help than the subjective assessment of satisfaction or dissatisfaction with outcomes of the actions taken. Yet, effective critical assessment of the wisdom of choices made, that is, fed back to the decision-makers in time to be used in future choices, may be the major stimulus for upgrading a family's consumership and innovating new practices.

This study has been one of the first to test the classical economists' assumption that rationality acts to increase satisfaction, more effectively joining ends and means, as compared with decision processes characterized by irrationality and impulsive actions. We have been able to confirm the soundness of this assumption with respect to rationality of choice but, to our surprise, found negative relations between planfulness (preplanning actions and fulfilling plans) and satisfaction with consumption outcomes. We theorized that the subjective appraisals by families of actions taken against the needs they were expected to meet were serving for some families as a monitoring feedback mechanism to upgrade their consumer performances where the evaluation was negative and for other families the assessment served as a halo-type tranquilizer masking deficiencies where the evaluation was positive. To be sure, objectively viewed, some consumer actions warrant positive evaluations and some other actions merit negative evaluations. It would be the tendency to distort the assessment that should receive our attention in programs of training.

The fact that some of the best educated and most competent families in the study tended to be the most discriminating and most frequently dissatisfied with their consumption outcomes, and that families with less education and resources tended to be undiscriminatingly positive in evaluating their consumer choices, suggests that a training program to improve on initial assessments might be undertaken most profitably with contrast groups. Couples might be recruited from the categories in this study which had the greatest discrepancy between consumership performance and satisfaction with outcomes who might, therefore, be suspected of utilizing the assessment mechanism as a tranquilizer to rationalize impulsive actions. For example, controlling for social class by matching each contrast group with its class counter-part families of high education and high income with records of low consumership (low preplanning of actions and low plan fulfillment) that have high satisfaction scores would qualify as one contrast group. A second group of families to be recruited might be drawn from low-income, low-education levels whose satisfaction scores are low but whose consumership achievements are high. In the present study both groups appear to have discrepant satisfaction scores and would be likely to contribute something and learn even more under training by professionals.

Do positive assessments serve latent functions of maintaining face for the decision maker or of affirming solidarity of the decision making group, or of minimizing dissonance about an action which has gone beyond the point of no return (What's done is done!)? A training program would seek to render some of these latent functions visible to improve on the critical capacities of family heads. Training procedures might, therefore, include exposure to scenarios which could be role-played involving choices and assessment of outcomes and careful examination of the types of assessment errors generated by couples in the course of these simulations of consumer situations. Every attempt would be made to discover the types of conditions and interpersonal situations which turn couples from critical type assessments appropriate to bad choices to the use of the assessment as a defense mechanism of denying errors of judgment. The training should include testing of the extent to which negative feedback improves subsequent performances and whether or not positive feedback is reinforcing of successful procedures or is used as an expressive mechanism to maintain solidarity between spouses.

Suggested Field Experiments

In closing this chapter on applications of the research findings for families we would like to suggest that certain of these applications be subjected to the rigors of a field experiment before being adopted in agency programs. The field experiment is an ideal way of validating research propositions which are to become part of educational programs since the procedures and outcomes of a field experiment can often be put to work at once in programs of education and service.

Several of the training programs suggested in the past several pages lend themselves to field experiments in educational or agency settings. As stated, however, most of the programs include too many variables to be manipulated for a single experiment. A field experimental design requires the selection of one outcome variable, change in which can be ascribed to one or more experimental treatments administered to members of one or more experimental groups but scrupulously withheld from members of one or more control groups.[1]

Much of the richness of the several programs suggested will be lost in complying with the requirements of a field experiment but greater confidence can be placed in the outcome of a training program which utilizes such a design since spurious and concommittant relationships among variables are demonstrated which might vitiate the impact of an otherwise valid educational program.

In selecting from among the several training programs suggested in the previous pages, it is quite clear that those focusing on the upgrading of consumership in the short run fit best the requirements of a field experiment. Assessing research propositions with respect to life cycle management and career management would require longitudinal designs to assess fully the impacts of training. Whatever educational treatments are administered must have relatively quick effects to be caught within the time span covered by an experiment.

---

[1] For discussion of quasi-experimental designs in educational and sociological research, see D. T. Campbell and J. C. Stanley, "Experimental and Quasi-Experimental Designs for Research on Teaching" in N. L. Gage, *Handbook of Research on Teaching*, Chicago: Rand McNally, 1963, pp. 546-553.

Impacts of Training in Judgment on Consumership

For the best illustrations of the possibilities of a field experiment let us choose *consumership* as our outcome variable as indicated by the behavior preplanning of consumer actions. As antecedent to be built into educational treatments let us choose the variable *judgment* as operationalized by the Carlson-Hill Scale of Rationality of Decisions. This scale has incorporated into it, it may be remembered, the activities undertaken by families to assure a good outcome; namely, the search for information and knowledge needed to choose a course of action by consultation inside and outside the family, the weighing of satisfaction of alternatives in the short run and the long run in choosing a course of action.

In order to eliminate the confounding effects of duration of marriage, income and education, the experiment would be limited to newly married couples drawn from the population of marriage license applicants over a three-month period who in a preliminary interview proved to be both high school graduates without college training and of blue collar occupations. The preliminary interview would also elicit evidence of the extent of demand for a wide range of durable goods to permit screening out couples with low needs.

Sixty couples meeting these initial requirements would be randomly assigned to three experimental groups of ten couples each and to two control groups of 20 couples each, one of which (Control Group #2) would not be pretested but would be post-tested.

Pre-tests of judgment (adapting for pencil-paper administration, the components in the Carlson-Hill Rationality of Decisions Scale) and of consumership (based upon the recall of the extent of pre-planning of actions taken in the previous three months) would be administered to all couples except those assigned to Control Group #2 as well as a battery of tests of marital communication (role taking accuracy, power structure, and self disclosure).

The educational treatments proposed would be undertaken in a series of twelve sessions utilizing the stimulation of role playing techniques and video-taped playbacks with separate programs of content for each of the three experimental groups:

Experimental Group #1. In twelve sessions, training would bear directly on the *cognitive components of judgment;* namely, the sharpening of the definition of the problem, the search for information and alternative solutions, and the evaluation of these alternatives against immediate and distant outcomes.

Experimental Group #2. In twelve sessions, training would bear indirectly on judgment by emphasis on the *interpersonal components of judgment* involving consultation and self-disclosure, role taking, the spouse's preferences and decision making procedures, and the search for consensus in decision-making.

Experimental Group #3. In this group, the entire gamut of issues in judgment would be included in the training program with emphasis on the interaction between the cognitive styles of problem solution and the interpersonal involvements of consultation, role taking, and consensus formation.

Independently of the experimental sessions the couples of the three experimental groups and Control Group #1 would have been interviewed in three waves with the first interview timed with the pre-test and the subsequent interviews scheduled for the eighth and and sixteenth weeks to obtain a record of the plans anticipated (in the first and second interviews), the actions taken, and the evaluation of these actions (in the second and third interviews) using the format of the interview guides developed for the three generation study. These guides enable the interviewer to check on the number of activities undertaken listed in the Carlson-Hill Rationality Scale for each of the actions initiated by the couples studied. At the time of the third interview, the members of Control Group #2 would be interviewed to obtain, in so far as possible by recall, the same information obtained from the other four groups over the 16-week period.

Identical post-test measures with those administered in the pre-test would be given to both control groups and the three experimental groups at the end of the treatment period, roughly in the fourteenth week of the study.

The results of the field experiment would be assessed by comparing the before and after tests of each experimental group on the measures of judgment, to ascertain if the differential training programs brought about more changes in judgment in one group than in another. The before and after measures of judgment in the three experimental groups would also be compared with Control Group #1 to ascertain whether the training brought greater change than no treatment and with Control Group #2 on the after scores only, to see if the effect of the pre-test given to Control Group #1 and not #2 rather than training might account for the results.

Finally, the validation of the relation observed in the present survey between judgment and consumership would be assessed by noting whether or not an increase in judgment scores in the experimental groups is indeed associated with a greater increase in consumership scores than the movement observed in these two sets of scores in the couples of the two untreated groups.

Other illustrations could be laid out in experimental design form but we resist the temptation to do so. Among the several programs of training by helping professionals, we do see clear advantages in undertaking field experiments for the following:

1. Impacts of training in parental role taking with children on the development of judgment about consumer choices among child rearing couples.

2. Effects of training in the construction of family policies on satisfaction with the outcome of consumer actions covered by those policies.

3. Effects of training in synchronization of multiple consumer plans and actions on satisfaction with the outcome of these actions.

4. Effects of training in assessment of congruity between ends and means in consumption on planfulness in subsequent consumer actions.

The many advantages of undertaking preliminary educational experiments have hardly been covered in these brief illustrations. Conducting a carefully designed experiment constitutes an important bridging step in assessing how far the survey findings or correlations among variables may be confidently applied in programs of training with family heads. If the experiment is carried out in the educational or agency setting in which the service is later to be rendered, and if the same professional personnel are involved in providing the educational treatments as will later provide the educational service, then these agencies are in the best possible position to adopt the results of a successful experiment immediately. The time and money costs and the likelihood of success can easily be calculated for future expansion of the service to reach a larger public.

Summary

From the several findings of this study an effort has been made to select those which might profitably be applied for the improvement of family practices in resource use and life cycle management. We distinguished between changes which are possible for families to undertake without professional help, those which are likely to necessitate professional attention and still others which are likely to require basic changes in economic and social policies through social legislation.

Family heads are invited to consider a number of changes in

family consumption practices which would upgrade their consumership achievements:

1. Setting a time for fulfilling a consumption plan increases the
likelihood of fulfillment.

2. Undertaking a major change such as a change of residence
without considering other contingency changes makes for unplanned
actions and irrational choices—it's best to look at the entire package
and budget accordingly.

3. Changes covered by family policies are more likely to be
evaluated as satisfactory later than non-policy covered changes, so
shouldn't families build policies for major recurring expenditures!

4. Some expensive durable goods are typically not planned for,
such as automobiles, which suggests this is an area of consumership
requiring attention.

5. Families that do the most discussing of plans in advance among
themselves, who talk things over with others outside the immediate
family, and who do more shopping around before they make changes
seem to have the most control over changes and seem to be happiest
with the decisions they finally make.

6. Families with close kinship ties are advantaged in getting ahead
financially even when they tend to be self reliant in accepting
financial help.

A number of changes in contemporary social policies may be
identified which would facilitate improved consumership and good
career management by increasing the general level of educational
competence and labor force participation of young people:

1. Greater financial support to increase the level of education
in the form of loans and scholarships and tax deductions to parents
to offset the costs of higher education of children.

2. To encourage the labor force participation of wives, provisions
should be made for day care nurseries for pre-school children, development of part time positions for mothers, maternity leave privileges, and a system of house cleaning services which would facilitate
employment and minimize the double load of the married mother.

3. Social policy should recognize the modified extended family
network as a problem solving resource and reward intergenerational
transfers for educational, professional and health objectives by making such transfers tax deductible just as charitable transfers now are.

Finally, in designing training programs in family consumership
we sought to bring a type of professional training to bear which was
not so much remedial or therapeutic as developmental, enabling families to realize their potentialities by increasingly excellent per-

formances. The programs, first of all, were to be differentiated for couples by stage of development, secondly career management vs. short run consumership issues were to be examined and third, training in evaluating consumership achievement was advocated.

In devising differentiated programs by stages of family development three points in the life cycle were singled out:

1. Training of the childless newly married put emphasis on greater specificity of short run planning, greater range in the search for information about alternative problem solutions and sharpening of the evaluation function while seeking to upgrade the couple's choice before taking action on them. The chief errors of consumership of this stage were low fulfillment of plans and relatively low rationality of decision-making.

2. Training programs for child rearing families focuses upon improving communication between children and parents and on greater involvement of children in the generating of plans and evaluating of actions taken. Construction of family policies for realizing educational plans for children and their social placement constitute issues of life cycle management with this developmental stage. Couples at this stage made few errors of consumership and were excellent on most counts of career management and would only need to be upgraded in their performances.

3. Training of launching and post parental families reaches a new set of issues involving different sources of consumership errors. They are not the most planful of consumers since they only achieve middle range rationality and pre-planning levels and make rather uncritical assessments of their consumer actions. A training program would seek to upgrade the pre-planning of these couples and would also move directly into issues of kin-keeping in which this cohort is actively engaged, examining the kinds of judgment needed to determine how much financial aid and counsel to give the children being launched into jobs and marriage.

Training in the strategies of career management is seen as having merit independent of expertise in short run consumership. It is proposed that the training include the principles of time and money budgeting to synchronize activities which are intercontingent over the life cycle. Training in the construction of family policies for newly married couples and in the review and assessment of family policies created for another era also appeared appropriate for older couples.

It was proposed that family life cycle management games be developed in which the players would need to role take with other decision-makers in their network whose decisions would interact with and modify their own. Scenarios for simulating changes over long time spans would illuminate the critical importance of timing career changes in getting ahead, such as marriage, births, home ownership and job changes making clear what decisions tended to close off or open up options much later in the family cycle when the costs of social placement of children and independent retirement would have high saliency.

In the continuous interplay of the components of the family consumption process and in family problem solving too, the provision of feedback is crucial to the improvement of subsequent cycles. It is in this facet of consumership that the individual family is most handicapped in attempting self improvement. A training program might include exposure to scenarios which could be role played, involving choices and assessment of outcomes and careful examination of the types of assessment errors generated by couples in the course of these simulations of consumer situations. It would be anticipated that the types of conditions and interpersonal situations would be rendered salient which turn couples from critical type assessments appropriate to bad choices to the use of the assessment as a defense mechanism of denying errors of judgment.

Most of the programs of training suggested would be better undertaken after being validated in a field experiment in the same setting in which the services would later be rendered. Five suggestions of program applications which lend themselves to educational experiments are made and one illustration is expanded at some length, the impacts of staff induced improvements in judgment on consumership among newly married couples. The experimental design involves random assignment of newly married couples to three experimental groups and two control groups with assessments of judgment and consumership occurring before and after exposure to the treatments. In a series of twelve sessions with a different content for each experimental group and no training for the control groups the impacts of the program are assessed by the relative improvement in the two variables of judgment and consumership in the experimental groups as against the control groups. Similar experiments might be undertaken for couples farther along in the family cycle dealing with issues such as the effects of improvements in parental role taking with children on the development of judgment or the effects of training in synchronizing multiple consumer plans and actions on satisfaction with the outcomes of these actions.

No attempt has been made in this chapter to examine the value biases of the authors in the translation of their several findings into applications to be utilized by families for their own development. Others are free to make their own translations and we trust that we have made the findings sufficiently salient for them to do so! We do recognize that we share with most of the families in the study the belief that efficiency in managment of one's resources is good both in the short run and the long run. Moreover, we think they share with us the values that a society should foster growth and development of its families over the life span and in so doing to challenge each generation to pass along to the next what it has learned in its own brief "pursuit of excellence."

APPENDIX A

Selected Bibliography

Adams, Bert N. 1967 "Interaction theory and the social network." Sociometry 30 (1967):64-78.

Adams, Bert N. 1967 "Occupational position, mobility, and the kin of orientation." American Sociological Review 32 (1967):364-377.

Adams, Bert N. 1968 Kinship in an Urban Setting. Chicago: Markham Publishing Company.

Addiss, Louise 1966 "Family patterns in today's economic world." Proceedings of the Symposium, Catastrophic Illness: Impact on Families' Challenge to the Professions, Cancer Care, Inc. of the National Cancer Foundation, p. 14.

Albrecht, Ruth 1954 "The parental responsibilities of grandparents." Marriage and Family Living 16 (1954):201-204.

Aldous, Joan 1963 "Family continuity patterns over three generations: content, degree of transmission and consequences." Unpublished Ph. D. Dissertation. University of Minnesota.

Aldous, Joan 1965 "The consequences of intergenerational continuity." Journal of Marriage and the Family 27 (November):462-468.

Aldous, Joan 1967 "Intergenerational visiting patterns: variation in boundary maintenance as an explanation." Family Process 6, 2 (1967):235-251.

Aldous, Joan and Reuben Hill 1965 "Social cohesion, lineage type, and intergenerational transmission." Social Forces 43, 4 (May):471-482.

Aldous, Joan, and Reuben Hill 1969 "Strategies for breaking the poverty cycle." Social Work (July):3-12.

Apple, Dorrian 1956 "The social structure of grandparenthood." American Anthropologist 58 (1956):656-663.

Axelson, Leland J. 1963 "The marital adjustment and marital role definitions of working and nonworking wives." Marriage and Family Living XXV (May):189-195.

Back, Kurt W. 1965 "A social psychologist looks at kinship structure." Pp. 326-340. in Ethel Shanas and Gordon F. Streib (eds.), Social

Structure and the Family: Generational Relations. Englewood Cliffs, N.J., Prentice Hall, Inc.

Barton, Allen H. 1955 "The concept of property space in social research." Pp. 40-54 in Paul Lazarsfeld and Morris Rosenberg (eds.), The Language of Social Research. Chicago: Free Press.

Becker, Howard S. 1961 "The implications of research on occupational careers for a model of household decision-making." Pp. 239-254 in Nelson N. Foote (ed.), Household Decision-Making. New York: University Press.

Becker, Howard S., and Anselm L. Strauss 1956 "Careers, personality, and adult socialization." American Journal of Sociology 62 (November):253-263.

Bennett, John W., and Leo A. Despres 1960 "Kinship and instrumental activities." American Anthropologist 62 (1960):254-267.

Benson, Purnell, Arlo Brown, Jr., and Sister Loretta Maria Sheehy 1956 "A survey of family difficulties in a metropolitan suburb." Marriage and Family Living 28 (August):249-253.

Beresford, John C. and Alice M. Rivlin 1964 "Privacy, poverty and old age." Demography 3, (1964):242-1258.

Beresford, John C., and Alice M. Rivlin 1964 "The multigeneration family." Prepared for a meeting on the multigeneration family at the University of Michigan Conference of Aging, Ann Arbor, Michigan (mimeographed).

Beresford, John C. and Alice M. Rivlin 1969 "The multi-generational family." in Living in a Multigenerational Family, Institute of Gerontology, University of Michigan and Wayne State University, Occasional Papers in Gerontology 31 (January):1-17.

Berkowitz, Leonard, and Louise R. Daniels 1964 "Affecting the salience of the social responsibility norm: effects of past help on the response to dependency relationships." Journal of Abnormal and Social Psychology 68 (1964):275-281.

Beyer, Glenn H., and Margaret E. Woods 1963 "Living and activity patterns of the aged." Research report No. 6. Ithaca, N.Y.: Center for Housing and Environmental Studies, Cornell University.

Bigelow, Howard F. 1948 "Financing the marriage." Pp. 393-418 in Howard Becker and Reuben Hill (eds.) Family, Marriage and Parenthood. Boston: D. C. Heath.

Birren, James E. (ed.) 1964 The Psychology of Aging, Englewood Cliffs, N.J.: Prentice-Hall, Inc.

Blackwell, Gordon W. 1942 "Correlates of the state of family development among farm families on relief." Rural Sociology 17 (June:161-74.

Blau, Peter 1955 The Dynamics of Bureaucracy. Chicago: University of Chicago Press.

Blau, Zena Smith 1956 "Changes in status and age identification." American Sociological Review 21 (1956):198-203.

Blau, Zena Smith 1961 "Structural constraints on friendships in old age." American Sociological Review 26 (1961):429-439.

Blood, Robert O., Jr. 1962 "The effects of the wife's employment on the husband-wife relationship." Pp. 282-305 in Ivan F. Nye and Lois W. Hoffman The Employed Mother. Chicago: Rand McNally.

Blood, Robert O., Jr., and Donald Wolfe 1960 Husbands and Wives: The Dynamics of Married Living. New York: The Free Press of Glencoe.

Bossard, James H. S., and Eleanor Stoker Boll 1955 "Marital unhappiness in the life cycle." Marriage and Family Living XVII (February):10-14.

Bott, Elizabeth 1957 Family and Social Network. London: Tavistock Publications, Ltd.

Bowerman, Charles 1957 "Adjustment in marriage: over-all and in specific areas." Sociology and Social Research XLI (March-April):257-263.

Brim, Orville Jr., et. al., 1962 Personality and Decision Processes. Stanford: Stanford University Press.

Brown, George H. 1961 "The automobile buying decision within the family." Pp. 193-199 in Nelson N. Foote (ed.), Household Decision-Making. New York: University Press.

Burgess, Ernest W., and Paul Wallin 1953 Engagement and Marriage. Philadelphia: J. B. Lippincott Company.

Burgess, Ernest W. (ed.) 1960 Aging in Western Societies. Chicago: University of Chicago Press.

Cain, Leonard D., Jr. 1964 "Life course and social structure." Pp. 272-309 in Robert L. Faris (ed.), Handbook of Modern Sociology. Chicago: Rand McNally and Co.

Campbell, D. T., and J. C. Stanley 1963 "Experimental and quasi-experimental designs for research on teaching." Pp. 546-553 in N. L. Gage, Handbook of Research on Teaching. Chicago: Rand McNally.

Cavan, Ruth S., et al. 1949 Personal Adjustment in Old Age, Chicago: Science Research Associates, Inc.

Clark, Lincoln H. (ed.) 1955 Consumer Behavior: The Life Ccyle and Consumer Behavior. New York: New York University Press.

Coult, Allan D., and Robert W. Habenstein 1962 "The study of extended kinship in urban society." The Sociological Quarterly 3 (April):141-145.

Crockett, Jean A. 1963 "Older people as consumers." Pp. 127-146 in H. L. Orbach and Clark Tibbits (eds.), Aging and the Economy. Ann Arbor: University of Michigan Press.

Cumming, Elaine, et al. 1960 "Disengagement—a tentative theory of aging." Sociometry XXIII (March):23-35.

Cumming, Elaine, and William E. Henry 1961 Growing Old: The Process of Disengagement. New York: Basic Books, Inc.

Cumming, Elaine, and David M. Schneider 1961 "Sibling solidarity: a property of American kinship." American Anthropologist 63 (1961):498-507.

de Grazia, Sebastian 1964 Of Time, Work, and Leisure. Garden City, New York: Anchor Books, Doubleday and Co.

Deutscher, Irwin 1959 Married Life in the Middle Years: A Study of the Middle Class Urban Postparental Couple. Publication No. 126. Kansas City: Community Studies, Inc.

Deutscher, Irwin 1964 "The quality of postparental life: definitions of the situation." Journal of Marriage and the Family XXVI (February):52-59.

Dinkel, Robert M. 1943 "Parent-child conflict in Minnesota families." American Sociological Review 8 (1943):412-419.

Dinkel, Robert 1944 "Attitudes of children toward supporting aged parents." American Sociological Review 9, 4 (August):370-379.

Durand, John D. 1948 The Labor Force in the United States, 1890-1960. New York: Social Science Research Council.

Duvall, Evelyn Millis 1970 Family Development. 4th edition. Philadelphia: J. B. Lippincott Co.

Farber, Bernard 1957 "An index of marital integration." Sociometry 20 (June):117-134.

Farber, Bernard 1959 Effects of a Severely Mentally Retarded Child on Family Integration, Monographs of the Society for Research in Child Development, XXIV, No. 2 (Serial No. 71), Lafayette, Indiana: Child Development Publications of the Society for Research in Child Development, Inc.

Farber, Bernard 1960 "Perceptions of crisis and related variables in the impact of the retarded child on the mother." Journal of Health and Human Behavior 1 (1960):108-118.

Farber, Bernard 1960 Family Organization and Crisis: Maintenance of Integration in Families with a Severely Mentally Retarded Child. Monographs of the Society for Research in Child Development, XXV, No. 1 (Serial No. 75), Lafayette, Indiana: Child Development Publications of the Society for Research in Child Development, Inc.

Farber, Bernard 1961 "The family as a set of mutually contingent careers." Pp. 276-297 in Nelson N. Foote (ed.), Household Decision-Making. New York: University Press.

Farber, Bernard (ed.) 1968 Kinship and Family Organization. New York: John Wiley Press.

Farber, Bernard and Leonard S. Blackman 1956 "Marital role tensions and number and sex of children." American Sociological Review 21 (October): 596-601.

Farber, Bernard, and Julia McHale 1959 "Marital integration and parents' agreement on satisfaction with their child's behavior." Marriage and Family Living 21 (February):65-69.

Farber, Bernard, William C. Jenne, and Romolo Tiogo 1960 Family Crisis and the Decision to Institutionalize the Retarded Child. Council for Exceptional Children Research Monograph Series, I, Series A, No. 1. Washington D. C.: Council for Exceptional Children.

Feldman, Harold 1965 Development of the Husband-Wife Relationship. Ithaca, New York: Cornell University Research Report.

Ferber, Robert 1955 Factors Influencing Durable Goods Purchases. Urbana: Bureau of Economic and Business Research.

Ferber, Robert 1954 "The role of planning in consumer purchases of durable goods." American Economic Review 44 (December):854-874.

Fink, H. H. 1957 "The relationship of time perspective to age, institutionalization, and activity." Journal of Gerontology 12 (1957):414-417.

Fisher, Janet A. 1955 "Family life cycle analysis in research on consumer behavior." Pp. 28-35 in Lincoln H. Clark (ed.), Consumer Behavior: The Life Cycle and Consumer Behavior. New York: New York University Press.

Foote, Nelson N. 1957 "The appraisal of family research." Marriage and Family Living 19 (February):92-99.

Foote, Nelson N., et. al. 1960 Housing Choices and Constraints. New York: McGraw-Hill.

Foote, Nelson N. 1963 "Matching of husband and wife in phases of development." Pp. 15-21 in Marvin B. Sussman, Sourcebook in Marriage and the Family, 2nd edition. Boston: Houghton Mifflin Co.

Fried, Edrita G., and Karl Stern 1948 "The situation of the aged within the family." American Journal of Orthopsychiatry 18 (1948):31-54.

Garigue, Philip 1965 "French canadian kinship and urban life." American Anthropologist 58 (December):1090-1101.

Geiger, Kent 1955 "Deprivation and solidarity in the Soviet urban family." American Sociological Review 20 (January):57-68.

Gilmore, Harlan W. 1932 "Five generations of a begging family." American Journal of Sociology 37 (March):768-774.

Glasser, Paul H., and Lois N. Glasser 1962 "Role reversal and conflict between aged parents and their children." Marriage and Family Living 24 (1962):46-51.

Glick, Paul C. 1947 "The family cycle." American Sociological Review 14 (April):164-74.

Glick, Paul C. 1955 "The life cycle of the family" Marriage and Family Living 17 (February):3-9.

Glick, Paul C. 1957 American Families. New York: John Wiley and Sons.

Glick, Paul C, and Robert Parke, Jr. 1965 "New approaches in studying the life cycle of the family." Demography 2 (1965):187-202. Chicago: The Population Association of America.

Godfrey, Eleanor 1951 A Construction of Family Typologies and Their Initial Verification. Cambridge: Radcliffe College.

Gold, Martin, and Carol Slater 1958 "Office, factory, store—and family: a study of integration." American Sociological Review 23 (February):64-74.

Goldstein, Sidney 1960 Consumption Patterns of the Aged. Philadelphia: University of Pennsylvania Press.

Goodman, Arlene Davis 1968 "Marital adjustment in a three generational sample." Unpublished masters thesis. University of Minnesota.

Gouldner, Alvin 1960 "The norm of reciprocity." American Sociological Review 25, 2 (April):161-178.

Gray, Robert M., and David O. Moberg 1962 The Church and the Older Person. Grand Rapids, Mich.: William B. Eerdmans Publishing Co.

Gray, Robert M., and Ted C. Smith 1960 "Effect of employment on sex differences in attitudes toward the parental family." Marriage and Family Living 22 (1960):36-38.

Gravatt, Arthur E. 1953 "Family relations in middle and old age, a review." Journal of Gerontology 8 (April):197-201.

Gravatt, Arthur E. 1957 "An exploratory study of marital adjustment in later maturity." The Coordinator 6 (December):23-25.

Gross, Neal, Ward S. Mason, and A. W. McEachern 1958 Explorations in Role Analysis. New York: John Wiley and Sons.

Gurin, Gerald, Joseph Veroff, and Sheila Feld 1960 Americans View Their Mental Health: A Nationwide Interview Study. New York: Basic Books, Inc.

Hagstrom, Warren O., and Jeffrey K. Hadden 1965 "Sentiment and kinship terminology in American society." Journal of Marriage and the Family 27 (August):324-332.

Hatch, David L., and Mary G. Hatch 1962 "An unhappy family: some observations on the relationship between the Calvinist ethic and interpersonal relations over four generations." Marriage and Family Living 24 (August):213-223.

Hausknecht, Murray 1962 The Joiners: A Sociological Description of Voluntary Association Membership in the United States. New York: The Bedminster Press.

Havighurst, Robert J., Bernice L. Neugarten, and Sheldon S. Tobin 1964 "Disengagement, personality, and life satisfaction in the later years." Pp. 419-425 in P. From Hansen (ed.), Age with a Future (Proceedings of the 6th International Congress of Gerontology, Copenhagen, 1963). Philadelphia: F. A. Davis Co.

Henry, W. E., and Elaine Cumming 1959 "Personality development in adulthood and old age." Journal of Projective Techniques 23 (1959):383-390.

Herbst, P. G. 1952 "The measurement of family relationships." Human Relations 5 (February):3-36.

Hill, Reuben 1949 Families Under Stress: Adjustment to the Crises of War Separation and Reunion. New York: Harper and Brothers.

Hill, Reuben 1961 "Patterns of decision-making and the accumulation of family assets." Pp. 57-81 in Nelson Foote (ed.), Household Decision-Making. New York: New York University Press.

Hill, Reuben 1963 "Judgment and consumership in the management of family resources." Sociology and Social Research 47, 4 (July):446-460.

Hill, Reuben 1964 "The American family of the future." Journal of Marriage and the Family 26, 1 (February):20-28.

Hill, Reuben 1964 "Methodological problems with the development approach to family study." Family Process 3, 1 (1964):5-22.

Hill, Reuben 1965 "Decision making and the family life cycle." Pp. 113-139 in Ethel Shanas and Gordon F. Streib (eds.), Social Structure and the Family: Generational Relations. Englewood Cliffs, N.J.: Prentice-Hall, Inc.

Hill, Reuben 1970 "The three generation technique for studying social change" in Reuben Hill and Rene Konig (ed.), Families in East and West: Socialization Processes and Kinship Ties. Paris: Mouton and Company.

Hill, Reuben, and Joan Aldous 1969 "Socialization for marriage and parenthood." Pp. 885-951 in David Goslin (ed.), Handbook of Socialization Theory and Research. Chicago: Rand McNally.

Hill, Reuben and Donald A. Hansen 1960 "The identification of conceptual frameworks utilized in family study." Marriage and Family Living 12 (November):299-311.

Hill, Reuben, J. Joel Moss, and Claudine G. Wirths 1953 Eddyville's Families. Chapel Hill, No. Carolina: Institute for Research in Social Science, University of North Carolina.

Hill, Reuben, and Roy H. Rodgers 1964 "The developmental approach." Pp. 171-211 in Harold T. Christensen (ed.), Handbook of Marriage and the Family. Chicago: Rand McNally.

Hill, Reuben, H. Mayone Stycos and Kurt W. Back 1959 The Family and Population Control. Chapel Hill, N.C.: University of North Carolina Press.

Hobart, Charles W. 1958 "Disillusionment in marriage and romanticism." Marriage and Family Living 20 (May):156-162.

Hoffman, Lois W. 1960 "Effects of the employment of mothers on parental power relations and the division of household tasks." Marriage and Family Living 22 (1960):27-35.

Hollingshead, August B. and Fredrick C. Redlich 1958 Social Class and Mental Illness. New York: John B. Wiley and Sons.

Homans, George 1958 "Social behavior as exchange." American Journal of Sociology 63, 6 (May):597-606.

Homans, George C. 1950 The Human Group. New York: Harcourt, Brace, and World, Inc.

Ingersoll, Hazel L. 1948 "A study of the transmission of authority in the family." Genetic Psychology Monographs 37:225-302.

Irish, Donald P. 1964 "Sibling interaction: a neglected aspect in family life research." Social Forces 42 (1964):279-288.

Ishwaran, K. 1959 "The impact of the war on the family." Pp. 92 ff. chapter in K. Ishwaran, Family Life in the Netherlands. The Hague: Van Keulen.

Jacobson, Paul H. 1959 American Marriage and Divorce. New York: Rhinehart and Co.

Jourard, S. M., and P. Lasakow 1958 "Some factors in self-disclosure." Journal of Abnormal and Social Psychology (January):91-98.

Juster, F. Thomas 1959 Consumer Expectations, Plans, and Purchases:

A Progress Report. Occasional Paper 70. New York: National Bureau of Economic Research, Inc.

Juster, F. Thomas 1960 "Prediction and consumer buying intentions." Papers and Proceedings of the American Economic Association 50 (May): 604-617.

Juster, F. Thomas 1961 "Durable goods purchase intentions, purchases, and the consumer planning horizon." Pp. 311-342 in Nelson N. Foote (ed.), Household Decision-Making. New York: University Press.

Karlsson, George 1951 Adaptability and Communication in Marriage. Uppsala: Almqvist & Wiksells Boktryckeri Ab.

Kelly, E. Lowell 1941 "Marital compatibility as related to personality traits of husbands and wives as rated by self and spouse." Journal of Social Psychology 13 (February):193-198.

Kenkel, William F. 1957 "Influence differentiation in family decision making." Sociology and Social Research 42 (September-October):18-25.

Kenkel, William F. 1961 "Family interaction in decision-making on spending." Pp. 140-164 in Nelson N. Foote (ed.), Household Decision-Making. New York: University Press.

Kenkel, William F. and Dean K. Hoffman 1956 "Real and conceived roles in family decision making." Marriage and Family Living 18 (November):211-216.

Kerckhoff, Alan C. 1965 "Nuclear and extended family relationships: a normative and behavioral analysis." Pp. 93-112 in Ethel Shanas and Gordon F. Streib (eds.), Social Structure and the Family: Generational Relations. Englewood Cliffs, N. J.: Prentice-Hall, Inc.

Kirkpatrick, Clifford, and John Cotton 1951 "Physical attractiveness, age and marital adjustment." American Sociological Review 16 (February): 81-86.

Kirkpatrick, E. L., Mary Cowles, and Roselyn Tough 1934 "The life cycle of the farm family." Research Bulletin 121. Madison: Agricultural Experiment Station, University of Wisconsin.

Kleemeier, R. W. (ed.) 1961 Aging and Leisure. New York: Oxford University Press.

Knox, William E. 1965 Filial Bonds: The Correlates of the Retired Father's Perception of Solidarity with His Adult Children. Ann Arbor, Mich: University Microfilms, Inc.

Kodlin, Dankward, and Donovan J. Tompson 1958 An Appraisal of the Longitudinal Approach to Studies of Growth and Development. Lafayette, Indiana: Society for Research in Child Development.

Koller, Marvin R. 1954 "Studies of three-generation households." Marriage and Family Living 16 (1954):205-206.

Komarovsky, Mirra 1961 "Class differences in family decision-making on expenditures." Pp. 255-265 in Nelson N. Foote (ed.), Household Decision-Making. New York: University Press.

Komarovsky, Mirra 1964 Blue-Collar Marriage. New York: Random House, Inc.

Koos, Earl Loman 1946 Families in Trouble. Morningside Heights, New York: King's Crown Press.

Kreps, Juanita M. 1965 "The economics of intergenerational relationships." Pp. 267-288 in Ethel Shanas and Gordon F. Streib (eds.), in Social Structure and the Family: Generational Relations. Englewood Cliffs, N. J.: Prentice-Hall, Inc.

Landis, Judson T. 1942 "Social psychological factors of aging." Social Forces 20 (May):468-470.

Landis, Judson T. 1946 "Length of time required to achieve adjustment in marriage." American Sociological Review 11 (December):666-677.

Lansing, John B., and Leslie Kish 1957 "Family life cycle as an independent variable." American Sociological Review 22 (October):512-519.

Lansing, John B., and James N. Morgan 1955 "Consumer finances over the life cycle." Pp. 36-51 in Lincoln H. Clark (ed.), Consumer Behavior, Vol. 2: The Life Cycle in Consumer Behavior. New York: New York University Press.

Larrabee, Eric, and Rolf Meyersohn, (eds.) 1958 Mass Leisure. Glencoe, Ill.: The Free Press.

Leichter, Hope, and William E. Mitchell 1967 Kinship and Social Casework. New York: Russell Sage.

Lenski, Gerhard 1961 The Religious Factor. Garden City, New York: Doubleday and Co., Inc.

Levy, Marion 1949 The Family Revolution in Modern China. Cambridge: Harvard University Press.

Lipman, Aaron 1960 "Marital roles of the retired aged." Merrill-Palmer Quarterly 6 (April):192-195.

Litman, Theodor J. 1969 "Health care and the family: a three generational analysis." Unpublished manuscript presented at the American Sociological Association meetings, September 3, 1969, San Francisco.

Littman, R. A., John Curry, and John Pierce-Jones 1957 "Where parents go for help." The Co-ordinator 6 (September):3-9.

Litwak, Eugene 1959-1960 "The use of extended family groups in the achievement of family goals." Social Problems 7 (1959-1960):177-187.

Litwak, Eugene 1960 "Geographic mobility and extended family cohesion." American Sociological Review 25 (1960):385-394.

Litwak, Eugene 1960 "Occupational mobility and extended family cohesion." American Sociological Review 25 (1960):9-21.

Litwak, Eugene 1965 "Extended kin relations in an industrial democratic society." Pp. 290-323 in Ethel Shanas and Gordon F. Streib (eds.), Social Structure and the Family: Generational Relations. Englewood Cliffs, N. J.: Prentice-Hall, Inc.

Litwak, Eugene and Ivan Szelenyi 1969 "Primary group structures and their functions: kin, neighbors, and friends." American Sociological Review 34:465-481.

Locke, Harvey J., and Muriel Mackeprang 1949 "Marital adjustment and the employed wife." American Journal of Sociology 54 (May):536-538.

Macdonald, Robert 1964 "Intergenerational family helping patterns." Unpublished doctoral dissertation. University of Minnesota.

Maddox, George L., Jr. 1964 "Disengagement theory: A critical evaluation." The Gerontologist 4 (June, Part I):80-82.

March, C. Paul, and A. Lee Coleman 1954 "The relationship of kinship, exchanging work, and visiting to the adoption of recommended farm practices." Rural Sociology 19 (September):291-293.

Martin, Norman, and Anselm L. Strauss 1956 "Patterns of mobility within industrial organizations." Journal of Business 29 (April):101-110.

McGuire, Carson 1952 "Conforming, mobile, and divergent families." Marriage and Family Living 14 (1952):109-115.

McKinley, Donald Gilbert 1964 Social Class and Family Life. New York: The Free Press of Glencoe.

Miller, Daniel R., and Guy E. Swanson 1958 The Changing American Parent: A Study in the Detroit Area. New York: John Wiley and Sons, Inc.

Mogey, J. M. 1956 Family and Neighborhood. London: Oxford University Press.

Mogey, John 1964 "Family and community in urban-industrial societies." Pp. 501-529 in Harold T. Christensen (ed.), Handbook of Marriage and the Family. Chicago: Rand McNally and Company.

Morgan, James 1958 "A review of recent research on consumer behavior." P. 100 in Lincoln Clark (ed.), Consumer Behavior: Research on Consumer Reactions. New York: Harper & Brothers.

Morgan, James N. 1961 "Household decision-making." Pp. 81-102 in Nelson N. Foote (ed.), Household Decision-Making. New York: University Press.

Morgan, James 1965 "Measuring the economic status of the aged." International Economic Review 6 (1965):1-17.

Morgan, James, Martin David, Wilbur J. Cohen, and Harvey E. Brazer 1962 Income and Welfare in the United States. New York: McGraw-Hill.

Morse, Nancy C., and Robert S. Weiss 1955 "The function and meaning of work and the job." American Sociological Review 20 (1955):191.

Mueller, Eva, and George Katona 1954 "A study of purchase decisions." Pp. 20-87 in L. H. Clark (ed.), Consumer Behavior Vol. 1. New York: New York University Press.

Muir, Donald E., and Eugene A. Weinstein 1962 The social debt: an investigation of lower-class and middle-class norms of social obligation." American Sociological Review 27 (1962):532-539.

Neugarten, Bernice L., et al., (eds.) 1964 Personality in Middle and Late Life. New York: Atherton Press.

Neugarten, Bernice L., and Karol K. Weinstein 1964 "The changing

American grandparent." Journal of Marriage and the Family 26 (1964): 199-204.

Nye, F. Ivan 1958-1959 "Employment status of mother and marital conflict, permanence and happiness." Social Problems 6 (Winter):260-267.

O'Donovan, Thomas P. 1962 "Intergenerational Educational Mobility." Sociology and Social Research 47 (October):57-67.

Orbach, Harold L. 1961 "Aging and religion: a study of church attendance in the detroit metropolitan area." Geriatrics 16 (1961):530-540.

Orbach, H. L., and Clark Tibbitts, (eds.) 1963 Aging and the Economy. Ann Arbor: University of Michigan Press.

Parsons, Talcott 1943 "The kinship system of the contemporary United States." American Anthropologist 45 (January-March):22-38.

Parsons, Talcott, and Robert F. Bales 1955 Family Socialization and Ineraction Process. Glencoe, Illinois: The Free Press.

Phillips, B. S. 1957 "A role theory approach to adjustment in old age." American Sociological Review 22 (1957):212-217.

Phillips, B. S. 1961 Role change, subjective age and adjustment: a correlational analysis." Journal of Gerontology 16 (1961):347-352.

Pineo, Peter C. 1961 "Disenchantment in the later years of marriage." Marriage and Family Living 23 (February):3-11.

Prasad, S. Benjamin 1964 "The retirement postulate of the disengagement theory." The Gerontologist 4 (March):20-23.

Quarantelli, Enrico 1960 "A note on the protective function of the family in disasters." Marriage and Family Living 22 (August):263-264.

Rainwater, Lee 1965 Family Design: Marital Sexuality, Family Size, and Contraception. Chicago: Aldine Publishing Company.

Rainwater, Lee, Richard P. Coleman, and Gerald Handel 1959 Workingman's Wife. New York: Oceana Publications, Inc.

Reiss, Paul J. 1962 "The extended kinship system: correlates of and attitudes on frequency of interactions." Marriage and Family Living 24 (November):333-339.

Robins, Arthur J. 1962 "Family relations in three-generation households." P. 470 in Clark Tibbitts and Wilma Donahue (eds.), Social and Psychological Aspects of Aging. New York: Columbia University Press.

Robins, Lee N., and Miroda Tomanec 1962 "Closeness to blood relations outside the immediate family." Marriage and Family Living 24 (November):340-346.

Rodgers, Roy H. 1962 "Improvements in the construction and analysis of family life cycle categories." Ph.D. Dissertation, University of Minnesota. Kalamazoo, Michigan: Western Michigan University Press.

Rodgers, R. H. 1964 "Some factors associated with homogeneous role patterns in family life cycle careers." Pacific Sociological Review 7 (1964): 38-48.

Rogers, Everett, and Hans Sebald 1962 "A distinction between familism, family integration, and kinship orientation." Marriage and Family Living 24 (1962):25-30.

Rogoff, Natalie 1953 Recent Trends in Occupational Mobility. Glencoe, Illinois: The Free Press.

Rose, Arnold M. 1955 "Factors associated with the life satisfaction of middle-class, middle-aged persons." Marriage and Family Living 17 (February):15-19.

Rose, Arnold M. (ed.) 1963 Aging in Minnesota, Minneapolis: University of Minnesota Press.

Rose, Arnold M. 1964 "A current theoretical issue in social gerontology." The Gerontologist 4 (March):46-50.

Rose, Arnold M., and Warren A. Peterson, (eds.) 1965 Older People and Their Social World. Philadelphia: F. A. Davis Co.

Rosow, Irving 1965 "Intergenerational relationships: problems and proposals." Pp. 341-378 in Ethel Shanas and Gordon Streib (eds.), Social Structure and the Family. Englwood Cliffs, N. J.: Prentice-Hall, Inc.

Rosow, Irving 1967 Social Integration of the Aged. New York: The Free Press.

Rossi, Peter H. 1955 Why Families Move: A Study in the Social Psychology of Urban Residential Mobility. Glencoe: The Free Press.

Ryder, Norman B. 1965 "The cohort as a concept in the study of social change." American Sociological Review 30 (1965):843-861.

Sandage, C. H. 1956 "Do research panels wear out." Journal of Marketing (April):399-401.

Sayres, William C. 1956 "Ritual kinship and negative affect." American Sociological Review 21 (June):348-352.

Schaie, K. Warner 1965 "A general model for the study of development problems." Psychological Bulletin 64 (1965):92-107.

Schneider, David M., and George C. Homans 1955 "Kinship terminology and the American kinship system." American Anthropologist 57 (1955):1194-1208.

Schorr, Alvin L. 1960 Filial Responsibility in the Modern American Family. Washington, D. C.: Social Security Administration, United States Department of Health, Education and Welfare.

Schorr, Alvin L. 1962 "Filial responsibility and the aging, or beyond pluck and luck." Social Security Bulletin 25 (1962):4-9.

Schorr, Alvin L. 1968 "Social security and filial responsibility." Explorations in Social Policy. New York: Basic Books.

Shanas, Ethel 1966 "Family help patterns and social class in three countries." Presented at the meetings of the American Sociological Association, Miami.

Shanas, Ethel, and Gordon Streib, (eds.) 1965 Social Structure and the Family: Generational Relations. Englewood Cliffs, N. J.: Prentice-Hall, Inc.

Sharp, Harry, and Morris Axelrod 1956 "Mutual aid among relatives in an urban population." Pp. 433-439 in Ronald Freedman et al. (eds.), Principles of Sociology. New York: Henry Holt and Company.

Sharp, Harry, and Paul Mott 1956 "Consumer decisions in the metropolitan family." Journal of Marketing 21 (October):149-156.

Sheldon, Henry D. 1958 The Older Population of the United States. New York: John Wiley and Sons.

Simmons, Leo 1945 Role of the Aged in Primitive Society. New Haven: Yale University Press.

Simpson, George L., Jr. 1956 The Cokers of Carolina: A Social Biography of a Family. Chapel Hill: University of North Carolina Press.

Simpson, Ida Harper, and John C. McKinney (eds.) 1966 Social Aspects of Aging. Durham, N. C.: Duke University Press.

Slater, Sherwood B. 1967 "The function of the urban kinship network under normal and crisis situations." Paper presented before the Annual Meetings of the American Sociological Association, San Francisco, California.

Smith, Joel, William H. Form, and Gregory P. Stone 1954 "Local intimacy in a middle-sized city." American Journal of Sociology 60 (November):276-284.

Smith, William M., Jr., Joseph H. Britton, and Jean O. Britton 1958 Relationships Within Three-Generation Households. College of Home Economics Research Publication No. 155. University Park: The Pennsylvania State University.

Stehouwer, Jan 1965 "Relations between generations and the three-generation household in Denmark." Pp. 142-162 in Ethel Shanas and Gordon F. Streib (eds.), Social Structure and the Family: Generational Relations. Englewood Cliffs, N. J.: Prentice-Hall, Inc.

Streib, Gordon F. 1965 "Intergenerational relations: perspectives of the two generations on the older parent." Journal of Marriage and the Family 27 (November):469-476.

Streib, Gordon 1958 "Family patterns in retirement." Journal of Social Issues 24 (1958):46-60.

Strodtbeck, Fred L. 1951 "Husband-wife interaction over revealed differences." American Sociological Review (August):468-473.

Stryker, Sheldon 1955 "The adjustment of married offspring to their parents." American Sociological Review 20 (April):149-154.

Stuckert, Robert P. 1963 "Occupational mobility and family relationships." Social Forces 41 (March):301-307.

Sussman, Marvin B. 1953 "The help pattern in the middle class family." American Sociological Review 18 (February):22-28.

Sussman, Marvin B. 1953 "Parental participation in mate selection and its effects upon family continuity." Social Forces 32 (October):76-81.

Sussman, Marvin B. 1954 "Family continuity: selective factors which affect relationships between families at generational levels." Marriage and Family Living 16 (May):112-120.

Sussman, Marvin B. 1955 "Activity patterns of post-parental couples and their relationship to family continuity." Marriage and Family Living 17 (1955):338-341.

Sussman, Marvin B. 1959 "The isolated nuclear family: fact or fiction." Social Problems 6 (Spring): 333-340.

Sussman, Marvin B. 1960 "Intergenerational family relationships and social role changes in middle age." Journal of Gerontology 15 (January): 71-75.

Sussman, Marvin B. 1965 "Relationship of adult children with their parents in the United States." Pp. 62-92 in Ethel Shanas and Gordon F. Streib (eds.), Social Structure and the Family: Generational Relations. Englewood Cliffs, N. J.: Prentice-Hall, Inc.

Sussman, Marvin B., and Lee Burchinal 1962 "Kin family network: unheralded structure in current conceptualizations of family functioning." Marriage and Family Living 24, 2 (August):231-240.

Sussman, Marvin B., and Lee Burchinal 1962 "Parental aid to married children: implication for family functioning." Marriage and Family Living 24, 4 (November):320-332.

Sweetser, Dorrain Apple 1963 "Asymmetry in intergenerational family relationships." Social Forces 41 (1963):346-352.

Sweetser, Dorrain Apple 1964 "Mother-daughter ties between generations in industrial societies." Family Process 3 (September):332-343.

Sweetser, Dorrain Apple 1966 "The effect of industrialization on inter-generational solidarity." Rural Sociology 31 (June):156-170.

Thomas, Edwin J. 1957 "Effects of facilitative role interdependence on group functioning." Human Relations 10 No. 4 (1957):347-366.

Thompson, W. E., Gordon F. Streib, and J. Kosa 1960 "The effects of retirement on personal adjustment: a panel analysis." Journal of Gerontology 15 (1960):165-169.

Tibbitts, Clark, and Wilma Donahue 1962 Social and Psychological Aspects of Aging. New York: Columbia University Press.

Tobin, Sheldon, and Bernice Neugarten 1961 "Life satisfaction and social interaction." Journal of Gerontology 16 (October):344-346.

Townsend, Peter 1957 The Family Life of Old People. London: Routledge and Kegan Paul.

Townsend, Peter 1963 "The family of three generations." Presented at the International Social Science Research Seminar in Gerontology, Markaryd, Sweden.

Townsend, Peter 1966 "The emergence of the four-generation family in industrial society." Proceedings, 7th International Congress of Gerontology, Vienna 8 (1966):555-558.

Udry, J. Richard, and Mary Hall 1965 "Marital role segregation and social networks in middle-class middle-aged couples." Journal of Marriage and the Family 27 (August):392-395.

Vincent, Clark 1963 "The family in health and illness: some neglected areas." The Annals of the American Academy of Political and Social Science 346 (March):109-125.

Wallach, Michael A., and Nathan Kogan 1961 "Aspects of judgment and decision-making: interrelationships and changes with age." Behavioral Scientist 6 (1961):23-36.

Waller, Willard, and Reuben Hill 1951 The Family: A Dynamic Interpretation. rev. ed. New York: The Dryden Press, Inc.

Weeks, H. Ashley, Marjorie Davis, and Howard Freeman 1958 "Apathy of families toward medical care." Pp. 148-158 in E. G. Jaco (ed.), Patients, Physicians and Illness. Glencoe, Ill.: Free Press.

Westoff, Charles F. 1961 "Some aspects of decision-making in the family growth process." Pp. 25-38 in Nelson N. Foote (ed.), Household Decision-Making. New York: University Press.

Wilensky, Harold 1961 "Life cycle, work situation, and participation in formal associations." Pp. 213-242 in Robert W. Kleemeier, (ed.), Aging and Leisure. New York: Oxford University Press.

Williams, Richard 1961 "Changing status, roles and relationships." Pp. 283-284 in Clark Tibbitts, Handbook of Social Gerontology. Chicago: University of Chicago Press.

Wolgast, Elizabeth H. 1958 "Economic decisions in the family." Journal of Marketing 23 (October):151-158.

Wolgast, Elizabeth H. 1958 "Do husbands or wives make the purchasing decisions." Journal of Marketing 22 (October):151-158.

Young, Michael, and Peter Willmott 1964 Family and Kinship in East London. Baltimore, Md: Penguin Book.

Zborowski, Mark, and Lorraine D. Eyde 1962 "Aging and social participation." Journal of Gerontology 17 (1962):424-430.

Zelditch, Morris, Jr. 1955 "Role differentiation in the nuclear family." Pp. 312 ff in Talcott Parsons and Robert F. Bales (eds.), Family, Socialization and Interaction Process. Glencoe, Illinois: Free Press.

Zola, Irving Kenneth 1962 "Feelings about age among older people." Journal of Gerontology 17 (1962):65-68.

Samples of Data Collection Instruments Used in the Study

I Interview Guide for Four Panel Interviews Over 12 Months Covering Inventories of Household Possessions, Career Histories over Marriage Span and Chronicle of Plans Made and Actions Taken.

II Interview Guide for Joint Couple Interview

III Interview Guide for Assessing Intergenerational Helping Patterns

IV Pencil-Paper Questionnaires and Tests Administered to Respondents

I

Interview Guide for Four Panel Interviews over a Year's Period Covering Inventories, Histories, Plans and Actions Taken

Face-Sheet Information

Interview Number: ...... Interviewer .... Editor ....
(Cued for Generation)

Full Address .... Ph. ......
　　　　　　　　Street　　　　Zone　　　　City

	Wife	*Husband*
Name	. . . .	. . . .
Month and Year of Birth	. . . .	. . . .
Religious Affiliation	. . . .	. . . .
Ethnic Background		
(e.g. 1st generation Norwegian)	. . . .	. . . .
Color (Determined by interviewer)	. . . .	. . . .
Years Schooling Completed	. . . .	. . . .
Size of Community in Which Reared	. . . .	. . . .
Years of Residence in the Twin Cities	. . . .	. . . .

Names, addresses, and relationship of related families in study:

1. Name . . . .
               Husband   Wife

   Address . . . . Ph. . . . .
               Street   Zone   City

   Relationship . . . .   Generation . . . .
                             (Child, Parent, Grandparent)

2. Name . . . .
               Husband   Wife

   Address . . . . Ph. . . . .
               Street   Zone   City

   Relationship . . . .   Generation . . . .
                             (Child, Parent, Grandparent)

I. RESIDENTIAL STATUS

    To begin with, let's talk a little about your home.

    1. Is this building a single unit, double unit, or multi-unit?
    2. And of what material is it constructed?
    3. How old is the building?
    4. How many bedrooms do you have?
    5. How many bathrooms do you have?
    6. How many bathtubs do you have?
    7. Do you have a dining room?
    8. How many rooms do you have all together? (Not including bathrooms, halls, attics, basements, closets).
    9. Do you have electricity?
   10. How many telephones do you have?
   11. Do you own your residence? Is it mortgaged?
       Do you rent your residence? Is it mortgaged?
   12. Do you have a garage? If yes, how large is it?

13. Have you changed residence in the last six months?
    a) If yes, What move did you make?
    Why did you choose this particular time?
    How early did you start to make plans for moving?
    What went into these plans?
    b) If no, Are you thinking seriously of moving?
    If yes, where are you thinking of moving?
    Have you a definite time in mind for making the move?
    If yes, when? 0-3 mos., 3-6 mos., 6-9 mos., 9-12 mos., 12+ mos.?
    Why do you plan to move at this time?
    What plans have you made?

14. Have you done any remodeling on your house and property during the past six months? If yes, what did you have done?
    What would you estimate the value of the work to be?
    Why did you choose this particular time to have the remodeling done?
    How early did you start making plans for remodeling?
    What went into these plans?
    If no, are you seriously thinking of having any remodeling done on your home or property? If yes, what are you thinking of having done?
    Do you have a definite time in mind for having the work done?
    If yes, when? 0-3 mos., 3-6 mos., 6-9 mos., 9-12 mos., 12+ mos.?
    Why would you have it done at this time?
    What plans have you made for having the work done?

15. Have you done any major redecorating in your house over the past six months?
    If yes, what did you have done?
    What would you estimate to be the value of this work?
    Why did you choose this particular time to have the work done?
    How early did you start making plans for redecorating?
    What went into these plans?
    If no, are you seriously thinking of having any major redecorating done in your house?
    If yes, what are you thinking of having done?
    Do you have a definite time in mind for having the work done?
    If yes, when? 0-3 mos., 3-6 mos., 6-9 mos., 9-12 mos., 12+ mos.?
    Why would you have it done at this time?
    What plans have you made for having the work done?

II. RESIDENTIAL HISTORY

Now, I wonder if you could think back with me to the year you were married. What year was that? Could you tell me about the different houses and apartments you've lived in since that time—starting with the first one after marriage. (Ask the following questions for each residence).

1. Where was it located?
2. What year did you move in?
3. And in what year did you vacate that residence?
4. What type of dwelling was it?   a. Single unit
                                    b. Double unit
                                    c. Multi-unit
5. Was it furnished or unfurnished?
6. How many bedrooms did you have there?
7. And how many baths?
8. How many bathtubs were there in that residence?
9. Was there a dining room?
10. And how many rooms were there all together, not including halls, attics, basements, and closets?
11. Did it have electricity?
12. How many telephones did you have? (Numbers and extensions)
13. Did you own that residence or did you rent it?
14. How much did you pay (for the house)/(for monthly rent)?
15. (If owned) Was the house mortgaged?
16. Did you have a garage? (If "yes" What was its size (number of cars)?

III. Inventory of Durable Goods

Durable Goods Sometimes Found in Homes

The list below shows a number of items which are sometimes found in homes.

1.   Air conditioners
2.   Blankets, electric
3.   Coffee-maker, electric
4A. Cooking range, gas
4B. Cooking range, electric
4C. Cooking range, wood-coal
4D. Cooking range, other
5A. Sofa, non-convertible
5B. Sofa, convertible
5C. Sofa, studio-couch
6.   Dining room table
7.   Dishwasher
8A. Dryer, electric
8B. Dryer, gas
9A. Floor covering, linoleum
9B. Floor covering, tile
9C. Floor covering, throw rugs, cotton loop rugs, fiber rugs

9D. Floor covering, woolen rugs
9E. Floor covering, wall to wall carpeting
10. Food freezer
11. Fry pans, electric
12. Garbage disposal
13A. High fidelity equipment, radio only
13B. High fidelity equipment, phonograph only
13C. High fidelity equipment, radio-phono combination
14. Musical instruments (specify which)
15. Pets (specify which)
16A. Radios (non-high fidelity), table
16B. Radios (non-high fidelity), console
16C. Radios (non-high fidelity), portable
16D. Radios (non-high fidelity), radio-phono combination
17. Record players (not including hi-fi or radio-phono combinations)
18A. Refrigerators, ice cube freezer only
18B. Refrigerators, food freezer space
18C. Refrigerators, ice box
19A. Sewing machine, electric
19B. Sewing machine, treadle
20A. Television set, black and white—console
20B. Television set, black and white—table
20C. Television set, black and white—portable
20D. Television set, color, any type
20E. Television set, radio-phono combination
21A. Vacuum cleaner, upright
21B. Vacuum cleaner, tank or canister
22A. Washing machine, automatic
22B. Washing machine, wringer

1. Which of the items listed on the sheet do you possess at the present time?

   a. How many do you have?
   b. What brand is the item?

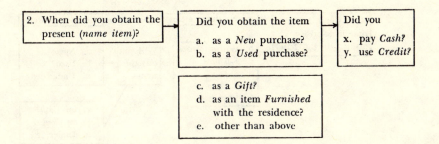

IV. Inventory History

1. Is the present (name item) the only one you've ever owned?

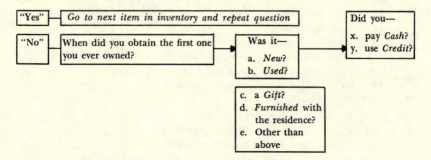

| "Yes" | Go to next item in inventory and repeat question |

| "No" | When did you obtain the first one you ever owned? |

Was it—
a. *New?*
b. *Used?*

c. a *Gift?*
d. *Furnished* with the residence?
e. Other than above

Did you—
x. pay *Cash?*
y. use *Credit?*

2. When did you obtain the one after your first one?

If original was the only other one owned, go to next item in inventory and repeat question #1 above.
If original and the present item are not the only others ever owned, obtain all others in chronological order. Then go to next item in inventory and repeat question #1 above.

V. Gifts and Planned Purchases

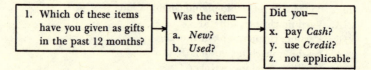

1. Which of these items have you given as gifts in the past 12 months?

Was the item—
a. *New?*
b. *Used?*

Did you—
x. pay *Cash?*
y. use *Credit?*
z. not applicable

2. a. Are you seriously considering purchasing any of these items or any similar items?
   b. Is there anything in particular that your husband (wife) might be seriously considering purchasing that you haven't mentioned?

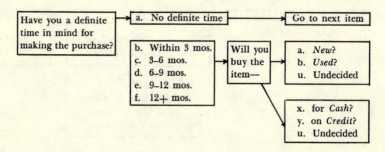

| "Yes" | What would that purchase be? |

Have you a definite time in mind for making the purchase?

a. No definite time

Go to next item

b. Within 3 mos.
c. 3–6 mos.
d. 6–9 mos.
e. 9–12 mos.
f. 12+ mos.

Will you buy the item—

a. *New?*
b. *Used?*
u. Undecided

x. for *Cash?*
y. on *Credit?*
u. Undecided

VI. AUTOMOBILE HISTORY

    1. Now, tell me about the cars you have owned since you've been married.

        a. When did you buy the first one?

        b. What make and year was it?

        c. Was it a new or used car?

        d. How did you finance it?

        e. When and how did you dispose of it?

        f. When did you buy the next one?

        g. *Return to (b) above and continue until you have information on all cars owned.*

    2. Are you seriously thinking of purchasing an automobile?
If yes, Have you a definite time in mind for making the purchase?
Within 3 mos., 3-6 mos., 6-9 mos., 9-12 mos., 12+ mos.?

VII. FAMILY COMPOSITION, EDUCATIONAL STATUS, EMPLOYMENT STATUS, AND HISTORY AND INSURANCES COVERAGES

Now, I'd like to find out a little about the different members of your immediate family. Let's start with your husband. *(Then repeat for each member of the family, including Respondent.)*

A. Family Composition and Social Status

    1. What is the name of each member of your family?

    2. What is the month and year of his/her birth?

    3. How many years of schooling has he completed? (Do not count kindergarten or nursery school.)

    4. Ask as necessary to determine occupational information for each member of the family.

        a. What is his occupation? What does he do in that job?

        b. Who is his employer? (Not applicable for students)

        c. Levels of supervision in place of work

        d. Number of employees in place of work

    5. What other jobs does he hold?

    6. How many hours a week does he spend on this (these) part-time jobs?

    7. Are there any members of your immediate family who do not live here?

        ....No.

        ....Yes.   What are their names? Position in family? What is month and year of their birth? Where are they now?

    8. Are you supporting any other relatives whom you haven't already mentioned?

        ....No.

        ....Yes.   Who are they? What is their relationship to you?

9. Are there others living here who are not members of your family?
   ....No.
   ....Yes. Who are they? How do they happen to be living here?
10. Since you've been married have there been others living in your household who are no longer here?
    ....No.
    ....Yes. Who were they? Why did they leave? How did they happen to be here?
11. Have there been any additions to your household in the last six months?
    ....No.
    ....Yes. Who? Why did they come to live with you? (If not obvious) Why did they come at this particular time? (if not obvious) How early did you start to develop plans for their coming? What went into these plans?
12. Are you seriously thinking of the addition of any persons to your household?
    ....No.
    ....Yes. Who? Do you have a definite time in mind as to when they would join the household?
       ....No.
       ....Yes. 0-3 mos., 3-6 mos., 6-9 mos., 9-12 mos. 12+ mos.? Why would they come at this time? What plans have you made for their coming?
13. Has anyone in the family changed jobs or taken up a new job over the past six months?
    ....No.
    ....Yes. What was the change? Why did the change come at this particular time? When did you begin to develop plans for this change? What went into these plans?
14. Is anyone in the family seriously thinking of changing jobs or taking up a new job?
    ....No.
    ....Yes. Who? What change does he have in mind? Does he have a definite time in mind for making the change (or taking up the new job)?
       ....No.
       ....Yes. 0-3 mos., 3-6 mos., 6-9 mos., 9-12 mos., 12+ mos.? Why would he do it at this time? What plans has he made with regard to the change?

B. Employment History

1. I wonder if you could think back with me to the year you were

married. Do you recall the work your husband was doing then? (If husband available get information from him:)

  a. What was that job? What exactly did he do—what were his duties?

  b. Did he hold another part-time job during this time? What was it? When did he quit that job?

  c. When did he leave the full-time job?

  d. Did he take another job right away? (If not, how long was he unemployed?)

  e. Return to "a" and repeat series until you have the entire employment history.

2. Have you (the wife) held any jobs since your marriage? (If yes) Tell me about them. (Use same sets of questions a-e above).

C. What is the coverage of insurances for family members: Life insurance, Blue Cross, Blue Shield? Other health insurance, accident insurance, social security?

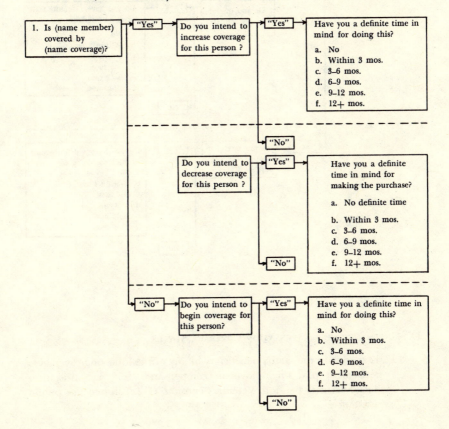

VIII. INVENTORY OF FINANCIAL STATUS

    1. Which of the following items do you have: savings account, checking account, government bonds, stocks, corporate bonds, other investments, retirement program?

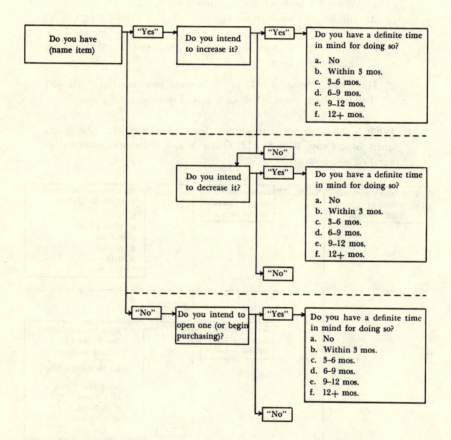

IX. INVENTORY OF COMPENSATION COVERAGE STATUS

    1. Is anyone in the family beneficiary of any of the following coverages: retirement pay, unemployment compensation, old age assistance, Social Security pension, Veteran's pension, G. I. Bill benefits, public assistance?

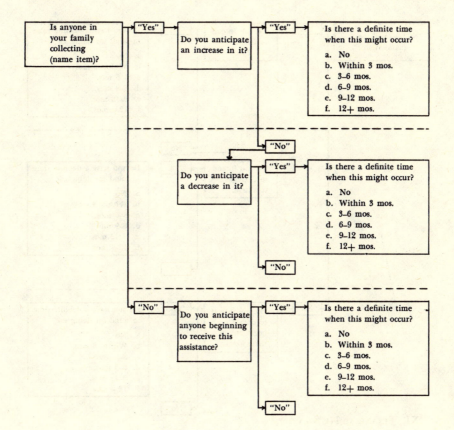

X. INSURANCE AND PROPERTY INCOME STATUS

1. Are you carrying protective insurances or have other hedging income from property: fire insurance on house and contents, auto liability and collision insurance and theft insurance, or liability property, mortgage insurance, income from property and tenants?

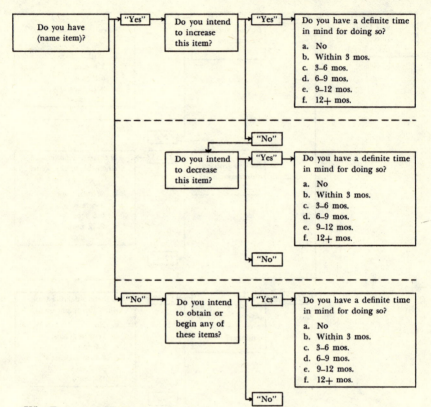

XI. FINANCIAL HISTORY

In my previous visits with you, we have talked about the various kinds of insurance, savings, and the like which you have at the present time. I wonder now if we can talk a bit about your possession of these things in the past. Thinking back to when you were first married—

A. Savings

    1. Have you ever had a savings account?
    2. In what year of your marriage did you first open a savings account?
    3. Is that account still open?
    4. In what year of your marriage did you close that account?
    5. Did you ever open another account?

    6. What would you say the reasons are for your saving? For what purpose or for what goals are you saving?
    7. In your family, how do you decide how much to save?
    8. Do you have an emergency fund? If yes, where is it located?
    9. What is the lowest amount you'd hold to use for emergencies?
  10. What top 3 emergencies do you have this fund for?

Year of Marriage

	Opened	Closed
1st Account		
2nd Account		
3rd Account		
4th Account		
5th Account		

B. Government Bonds

1. Have you ever owned any government bonds?
2. In what year of your marriage did you first purchase government bonds?
3. Do you still hold them?
4. In what year of marriage did you sell them?
5. Did you ever purchase any other government bonds?
6. What would you say are your reasons for purchasing government bonds?
7. How do you decide in your family what to purchase?

C. Stocks and Bonds

1. Have you ever owned any corporate stocks or bonds of any kind? (Other than government bonds)

Year of Marriage

	Bought	Sold
1st Purchase		
2nd Purchase		
3rd Purchase		
4th Purchase		
5th Purchase		

2. In what year of your marriage did you first purchase stocks or bonds?
3. Do you still hold them?
4. In what year of your marriage did you sell them?
5. Did you ever purchase any other stocks or bonds?
6. What would you say are your reasons for purchasing stocks and bonds? (Probe for whether strictly savings or manipulated for profit.)
7. How do you decide in your family what to purchase?

D. Insurance

1. Have you ever owned a life insurance policy for any member of the family?
2. In what year of your marriage (or before marriage) did you first take out an insurance policy? On which member of the family?
3. Is this policy still in force?
4. In what year of your marriage did you drop the policy?
5. Did you ever purchase any other policies?
6. What type of policies have you purchased? What are your reasons for purchasing insurance? (NOTE TO INTERVIEWER: Probe for a life insurance policy on the wage earner to cover the home mortgage and auto financing where applicable).
7. How do you decide in your family what kind of insurance and the amount to purchase?

E. Retirement Provisions

1. Have you ever had any kind of provision or plan for retirement?
2. What was your original plan for retirement?
3. In what year of your marriage did you first make provisions for retirement?
4. Have you changed these provisions since then?
5. What were these changes and in what year of your marriage did they occur?
6. Are there other plans for retirement which we have missed?
7. How did you decide in your family on retirement plans?

F. Budgeting

1. What does or did your family consider budgeting to be?
   Check and probe for:
   An estimate of coming expenses
   Plan for distribution of money
   An accounting system
   Examination of plan for changes

Does your budget include the total income for the family? What expenses, if any, are not included in your budget? What expenses *are* included?

2. Where and when did you and your spouse first learn about budgeting? (Use specific probes as to whether this learning occurred in families, school, work from friends, social service organizations.)
3. When did you begin budgeting in your family?
   a. Why did you begin?
   b. Whose idea was it to budget? (Wife, husband, parents, others?)
   c. Who works on the budget? Who takes the initiative?
   d. What period is included in your planning—weekly, monthly, yearly?
4. Have you continued budgeting since the first date listed above?
5. In what year of your marriage did you stop?
6. Did you begin again?
7. (If budgeting is discontinued or had been discontinued) Why did you discontinue budgeting?

XII. CHANGES IN RESIDENCE, REMODELING AND REDECORATING, DURABLE GOODS PURCHASED, JOB CHANGES, AND FINANCIAL CHANGES IN SECOND AND SUBSEQUENT INTERVIEWS OVER A YEAR'S PERIOD.

Introductory Statement: The last time I was here we talked about some of the plans you had made for the immediate future; things you were seriously interested in doing soon. Everybody knows that things don't always turn out the way we expect them to. Now I want to go back over the things we talked about one by one to see which way they turned out.

A. Change in Residence

.... Respondent DID expect to move.

.... 1. I notice that you have moved since my last visit, as you had expected to do.

     a. How did it work out?   ....Satisfied
                          ....Dissatisfied

     b. How did you arrive at the decision to move? Tell me what happened?

     c. How did you decide on this place over others that you might have chosen?

.... 2. I notice that you have not moved since my last visit, though you thought at that time there was some possibility that you would do so.

     a. How do you and the family feel about this?
          ....Satisfied
          ....Dissatisfied

     b. Have you just postponed moving or does this mean a permanent change in plans?

.... Respondent DID NOT expect to move.

.... 3. I notice that you have moved since my last visit.

     a. How did it work out?   ....Satisfied
                          ....Dissatisfied

     b. How did you arrive at the decision to move? Tell me what happened?

     c. How did you decide on this place over others that you might have chosen?

.... 4. Respondent did not move.

     a. Has the question of moving come up in the last three months?

          ....Yes
          ....No

c. (If change in plans) Tell me what happened.

Interviewer Rating: (After each confrontation of places with actions taken, the interviewer is expected to elicit the data about the decisions made to make the rating below).

1. Did couple discuss or confer:
   ....(a) within the family
   ....(b) outside the family?

2. Was there a search for information about alternatives—shopping around?
   ....Yes ....No

3. Were relative costs and satisfactions weighed among alternatives?
   ....Yes ....No

4. Were long-range and immediate satisfactions taken into account?
   ....Yes ....No

Underline
those
taken
into
account

5. Is there a *family* policy?   ....Yes   ....No
   What is it, if any?

B. Redecoration and Remodeling

Have you done any major redecorating since my last visit?   ....Yes   ....No
Have you done any major remodeling since my last visit?   ....Yes   ....No

Respondent DID   ....expect to redecorate
                  ....expect to remodel

Respondent DID NOT   ....expect to redecorate
                      ....expect to remodel

....1a. You say that you have redecorated as you expected to do on my last visit.

....1b. You say that you have remodeled as you expected to do on my last visit.

   (a) What did you do?

   (b) How do you feel about results?

     ....Satisfied

     ....Dissatisfied

   (c) Trace through decision process.

....2a. You say you haven't redecorated since my last visit though at that time you had expected that you might.

   (1) How do you feel about this postponement?

     ....Satisfied   ....Dissatisfied

....2b. You say that you haven't remodeled since my last visit though at that time you had expected that you might.

   (1) How do you feel about this?

   (a) Have you postponed this or have you changed your plans?

   (b) (If change in plans) Tell me what happened.

....3a. You say you have redecorated since my last visit.

....3b. You say you have remodeled since my last visit.

   (a) What did you do?

   (b) How do you feel about results?

     ....Satisfied

     ....Dissatisfied

   (c) Trace through decision process.

....4a. Respondent did not redecorate.

....4b. Respondent did not remodel.

   (a) Has the question come up since my last visit?

     ....Yes   ....No

(Interviewer's rating on these decisions as listed earlier)

C. Durable Goods and Automobile Inventory Additions

(Hand respondent list of durable goods shown above)

Have you purchased any of these items or any similar items since my last visit three months ago?   ....Yes   ....No

Have you purchased an automobile since my last visit three months ago?   ....Yes   ....No

....Respondent expected to make NO PURCHASES.

Respondent DID expect to add—

1................   2................
3................   4................

....1. For each purchase completed, get satisfaction and trace purchasing decision.

   a. How do you feel about the purchase? Would you like to return it and get your money back?
      ....Satisfied   ....Dissatisfied

   b. How did you arrive at the decision to buy? What happened?

....3. For each purchase completed, get satisfaction and trace purchasing decision.

   a. How do you feel about the purchase? Would you like to return it and get your money back?
      ....Satisfied   ....Dissatisfied

   b. How did you arrive at the decision to buy? What happened?

....2. For each purchase not completed, ask:

   a. When I was last here you said you might buy ....Is this just a postponement or a change in plans?

      (1) How do you feel about it?
         ....Satisfied   ....Dissatisfied

   b. (If change in plans) Tell me what happened.

....4. No purchases made.

   a. Have you talked about the possibilities of purchasing any of these items in the last three months?

      (1) Which items?
         ....

(Interviewer rating on each purchase plan fulfilled, postponed or unplanned purchase following outline provided earlier)

D. Changes in Household Membership, Job, Schools

Have you added any persons to the household?   ....Yes   ....No
Has anyone in the family changed jobs or taken a new job?   ....Yes   ....No
Has anyone in the family changed schools or gone back to school?   ....Yes   ....No

Respondent expected to:

A.   ....Add household members
B.   ....Change job
C.   ....Change schools

.... 1. For each change made, get satisfaction and trace decision process.

    a. How has it worked out?   ....Satisfied
                              ....Dissatisfied

    b. How did you arrive at the decision? What happened?

.... 2. For each change not made, get satisfaction and trace decision process.

    a. When I was here last, you thought you might .... Have you changed your plans permanently? ....Yes ....No
      (1) Are you satisfied with this decision?
         ....Yes ....No

    b. Tell me what happened.

Respondent expected to make no changes in:

  ....Household
  ....Job
  ....School

.... 3. For each change made, get satisfaction and trace decision process.

    a. How has it worked out? ....Satisfied
                             ....Dissatisfied

    b. How did you arrive at the decision? What happened?

.... 4. Respondent made no changes

    a. Have you talked about the possibilities since my last visit?

(Interviewer rating on each decision required following outline provided earlier)

E. Changes in Financial Status

Have you made any changes in your holdings of any of the items listed here? That is, have you either increased your holdings, decreased them, obtained them for the first time, or dropped them?

Respondent expected to make following changes:

....A. Increase ...., ...

....B. Decrease ...., ...

....C. Stop ...., ...

....D. Start ...., ...

....1. For each change made, get satisfaction and trace decision process.

a. How has it worked out? ....Satisfied
..........Dissatisfied

b. How did you arrive at the decision? What happened?

....2. For each change not made, get satisfaction and trace decision process.

a. When I was here last, you thought you might

Have you changed your plans permanently?
....Yes ....No

(1) Are you satisfied with this decision?
....Yes ....No

b. Tell me what happened

(Interviewer rating required for each change as per earlier outline)

Respondent expected to make no changes in financial matters.

....3. For each change made, get satisfaction and trace decision process.

a. How has it worked out? ....Satisfied
..........Dissatisfied

b. How did you arrive at the decision? What happened?

....4. Respondent made no changes.

a. Have you talked about the possibilities since my last visit?

F. History of Family Income Over Marriage Span

Instructions For Family Income Sheet
(To Be Read to Husband)

Past research on the income of families shows that it seems to follow a definite pattern. As you can see in this graph (show R graph), it generally starts at a relatively low level and gradually rises to a peak and then drops off rather rapidly. Now, we are interested in knowing if our families are like this, too. Would you please put an "X" in the boxes to indicate the approximate total family income at marriage and to indicate changes, either up or down, which have taken place since that time. Please notice that this is total family income, not just the husband's salary. For example, if your total family income was about $2600 at marriage, you would place an "X" under the 2 and opposite the line marked "year." Then, if your income increased to $4000 after about 3 years of marriage, you would put an "X" under the 4 and opposite the line marked "3" years. If it will help, you can put the year of your marriage in the margin and then the other years on down so that it will be easier to remember. (Note to interviewer: *Give aid as necessary, but allow the respondent to complete the form by himself. Then when he gives it back to you, Say, "I notice that the last is in the box opposite . . . . . . years of marriage. Have there been any changes since then?" This is to insure that the respondent has indicated his present level to us.*)

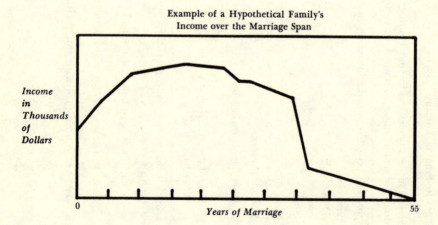

Example of a Hypothetical Family's
Income over the Marriage Span

Income in Thousands of Dollars

0

Years of Marriage   55

FAMILY INCOME IN THOUSANDS OF DOLLARS

Years Married	Less Than 1,000	1	2	3	4	5	6	7	8	9	10	11	12	13	14	15	20	25	30	35	40	45	50+
1 yr.																							
2 yrs.																							
3 yrs.																							
4 yrs.																							
5 yrs.																							
6 yrs.																							
7 yrs.																							
8 yrs.																							
9 yrs.																							
10 yrs.																							
12 yrs.																							
14 yrs.																							
16 yrs.																							
18 yrs.																							
20 yrs.																							
22 yrs.																							
24 yrs.																							
26 yrs.																							
28 yrs.																							
30 yrs.																							
32 yrs.																							
34 yrs.																							
36 yrs.																							
38 yrs.																							
40 yrs.																							
42 yrs.																							
44 yrs.																							
46 yrs.																							
48 yrs.																							
50 yrs.																							
51–54 yrs.																							
55–59 yrs.																							
60–64 yrs.																							
65–69 yrs.																							
70 & over																							

G. Financial Outlook

    1. Do you think your financial situation is:
        (a) ( ) Better than at the beginning of our visits.
                (Interviewer give the respondent the date of first visit)
        (b) ( ) Worse than at the beginning of our visits.
        (c)   ( ) About the same. No change has taken place.
        (d) ( ) Uncertain, cannot make an evaluation.
    2. If the financial situation is better:
        (a) Why are you better off? What factors have made for an improved
            financial situation during the past year?
    3. If worse,
        (a) Why are you worse off? What factors and/or expenses have made
            for a less satisfying financial situation during the past year?
    4. Family Income:
        (a) Estimated income for next year: . . . .
           (1) How sure? . . . .

H. Effects of Being Interviewed

We have visited with you four times this past year asking lots of questions. Some experts say visits and interviews shouldn't make much difference in the way families plan their lives, others say it does make a real difference, that people who have been interviewed are changed families as a result.

    1. Have you noticed any changes at all in what you have been doing that may have been caused by our visits? What changes or in what way?

Probe if not forthcoming spontaneously:

    1. Have you talked over the problems we have discussed, where to live, whether to remodel, what to purchase, finances and jobs, more together than you were doing a year ago?
        (a) If yes, which of these? (Probe for areas)
    2. Do you approach these problems any differently than you did a year ago?
        (a) If yes, in what ways? (Probe for increased planfulness, weighing pros and cons, long-range planning, learning from experience)
    3. Have you ever found yourselves bringing up what we have talked about in these visits in arriving at a decision to make a move, or a purchase, or change jobs?
        (a) If yes, tell me what happened—(Probe for each instance where this has occurred)

II

Interview Guide for Joint Couple Interview

I. GOALS AND OBJECTIVES

   A. *Marriage and Children*

      1. When I was here the last time, you told me that you had been married in ...... (interviewer fill in year). Tell me—how did you decide to marry then? Why not sooner or later?

(Probe if not mentioned *after usual clarity and completion* probes:)

         a. Did you think at all about general conditions in the country at the time?

         b. Did you take into account your personal situation at the time?

         c. Were there considerations having to do with either of your parents' opinions concerning your marriages?

      2. Now, thinking about when you were first married, did you have any ideas about what you wanted as far as a family was concerned —such things as the number of children, when the first one would be born, how far apart they would be born, or whether they would be boys or girls?

        ....Yes. What were these ideas?

        ....No. Well, did you develop ideas about this later on in marriage?

            ....Yes. When was this? ....

            What were these ideas?

(Interviewer summarize: preferred number ...., preferred interval between marriage and first child ...., preferred interval between children ...., preferred sex distribution ....)

      3. Again thinking about when you were first married, did you have some ideas about what you wanted in the way of education for the children you intended to have?

        ....Yes. What were these ideas?

        ....No. Did you develop ideas about education later in the marriage?

            ....Yes. When was this? ....

            What were these ideas?

(Interviewer summarize: (a) Through elementary school: ....boys ....girls, through high school: ....boys ....girls, through college: ....boys ....girls, professional or graduate degree: ....boys ....girls.)

      4. Did (or do) you have any special plans for any child? (Place name of child in blank)

         a. Private school or tutor, military school

ḅ. Conservatory training, private lessons for art, drama, music, dancing?

c. Foreign study, travel, etc.

d. Other (Specify)

e. No ....

B. *House and Neighborhood*

5. Where did you eventually want to be when you settled down residentially? Did you have any special section of the United States you wished to settle in?

a. Where?

b. Why?

6. Did you want to live in:

....a. The central city?

....b. The city but farther out?

....c. The suburbs?

....d. Small town?

....e. The country?

Why?

7. Do you have certain characteristics which you look for in choosing a neighborhood in which you would like to live?

8. Do (or did) you have a clear picture of a "dream house" which you have felt it was reasonable to expect that you might live in someday? Tell me about it. Is it?—

a. An apartment, flat?

b. A duplex?

c. A single family dwelling?

Does it have?—

....a. 1–2 bedrooms	....g. Den
....b. 3 bedrooms	....h. Number of baths
....c. 4 bedrooms	....i. Utility room
....d. 5 or more bedrooms	....j. Basement
....e. Dining room	....k. Sunroom-porch
....f. Family room	....l. Sewing room

........Total Rooms

9. Of the items in the list of durable goods, which would you regard as essential to furnish your "dream house"? Remember, you will need to pay for them eventually! (List husband's choice, wife's choice and joint choices separately).

C. *Work Goals*

10a. Now, thinking about employment for the husband, what kind of work have you wanted him to do? (Note: Get responses from *both* H and W. If only one answers, probe the other with a reactive probe of the type, "How do you feel about this?" to other respondent).

10b. Why did you want this sort of a job? (Note who gives the reasons below)
   a. Pay bills.
   b. Provide prestige for family.
   c. Fits well with raising family.
   d. Enjoys, has a talent for.
   e. Other (specify nature and who provided response) . . . .

11a. What sort of work has the wife wanted to do?

11b. Why did she want this sort of work? (Check *all* applicable)
   a. Pay bills.
   b. Provide prestige to family.
   c. Fits well with raising a family.
   d. Enjoys, has a talent for.
   e. Other (specify) . . . .

12a. What plans have you had for dividing housekeeping and bread-winning activities? (Note any qualifications of response, especially those associated with family cycle stages.)

	Husband	Wife	Qualifications
Breadwinner only			
Housekeeper & breadwinner			
Housekeeper only			

12b. Under what conditions, if any, should a wife who has a year-old child work?

D. *Summary*

As I look over your answers, you have told me you wanted a certain kind of family and that you wanted to do certain things for and with them. Now let's see—you've said you wanted . . . . . . children, about . . . . . . years apart, the first ones coming about . . . . . . (years or months) after you were married. You wanted them to have schooling through . . . . You thought you wanted to live in . . . . (region) and in . . . . (city, suburb, etc.) in a house with . . . . (bedrooms and total rooms.) You thought that the husband should work at . . . . (kind of work) while the wife should work at . . . . (kind of work). Would you say that's a fair picture of what you've told me?

E. *Evaluation of Progress or Extent of Realization of Goals*

13a. *For grandparents and parents:*
   Looking back over your marriage, how close would you say you've come to realizing your desires for your family?

....a. Almost none

....b. About half of them

....c. All of them

....d. Over-achieved

13b. For *children:*

In your marriage so far, where would you say you are in your "timetable" for achieving these desires?

a. About on schedule

b. Ahead of schedule

c. Behind schedule

d. Probably never get there

14. Were there periods in your marriage when you seemed to make more progress towards your goals and other periods when you made less progress?

15. What sorts of sacrifices have been made to get as far as you have?

(Probes: a. What things were given up entirely? b. What things were postponed for the present?)

F. *Change in Objectives Through Hindsight*

16. If you could press a button and begin all over again, what would you do differently?

17. As you look over the way you've done things in your family, what things do you hope that your children will carry on in their marriages?

II. QUESTIONS ABOUT OPINIONS OF HUSBAND AND WIFE DESIGNED TO GENERATE DISCUSSION BETWEEN SPOUSES BY REVEALING DIFFERENCES

(Instructions to Interviewer:

1. List "H" for husband and "W" for wife before comments are made.

2. Whenever a difference appears, push gently for a joint statement: "What do you both feel about this? What is your view as a family?"

3. Ratings will be easier if number and order of comments are shown in place as verbatim as possible.)

A. *Questions Posed*

18. Do you feel that husband wife should each have their own circle of friends?

19. Who should spend more on clothing?

20. How should you treat exasperating behavior on the part of your child?

21. Who should be the spokesman for the family in dealing with school officials, bank, landlord, etc.?

22. What should your relations with your in-laws be?
23. What in your opinion is the single biggest difference the coming of the first child makes?

B. *Interviewer's Ratings of Husband-Wife Interaction in Arriving at Consensus on Preceding Opinion Questions*

26. Relative amount of talking:
    wife talks most   ....
    husband talks most   ....
    about the same   ....
27. Domination-subordination: Who has decision role in the family decisions?
    H—always   ....
    H—most of the time   ....
    W—most of the time   ....
    W—always   ....
    Indeterminate   ....
28. Who contributes the most ideas?
    About the same   ....
    Wife   ....
    Husband   ....
29. Initiative vs. passivity?
    Husband shows most initiative   ....
    about equal   ....
    Wife shows most initiative   ....
30. Degree of Partnership: High Med. Low
    Companionship   ...   .
    Communication   ....
    Each going own way almost independently ....
    Specify other ....
31. Marriage is more companionate, or more segregated roles?
    Companionate   ....
    Segregated   ....
32. Harmony vs. conflict:
    Open conflict frequent   ....
    Occasional conflict   ....
    Suppressed conflict   ....
    No conflict   ....
    Agreement after discussion   ....
    Agreement without discussion ....
    Very high consensus   ....
33. Who does more about face-saving and smoothing over differences?

	Smoothing over	*Identifying differences*
H—More	......	......

W—More   . . . .
Indeterminate   . . . .
. . . . . . No differences identified
. . . . . . Differences identified, but smoothing over not attempted.
34. Do they seem to be happy together?
    Yes   . . . .
    No   . . . .
35. Are gestures of affection or hostility made?
                        Hostility   *Affection*
    Husband
        Yes   . . . .
        No   . . . .
    Wife
        Yes   . . . .
        No   . . . .
36. Are there conspicuous features of the husband-wife relationship
    which you feel have been left out by these ratings? Please state.

III

Interview Guide for Assessing Intergenerational Helping Patterns

1. Introduction

"We're going to discuss ways in which people help one another. Some do it
financially; some by sharing *goods*; some by lending a hand in *providing services*; some by sharing of their *ideas, knowledge and experience*. We know
some families only help their family members; that is, children, parents, and
grandparents—.Some families only help others outside, such as friends, neighbors, underprivileged people, and so forth. Some families help each other only
by money, loans, gifts, and the like. Some don't believe in this and only give
goods or provide services.

"When families *want* help, they have their preferences, too. Some families
never go outside their immediate families, for professional advice or counseling, to agencies such as Country Welfare Departments, Family Service Agencies or Catholic Charities. And some families *never* discuss their own troubles
with other family relatives and in-laws but instead go to friends, neighbors,
doctors, ministers or social agencies for help with their personal problems.

"First I'm going to ask about the people and organizations you and your
husband *have helped* in the past year. Then I'll ask the situation or reason
that prompted you to give this help and whether or not you expect some return
for the help you gave.

"Let's begin with financial or money help. In the *past year*, to whom have
you given or loaned money:"

A. Financial Help Given

Total Amount Given Last Year to All Sources $ . . . .

Financial Help to	Amount, $	Circumstances* (What was the need?)	Conditions** (See next page)

*Code for Circumstances Which Prompted Help or Giving

A. *Children*
1. Birth of child
2. Special occasion, such as anniversary or Christmas
3. Improvement of grades
4. Child-care problems
5. Child-teacher problems
6. Child-parent problems
7. Improvement of play space
8. Improvement of play equipment
9. Special Schooling
10. Parent replacement

B. *Couples*
1. Special occasion
2. Education and/or rehabilitation
3. In-laws
4. Money
5. Drinking/gambling
6. Infidelity
7. Sexual relations
8. Peer group problems—friends, neighbors
9. Old age

C. *Disasters*

Major Wage Earner
1. Death
2. Incapacity/disability
3. Loss of employment
4. Insufficient income
5. Illness

Spouse
6. Death
7. Incapacity/disability
8. Loss of employment
9. Illness

General Loss or Failure
10. Fire or flood
11. Major appliance
12. Major equipment of business
13. Replacement—wear and tear

D. *Raise Scale of Living*

E. *Living Costs—General Assistance*

** Code for Types of Conditions Set on Giving or Helping

Code	Finances	Goods	Lend-a-Hand Services	Share the Brain Knowledge
1	Gift	Gift	Gives or receives total capacity to do the job—others take over job entirely.	Assumption of problem and the solution—others take over problem entirely.
2	Loan—Not expected or intended repayment.	Loan—Not expected to repay or return.	Helps out—Lends a hand and expects no repayment or return.	Seeks or gives constant information "Tell me what to do" or "I'll tell you what to do."
3	Loan—Expects return or to return services.	Loan—Expects replacement or to replace with other items of less value.	Expect other or intend to reciprocate in own way (less).	Swaps information only, shares experiences and problems. Sympathize with one another.
4	Loan—Expects or intends to return. No time limit.	Return as is when finished using.	Reciprocate—Expect or intend to repay in same way sometime.	Good listener—Seeks or is a broad shoulder to cry on. Available when needed and know would use other similarly.
5	Loan—Expects or intends return. Stated time.	Return and replace if worn, fix up.	Reciprocate—Expect or intend equivalent service at or within specified time (with maximum skills).	Seek and use specific information or counsel. Limited time counseling—if counseling is accepted. Or refers or helps to go to more appropriate source for help.
6	Loan and expect or intend return with interest	Replace with a new one.	Pay or reciprocity and additional service.	Seeks or gives support, counseling—but helps other person assume total problem for self.

B. *Goods—Given Last Year*

"Now let's think of the goods you gave or loaned to people or organizations in the past year"

Goods Given To	Type of Article	Circumstances (What was the need?)	Conditions (Gift, loan, exchange, expect return?)

C. *Services Given Last Year*

"Now how about services given to others in the past year, such as help in child care or baby-sitting, nursing, housework, redecorating, helping your club, church or some welfare agency, etc."

Services Given To	Type	Circumstances (What was the need?)	Conditions (Gift, exchange, etc.)

D. *Giving Knowledge, Sharing Experiences, Ideas, Counseling*

"Now let's talk about whether or not you or your husband helped others last year by sharing with them the knowledge you have gained from experience. Have you helped others by giving information or counseling or by being a good listener when others had family or personal problems, school, money or business problems?"

Knowledge Help Given To Whom	Circumstances (What was the need or problem?)	Conditions (How did you help?) (Helped decide; Shared problem, Advice; Listen?)

Help Received—Introduction

"We've talked about all the ways in which you and your immediate family helped others last year. Now let's talk about the ways in which you *received* help from others. This time I would like to know from what people and organizations you received the kinds of help we've just discussed and the circumstances or reasons for receiving their help.

"Let's begin with financial or money help—in the *past year* from what people or organizations have you received or borrowed money?"

E. *Financial Help Received*   *Total Amount Received from All Sources Last Year* $ ....

Financial Help From   *Amount, $*   *Circumstances* (What was the need?)   *Conditions* (Gift, loan, exchange, etc.)

F. *Goods Received Last Year*
"Now let's think of the *goods* you were given or had loaned to you from people or organizations in the past year—."

Goods Received From   *Type of Article*   *Circumstances* (What was the need?)   *Conditions* Gift, Loan, Exchange, Expect Return?)

G. *Services Received Last Year*
"Now how about *services* received from others in the past year, such as help in child care or babysitting, nursing, housework, redecorating, help from your club, church or some welfare agency, etc."

Services Received From   *Type*   *Circumstances* (What was the need?)   *Conditions* (Gift, Exchange, etc.)

H. *Receiving Knowledge, Sharing Experience, Ideas, Counseling*
"Now let's talk about whether or not you or your husband received help from others last year by sharing with them the knowledge they had gained from experience. Have you been helped by others by getting information or counseling or by seeking a good listener when you had family or personal problems, school, money or business problems?"

Knowledge Help Received From Whom   *Circumstances* (What was the need or problem?)   *Conditions* (How were you helped?) (Helped decide; Shared problem, Advice; Listening?)

(NOTE—In the original format, each question posed in the following pages, was followed by two blank pages for the interviewer's use in recording responses, comments and impressions.)

2. For the family and personal problems you met or solved during the past year or are presently working on, to whom did you go for advice and counseling?

      . . . . . Doctor
      . . . . . Lawyer
      . . . . . School Nurse
      . . . . . Social Worker
      . . . . . Religious Leader
      . . . . . Family Members
      . . . . . None of These
      . . . . . No family or personal problems last year?
              (Probe: If did have, to whom would you have gone?)

Comments:

3. Social Activities and Rituals

Instructions: Use the code below to indicate on the chart with whom the family Always, Almost Always and Sometimes does these activities.

Code:

I	= Immediate family (wife, husband, and resident children)	HP	= Husband's parents
		HGP	= Husband's grandparents
H-W	= Husband and wife only		
MC	= Married children	HS or HB	= Husband's sister(s) or brother(s)
MGC	= Married grandchildren	F or N	= Friends, neighbors (other than fellow club members)
WP	= Wife's parents	CM	= Club or organization members
WGP	= Wife's grandparents		
WS or WB	= Wife's sister(s) or brother(s)	RO	= Cousins, aunts and uncles and other relatives (specify which of these)

Note I—If one member only of the family engages in an activity with a certain person, indicate this separately by circling the code letter and placing this alongside the code letter(s) of whomever the family member does this activity with; e.g., if the husband *Always* goes *bowling* with *his brother* and the wife *Sometimes* goes *bowling* with *fellow P.T.A. members*, then you would check item (f) as below:

	Always	Almost Always	Sometimes
(f) Sports	(H) HB		(W) CM

Note II—For *Special Holidays* (item C) and *Recreation* (item H), *circle* the one activity (or two at the most) considered by the family to be the most important single holidays for their family or the most usual type of recreation.

Note III—If the family alternates between grandparents on some holidays or anniversaries; e.g., Christmas one year with the wife's parents, one year with the husband's parents, check both under "Sometimes".

Introduction: "On this page below we have a list of common activities and special events in which many families participate. I will ask you, *for each activity, with whom* you participate—then ask you whether you *Always* participate with those you mention or is it only *Almost Always,* or only *Sometimes?*

"Let's begin with Birthdays. How about your birthday (or your husband's) —with whom do you spend your birthday."

With Whom Do You Participate in These Activities

Activities	Always (Weight 5)	Almost Always (Weight 3)	Sometimes (Weight 1)
(a) Birthdays: Your own and your husband's Your children's Your parent's			
(b) Mother's Day			
(c) Special Holidays (July 4, Thanksgiving, New Year's, Easter, etc.) (Circle the most important one)			
(d) Anniversaries, weddings: Your own Your parent's Your children's			
(e) Vacation trips			
(f) Sports (bowling, golf, fishing, ball games, etc.)			
(g) Picnics, drives			
(h) Recreation (movies, dancing, bingo, card games, etc.) (Circle usual type of recreation)			
(i) Religious observances (church, synagogue, etc.)			
(j) Dining out			
(k) Club or organization activities			

Note IV—After completing the form review it with the respondent, probing particularly for friends, neighbors, club members or for others not mentioned by the respondent.

Intergenerational Family Policy on Gift Giving

4. "In your family, do you have a general policy about giving of gifts; that is, some general agreement on things such as to whom should gifts be given (or not given), on what occasions should gifts be given, how much should be spent, what to select, etc.?" (Use example, if necessary; e.g., gifts to younger children only, greeting cards only, etc.)
   . . `. . Yes   . . . . No
5. (If yes) What it the policy?
6. Is the policy followed or practiced by all the family?   . . . . Yes   . . . . No
7. (If no) What exceptions are there?

Frequency of Family Contacts

"How often do you actually visit, phone, or write various members of your family; e.g., every day, every week, every month, every three or four months, once a year or less?"

Instructions:

   Note I—Code the replies by circling the appropriate letters:

D—Once or more per day   W—Once or more per week

M—Once or more per month

Q—Once or more quarterly (3-4 months)   Y—Once each year or less often

Note II—Where there is a range for various relatives in any one category; e.g., "One child we see once every three to four years, the others at least once a month," check one of the relatives immediately accessible and note the other(s) as "*Special Case.*"

Family Members	Method and Frequency of Contact			
	(Circle:)			
(a) Married children	*Visit* D W M Q Y	*Phone* D W M Q Y	*Write* D W M Q Y	*Ask about only* D W M Q Y (from others) D W M Q Y
	Special Case:			
(If none, check ....)				
(b) Married grandchildren	(Circle:)			
	Visit D W M Q Y	*Phone* D W M Q Y	*Write* D W M Q Y	*Ask about only* D W M Q Y (from others) D W M Q Y
	Special Case:			
(If none, check ....)				
(c) Wife's parents	(Circle:)			
	Visit D W M Q Y	*Phone* D W M Q Y	*Write* D W M Q Y	*Ask about only* D W M Q Y (from others) D W M Q Y
	Special Case:			
(If none, check ....)				
(d) Husband's parents	(Circle:)			
	Visit D W M Q Y	*Phone* D W M Q Y	*Write* D W M Q Y	*Ask about only* D W M Q Y (from others) D W M Q Y
	Special Case:			
(If none, check ....)				
(e) Wife's grandparents	(Circle:)			
	Visit D W M Q Y	*Phone* D W M Q Y	*Write* D W M Q Y	*Ask about only* D W M Q Y (from others) D W M Q Y
	Special Case:			
(If none, check ....)				
(f) Husband's grandparents	(Circle:)			
	Visit D W M Q Y	*Phone* D W M Q Y	*Write* D W M Q Y	*Ask about only* D W M Q Y (from others) D W M Q Y
	Special Case:			
(If none, check ....)				

(g) Wife's brother(s)
    or sister(s)

(If none, check .....)

(Circle:)

Visit D W M Q Y *Phone* D W M Q Y *Write* D W M Q Y *Ask about only*
(from others)
D W M Q Y

Special Case:

(h) Husband's brother(s)
    sister(s)

(If none, check .....)

(Circle:)

Visit D W M Q Y *Phone* D W M Q Y *Write* D W M Q Y *Ask about only*
(from others)
D W M Q Y

Special Case:

IV

Pencil-Paper Questionnaires and Tests Administered to Respondents

Farber Marital Consensus Test

Below are listed standards by which family success has been measured. Look through the list and mark *1* after the item you consider most important in judging the success of families (in the column headed *Rank*). Look through the list again and mark *2* after the item you consider next important. Keep doing this until you have a number after each item.

There is no order of items which is correct; the order you choose is correct for you. Remember, there can be only one item marked *1,* one item marked *2,* one item marked *3, ...* one item marked *10.*

Rank

A place in the community. The ability of a family to give its members a respected place in the community and to make them good citizens (not criminals or undesirable people) . . . .

Healthy and happy children. . . . .

Companionship. The family members feeling comfortable with each other and being able to get along together . . . .

Personality development. Continued increase in family members' ability to understand and get along with people and to accept responsibility . . . .

Satisfaction in affection shown. Satisfaction of family members with amount of affection shown and of the husband and wife in their sex life   . . . . .

Economic security. Being sure that the family will be able to keep up or improve its standard of living . . . .

Emotional security. Feeling that the members of the family really need each other emotionally and trust each other fully . . . .

Moral and religious unity. Trying to live a family life according to religious and moral principles and teachings . . . .

Everyday interest. Interesting day-to-day activities having to do with house and family which keep family life from being boring . . . .

A home. Having a place where the family members feel they belong, where they feel at ease, and where other people do not interfere in their lives . . . .

Farber Family Role Tension Test

Please compare personality traits of your partner, your children, and yourself below. The traits are listed on the left side of the page. The degrees to which people have these traits are listed across the top—from "very much" to "not at all." For each trait, in the box describing the degree to which the person has the trait, mark:

W   for wife
H   for husband
1   for oldest child
2   for next oldest child
3   for next oldest child, etc.

For example, if you and your partner had a trait very much and your oldest child did not have the trait at all, you would mark W and H in the "very much" box and 1 in the "hasn't the trait at all" box.

Rate your partner first, then yourself, and then your children. Circle any rating you are not sure of.

| Traits | *Degree to which Person Has Trait* | | | | |
	Has trait very much	*Has trait considerably*	*Has trait somewhat*	*Has trait a little*	*Hasn't the trait at all*
EXAMPLE					
Likes to be with people	Ⓗ W				1
Sense of humor					
Sense of duty					
Stubborn					
Gets angry easily					
Nervous or irritable					
Easygoing					
Moody					
Jealous					
Likes to take responsibility					
Dominating or bossy					
Critical of others					
Easily excited					
Feelings easily hurt					
Likes belonging to organizations					
Easily depressed					
Self-centered					
Shy					

Marital Communication and Agreement Test

Instructions: As you know, there are married couples who discuss things that other married couples do not discuss. We would like to have you indicate by an "x" in the proper box how often you discuss the following matters and how closely you think you agree on them even if you do not discuss them. Please do not consult with your partner, since we want both of you to fill out the same form and we would like to have your individual ideas on these.

Topic	We Discuss			I Think We—				
	Often	Once in a While	Never	Always Agree	Almost Always Agree	Occasionally Disagree	Frequently Disagree	Always Disagree
a. Handling family finances								
b. Matters of recreation								
c. Religious matters								
d. Showing affection								
e. Friends								
f. Caring for children								
g. Sexual relations								
h. Table manners								
i. Ways of acting in public								
j. Ideas about what is best in life								
k. Ways of dealing with your in-laws								
l. Wife's working								
m. Sharing household tasks								

Social Participation Test

Instruction: Please list below all organizations which you or your husband (wife) are a member of or participate in at the present time. Put down the name of the organization (church, club, lodge, charity organization, professional organization, PTA, etc.) and then place an "H" for husband and/or a "W" for wife in each column that is applicable. In the example, for instance, both husband and wife are members of the "Happy Homemaker's Club", both attend meetings, they make no financial contributions, the wife is a committee member, and the husband is an officer.

Name of Organization	*Member*	*Attend*	*Financial Contributions* (Yes) or (No)	*Committee Member*	*Officer*
Example: Happy Homemaker's Club	HW	HW	No	W	H
1.					
2.					
3.					
4.					

Role Allocation and Power Structure Test

A. Please check (√) below who it is in the family who usually does the jobs listed.

Task	*Wife Always*	*Wife Usually*	*Husband Usually*	*Husband Always*	*Both Together*	*Neither Does it*
1. Who gets husband's breakfasts?	......	......	......	......	......	......
2. Who washes supper dishes?	......	......	......	......	......	......
3. Who straightens up living room when company comes?	......	......	......	......	......	......
4. Who mows lawn?	......	......	......	......	......	......
5. Who shovels snow from sidewalks?	......	......	......	......	......	......

6. Who keeps track of
   money and bills?   . . . .

B. Please check (√)below who it is who usually makes the final decision about the problems listed.

Problem	Wife Always	Wife Usually	Husband Usually	Husband Always	Both Together	Neither Does it
1. What house or apartment to take?	. . . . . .	. . . . . .	. . . . . .	. . . . . .	. . . . . .	. . . . . .
2. How much life insurance and what type?	. . . . . .	. . . . . .	. . . . . .	. . . . . .	. . . . . .	. . . . . .
3. Whether the wife shall work gainfully?	. . . . . .	. . . . . .	. . . . . .	. . . . . .	. . . . . .	. . . . . .
4. Whether the husband changes his job or not?	. . . . . .	. . . . . .	. . . . . .	. . . . . .	. . . . . .	. . . . . .
5. Whether or not a doctor is called when a family member is ill?	. . . . . .	. . . . . .	. . . . . .	. . . . . .	. . . . . .	. . . . . .
6. Where to spend vacations?	. . . . . .	. . . . . .	. . . . . .	. . . . . .	. . . . . .	. . . . . .

Cognitive Values Test
(Adapted from Brim *et al*)

These are proverbs and statements about life. You will find you agree with some, disagree with others.

For each of these sayings, circle the answer at the right which best expresses how you feel about it.

	Strongly Agree	Agree	?	Disagree	Strongly Disagree
1. Happiness comes from living day to day.	SA	A	?	D	SD
2. The highest wisdom is continual cheerfulness.	SA	A	?	D	SD
3. Nothing is less in our power					

than the heart, and far
from commanding it we
are wiser to obey it.   SA   A   ?   D   SD

4. Flowers know where the sun
is, and feel its warmth.   SA   A   ?   D   SD

5. Every human problem can be
solved and every hunger satisfied and every promise can be
fulfilled if God so wills.   SA   A   ?   D   SD

6. Man's existence is completely
under the control of destiny.   SA   A   ?   D   SD

7. For every action there's a
limited number of outcomes;
it's smart to consider them
all beforehand.   SA   A   ?   D   SD

8. It's important to decide upon
one thing and stick to it.   SA   A   ?   D   SD

9. Our grand business is not to
see what lies dimly at a
distance, but to do what
clearly lies at hand.   SA   A   ?   D   SD

10. To fear the worst is to go
through life with an
unnecessary burden.   SA   A   ?   D   SD

11. Happiness comes from impulse,
rather than reason.   SA   A   ?   D   SD

12. Old houses, like old people,
feel very tired at times.   SA   A   ?   D   SD

13. As God created the world,
so He can change or end it
as He pleases.   SA   A   ?   D   SD

14. There is a divinity that shapes
our ends, rough-hew them
as we will.   SA   A   ?   D   SD

15. You can only confuse yourself
by thinking of all that
might happen.   SA   A   ?   D   SD

16. Each important thing that
happens to man can be traced
to a single cause.   SA   A   ?   D   SD

17. The pleasures of one today
are worth those of two
tomorrows.   SA   A   ?   D   SD

18. It is worth a thousand dollars
a year to have the habit of

	Strongly Agree	Agree	?	Dis- agree	Disagree Disagree
looking on the bright side of things.	SA	A	?	D	SD
19. Our first impulses are good; thought usually weakens them.	SA	A	?	D	SD
20. The unlighted match feels its own heat when lighted.	SA	A	?	D	SD
21. God is powerless in the face of natural laws and to ask him for help is to shout at the wind.	SA	A	?	D	SD
22. Nothing comes to pass but what fate wills.	SA	A	?	D	SD
23. In deciding whether or not to do something, it's wise to make as long a list as you can of all the outcomes.	SA	A	?	D	SD
24. To try to do many things is to do none of them well.	SA	A	?	D	SD
25. To live each day as if it were the last would soon lead one to disaster.	SA	A	?	D	SD
26. In the lottery of life there are more prizes drawn than blanks.	SA	A	?	D	SD
27. Thinking is a luxury, sometimes useless, sometimes fatal.	SA	A	?	D	SD
28. Trees can't feel the wind pass, no matter how hard it blows.	SA	A	?	D	SD
29. The volcano erupts to show its power over man.	SA	A	?	D	SD
30. Whatever may happen to thee, it was prepared for thee from all eternity.	SA	A	?	D	SD
31. A man who tries to figure out everything that will happen can never decide anything.	SA	A	?	D	SD
32. You can spend so much time trying different ways of handling a situation that none of them is given a fair trial.	SA	A	?	D	SD
33. If one is faithful to the duties of the present, the future will take care of itself.	SA	A	?	D	SD

34. It's easy to get what one
    wants out of life.   SA   A   ?   D   SD
35. Impulse rarely works; thought
    is the key to success.   SA   A   ?   D   SD
36. The sea, moving restlessly,
    knows where the sunken
    ships are on its floor.   SA   A   ?   D   SD
37. The Devil lurks constantly,
    waiting to push those over
    who wander too close to the
    precipice of temptation.   SA   A   ?   D   SD
38. A childlike and abiding trust
    in destiny is anxiety's best
    preventive and remedy.   SA   A   ?   D   SD
39. The more results you can
    think of ahead of time, the
    better off you'll be.   SA   A   ?   D   SD
40. Life is best handled by
    having a whole bag of tricks,
    not by a simple rule or two.   SA   A   ?   D   SD

Beliefs About Childhood and Parenthood

(Adapted from Blood)

A number of statements are listed below about what fathers, mothers, and children ought to be today. Choose in each set the five you most agree with.

A. Choose and circle the appropriate numbers for the five most desirable characteristics of a father:

  1. Seeks to understand his children.
  2. Works hard to support his family.
  3. Answers his children's questions frankly.
  4. Joins his children in their play.
  5. Develops habits of obedience in his children.
  6. Encourages his children to grow up in their own ways.
  7. Decides what is best for his children.
  8. Disciplines his children.
  9. Works with his family on household tasks.
  10. Buys nice things for his children.

B. Choose and circle the appropriate numbers for the five most desirable characteristics of a mother:

  1. Helps her children learn how to get along with others.
  2. Has her children engage in character-building activities.

3. Keeps her children clean and well-dressed.
4. Stimulates her children's mental growth.
5. Understands her children's feelings.
6. Makes her children mind.
7. Is affectionate toward her children.
8. Trains her children to regular habits (eating, sleeping, etc.)
9. Promotes her children's emotional well being.
10. Is a good housekeeper.

C. Choose and circle the appropriate numbers for the five most desirable characteristics of a child:

1. Is courteous and respectful to adults.
2. Confides in his parents.
3. Likes to play with other children.
4. Respects property, takes care of his things.
5. Is curious, eager to learn.
6. Keeps clean and neat.
7. Enjoys growing up.
8. Does his chores and assignments thoroughly.
9. Is honest and truthful.
10. Is happy and contented.

Index